MW01044639

CAROLINA Sunshine

THEN & NOW

Charity League of Charlotte

Charity League's tradition of volunteers working for the betterment of the conditions of young children has been the driving force in its continued service to the Charlotte community. We are grateful to our many friends whose cooperation and generosity have helped us continue our charitable work. We do believe that, "We never stand so tall as when we stoop to help a little child."

1st Printing	5,000	October 1996
2nd Printing	5,000	May 1998
3rd Printing	7,500	July 2002

Copyright © 1996 by Charity League of Charlotte.

All rights reserved.

ISBN 0-9652020-0-3

LCCN: 96-084168

WIMMER COOKBOOKS

ConsolidatedGraphics

1-800-548-2537

Table of Contents

"Sunshine" recipes came from the Charity League Cookbook published in 1955.

"Dogwood" recipes came from Restaurants in the Carolinas.

Original Cookbook Committee

1996

Co-Chairmen

Bonnie Adams
Carolyn Bass

Editor

Linda Dowd

Committee

Jackie Brown
Kitty Bryson
Fay Coker
Judy Crowther
Lynda Eddy
Beth Harper
Julie Hartzell
Sarah Hennessee
Barbara Huckabee
Windy Leonard
WillieBell Martin
Betty Miller
Judy Thrash

Thanks to the generous time and talents of Charity League members, friends and family we are delighted to present this wonderful cookbook, ***Carolina Sunshine, Then & Now***. Thanks to all who participated in some way to make this book a reality.

Addendum

We wish to acknowledge the ladies who have chaired through the years ***Carolina Sunshine, Then & Now***.

1998 – Lynda Eddy
Carolyn Bass

2002 – Lynda Eddy
Barbara Huckabee
Carolyn Bass

About the Artist

Tom Douglas was born in Queens, New York. He grew up in Queens and moved to Charlotte, North Carolina in 1992. He produced the illustration for the cover of ***Carolina Sunshine, Then & Now*** specifically for the Charity League of Charlotte while studying Advertising Design at Central Piedmont Community College in Charlotte, North Carolina.

Tom worked at a full-time job to support himself while going to college. He credits the support of his parents over the years toward his schooling and dreams of being an artist. He thanks the Visual Arts Faculty of CPCC for their support, with special thanks to Evie Henderson, his Advertising/Graphic Design instructor at Central Piedmont Community College.

Underwriters Club

On behalf of Charity League, the Cookbook Committee would like to thank the following businesses, friends and families whose generosity has enabled us to publish this wonderful collection of tried and true recipes. This is only a partial listing as many of the contributors wished to remain anonymous.

Nelson & Carolyn Bass
Frank & Beverly Burgess
Bill & Gail Cowan
Clem & Judy Crowther
Ron & Lynda Eddy
Sarah Hovis
Jim & Barbara Huckabee
Julie Lewis
Ruby Mayes
Betty Miller
Earl & Doris Pope
Nova Realty
Jeanne Reynolds
Linda Snider
Faye Starnes
Catherine S. Weathers
Doris Wolf

Charity League, Incorporated

Charity League's roots run deep and strong in the Charlotte community. In 1922, under the guidance of Mrs. E. C. Marshall, a group of young girls from St. Peter's Episcopal Church began visiting and entertaining children at St. Peter's Episcopal Hospital. In 1921 Mrs. James L. Staton organized the Junior Hospital Guild with some of the same young women from St. Peter's Episcopal Church. Their work embraced services beyond hospital auxiliary work, and in 1926 young women from other denominations were invited to join. Two years later, this guild became Charity League of Charlotte.

Charity League operated a "Sunshine School" on Cecil Street for children in grades four and five who suffered from physical or emotional problems. While fighting the hardships of the Depression, the volunteers still were able to help children. In 1938 Charity League opened three cafeterias in Eastover, Myers Park and Elizabeth Elementary Schools. Ample revenue from the cafeterias sustained their services for young children. However, the 1948 Federal Lunch Room Act put Charity League out of the cafeteria business! During this decade Charity League was operating "Sunshine Rooms" for children who needed extra attention.

Charity League's focus then changed. They decided to concentrate exclusively on the needs of preschool children, thus a preschool program was established at Seigle Avenue Presbyterian Church. Less than ten years later, Charity League purchased property on Jackson Avenue to serve as the home for Children whose working parents could not afford day care. It was called Sunshine Day Nursery.

Charity League continues its commitment to children in the Charlotte area through fund-raisers; such as their annual Bazaar, annual Fashion Show, Cookbook sales and charitable donations.

Annual Coffee

Charlotte is a feast for the eyes in the Spring. Its beauty is unparalleled. The pink and white dogwood trees and redbud trees are in bloom. The forsythia is vibrant yellow; spent pear blossoms carpet bright green grass. A culinary feast is in the making too. The invitations have been sent, the responses received. Every nook and cranny of the host's home is decorated with fresh bouquets gathered from each other's gardens and arranged by talented committee members. Another committee prepared the recipes that have been handed down as traditional "Coffee" fare. The host member's home may never again shine quite like it does today. Her garden is manicured, and her azaleas are blooming. It is time for Charity League's annual Coffee.

Bite sized, warm, shaved ham biscuits are still passed in silver baskets. Incoming and outgoing Charity League Presidents still alternate pouring coffee for guests. One hundred or so active and retired Charity League members gather for the one social event of the year that they allow themselves, the Charity League Coffee.

Every Spring, League members have an opportunity to see old and new League friends. Gone are the days when members donned their spring hats, pulled on their gloves and spent the morning chatting over a catered affair. Charity League members prepare all food served at this annual event. They have long known that delicious food prepared and served lovingly in our homes is one the highest compliments we can pay to one another.

All recipes in this section are served at the Annual Charity League Spring Coffee.

Charity League Punch

- 4 quarts cheerwine, chilled
- 2 quarts unsweetened pineapple juice, chilled

Combine ingredients and pour over ice ring in punch bowl. Ice ring can be garnished with fruit or flowers.
Yield: 35 to 40 (5 ounce) servings

Cream Puffs for Chicken Salad

- 1 cup water
- ½ cup butter or margarine
- 1 cup all-purpose flour, sifted
- 4 eggs, at room temperature

Combine water and butter or margarine in saucepan and bring to a boil. Add flour, stirring constantly, and cook for about 1 minute or until mixture leaves the pan and forms a ball. Remove from heat and let stand until cool. Add eggs, 1 at a time, beating after each addition and until smooth and velvet consistency. Drop dough by teaspoonfuls on ungreased baking sheet. Bake at 400° for 20 minutes or until dry, reduce heat to 325° and bake for additional 20 minutes or until puffed, golden brown and dry. Allow to cool at room temperature. Store in airtight container until ready to serve. Using sharp knife, split puffs in halves. Fill each half with chicken salad and top with small piece of pimento or green olive slice.
Yield: 6 dozen

Cheese Biscuits

- 1 cup butter
- 2 cups (8 ounces) grated sharp cheese, at room temperature
- 2 cups all-purpose flour
- ¼ teaspoon (or more) cayenne pepper
- 2 cups crispy rice cereal

Melt butter in large saucepan. Blend in cheese, flour and cayenne pepper, mixing well. Stir in cereal. Roll mixture into small balls, place on baking sheet and flatten to wafer size. Bake at 375° for 10 minutes; do not brown.
Yield: 4 dozen

Nutty Fingers

½ cup margarine
½ cup butter
¼ cup plus 2 tablespoons sugar
1 cup ground or chopped pecans
2½ cups all-purpose flour
2 teaspoons vanilla
Powdered sugar

Combine margarine, butter, sugar, pecans, flour and vanilla, mixing well. Shape dough into fingers and place on baking sheet. Bake at 350° for 15 to 20 minutes or until lightly browned. Roll fingers in powdered sugar.
Yield: 6 to 8 dozen

Orange Sandwich Cookies

Cookies
3½ cups all-purpose flour
¾ cup sugar
2 teaspoons grated orange peel
¼ teaspoon salt
1¼ cups butter
¼ cup orange juice

Combine flour, sugar, orange peel and salt. Cut butter into dry ingredients until consistency of coarse meal. Stir in orange juice, mixing until dough forms. Shape dough into a ball and chill, covered, for 30 minutes. On lightly floured board, roll dough to ⅛-inch thickness. Cut with cookie cutters or 2-inch biscuit cutter and place on ungreased baking sheets. If desired, cut a small hole from center of half of cookies for use as top of cookie sandwich. Bake at 400° for about 8 minutes. Cool on wire rack. While cookies are cooling, prepare frosting. Spread frosting on half the cookies and top with remaining cookies.
Yield: 6 dozen

Orange Buttercream Frosting
½ cup butter, softened
3 cups powdered sugar
2 to 3 tablespoons orange juice
1½ teaspoons grated orange peel

Cream butter and powdered sugar together until smooth. Add orange juice and peel, mixing until smooth and spreading consistency.
Yield: 1 cup

Cheese Crescents with Date Nut Filling

1 cup butter, softened
2 cups (8 ounces) grated sharp cheese
1¾ cups (or more) all-purpose flour
½ teaspoon salt
1 teaspoon paprika
¼ teaspoon red pepper
¼ cup fresh lemon juice
1 (8 ounce) package chopped dates
½ cup sugar
½ cup water
½ cup chopped nuts

Cream butter, cheese, flour, salt, paprika, red pepper and lemon juice together until well blended, adding a small amount of lemon juice if needed. Chill dough while preparing filling. Combine dates, sugar, water and nuts. On lightly floured surface, roll chilled dough to ⅛-inch thickness and cut with 2-inch biscuit cutter. Place small amount of date mixture on half of each circle, fold other half over filling and press edges together to form crescent. Place on baking sheet. Bake at 325° for 20 to 30 minutes or until lightly browned.
Yield: 5 dozen

Corned Beef Sandwiches

2 (12 ounce) cans corned beef
6 hard-cooked eggs, finely chopped
2 cups finely chopped celery
2 cups mayonnaise
1 (8 ounce) jar sweet pickles, drained and chopped
¼ rounded teaspoon dry mustard
3 (32 slice) loaves white bread

Grind corned beef in food processor. Combine beef, eggs, celery, mayonnaise, pickles and mustard, mixing thoroughly. Spread filling on bread to make sandwiches, trimming crusts from slices if desired. Cut each sandwich into 4 fingers or 4 triangles.
Yield: 16 dozen sandwich quarters

Crème de Menthe Brownies

- 1 cup butter or margarine, softened, divided
- 1 cup sugar
- 4 eggs
- 1 cup all-purpose flour
- ½ teaspoon salt
- 1 (16 ounce) can chocolate syrup
- 1 teaspoon vanilla
- 2 cups sifted powdered sugar
- 2 to 3 tablespoons crème de menthe
- 1 (6 ounce) package semi-sweet chocolate chips

Cream ½ cup butter and gradually add sugar, beating until fluffy. Add eggs, 1 at a time, beating well after each addition. Combine flour and salt. Alternately add dry ingredients and chocolate syrup to creamed mixture, beginning and ending with dry ingredients. Stir in vanilla. Pour batter into greased and floured 13x9x2-inch baking pan. Bake at 350° for 25 to 28 minutes. Cool completely. Cream ¼ cup butter and gradually add powdered sugar and creme de menthe, mixing well. Spread evenly over cooled brownies. Chill for at least 1 hour. Combine chocolate chips and remaining ¼ cup butter in top of double boiler; bring water too a boil, reduce heat to low and cook until chocolate is melted. Spread over frosting layer on brownies. Chill for 1 hour. Cut into squares.
Yield: 3½ dozen

Sugar Cookies

- ½ cup butter, softened
- ¾ cup sugar
- 1 egg
- 1 teaspoon vanilla
- 1¾ cups all-purpose flour
- ¼ teaspoon baking powder
- ¼ teaspoon salt

Cream butter, sugar, egg and vanilla together until smooth. Combine flour, baking powder and salt. Add dry ingredients to creamed mixture and mix well. Drop dough by rounded teaspoon on ungreased baking sheet. Flatten each cookie with bottom of glass rubbed with butter and dipped in sugar. Bake at 425° for 5 to 9 minutes.
Yield: 3 dozen

Traditional Ham Biscuits

Filling

1 (15 pound) Smithfield ham

Mayonnaise

Place ham in boiling water in large stock pot. Reduce heat and simmer until ham separates from bone. While ham is cooking, prepare biscuits or biscuits can be made in advance and frozen. Remove meat from water and trim all fat. Grind ham in food processor. Ground ham can be frozen for later use. When ready to stuff biscuits, add just enough mayonnaise to bind ham. Spread in split biscuits. To heat biscuits, wrap in aluminum foil and bake at 400° until warm. Extra biscuits can be frozen.

Yield: 10 dozen

Angel Biscuits

1 packet dry yeast
2 tablespoons warm water
2 cups buttermilk
5 cups all-purpose flour
1 tablespoon baking powder
1 teaspoon baking soda
1 teaspoon (or more) salt
¼ cup (or less) sugar
1 cup vegetable shortening

Dissolve yeast in warm water, then mix with buttermilk and set aside. Combine flour, baking powder, baking soda, salt and sugar. Cut shortening into dry ingredients. Add liquid to dry ingredients and mix well. Place dough in plastic bag in refrigerator and use as needed. On lightly floured surface, roll dough, cut with 1¼-inch cutter and place on greased baking sheet. Bake at 400° for 10 to 12 minutes. Biscuits can be frozen until ready to use.

Yield: 10 dozen

Hartsville Special

2 hard-cooked eggs, mashed
¼ cup chopped pimento-stuffed green olives
1 tablespoon grated onion
1 cup chopped pecans
¼ teaspoon dry mustard
1 cup mayonnaise
Salt and black pepper to taste
24 slices white or wheat bread

Combine eggs, olives, onion, pecans, mustard, mayonnaise, salt and black pepper, mixing well. Spread mixture on bread slices to form sandwiches.

Yield: 1 dozen

Vegetable Sandwiches

2 medium cucumbers, peeled
2 carrots
2 green onions, chopped
1 medium-size green bell pepper, seeded
¼ teaspoon dry mustard
1 cup mayonnaise
Salt and black pepper to taste
1 packet unflavored gelatin
24 slices white bread

Combine cucumbers, carrots, onions and bell pepper in food processor and chop to fine consistency. Drain liquid, reserving 3 tablespoons. Add mustard, mayonnaise, salt and black pepper to vegetables. Dissolve gelatin in reserved vegetable juice and stir into vegetables, mixing well. Chill overnight. Spread vegetable mixture on bread slices to form sandwiches.
Yield: 1 dozen

Peanut Butter Cups

1 (8 ounce) package refrigerated sugar or peanut butter slice and bake cookie dough
48 miniature peanut butter cup candies

Cut cookie dough in 12 slices and cut each slice in 4 pieces. Place 1 piece in each cup of greased miniature muffin pan. Bake at 375° for 10 minutes. While cookies are baking, unwrap candy. Remove baked cookies from oven and immediately press 1 piece candy in center of each hot cookie. Cool in pan for 10 minutes. Carefully remove and place on paper towel to cool.
Yield: 4 dozen

Spinach Sandwiches

- 1 (10 ounce) package frozen chopped spinach, thawed
- ½ cup chopped parsley
- ½ cup finely chopped green onion
- ½ teaspoon dill weed
- 1 tablespoon salad dry seasoning
- ½ cup mayonnaise
- ½ cup sour cream
- 1 teaspoon oregano
- Juice of ½ lemon
- 6 slices bacon
- 10 slices bread

Press spinach in colander to remove all excess moisture. Combine spinach, parsley, onion, dill weed, salad seasoning, mayonnaise, sour cream, oregano and lemon juice, mixing well. Chill. Fry bacon until crisp, drain on paper towel and crumble. Add bacon bits to spinach mixture. Spread spinach filling on buttered bread slices to form sandwiches. Cut each into 4 fingers or triangles.
Yield: 1⅔ dozen

Tea Time Tassies

- 1 (3 ounce) package cream cheese, softened
- ½ cup margarine, softened
- 1 cup sifted all-purpose flour
- 1 egg
- ¾ cup firmly-packed brown sugar
- 1 tablespoon margarine, softened
- 1 teaspoon vanilla
- Dash of salt
- ⅔ cup chopped pecans

Blend cream cheese and margarine together. Stir in flour and mix well. Chill for 1 hour. While dough is chilling, prepare filling. Beat egg, brown sugar, margarine, vanilla and salt together until smooth. Shape chilled dough into 2 dozen balls. Place in miniature muffin pans, pressing dough on bottom and sides of cups. Spoon ½ of pecans into pastry-lined cups, add egg mixture and top with remaining pecans. Bake at 325° for 25 minutes or until filling is firm. Cool in pan.
Yield: 2 dozen

Appetizers & Beverages

Gracious beginnings are as much a part of being a Carolinian as are the Blue Ridge Mountains and the Atlantic beaches. Carolinians are blessed with the most beautiful landscapes in the South. You develop the Carolina's style of the Southern "ease" by spending your weekends with your feet in the hot sand or a cool mountain stream. Most of us are getting ready to go to or have just returned from a weekend at the mountains or beach. We travel with our family or friends for a game of golf or bridge or for a weekend of fishing or skiing. We chaperone enthusiastic youth groups and, on occasion, even get away for adult retreats!

If you grew up summering barefoot at a Barrier Island cottage, the piquant aroma of baked crab dip drifted out the screen door when friends were coming over. Because peaches grow abundantly in both Carolinas, peach daiquiris make one of the prettiest summer drinks you can offer to your guests. If snowy wintry evenings in a mountain cabin are more to your liking, then, after a day of cross country skiing on the trails near Beech Mountain, you might serve hot chocolate with peppermint schnapps and hearty Sausage Cheese Balls fresh from the oven. One requisite for either mountain cabin or beach cottage is a rocking chair for each guest.

However, if you do not have the required number of rocking chairs, we hope you will be inspired to prepare a gracious beginning the next time you are entertaining your guests. Practice a little Carolina style Southern hospitality!

Taffy Apple Dip

- 1 (8 ounce) package cream cheese, softened
- ¾ cup firmly-packed brown sugar
- 1 tablespoon vanilla extract
- ½ cup chopped pecans
- 2 large apples, cut in wedges

Combine cream cheese, sugar and vanilla, beating until smooth. Stir in pecans. Spread mixture on small serving plate. Serve with apple wedges.
Yield: 2 cups

Hot Pepper Cheese Ball

- 1 cup (4 ounces) grated New York State cheese
- ½ (8 ounce) package cream cheese, softened
- 1 cup (4 ounces) pimento cheese
- 1 cup chopped pecans
- 2 or 3 jalapeño peppers, chopped, with small amount of juice
- Juice of 1 lemon
- 2 large onions, minced
- Red pepper sauce to taste
- Worcestershire sauce to taste
- Paprika

Combine New York State cheese, cream cheese, pimento cheese, pecans, jalapeño peppers, lemon juice, onion, red pepper sauce and Worcestershire sauce, mixing thoroughly. Chill overnight. Shape mixture into 1 ball and roll in paprika. Serve with assorted crackers.
Yield: 6 cups

Pineapple Cheese Ball

- 2 (8 ounce) packages cream cheese, softened
- 1 (8½ ounce) can crushed pineapple, drained
- 2 tablespoons minced onion
- ¼ cup chopped green bell pepper
- 1 tablespoon seasoned salt (optional)
- 2 cups chopped pecans

Combine cream cheese, pineapple, onion, bell pepper and seasoned salt, mixing thoroughly. Shape into ball. Roll in pecans. Chill until ready to serve. Serve with assorted crackers.
Yield: 4 cups

Roquefort Cheese Dip

- 1 (3 ounce) package cream cheese, softened
- ⅓ of (4 ounce) package Roquefort cheese
- 1 teaspoon Worcestershire sauce
- 1 teaspoon lemon juice
- Dash of onion salt
- Dash of garlic salt
- 2 tablespoons mayonnaise

Combine cream cheese and Roquefort cheese, mixing thoroughly. Gradually blend in Worcestershire sauce, lemon juice, onion salt, garlic salt and mayonnaise. Serve with assorted crackers.
Yield: 2⁄3 cup

Appetizer Cheesecake

- 1 cup sour cream
- ¼ cup finely chopped green bell pepper
- ¼ cup finely chopped celery
- 2 tablespoons minced onion
- 2 tablespoons finely chopped pimento-stuffed green olives
- 1 teaspoon lemon juice
- ¼ teaspoon Worcestershire sauce
- Dash of paprika
- 3 drops hot pepper sauce
- ⅔ cup crushed round cheese crackers

Combine sour cream, bell pepper, celery, onion, olives, lemon juice, Worcestershire sauce, paprika and hot pepper sauce, mixing thoroughly. Line 2½ cup bowl with plastic wrap. Spread about ½ cup sour cream mixture in bottom of bowl, sprinkle with about ¼ cup crumbs and repeat layers, reserving 2 tablespoons crumbs for garnish. Chill overnight. Invert on serving plate, remove plastic wrap and sprinkle with reserved crumbs. Serve with assorted crackers.
Yield: 2 cups

Crab Delight Dip

- 1 cup mayonnaise
- ½ cup sour cream
- 1 tablespoon chopped parsley
- 1 teaspoon lemon juice
- 1 tablespoon sherry
- 1 (6½ ounce) can crabmeat, drained and cleaned
- Salt and black pepper to taste

Combine mayonnaise, sour cream, parsley, lemon juice and sherry. Fold in crabmeat and season with salt and black pepper. Chill for at least 2 hours before serving. Serve with club crackers or fresh vegetables cut for dipping.
Yield: 2 cups

Smoked Salmon and Onion Cheesecake

- **5 tablespoons grated Parmesan cheese, divided**
- **2 tablespoons fine dry breadcrumbs**
- **1 small Vidalia or other sweet onion, chopped**
- **1 cup chopped green bell pepper**
- **3 tablespoons butter**
- **3 (8 ounce) packages cream cheese, softened**
- **⅓ cup evaporated milk**
- **4 eggs**
- **½ pound nova lox trimmings, finely chopped**
- **½ cup (2 ounces) shredded Swiss cheese**
- **Salt and black pepper to taste**

Butter bottom and sides of 8-inch spring form pan. Combine 2 tablespoons Parmesan cheese and breadcrumbs. Sprinkle in bottom and on sides of prepared pan, coating evenly. Wrap aluminum foil around pan, covering bottom and 2 inches of sides. Sauté onion and bell pepper in butter just until tender. Combine cream cheese, milk and eggs. Using electric mixer, beat until smooth and blended. Fold in nova lox and Swiss cheese. season with salt and black pepper. Pour mixture into prepared pan. Place pan in large roasting pan and add boiling water to 2-inch depth. Bake at 300° for 1 hour and 40 minutes or until firm. Turn off oven temperature. Remove spring form pan from water and return to oven for 1 hour. Remove and let stand for at least 2 hours. Store, covered, in refrigerator. Serve at room temperature. Cut in wedges or serve with assorted crackers.

Note: The cheesecake has an attractive color and can be served as an appetizer or luncheon dish.

Do not use low-fat cream cheese.

Yield: 16 servings

Shrimp Spread

- **1 (8 ounce) package low-fat cream cheese, softened**
- **½ cup low-fat sour cream**
- **¼ cup low-fat mayonnaise**
- **1 cup seafood cocktail sauce**
- **1 cup (4 ounces) shredded low-fat mozzarella cheese**
- **2 (4¼ ounce) cans shrimp, rinsed and drained**
- **¾ cup seeded, finely chopped tomato**
- **3 green onions, sliced**

Combine cream cheese, sour cream and mayonnaise, beating until smooth. Spread mixture on 12-inch round serving platter. Spread seafood sauce on cheese layer. Sprinkle mozzarella cheese, shrimp, tomato and onion on sauce. Chill, covered, until ready to serve. Serve with assorted crackers.
Yield: 5 cups

Edisto Shrimp Dip

- **1 (3 ounce) package cream cheese, softened**
- **½ medium-sized green bell pepper, finely chopped**
- **2 stalks celery, finely chopped**
- **2 tablespoons pepper relish**
- **1 pound shrimp, cooked, shelled, deveined and shredded**
- **½ cup mayonnaise**

Combine cream cheese, bell pepper, celery, pepper relish and shrimp. Stir in enough mayonnaise for spreading consistency. Chill overnight or for several hours. Serve with crackers.
Yield: 4 cups

Spring Garden Dip

- **1 cup sour cream**
- **½ cup mayonnaise**
- **1 teaspoon salt**
- **Dash of pepper sauce**
- **½ cup minced green onion**
- **¼ cup finely chopped radish**
- **¼ cup finely chopped cucumber, well drained**
- **¼ cup finely chopped green bell pepper**
- **Sugar to taste**

Combine sour cream, mayonnaise, salt and pepper sauce. Fold in onion, radish, cucumber and bell pepper. Season with sugar. Serve with fresh carrots, celery, turnips, cauliflower and other vegetables cut for dipping.
Yield: 2½ cups

Betty Brown's Trio of Shrimp Paste

Shrimp Paste I

2 pounds shrimp, cooked, shelled and deveined
2 medium-sized green bell peppers
1 small red onion
1 tablespoon Worcestershire sauce
½ teaspoon prepared mustard
1 teaspoon vinegar
Red pepper to taste
3 tablespoons butter
⅓ cup all-purpose flour
¼ teaspoon salt
1 cup milk

Press shrimp through grinder, then grind bell pepper and onion. Mix shrimp and vegetables. Add Worcestershire sauce, mustard, vinegar and red pepper. Prepare white sauce by melting butter in saucepan. Blend in flour and salt and gradually add milk, cooking until thickened. Add white sauce to shrimp mixture. Press firmly into large or individual molds. Chill and unmold to serve.

Note: Recipe was given to Alice Lucas Rutledge in 1936 by Sara Simons of Charleston, South Carolina.

Yield: 8 servings

Shrimp Paste II

½ cup butter, softened
1 pound shrimp, cooked, shelled and deveined
Salt to taste

Cream butter until very soft and smooth. Press shrimp through grinder. Add shrimp and salt to butter. Press firmly in rectangular baking dish. Bake at 350° for 30 minutes or until mixture separates slightly from sides of dish and surface is lightly browned. Let stand until cool, then chill overnight before serving. Serve with cold meat platter or use for stuffing celery or sandwich filling.

Note: From Alice Lucas Rutledge's recipe collection, first served in 1936.

Yield: 4 servings

Betty Brown's Trio of Shrimp Paste (continued)

Shrimp Paste III

- 4 cups ground cooked shrimp
- 1½ cups mayonnaise
- 1 teaspoon Worcestershire sauce
- ½ teaspoon nutmeg
- ½ teaspoon celery salt

Combine shrimp, mayonnaise, Worcestershire sauce, nutmeg and celery salt, mixing thoroughly. Press firmly into mold and chill. Serve with crackers.
Yield: 5½ cups

Vegetable Spread

- 1½ medium cucumbers
- 2 large tomatoes
- 1 large onion
- 2 medium carrots
- 1 teaspoon salt
- 1 packet unflavored gelatin
- 1 tablespoon cold water
- Very hot water
- 2 cups mayonnaise

Using food processor or blender, separately grind each vegetable to coarse consistency; do not overgrind. Combine vegetables in colander, sprinkle with salt and set aside to drain thoroughly. Place gelatin in small bowl and add cold water. Place bowl with gelatin in larger bowl and add very hot water to larger bowl. Stir until gelatin is dissolved. Gradually blend mayonnaise into gelatin. Combine mayonnaise mixture and well-drained vegetables, mixing well. Chill for 24 hours. Use as spread for tea sandwiches, open faced sandwiches garnished with olive or radish slice or as a delicious spread on crackers.
Yield: 4 to 5 cups

Avocado Dip

- 2 avocados, peeled
- 4 hot jalapeño peppers, seeded
- 1 medium tomato
- ½ medium-sized onion, chopped
- 1 (12 ounce) carton cottage cheese
- ⅛ teaspoon salt

Combine avocado, jalapeño peppers, tomato, onion, cottage cheese and salt in blender or food processor container. Blend to puree consistency. Serve with corn chips or tortilla chips.
Yield: 3 cups

Broccoli or Spinach Dip

- 1 packet vegetable soup mix
- 2 cups sour cream
- ½ cup mayonnaise
- 1 teaspoon lemon juice
- 1 (10 ounce) package frozen chopped spinach or broccoli, thawed and well-drained
- 1 (8 ounce) can water chestnuts, drained and chopped

Combine soup mix, sour cream, mayonnaise and lemon juice. Fold in spinach or broccoli and water chestnuts. Chill thoroughly. Serve with bread fingers or fresh vegetables cut for dipping.
Yield: 3 cups

Peasant Caviar

- 3 pounds eggplant
- 12 cloves garlic, sliced
- 1 tablespoon salt
- ¼ cup plus 2 tablespoons lemon juice
- 1 tablespoon olive oil
- Salt to taste
- 1 teaspoon black pepper
- ¾ cup golden raisins
- ½ cup chopped black olives
- ½ cup toasted pine nuts or walnuts
- ½ cup chopped parsley
- ¼ cup chopped red onion
- 2 tomatoes, seeded and diced

Slice eggplants in halves lengthwise. Cut deep slips in eggplant flesh and insert garlic slices. Place in roasting pan, skin side down, and sprinkle with salt. Bake, covered, at 400° for 1 hour or until tender. Scoop eggplant pulp from shells, discarding shells. Thoroughly mash eggplant pulp, using food processor if preferred. Blend in lemon juice, oil, salt to taste and black pepper, mixing well. Fold in raisins, olives, pine nuts or walnuts, parsley, red onion and tomato. Chill until ready to serve. Serve with crackers or pita bread. Spread can be frozen.
Yield: 4 cups

Mexican Vegetable Dip

1 (4 ounce) can green chilies, chopped, with liquid
1 (4 ounce) can ripe olives, chopped and drained
4 medium tomatoes, chopped
4 green onions with tops, chopped
1 (4 ounce) jar sliced mushrooms, drained (optional)
1 teaspoon garlic salt
3 tablespoons vegetable or olive oil
1 tablespoon white vinegar
3 dashes hot pepper sauce (optional)
Salt and black pepper to taste

Combine chilies, olives, tomatoes, green onion and mushrooms. Stir in garlic salt, vegetable or olive oil, vinegar, hot pepper sauce, salt and black pepper. Chill for 3 to 4 hours or overnight; the longer the better. Serve with tortilla chips or taco flavored chips.

Note: Ingredients make this a low-calorie dip.

Yield: 4 cups

Mark's Layered Mexican Dip

1 (8 ounce) package cream cheese, softened
1 cup (8 ounces) cottage cheese
½ teaspoon garlic powder
1 (14 ounce) can refried beans
½ cup regular, low-fat or fat-free sour cream
1 (6 ounce) can green chilies, diced and drained
1 to 2 cups hot or mild tomato salsa
½ cup chopped green onion
1 green bell pepper, chopped
1 tomato, coarsely chopped
½ cup (2 ounces) finely shredded Cheddar cheese

Combine cream cheese, cottage cheese and garlic powder, beating thoroughly. Spread cheese mixture in 10-inch pie plate or round serving platter. Combine beans, sour cream and chilies. Spread on cheese layer. Spoon salsa evenly on bean mixture. Sprinkle green onion, bell pepper and tomato on salsa and top with Cheddar cheese. Serve with tortilla chips.

Yield: 6 cups

Martha's Hot Asparagus Dip

- 3 (10¼ ounce) cans cut asparagus spears, drained
- 1 cup mayonnaise
- 1½ cups (6 ounces) grated Parmesan cheese
- 1 clove garlic, crushed
- Salt and black pepper to taste

Place asparagus, mayonnaise, Parmesan cheese, garlic, salt and black pepper in blender or food processor container. Blend thoroughly. Spread mixture in 1½-quart round casserole. Bake at 350° for 20 to 30 minutes. Serve with tortilla chips or crackers.
Yield: 5 cups

Hot Artichoke Dip

- 1 (14 ounce) can artichoke hearts, drained and chopped
- 1 cup mayonnaise
- 1 cup (4 ounces) grated Parmesan cheese
- 4 drops hot pepper sauce
- 4 drops Worcestershire sauce
- ½ teaspoon garlic powder
- 1 tablespoon lemon juice

Combine artichoke hearts, mayonnaise, Parmesan cheese, hot pepper sauce, Worcestershire sauce, garlic powder and lemon juice. Spread mixture in 1-quart casserole. Bake at 350° for 30 minutes or until bubbly. Serve hot with melba rounds, shredded wheat crackers or other crackers.
Yield: 3½ cups

Chipped Beef Roll

- 1 (4 ounce) package or jar dried beef, coarsely chopped
- 1 tablespoon margarine
- 1 (8 ounce) package regular or low-fat cream cheese, softened
- 2 teaspoons horseradish
- 1 teaspoon prepared mustard

Sauté beef in margarine until sizzling but not overbrowned. Drain excess fat. Combine cream cheese, horseradish and mustard. Shape into a ball or log and roll in beef. Wrap in wax paper and chill. Serve with assorted crackers.
Yield: 1½ cups

Sourdough Beef Dip

- 1 (8 ounce) package low-fat cream cheese, softened
- 1 cup sour cream
- 1 (4 ounce) package wafer-sliced beef, chopped
- ¼ cup chopped green onion
- 2 tablespoons chopped green bell pepper
- 1 (8 inch) round loaf sourdough bread

Combine cream cheese, sour cream, beef, green onion and bell pepper, blending thoroughly. Slice top from bread loaf, reserving slice. Hollow loaf, reserving chunks of bread for dipping. Spoon dip into bread "bowl", top with reserved slice and wrap in aluminum foil. Bake at 300° for 1½ hours. Remove top slice from bread and cut into cubes for dipping.

Yield: 2½ cups

BoPeep Gupton's Pecan Dip

- 1 (8 ounce) package cream cheese, softened
- 2 tablespoons milk
- ½ cup sour cream
- ¼ cup finely chopped green bell pepper
- 1 tablespoon minced onion
- ½ teaspoon garlic salt
- 1 (2½ ounce) jar dried beef, shredded
- 2 tablespoons butter
- ½ cup coarsely chopped pecans
- ½ teaspoon salt

Combine cream cheese, milk and sour cream, blending thoroughly. Add bell pepper, onion and garlic salt. Fold beef into cheese mixture. Spoon mixture into 8-inch pie plate or baking dish. Sauté pecans with salt in butter in small skillet until crisp. Sprinkle on cheese mixture. Bake at 350° for 20 minutes. Serve with crackers.

Note: For a variation, omit garlic salt, butter and salt; add a dash of black pepper. For a variation using nuts other than pecans, combine all ingredients except nuts; spread mixture in 1½-quart casserole and sprinkle nuts on mixture; bake at 350° for 25 minutes or until bubbly and browned. Serve with crackers or chips.

Yield: 2½ cups

Hot Cheese Dip with Apple Slices

6 slices bacon
1 (8 ounce) package cream cheese, softened
2 cups (8 ounces) shredded Cheddar cheese
¼ cup plus 2 tablespoons half and half
1 teaspoon Worcestershire sauce
¼ teaspoon dry mustard
¼ teaspoon onion salt
¼ teaspoon hot pepper sauce
Apple slices, unpeeled
Lemon juice

Sauté bacon until crisp, drain well and crumble. In top of double boiler, combine cream cheese, Cheddar cheese, half and half, Worcestershire sauce, mustard, onion salt and hot pepper sauce. Heat over water over low heat, stirring occasionally, until cheese is melted and mixture is hot. Stir in crumbled bacon. Cut apples into slices, dipping in lemon juice to prevent browning. Serve dip with apple slices.

Note: This is a colorful dip for fall holiday parties.

Yield: 2½ cups

Crab Soufflé Spread

1 (6 ounce) can crabmeat, drained and flaked
1 cup mayonnaise
1 egg, beaten
1½ tablespoons capers, drained
1 tablespoon horseradish
½ teaspoon prepared mustard
¼ teaspoon hot pepper sauce
¼ cup (1 ounce) shredded Cheddar cheese

Combine crabmeat, mayonnaise, egg, capers, horseradish, mustard and hot pepper sauce, mixing thoroughly. Spoon mixture into 1-quart casserole. Sprinkle with Cheddar cheese. Bake at 350° for 20 minutes. Serve with crackers.

Yield: 2 cups

Claire's Mexican Dip

- 2 cups (8 ounces) shredded Cheddar cheese
- ¼ teaspoon garlic powder
- 1 cup mayonnaise
- 1 (4 ounce) can green chilies, chopped
- Dash of hot pepper sauce
- 1 (4½ ounce) can ripe olives, chopped and divided
- 1 medium tomato, chopped and divided
- ¼ cup chopped green onion, divided

Combine Cheddar cheese, garlic powder, mayonnaise, chilies, hot pepper sauce, ½ of olives, ½ of tomato and ½ of green onion. Spread mixture in 9-inch pie plate. Bake at 350° for 20 minutes. Top with remaining olives, tomato and onion. Serve with tostito chips.
Yield: 3 cups

Vegetable Sandwiches

- 2 medium cucumbers
- 2 medium carrots
- 2 green onions
- 1 medium-sized green bell pepper, seeds removed
- 1 packet unflavored gelatin
- ¼ teaspoon dry mustard
- 1 cup mayonnaise
- Salt and black pepper to taste

Grind cucumbers, carrots, green onion and bell pepper together. Drain well, reserving liquid. Dissolve gelatin in 3 tablespoons vegetable liquid. Mix dry mustard, mayonnaise, salt and black pepper with vegetables. Stir in gelatin and mix well. Chill overnight. Use as spread for party sandwiches.
Yield: 4 cups

Vidalia Onion Appetizer

- 2 cups water
- 1 cup sugar
- ½ cup vinegar
- 3 medium-sized Vidalia onions, sliced and quartered
- ½ cup mayonnaise
- 2 tablespoons celery seed

Combine water, sugar and vinegar, mixing until sugar is dissolved. Add onions and let stand for 8 hours. Drain thoroughly. Add mayonnaise and celery seed to onion. Serve with crackers.
Yield: 18 to 24 servings

Italian Roll-ups

- **1 (8 ounce) package fat-free cream cheese, softened**
- **3 tablespoons fat-free sour cream**
- **2 tablespoons chopped parsley**
- **1 tablespoon garlic powder**
- **5 (8 inch) flour tortillas**
- **30 fresh spinach leaves, stems removed**
- **20 slices Italian salami**
- **12 slices provolone cheese**

Using electric mixer at medium speed, blend cream cheese, sour cream, parsley and garlic powder for 1 to 2 minutes or until smooth. Spread about 3 tablespoons cream cheese mixture evenly on each tortilla. Arrange 5 or 6 spinach leaves on cream cheese, place 4 slices salami on spinach layer and arrange 2½ slices provolone cheese on salami, cutting to fit. Roll each tortilla tightly and wrap with plastic wrap. Chill for at least 4 hours or overnight. To serve, cut each roll into 1-inch slices.
Yield: 2½ dozen

Beth's Mexican Pinwheels

- **1 (8 ounce) package cream cheese, softened**
- **1 cup sour cream**
- **1 cup (4 ounces) shredded Cheddar cheese**
- **1 (4 ounce) can green chilies, drained and chopped**
- **1 (3 4/5 ounce) can ripe olives, drained and chopped**
- **½ cup chopped green onion**
- **¼ teaspoon garlic powder**
- **1 (10 count) package flour tortillas**

Combine cream cheese, sour cream, Cheddar cheese, chilies, olives, green onion and garlic powder, mixing well. Spread evenly on tortillas. Roll each tortilla snugly and wrap with plastic wrap. Chill for several hours or overnight. To serve, cut each roll into pinwheels. These are great served with salsa.
Yield: 5 dozen

Grandma's Pickled Shrimp

Shrimp
Water
½ cup chopped celery tips
¼ cup mixed pickling spices
3½ teaspoons salt
2½ pounds shrimp, shelled and deveined
2 cups sliced onion
7 or 8 bay leaves

Combine water (enough to cover shrimp), celery, pickling spices and salt. Bring to a boil. Add shrimp and cook for 3 to 5 minutes or until done. Drain well. Layer shrimp and onion in shallow dish. Add bay leaves. Prepare sauce. Pour over shrimp and onion. Store, covered, in refrigerator for at least 24 hours to develop flavor. Shrimp can be stored in refrigerator for up to 1 week.

Sauce
1¼ cups vegetable oil
1½ teaspoons salt
2½ tablespoons capers with juice
¾ cup white vinegar
2½ teaspoons celery seed
Dash of hot pepper sauce

Combine oil, salt, capers, vinegar, celery seed and hot pepper sauce.

The grandmother of Guynn Francis kept pickled shrimp in the refrigerator throughout the summer. For a holiday appetizer, drain shrimp well and serve with a plain cracker.

Yield: 20 to 24 servings

Bacon Wrap-ups

10 slices bread, crusts trimmed
1 cup cream of mushroom soup, undiluted
15 slices bacon
33 wooden toothpicks

Cut each bread slice into 3 strips. Generously spread soup on each strip. Cut each bacon strip in halves. For each appetizer, place ½ slice bacon under 1 bread strip, wrap tightly and secure with wooden pick. Place on rimmed baking sheet. Bake at 325° for 1 hour.

Note: Men love these! Can be made a day ahead.

Yield: 2½ dozen

Beef Tenderloin

1 (6 pound) beef tenderloin, fat trimmed
Worcestershire sauce
Texas Pete hot pepper sauce
Ground celery seed
Hickory smoke salt
Seasoned salt
Garlic powder
Freshly ground black pepper
Ground ginger
Whole thyme
Paprika

Generously rub tenderloin with Worcestershire sauce and Texas Pete sauce. In order listed, sprinkle on spices, rubbing in well: celery seed, hickory smoke salt, seasoned salt, garlic powder, black pepper, ginger and thyme. Sprinkle tenderloin heavily with paprika. Chill for several hours or overnight. Tucking thinner end under and securing with wooden pick, place tenderloin in roasting pan. Bake at 500° for 10 minutes, decrease oven temperature to 350° and bake for about 25 minutes for rare roast (a meat thermometer is recommended).
Yield: 12 to 16 appetizer servings or 8 dinner servings

Chestnut Meatballs

2 cups breadcubes
½ cup milk
½ pound ground beef chuck
½ pound hot bulk pork sausage
1 teaspoon onion powder
1 tablespoon soy sauce
½ teaspoon hot pepper sauce
1 teaspoon garlic salt
½ teaspoon monosodium glutamate
1 (8 ounce) can water chestnuts, drained and minced
¼ cup vegetable oil

Soak breadcubes in milk. Press to remove as much milk as possible. Add bread to beef and sausage, mixing well. Stir in onion powder, soy sauce, hot pepper sauce, garlic salt and monosodium glutamate. Add water chestnuts and blend thoroughly. Shape mixture into 4 dozen balls. Brown a few at a time in vegetable oil, removing to chafing dish to keep warm.
Yield: 4 dozen

Hanky-Panky Cocktail Sandwiches

- **1 pound ground beef**
- **1 pound hot bulk pork sausage**
- **4 cups (16 ounces) grated cheese**
- **1 teaspoon oregano**
- **1 teaspoon garlic salt**
- **1 teaspoon red pepper flakes**
- **2 loaves cocktail rye bread**

Cook beef and sausage together until browned. Remove from heat and drain excess fat. Stir in cheese, oregano, garlic salt and red pepper flakes. Let stand until slightly cooled. Spread mixture thickly on bread slices and place on baking sheet. Bake at 350° for 10 to 12 minutes.

Note: Do not microwave sandwiches. The sandwiches can be assembled, placed on baking sheets, frozen and stored in plastic bags in freezer until needed. To complete, bake frozen pieces following regular directions. To reduce spiciness, use mild sausage or omit red pepper flakes.

Yield: 4 to 5 dozen

Sausage Balls in Chutney Sauce

- **2 pounds bulk pork sausage**
- **1 cup regular or fat-free sour cream**
- **1 (8-ounce) bottle chutney**
- **½ cup dry sherry**

Shape sausage into small balls and place on rimmed baking sheet. Bake at 400° until browned and cooked, shaking occasionally to turn to brown evenly. Combine sour cream, chutney and sherry. Pour into chafing dish and add sausage balls.

Yield: 2½ dozen

Popcorn will stay fresh and you will eliminate "old maids" if you store it in the freezer.

Sausage Rounds

1 pound ground beef
1 pound bulk pork sausage
1 (16 ounce) package Velveeta cheese, cubed
1 teaspoon basil
1 teaspoon oregano
¼ teaspoon garlic powder
1 to 2 tablespoons parsley flakes
2 loaves cocktail rye bread

Cook beef and sausage together until browned. Drain excess fat. Stir in cheese and cook over low heat until melted. Stir in basil, oregano, garlic powder and parsley. Spoon mixture on bread slices and place on baking sheet. Broil until bubbly.

Note: An easy hot appetizer which appeals especially to men. It can also be used as a regular open-faced sandwich filling and broiled.

Yield: 4 to 5 dozen

Sausage Pinwheels

1 (8 ounce) package refrigerated crescent dinner roll dough
1 pound hot or mild bulk pork sausage

Unroll dough and separate into 4 rectangles, lightly pressing perforations between pairs of triangles to form each rectangle. Divide sausage into 4 parts. Spread each evenly on dough rectangle and roll-up from long edge. Wrap in wax paper or aluminum foil and freeze until ready to use. To complete, thaw slightly until easy to cut. Cut in ¼-inch slices and place on baking sheet. Bake at 400° for 8 to 10 minutes. Serve hot.
Yield: 3½ dozen

***Holiday fragrance**: 3 to 4 cinnamon sticks, 3 bay leaves, ¼ cup whole cloves, ½ unpeeled lemon (cut into wedges), ½ unpeeled orange (cut into wedges) and 1 quart water. Place all ingredients in saucepan. Bring to boil, reduce heat and simmer, adding more water as needed. Cool and refrigerate between uses.*

Miniature Drumsticks

- 3 pounds broiler-fryer chicken wings
- ½ cup all-purpose flour
- ½ cup (2 ounces) grated Parmesan cheese
- 1 teaspoon monosodium glutamate
- 1 teaspoon salt
- 1 teaspoon paprika
- ½ teaspoon oregano
- ¼ teaspoon hot pepper sauce
- ¾ cup buttermilk
- Vegetable oil

Separate wings at joints, using "drumstick" portion for appetizer and reserving tip segments for soup or stock. Combine flour, Parmesan cheese, monosodium glutamate, salt, paprika and oregano. Add hot pepper sauce to buttermilk. Dip chicken pieces in liquid, drain excess and roll in dry ingredients. Fry pieces in 2 inches hot oil for about 5 minutes or until browned. Drain on paper towel. Serve hot.
Yield: 1½ dozen

Duck Hors D'oeuvres

- 2 duck breasts
- Water
- 3 tablespoons vinegar
- 1 teaspoon salt
- Wine Worcestershire sauce
- 2 cups regular or fat-free sour cream or yogurt
- 3 tablespoons Dijon mustard
- 1 (16 ounce) package bacon
- Garlic powder to taste
- Greek seasoning salt to taste

Place duck in water to cover, adding vinegar and salt. Soak for 4 hours or overnight. Rinse and soak in clear water, changing it once or twice, for 30 minutes. Cut breasts into 1-inch squares. Rinse again and marinate in Worcestershire sauce for 1 to 4 hours. Drain well. Combine sour cream, mustard, garlic powder and seasoning salt. Divide sauce and place duck squares in sauce. Cut bacon slices in halves. Wrap bacon slice around each duck piece. Broil on grill until bacon is crisp. Use remaining sauce for dipping.
Yield: 1¼ dozen

Tiny Tuna Puffs

- 1 cup water
- ½ cup margarine
- 1 cup sifted all-purpose flour
- 4 eggs
- 1 teaspoon minced onion flakes
- 1½ teaspoons lemon juice
- 1 (6½ ounce) can tuna, drained and flaked
- ½ cup mayonnaise
- 1 (8 ounce) can water chestnuts, drained and finely chopped

Combine water and margarine. Bring to a rolling boil. Stir in all of flour. Cook, stirring often, over low heat until mixture forms ball. Remove from heat. Add eggs 1 at a time, beating well after each addition. Drop dough by teaspoonful on ungreased baking sheet. Bake at 400° for 30 minutes. Let stand until cool. Combine onion flakes, lemon juice, tuna, mayonnaise and water chestnuts, mixing thoroughly. Spoon mixture into puffs and place on baking sheet. Bake at 400° for 3 minutes. To prepare in advance, bake puffs and freeze, then thaw and fill as needed.
Yield: 5 dozen

Artichoke Squares

- 1 small onion, chopped
- 1 clove garlic, minced
- 1 tablespoon butter
- 4 eggs, beaten
- ½ cup fine dry breadcrumbs
- ¼ teaspoon salt
- ⅛ teaspoon black pepper
- ⅛ teaspoon oregano
- ⅛ teaspoon hot pepper sauce
- 2 tablespoons chopped parsley
- 1 (13¾ ounce) can artichoke hearts, drained and chopped
- 2 cups (8 ounces) grated Cheddar cheese

Sauté onion and garlic in butter until softened. Add eggs, breadcrumbs, salt, black pepper, oregano, hot pepper sauce and parsley, mixing thoroughly. Fold artichokes and cheese into egg mixture. Pour into 8x8x2-inch baking dish. Bake at 350° for 30 minutes. Let stand to cool slightly before cutting into bite-sized squares. Serve hot.
Yield: 3 dozen

Asparagus Canapés

1 (8 ounce) package cream cheese, softened
1 (8 ounce) package blue cheese, crumbled
1 tablespoon mayonnaise
1 egg, beaten
3 drops Worcestershire sauce
3 drops hot pepper sauce
1 tablespoon lemon juice
1½ loaves white sandwich bread
1¼ pounds fresh asparagus or 2 (15 ounce) cans asparagus spears, drained
½ cup butter, melted

Combine cream cheese, blue cheese, mayonnaise, egg, Worcestershire sauce, hot pepper sauce and lemon juice, blending thoroughly. Trim crusts from bread and use rolling pin to flatten each slice. Spread cheese mixture on each slice, place asparagus spear on each and roll up. Place rolls on ungreased baking sheet and brush with butter. Bake at 425° for 15 minutes. Serve hot.

Note: Canapés can be assembled, frozen on baking sheets and stored in plastic bag in freezer until ready to use. Bake and serve as directed. For bite-sized canapés, cut assembled rolls into thirds before baking.

Yield: 2 to 2½ dozen

Cheese and Onion Broil

½ cup mayonnaise
2 teaspoons prepared mustard
1 cup minced scallions
½ cup (2 ounces) grated sharp Cheddar cheese
Salt and black pepper to taste
Shredded wheat crackers, such as Triscuits

Combine mayonnaise and mustard. Add scallions and Cheddar cheese. Season with salt and black pepper. Spread mixture on shredded wheat crackers. Bake at 400° until lightly browned. Serve warm.
Yield: 2 cups

Cheese Squares

2 (8 ounce) cans refrigerated crescent roll dough
1 (8 ounce) package cream cheese, softened
2 eggs, beaten
2 cups (8 ounces) grated sharp Cheddar cheese
2 cups (8 ounces) grated Muenster cheese
2 cups (8 ounces) grated Monterey Jack cheese
2 cups (8 ounces) grated Swiss cheese
¼ cup margarine, melted
¼ cup sesame seeds, toasted
1 teaspoon dried parsley

Unroll and arrange 1 can dough in bottom of 13x9x2-inch baking pan, lightly pressing perforations and seams. Blend cream cheese and eggs. Fold Cheddar, Muenster, Monterey Jack and Swiss cheeses into egg mixture. Spread evenly on dough on pan. Unroll remaining dough and arrange on cheese layer to form upper crust. Brush with margarine and sprinkle with sesame seeds and parsley. Using fork tines, puncture dough in several places to vent steam during baking. Bake at 350° for 30 minutes. Let stand for 15 minutes before cutting into bite-sized pieces.

Note: Squares can be baked, cut, frozen on baking sheets and stored in freezer until ready to use. Thaw, then reheat at 350° for about 10 minutes before serving.

Yield: 4 dozen

Cheese Cookies

½ cup butter
1 cup (4 ounces) grated sharp cheese
1 cup self-rising flour
Dash of cayenne pepper

Combine butter, cheese, flour and cayenne pepper, blending thoroughly. Using cookie press, squeeze dough in cookie shapes onto ungreased baking sheets. Bake at 350° for 15 minutes.
Yield:

Cheese Toast

1 loaf white thin sliced sandwich bread
½ cup mayonnaise
½ cup (2 ounces) grated Parmesan cheese
1 tablespoon chopped onion
¼ teaspoon red pepper

Trim crusts from bread and cut into shapes with cookie cutter. Place on baking sheet and set aside to air dry. Combine mayonnaise, Parmesan cheese, onion and red pepper in food processor. Process until spreading consistency. Spread mixture on bread shapes. Bake at 350° for 10 minutes or until browned.

Note: A hit at parties, the toast is also a good accompaniment to soup or salad.

Yield: 1 cup

Sausage Cheese Balls

1 pound hot bulk lean pork sausage
2½ cups (10 ounces) grated sharp Cheddar cheese
2½ cups biscuit baking mix

Crumble uncooked sausage and let stand at room temperature until softened. Add Cheddar cheese and biscuit mix, blending thoroughly until mixture can be formed into a large ball. Pinching off small pieces, roll between palms to form 1-inch balls and place on baking sheet; do not allow balls to touch. Bake, on rack below center of oven, at 350° for about 20 minutes or until balls are puffed and golden brown. Serve hot with chili or mustard sauce.

Note: Balls can be baked until firm but not browned, frozen on baking sheets and stored in plastic bags in freezer. Thaw slightly before reheating at 350° until golden brown.

Yield: 8 to 9 dozen

To quickly chill wine, beer or champagne, add a cup of salt to the ice. It will lower the temperature of ice and chill faster.

Williamsburg Cheese Straws

- **1 cup sifted all-purpose flour**
- **½ teaspoon salt**
- **¼ teaspoon dry mustard**
- **⅛ teaspoon cayenne pepper**
- **⅓ cup butter**
- **1 cup (4 ounces) grated sharp Cheddar cheese, divided**
- **1½ tablespoons ice water**
- **1 teaspoon celery seed**

Sift flour, salt, mustard and cayenne pepper together. Using pastry blender, cut in butter and ½ cup Cheddar cheese, until mixture is consistency of coarse crumbs. Add water and stir lightly to blend. Shape into ball. On lightly floured surface, roll pastry to ⅛-inch thickness. Sprinkle with remaining ½ cup cheese. Fold pastry in half and roll again to ⅛-inch thickness. Using pastry wheel or knife, cut pastry into 3x½-inch strips. Sprinkle with celery seed. Place on ungreased baking sheet. Bake at 350° for about 12 minutes or until lightly browned. Serve warm.

Note: Straws are especially good with hot spiced tomato juice or Bloody Mary mixed drinks.

Yield: 5 dozen

Pecan Stuffed Mushrooms

- **1 pound large mushrooms**
- **1 large clove garlic, minced**
- **¼ cup butter**
- **½ cup chopped pecans**
- **½ cup fine dry breadcrumbs**
- **¼ teaspoon salt**
- **¼ teaspoon black pepper**
- **¼ teaspoon ground thyme**

Remove stems from mushrooms. Reserve caps and chop stems. Sauté stems and garlic in butter until tender. Stir in pecans, breadcrumbs, salt, black pepper and thyme, mixing well. Spoon mixture into mushroom caps and place in buttered 8x8x2-inch baking dish. Bake at 350° for 15 minutes. Serve warm.

Note: Mushrooms are also a good side dish with steak entree.

Yield: 1½ to 2 dozen

Spinach Stuffed Mushrooms

1 package frozen spinach soufflé
1 pound large mushrooms
Melted butter

Prepare soufflé according to package directions. While soufflé bakes, remove stems from mushrooms and reserve for other use. Place caps, hollow side down, on baking sheet and brush with butter. Bake at 350° for about 5 minutes. Invert caps, fill with soufflé mixture and bake for about 10 minutes or until hot.
Yield: 1½ to 2 dozen

Spinach Balls

2 (10 ounce) packages frozen chopped spinach, cooked and drained
1 (8 ounce) package herb-seasoned stuffing mix
2 large onions, minced
½ cup (2 ounces) grated Parmesan cheese
5 eggs, lightly beaten
½ cup butter or margarine, melted
1 tablespoon garlic salt
1 teaspoon black pepper

Combine spinach, stuffing mix, onion, Parmesan cheese, eggs, butter or margarine, garlic salt and black pepper, mixing thoroughly. Shape into walnut-sized balls and place on well-greased baking sheets. Freeze until firm, then store in plastic bags in freezer until ready to use. To complete, place frozen balls on baking sheets. Bake at 350° for 20 to 25 minutes.

Note: Ingredients can be combined and stored, covered, in refrigerator overnight. Once baked, the balls should not be frozen.

Yield: 6 dozen

Quick microwave cleanup - heat 1 cup water and 3 tablespoons lemon juice in microwave-safe cup on High for 5 minutes.

Spinach Squares

- 1 cup all-purpose flour
- 1 teaspoon baking soda
- 1 teaspoon salt
- 2 eggs, beaten
- 1 cup milk
- ¼ cup margarine, melted
- ½ cup chopped onion
- 4 cups (16 ounces) grated Cheddar cheese
- 1 (10 ounce) package frozen chopped spinach, thawed and well drained

Combine flour, baking soda and salt. Blend eggs, milk and margarine together. Add to dry ingredients. Stir in onion, Cheddar cheese and spinach, mixing thoroughly. Pour mixture into 11x7x1½-inch baking pan. Bake at 350° for 30 to 35 minutes. Cut into squares and serve warm.

Note: Baked squares can be frozen. Thaw, then reheat at 350° for 10 minutes.

Yield: 2½ dozen

Vegetable Pizza

- 2 (8 ounce) packages refrigerated crescent roll dough
- 2 (8 ounce) packages cream cheese, softened
- 1 cup mayonnaise
- ¾ packet ranch salad dressing mix
- ½ bunch broccoli, chopped
- ½ head cauliflower, chopped
- 1 medium-sized red bell pepper, chopped
- 1 medium-sized green bell pepper, chopped
- 2 or 3 green onions, chopped
- 1 large tomato, chopped
- 2 cups (8 ounces) shredded Cheddar cheese

Unroll dough and arrange on large baking sheet to form crust, lightly pressing perforations and seams together. Bake, at temperature indicated on package directions, for 11 minutes. Combine cream cheese, mayonnaise and dressing mix. Spread on cooled crust. Combine broccoli, cauliflower, bell peppers, onion and tomato. Distribute evenly on cream cheese layer, pressing slightly. Sprinkle with Cheddar cheese. Cut into squares.

Yield: 4 dozen

Small Individual Pizzas

- 1 pound hot bulk pork sausage
- 1 (10½ ounce) can tomato soup, undiluted
- 1 (6 ounce) can tomato paste
- 1½ teaspoons oregano
- 1 teaspoon onion salt
- 2 loaves party rye bread
- ½ cup vegetable or olive oil
- 1 cup (4 ounces) grated sharp Cheddar cheese
- Grated Parmesan cheese (optional)

Cook sausage until browned, stirring to crumble. Drain excess fat. Combine tomato soup, tomato paste, oregano and onion salt. Lightly brush one surface of bread slices with oil to prevent sogginess. Sprinkle Cheddar cheese on bread, spread soup mixture on cheese and top with sausage. Sprinkle with Parmesan cheese. Place on baking sheets. Bake at 350° for 10 minutes.

Note: Pizzas can be baked, frozen on baking sheets and stored in plastic bags in freezer until ready to use. Reheat at 350° for 5 to 8 minutes before serving.

Yield: 4 dozen

Zucchini Appetizer

- 3 cups thinly sliced zucchini
- ½ cup minced onion
- 1 clove garlic, minced
- 2 tablespoons chopped parsley
- ½ cup (2 ounces) grated Parmesan cheese
- 1 cup Bisquick
- ½ teaspoon salt
- Black pepper to taste
- ½ teaspoon oregano
- ½ teaspoon marjoram
- ½ cup vegetable oil
- 4 eggs, lightly beaten

Combine zucchini, onion, garlic and parsley. Stir in Parmesan cheese, biscuit mix, salt, black pepper, oregano and marjoram. Add oil and eggs, mixing thoroughly. Pour batter into 13x9x2-inch baking pan. Bake at 350° until golden brown. Cut in bars or squares.

Yield: 4 dozen

Mexican Black-Eyed Susans

1 package Pillsbury pie crust mix
1 (5 ounce) jar sharp cheese spread
1 (8 ounce) package whole pitted dates
Pecan halves

Combine pie crust mix and cheese spread; do not add any water or milk. Place dough between 2 sheets wax paper and roll to ⅛-inch thickness. Using cheese spread jar rim, cut circles in dough. Insert pecan half into each date, place stuffed date in center of each dough circle, fold over, pinch edges together and place on baking sheet. Bake at 300° for 20 to 25 minutes.
Yield: 3 to 4 dozen

Sweet Orange Pecans

1 tablespoon grated orange peel
½ cup orange juice
1 cup sugar
4 cups pecan halves

Combine peel, juice and sugar in heavy saucepan. Bring to a boil. Add pecans and stir until syrup is absorbed. Remove and heat and stir until pecans separate. Spread coated pecans on waxed paper. Let stand until completely cooled.
Yield: 5½ cups

Sugared Peanuts

1½ cups sugar
3 cups raw shelled peanuts
¾ cups water

Combine sugar and water in large saucepan, mixing until sugar is dissolved. Stir in peanuts. Bring to a boil, reduce heat to medium and cook, stirring occasionally and then constantly, until all liquid is absorbed. Pour peanuts into large baking pan. Bake at 275 to 300° for 25 to 30 minutes, stirring at 10 minute intervals. Cool completely before storing in air-tight container. Peanuts keep well.
Yield: 3 cups

Signal Battalion Punch

2 (750 ml) bottles champagne
1 (750 ml) bottle dry red wine
1 cup gin
½ cup dark rum
½ cup cherry vodka
1 (46 ounce) can red punch drink
½ (8 ounce) package frozen whole strawberries
1 (16 ounce) bottle ginger ale or 7-Up

Combine champagne, wine, gin, rum, vodka, punch and strawberries in punch bowl. Stir in ginger ale or 7-Up just before serving.

Note: The punch is very pretty and very potent.

Yield: 25 to 30 (6 ounce) servings

Pink Punch

2 (10 ounce) packages frozen sliced strawberries, thawed
1 (15¼ ounce) can crushed pineapple
1 (12 ounce) can frozen lemonade concentrate, thawed
3 (12 ounce) cans water
2 (32 ounce bottles) ginger ale
½ gallon pineapple sherbet

Combine strawberries, pineapple, lemonade concentrate and water in punch bowl. Stir in ginger ale and sherbet just before serving.
Yield: 45 (5 ounce) servings

Holiday Sparkle Delight

1 (6 ounce) can frozen orange juice concentrate, thawed
Ice cubes or ice ring
1 (32 ounce) bottle regular or sugar-free 7-Up
1 (32 ounce) bottle club soda
1 (32 ounce) bottle cranberry juice cocktail
Lemon, lime or orange slices (optional)

Place orange juice concentrate and ice cubes or ice ring in punch bowl. Stir in 7-Up, club soda and cranberry juice. Float lemon, lime or orange slices on punch.
Yield: 20 (5 ounce) servings

Fruit Slush

- 1 (6 ounce) can frozen orange juice concentrate, thawed
- 1 (6 ounce) can frozen lemonade concentrate, thawed
- 1 cup sugar
- 1 (20 ounce) can crushed pineapple, undrained
- 2 (10 ounce) packages frozen strawberries, partially thawed
- 1 medium banana, mashed
- 1 (32 ounce) bottle 7-Up

Combine orange juice and lemonade concentrates, sugar, pineapple, strawberries and banana in mixing bowl. Stir in 7-Up. Pour mixture into clear plastic glasses, filling ½ full. Cover top of each with plastic wrap or aluminum foil and freeze. About 1 hour before serving, remove from freezer. Slush may be refrozen.

Note: This is a refreshing drink for a brunch or before dinner.

Yield: 10 to 14 (7 ounce) servings

Easy Peach Daiquiri

- 1 (10 ounce) can frozen peach daiquiri concentrate
- ½ (10 ounce) can rum, or to taste
- 2 or 3 fresh peaches, peeled and sliced
- Crushed ice

Combine daiquiri concentrate, rum and peaches in blender container. Top with crushed ice and blend until smooth. Serve in large wine glasses with straw.

Note: Makes a delicious frozen drink for a warm summer evening. Omit alcohol for an equally refreshing fruit drink.

Yield: 5 (8 ounce) servings

Frozen Daiquiri

1 (6 ounce) can frozen lemonade concentrate
1 (6 ounce) can frozen limeade concentrate
1 (6 ounce) can frozen orange juice concentrate
5 (6 ounce) cans water
3 (6 ounce) cans rum
9 packets sugar substitute
Fruit of choice

Using ½ of each ingredient, combine lemonade, limeade and orange juice concentrates, water, rum and sugar substitute in blender container. Blend until smooth and pour into freezer-proof container. Repeat with remaining ingredients, add to first batch, stir and freeze until ready to serve. Just before serving, mix portion of slush with fruit of choice in blender.
Yield: 12 (6 ounce) servings

Almond Tea

3 tea bags
6 cups water, divided
1 cup sugar
⅔ cup fresh lemon juice (3 lemons)
2 to 4 teaspoons almond extract
1 teaspoon vanilla extract

Steep tea in 2 cups boiling water. Combine sugar and remaining 4 cups water, bring to a boil and cook for 5 minutes. Stir in lemon juice and almond and vanilla extracts. Add tea liquid and heat thoroughly. Serve hot or cold. Tea can be stored in refrigerator for up to 2 weeks.
Yield: 7 (6 ounce) servings

Karen's Russian Tea

8 to 10 whole cloves
1 cinnamon stick
1 cup water
1 cup orange juice
Juice of 1 lemon
½ cup pineapple juice
2 cups brewed tea
½ cup sugar

Combine cloves and cinnamon with water in saucepan. Bring to a boil. Discard cloves and cinnamon. Add orange, lemon and pineapple juices, tea and sugar to spiced water. Heat thoroughly.
Yield: 6 (6 ounce) servings

Jazzy Tea

½ cup lemon-flavored iced tea mix
1 (6 ounce) can frozen lemonade concentrate, thawed
11 cups water
1 (32 ounce) bottle lemon-lime carbonated soft drink

Combine tea mix, lemonade and water. Add soft drink just before serving. Serve chilled.

This tea is served at the Mint Museum.

Yield: 20 (6 ounce) servings

Winter's Day Hot Chocolate

¼ cup cocoa
½ cup sugar
Dash of salt
½ cup hot water
4 cups milk
1 teaspoon vanilla extract
Peppermint schnapps
Whipped cream
Peppermint or cinnamon sticks

Combine cocoa, sugar and salt in saucepan. Blend in hot water, bring to a boil and cook for 2 minutes over medium heat, stirring constantly. Stir in milk and heat thoroughly; do not boil. Add vanilla and mix well. Pour into mugs and add 1 to 2 teaspoons schnapps, according to taste. Top with dollop of whipped cream. Use peppermint stick or cinnamon stick as a stirrer.

Note: This is an adults-only beverage.

Yield: 6 (6 ounce) servings

Silver will gleam after a rubbing with damp baking soda on a soft cloth.

To keep silver tarnish free: Place square of camphor in china cabinet or other closed place.

Salads & Salad Dressings

If we do not have our own backyard vegetable garden, we have a neighbor or a friend who does and is most eager to share their bounty, particularly tomatoes, squash and cucumbers. For any of us bereft of gardening friends, we have Farmers' Markets and vegetable stands nearby. In Mecklenburg and surrounding counties, we have numerous "Pick Your Own" farms. One of everyone's favorite May morning activities is to go strawberry picking.

Carolinians have a tradition of arriving at the home of a friend in need with a gift of food. We might take a basket of freshly picked strawberries along with a vegetable salad to a friend just home from the hospital. If a neighbor needs his spirits lifted, we make a double quantity of Aunt Irene's Chicken and Fruit Salad and take half to him for his evening meal. Sunshine Carrot Salad is just the dish to make quickly for a friend flooded with unexpected company.

Our lives are busier now than in the past; but, the tradition of offering a home cooked dish to say, "I'm thinking of you," and, "I care about you," has never changed.

Salads and Salad Dressings

Greens

Arugula—Also called rocket, arugula has a bittersweet flavor and small narrow dark-green leaves. It's generally used as an accent.

Butter or Boston—Rich and delicate in flavor with a buttery texture, butter or Boston lettuce is typically a small rounded head of soft medium-green leaves.

Cabbage—Always available in produce markets, varieties include green, red, savory, curly and Chinese. Cabbage is delicious in salad and is the base for coleslaw.

Endive—This is the term given to a family of strongly flavored salad greens. Belgian, a small pointed head, is the most expensive because it is usually imported. Escarole with wide dark-green leaves is used in Italian cooking. Chicory with large curly leaves has a bitter taste.

Iceberg—Round, smooth, compact head with pale crisp leaves, iceberg retains its crispness and is especially good for sandwiches and salads.

Leaf—Common types are red leaf, green leaf and Australian lettuce. Leaf lettuce includes all ruffled types that do not form heads.

Radicchio—Imported and resembling a small cabbage, radicchio has a bitter flavor which can be overwhelming when served alone but is good when used sparingly and tossed with other greens.

Romaine—Also known as cos lettuce, romaine has an elongated head with narrow dark-green leaves. It is preferred for Caesar salad and is crisp and flavorful.

Spinach—Wonderful in salads by itself or in combination with others greens, spinach must be washed very well to remove sand and grit.

Sprouts—Usually available in any produce market, these are interest additions to a salad. Alfalfa sprouts are wispy green shoots, bean sprouts are pale and tender and radish sprouts have a strong, distinctive flavor.

Watercress—Pungent and peppery in flavor, watercress has small round leaves which are delicious when young but bitter and tough when old.

Lettuce and Salad Greens

- Salad greens retain their freshness and longevity if they are first rinsed, wrapped in paper towels and then stored in a sealable bag in the refrigerator.
- Lettuce will keep about two weeks if purchased fresh and stored at 33°.
- Parsley and watercress should be washed, drained and stored in air-tight containers in the refrigerator.
- Revive wilted salad greens by dousing them quickly in warm water, then in ice water containing a small amount of vinegar.
- To core a head of lettuce, bang the core end on the kitchen counter, then twist and lift out the core. Avoid cutting the core with a knife as it will cause discoloration.
- Always tear lettuce into bite-sized pieces rather than cutting. Cutting causes discoloration.

Molded Salads

- Always add boiling water to flavored gelatins to dissolve but do not boil the gelatin-liquid mixture.
- One tablespoon unflavored gelatin (one packet) will gel 2 cups liquid.
- Before adding ingredients to gelatin, allow to stand until consistency of unbeaten egg whites.
- Add carbonated beverages by pouring slowly down side of bowl and stirring with an up and down motion.
- Drain frozen or canned fruits thoroughly before adding to gelatin mixture.
- To chill gelatin quickly, place in freezer for ten minutes or place bowl in ice water and stir.
- When unmolding gelatin, moisten serving plate with cold water to make it easier to position the gelatin.
- To unmold, run a spatula around the edge to loosen, invert on moistened serving platter, place a warm damp dish towel over the mold and shake gently.

My Own Pasta Salad

Salad

- 2 cups frozen snow peas
- Boiling water
- 2 cups broccoli flowerets
- 2½ cups cherry tomatoes, halved
- 2 cups sliced fresh mushrooms
- 1 (7¾ ounce) can pitted ripe olives, drained
- 1 (15 ounce) can garbanzo beans, drained
- 1 large green bell pepper, diced
- 2 stalks celery, diced
- 6 to 8 green onions, diced
- ½ (4 ounce) package cheese-stuffed tortellini
- ⅓ (8 ounce) package spinach fettucine, broken
- ½ (8 ounce) package rotini pasta
- 1 (8 ounce) package provolone cheese, broken
- 2 tablespoons grated Parmesan cheese
- 1 pound crab meat, imitation crab or shrimp

Blanch snow peas in boiling water for 1 minute, remove with slotted spoon and rinse with cold water. Blanch broccoli in boiling water for 1 minute, remove with slotted spoon and rinse with cold water. Combine snow peas, broccoli, tomatoes, mushrooms, olives, beans, bell pepper, celery and onion. Prepare pasta according to package directions, drain and cool slightly. While pasta is cooking, prepare salad dressing. Combine vegetables, pasta, provolone and 1 tablespoon Parmesan cheese. Add crab or shrimp and salad dressing, tossing well. Chill several hours before serving. Sprinkle with remaining 1 tablespoon Parmesan cheese.

Yield: 12 to 20 servings

Dressing

- ⅓ cup red wine vinegar
- ⅓ cup vegetable oil
- ⅓ cup olive oil
- ¼ cup sliced green onion
- 2 tablespoons chopped fresh parsley
- 2 cloves garlic, minced
- ½ teaspoon sugar
- 1 teaspoon salt
- ½ teaspoon black pepper
- 2 teaspoons dried whole basil
- 1 teaspoon whole dill weed
- ½ teaspoon dried whole oregano
- 1½ teaspoons Dijon mustard

Combine vinegar, vegetable oil, olive oil, green onion, parsley and garlic in jar with tight-fitting lid. Add sugar, salt, black pepper, basil, dill, oregano and mustard and shake vigorously until well mixed.

Note: This is great for a party.

Yield: 1¼ cups

Pasta Salad

- ½ (8 ounce) package shell pasta
- 1 (4 ounce) jar marinated artichoke hearts, undrained
- 1 (4 ounce) can pitted ripe olives, drained
- 1 cup cherry tomatoes, halved
- 1 tablespoon chopped fresh parsley
- Salt and black pepper to taste
- ½ teaspoon chopped fresh basil

Prepare pasta according to package directions, drain, rinse with cold water and drain well. Add artichoke hearts, olives, tomatoes, parsley, salt, black pepper and basil, tossing to mix. Chill until ready to serve.
Yield: 4 to 6 servings

Rotini Salad

- 1 (8 ounce) package rotini pasta
- 1 cup finely chopped celery
- ½ cup finely chopped green bell pepper
- ½ cup minced onion
- 1 (15 ounce) can kidney beans, drained
- 1 (15 ounce) can garbanzo beans, drained
- 1 (10 ounce) package frozen green peas, thawed
- 1 (2 ounce) jar pimento, chopped
- ½ cup vinegar
- ½ cup vegetable oil
- ¼ cup sugar
- 1 teaspoon black pepper
- 1 tablespoon garlic salt
- 1 teaspoon basil
- 1 tablespoon parsley flakes

Prepare pasta according to package directions, drain, rinse with cold water and drain well. Add celery, bell pepper, onion, kidney beans, garbanzo beans, peas and pimento. Combine vinegar, oil, sugar, black pepper, garlic salt, basil and parsley. Add to vegetables and toss well. Chill, covered, overnight.

Note: This is great for tailgating.
Yield: 8 servings

Crab Stuffed Tomatoes

- 5 large tomatoes
- 1 (7½ ounce) can crabmeat, drained and shredded
- 2 hard-cooked eggs, chopped
- 1 cup diced celery
- ½ cup mayonnaise
- 1 teaspoon salt
- 1 teaspoon dry mustard
- 1 tablespoon minced parsley
- 1 teaspoon Worcestershire sauce.
- Lettuce leaves

Cut thin slice from top of tomatoes. Remove, chop and reserve pulp. Turn tomatoes upside down to drain. Combine crabmeat, egg, celery and tomato pulp. Blend mayonnaise, salt, mustard, parsley and Worcestershire sauce. Fold into crabmeat mixture and spoon into tomatoes. Place stuffed tomato on lettuce leaves on individual serving plates.

Note: This is a favorite for bridge and bridal luncheons.
Yield: 5 servings

Cabbage Chicken Salad

Salad

- 1 (3 pound) broiler-fryer or 4 chicken breast halves, cooked, skin removed, boned and chopped
- 2 cups cooked pasta
- ½ medium head cabbage, thinly sliced
- 2 green onions with tops, chopped
- ½ red bell pepper, thinly sliced
- 2 tablespoons sesame seeds, toasted
- 2 tablespoons slivered almonds, toasted

Combine chicken, pasta, cabbage, green onion, bell pepper, sesame seeds and almonds, mixing lightly. Prepare dressing, add to salad and toss to coat thoroughly.
Yield: 6 servings

Dressing

- ½ cup olive oil
- 3 tablespoons vinegar
- 2 tablespoons sugar
- 1 teaspoon salt
- ½ teaspoon black pepper

Combine oil, vinegar, sugar, salt and black pepper, blending thoroughly.
Yield: ⅔ cup

Aunt Irene's Chicken and Fruit Salad

- **6 cups diced cooked chicken or turkey breast**
- **2 tablespoons orange juice**
- **2 tablespoons vinegar**
- **2 tablespoons vegetable oil**
- **1 teaspoon salt**
- **3 to 4 cups cooked rice**
- **1½ cups diced apple**
- **1½ cups diced celery**
- **1 (20 ounce) can pineapple tidbits, drained**
- **1 (11 ounce) can mandarin oranges, drained**
- **1 cup slivered almonds (optional)**
- **1½ cups Miracle Whip salad dressing**

Combine chicken or turkey, orange juice, vinegar, oil and salt in large bowl. In separate bowl, combine rice, apple, celery, pineapple, oranges, almonds and salad dressing, mixing thoroughly. Add rice mixture to chicken or turkey and mix well. Chill, covered, until ready to serve.

Note: The large quantity makes this salad especially suitable for church dinners, showers and other gatherings. The salad is best made a day in advance.

Yield: 16 to 20 servings

Hot Chicken Salad

- **2 cups diced cooked chicken**
- **2 cups diced celery**
- **½ cup slivered blanched almonds**
- **½ teaspoon grated onion**
- **1 cup mayonnaise**
- **2 tablespoons fresh lemon juice**
- **½ teaspoon salt**
- **½ cup (2 ounces) shredded medium-sharp Cheddar cheese**
- **⅔ cup coarsely crushed potato chips**

Combine chicken, celery, almonds, onion, mayonnaise, lemon juice and salt, mixing lightly but thoroughly. Spread mixture in buttered shallow 2-quart casserole. Combine Cheddar cheese and chips and sprinkle on chicken mixture. Bake, uncovered, at 375° for 20 minutes.

Yield: 6 servings

Salmon Rice Salad

- 2 cups cooked rice
- 1 (16 ounce) can cut green beans, drained
- ½ cup sliced ripe olives
- ¼ cup mayonnaise
- 2 tablespoons lemon juice
- 1 teaspoon salt
- ¼ teaspoon black pepper
- 1 (7¾ ounce) can pink salmon, drained and flaked
- Lettuce leaves

Combine rice, green beans, olives, mayonnaise, lemon juice, salt and black pepper, mixing thoroughly. Add salmon and toss to mix well. Chill. Serve on lettuce leaves.

Yield: 4 servings

Chicken and Cranberry Salad

First Layer

- 1 packet unflavored gelatin
- ¾ cup water, divided
- 2½ cups chopped cooked chicken
- ½ cup diced celery
- 2 tablespoons chopped parsley
- 1 cup mayonnaise
- 3 tablespoons lemon juice
- 1 teaspoon salt

Dissolve gelatin in ¼ cup water according to package directions and set aside. Combine chicken, celery, parsley, mayonnaise, remaining ½ cup water, lemon juice and salt. Add to gelatin. Spread mixture in 1½-quart casserole and chill until firm.

Second Layer

- 1 packet unflavored gelatin
- ¼ cup water
- 1 (16 ounce) can whole cranberry sauce
- 1 (8 ounce) can crushed pineapple, undrained
- ½ cup chopped pecans

Dissolve gelatin in ¼ cup water according to package directions and set aside. Combine cranberry sauce, pineapple and pecans. Add to gelatin. Spread over congealed first layer. Chill until ready to serve. Recipe may be doubled.

Note: This recipe originally appeared in the Charlotte Observer 20 years ago.

Yield: 6 servings

Crab Tomato Aspic

2 packets unflavored gelatin
1 cup cold condensed beef broth, divided
3 cups tomato juice
2 slices onion
2 bay leaves
¼ teaspoon celery salt
2 tablespoons lemon juice
1 cup chopped celery
1 (7½ ounce) can crabmeat, drained and flaked
1 or 2 hard-cooked eggs, sliced

Soften gelatin in ½ cup beef broth and set aside. Combine tomato juice, onion, bay leaves and celery salt in sauce pan. Bring to boiling. Remove onion and bay leaves. Add gelatin and stir until dissolved. Add remaining ½ cup beef broth and lemon juice. Chill until partially firm. Fold in celery and crabmeat. Pour into 5½ cup mold and chill until firm. Invert to unmold and garnish with egg slices.
Yield: 6 to 8 servings

Salmon Cucumber Salad

2 tablespoons unflavored gelatin
2 tablespoons cold water
2 tablespoons lemon juice
1 cup boiling water
1 cup thinly sliced cucumber
1 (7¾ ounce) can salmon, drained, skin and bones removed and flaked
1 cup cooked peas
¼ cup mayonnaise
1 teaspoon onion salt
½ teaspoon horseradish
¼ cup non-fat dry milk

Soften gelatin in mixture of cold water and lemon juice. Add boiling water and stir to dissolve gelatin. Pour ⅓ cup of liquid into 4-cup mold. Arrange cucumber slices, overlapping pieces, in mold. Chill until firm. Combine remaining gelatin, salmon, peas, mayonnaise, onion salt, horseradish and dry milk. Spoon mixture into mold and chill for about 2 hours or until firm.
Yield: 6 to 8 servings

Deep Sea Mold

- 2 packets unflavored gelatin
- 1 cup cold water
- 1 cup sour cream
- 1 cup mayonnaise
- 3 tablespoons lemon juice
- ¼ teaspoon hot pepper sauce
- ¾ teaspoon salt
- 1 teaspoon Worcestershire sauce
- 1 teaspoon dill weed
- ½ teaspoon minced onion flakes
- 2 (12 ounce) cans waterpack tuna, drained and flaked
- 1 (4 ounce) can Louisiana shrimp, drained
- ¾ cup chopped celery
- ¼ cup chopped green bell pepper
- 2 tablespoons diced pimento

Sprinkle gelatin on water in saucepan. Cook over low heat, stirring constantly, until gelatin is dissolved. Remove from heat and let stand until cool. Combine sour cream, mayonnaise, lemon juice, hot pepper sauce, salt, Worcestershire sauce, dill weed and onion flakes in large mixing bowl. Blend in cooled gelatin. Add tuna, shrimp, celery, bell pepper and pimento, mixing thoroughly. Pour into 8-cup mold and chill until firm.
Yield: 8 to 10 servings

Congealed Tuna Salad

- 1½ packets unflavored gelatin
- ¼ cup cold water
- 1 cup boiling water
- 2 cups mayonnaise
- 2 (6½ ounce) cans waterpack tuna, drained and flaked
- 2 hard-cooked eggs, chopped
- ½ cup chopped pimento-stuffed olives
- 1 teaspoon minced onion
- 2 teaspoons capers
- Salt and black pepper to taste
- Dash of red pepper
- Lettuce leaves

Soften gelatin in cold water. Add boiling water and stir to dissolve gelatin. Let stand until cool. Using rotary beater, blend mayonnaise into cooled gelatin and beat until smooth. Add tuna, eggs, olives, onion, capers, salt, black pepper and red pepper. Pour into 6-cup mold and chill until firm. Serve on lettuce leaves.
Yield: 8 servings

Beet Salad

1 (16 ounce) can sliced beets
½ cup sugar
½ cup cider vinegar
Salt and black pepper to taste
1 (3 ounce) package raspberry gelatin
1 packet unflavored gelatin
Water
Lettuce leaves
Mayonnaise

Drain beets, reserving juice. Dice beets. Combine sugar, vinegar, salt and black pepper. Add to beets. Combine raspberry gelatin and unflavored gelatin. Add water to reserved beet liquid to measure 2 cups and pour into saucepan. Bring to a boil, add to gelatin mixture and stir until dissolved. Add diced beet mixture. Pour into 12 individual molds or rectangular baking dish. Chill until firm. Serve on lettuce leaves with dollop of mayonnaise.
Yield: 12 servings

Congealed Cucumber Salad

1 (3 ounce) package sugar-free lime gelatin
¾ cup boiling water
¾ cup grated unpeeled cucumber
2 tablespoons minced onion
½ cup fat-free mayonnaise
1 cup fat-free cottage cheese
½ cup slivered almonds (optional)

Dissolve gelatin in boiling water. Stir in cucumber, onion, mayonnaise, cottage cheese and almonds; mixing thoroughly. Pour into 10½x6x1½-inch baking dish. Chill for 30 to 45 minutes or until firm. Serve on lettuce leaves.
Yield: 8 servings

Tomato Salad

1 (15 ounce) can stewed tomatoes
¼ cup water
2 (3 ounce) packages lemon gelatin
¾ cup mayonnaise
1 cup chopped celery
¼ cup chopped green bell pepper
1 medium-sized onion, chopped
Lettuce leaves

Pour tomatoes into saucepan and bring to a boil. Add water. Dissolve gelatin in tomato liquid and blend in mayonnaise. Add celery, bell pepper and onion. Chill until firm. Serve on lettuce leaves.
Yield: 4 to 6 servings

Tomato Aspic

- 1 packet unflavored gelatin
- ½ cup cold water
- 1 (28 ounce) can tomatoes, chopped
- 1 large onion, thinly sliced
- 1 tablespoon salt
- 2 tablespoons vinegar
- 15 whole cloves
- 1 medium-sized green bell pepper, thinly sliced
- Lettuce leaves
- 1 tablespoon whipping cream
- Mayonnaise

Soften gelatin in cold water and set aside. Combine tomatoes, onion, salt, vinegar and cloves in saucepan. Bring to a boil, reduce heat and simmer at near-boil for 20 minutes. Strain liquid from pulp. Add gelatin to liquid and stir in bell pepper. Pour into 4-cup mold and chill until firm. Serve on lettuce leaves. Whip cream into small portion of mayonnaise and spoon on top of molded salad.
Yield: 4 to 6 servings

Congealed Vegetable Salad

- 1 (3 ounce) package lemon gelatin
- 1 (3 ounce) package lime gelatin
- 2 cups boiling water
- 1 (5 ounce) can evaporated milk
- 1 cup mayonnaise
- 1 cup cottage cheese
- 1 medium-sized green bell pepper, chopped
- 2 carrots, grated
- 2 tablespoons grated onion

Dissolve lemon and lime gelatin in boiling water. Let stand until cool. Stir milk into gelatin liquid. Add mayonnaise, cottage cheese, bell pepper, carrots and onion, mixing thoroughly. Chill until firm.
Yield: 10 to 12 servings

Keep tomatoes in storage with the stems pointing downward and they will retain their freshness longer.

Molded Waldorf Salad

- 2 (3 ounce) packages lemon gelatin
- 1½ cups boiling water
- 1 tablespoon lemon juice
- 1 cup cold water
- Ice cubes
- ½ cup Miracle Whip salad dressing
- 1½ cups diced unpeeled red apples
- ¾ cup finely chopped celery
- ¼ cup chopped walnuts

Dissolve gelatin in boiling water and add lemon juice. Combine cold water and ice to measure 2 cups. Add to gelatin, stir until slightly thickened and remove ice. Whisk in salad dressing. Chill until partially firm. Fold apples, celery and walnuts into gelatin. Pour into 5-cup mold or 10 individual molds prepared with cooking spray. Chill for about 4 hours or until firm.
Yield: 10 servings

Blueberry Salad

Salad

- 1 (3 ounce) black raspberry gelatin
- 1 cup boiling water
- 1 (16 ounce) can blueberries, drained, or 1 (8 ounce) package frozen blueberries
- 1 (15¼ ounce) can crushed pineapple, drained

Dissolve gelatin in boiling water. Add blueberries and pineapple. Pour into shallow 2-quart casserole. Chill until firm. Spread topping over congealed salad.
Yield: 8 to 10 servings

Topping

- 1 (3 ounce) package instant vanilla pudding mix
- 1 cup milk
- 1 (8 ounce) carton frozen whipped topping, thawed

Blend pudding mix and milk. Fold whipped topping into pudding.

Apricot Cheese Delight Salad

Salad

- **1 (17 ounce) can apricots, juice reserved**
- **1 (20 ounce) can crushed pineapple, juice reserved**
- **1 cup miniature marshmallows**
- **2 (3 ounce) packages orange gelatin**
- **2 cups boiling water**
- **1 (8 ounce) carton frozen whipped topping, thawed**
- **¾ cup (3 ounces) grated Cheddar cheese**

Drain apricots, reserving juice and chopping fruit. Drain pineapple, reserving juice. Combine fruit but do not blend juices. Chill fruit. Dissolve gelatin in boiling water. Stir in 1 cup reserved apricot juice. Fold in fruit and marshmallows. Pour into 13x9x2-inch baking dish. Chill until firm. Spread whipped topping over congealed salad and sprinkle with cheese or prepare sauce and substitute for whipped topping, sprinkling with cheese.

Yield: 12 to 16 servings

Sauce

- **½ cup sugar**
- **2 to 3 tablespoons all-purpose flour**
- **1 egg, lightly beaten**
- **2 tablespoons butter or margarine (optional)**
- **1 cup pineapple juice**
- **1 cup whipping cream, whipped, or frozen whipped topping, thawed**

Combine sugar and flour in saucepan. Blend in egg and butter. Add reserved pineapple juice and cook over low heat, stirring constantly, until thickened. Let stand until completely cooled. Fold whipped cream or topping into sauce.

Perk up soggy lettuce by adding lemon juice to a bowl of cold water and soak for an hour in the refrigerator.

Cranberry Fruit Salad

2 cups ground cranberries
1½ cups sugar
2 (3 ounce) packages cherry gelatin
½ packet unflavored gelatin
2 cups boiling water
1 whole orange
½ cup chopped celery
¾ cup chopped nuts
1 (20 ounce) can crushed pineapple, undrained

Combine cranberries and sugar. Let stand for 2 hours. Dissolve cherry gelatin and unflavored gelatin in boiling water, stirring until dissolved. Cut unpeeled orange into slices, remove seeds and grind (food processor can be used). Add orange, celery, nuts and pineapple to gelatin. Pour into shallow 2-quart casserole. Chill until firm.
Yield: 10 to 12 servings

Congealed Grapefruit Salad

3 packets unflavored gelatin
½ cup plus 1 tablespoon cold water
1 cup boiling water
1 cup sugar
Pinch of salt
3 (3 ounce) packages cream cheese, softened
1 cup chopped pecans
Dash of lemon juice
3 cups grapefruit sections

Soften gelatin in cold water. Add boiling water, sugar and salt to gelatin and stir until dissolved. Combine gelatin liquid and grapefruit. Pour ½ of mixture into 9x5x3-inch loaf pan. Chill until firm. Blend cream cheese, pecans and lemon juice. Spread mixture on congealed gelatin. Pour remaining grapefruit mixture over cream cheese layer. Chill until firm.
Yield: 8 to 10 servings

Orange Delight Salad

2 (3 ounce) packages orange gelatin
1 cup boiling water
1 (6 ounce) can frozen orange juice concentrate
1 cup cold water
1 cup ginger ale
1 (11 ounce) can mandarin oranges, drained

Dissolve gelatin in boiling water. Add orange juice concentrate, cold water, ginger ale and oranges. Pour into 5-cup mold which has been rinsed in cold water. Chill until firm. Serve on lettuce.
Yield: 6 to 8 servings

Orange Fluff

1 (8 ounce) container fat-free cottage cheese
1 (3 ounce) package sugar-free orange gelatin
1 (8 ounce) can crushed pineapple, partially drained
1 (11 ounce) can mandarin oranges, drained
1 (8 ounce) container low-fat frozen whipped topping, thawed

Combine cottage cheese and gelatin. Add pineapple, oranges and whipped topping, mixing thoroughly. Chill for about 30 minutes or until firm.

Note: Other gelatin flavors may be substituted.
Yield: 6 to 8 servings

Fresh Peach Salad

1 (8 ounce) package marshmallows
½ cup milk
2 (3 ounce) packages peach gelatin
1 cup boiling water
½ cup cold water
2 cups sliced peaches
1 (12 ounce) container frozen whipped topping, thawed

Place marshmallows in microwave-safe bowl. Cook at high setting (100%) for 15 seconds, stir and repeat cycle until marshmallows are melted. Remove from microwave oven and add milk. Chill. Dissolve gelatin in boiling water. Stir in cold water and pour into 13x9x2-inch baking dish. Chill until partially thickened. Add peaches to gelatin. Fold whipped topping into marshmallows. Swirl marshmallow mixture through gelatin for marbled effect. Chill until firm.

Note: For dessert, pour mixture into graham cracker crust and chill until firm.
Yield: 24 servings

Gayle's Crushed Pineapple Salad

1 (20 ounce) can crushed pineapple, juice reserved
Juice of 1 lemon
1 cup sugar
2 packets unflavored gelatin
½ cup cold water
1 cup (4 ounces) grated American cheese
2 cups whipping cream, whipped
½ cup red or green maraschino cherries (or combination), halved and drained

Combine pineapple, lemon juice and sugar in saucepan. Heat until sugar is dissolved. Soften gelatin in cold water for 5 minutes, then add to pineapple mixture and let stand until cool. Add cheese and whipped cream to pineapple mixture. Fold in cherries. Pour into 6-cup mold and chill until firm.

Note: Gayle Claus of West Bend, Wisconsin, shared this recipe with Dorris J. Edmond in 1950.
Yield: 8 to 12 servings

Pineapple Party Salad

1 (15 ounce) can crushed pineapple, juice reserved
Water
1 (3 ounce) package lime gelatin
1 (3 ounce) package lemon gelatin
¼ teaspoon salt
1 cup fat-free cottage cheese
1 cup fat-free mayonnaise
¼ cup slivered almonds, chopped

Drain pineapple, reserving fruit and juice. Add water to juice to measure 2 cups and pour into saucepan. Bring to a boil, remove from heat and add gelatin, stirring until dissolved. Add salt and let stand until partially thickened. Fold cottage cheese, mayonnaise, almonds and pineapple into gelatin. Pour into shallow 2-quart baking dish and chill until firm.

Note: Grace Reed, mother of Julie Hartzell, served this every Christmas in small tree molds.
Yield: 10 to 12 servings

Strawberry Salad

1 (3 ounce) package strawberry gelatin
1 cup boiling water
⅓ cup cold water
½ cup red or white wine
2 tablespoons lemon juice
1 (3 ounce) package cream cheese
1 cup fresh strawberry halves or frozen strawberries, thawed

Dissolve gelatin in boiling water. Stir in cold water, wine and lemon juice. Chill until partially thickened. Cut cream cheese into small cubes. Fold cheese and strawberries into gelatin. Spoon into 8 individual molds and chill until firm.
Yield: 8 servings

Strawberry Pretzel Salad

First Layer
2 cups broken thin pretzel sticks
¾ cup margarine, melted
3 tablespoons sugar

Combine pretzels, margarine and sugar. Spread mixture in bottom of 13x9x2-inch baking dish. Bake at 400° for 6 to 7 minutes; do not over-bake. Let stand until cool.

Second Layer
1 (8 ounce) package regular or low-fat cream cheese
1 cup sugar or equivalent sugar substitute
2 cups frozen whipped topping, thawed

Combine cream cheese, sugar and whipped topping, mixing thoroughly. Spread over pretzel layer.

Third Layer
2 (3 ounce) packages regular or sugar-free strawberry gelatin
2 cups boiling water
2 (10 ounce) packages frozen strawberries, thawed and undrained

Dissolve gelatin in boiling water. Stir in strawberries with juice. Chill until partially thickened. Pour strawberry mixture over cream cheese layer. Chill until firm.
Yield: 12 to 16 servings

Christmas Layer Salad

First Layer

- 1 (3 ounce) package lime gelatin
- 1 cup boiling water
- ½ cup cold water
- 1 (8 ounce) can crushed pineapple, drained

Dissolve gelatin in boiling water. Stir in cold water and pineapple. Pour into 11x7x1 ¾-inch baking dish. Chill until firm.

Second Layer

- 2 (3 ounce) packages cream cheese, softened
- 1 (3 ounce) package lemon gelatin
- 1 cup boiling water
- 1 cup cold water

Combine cream cheese and gelatin, mixing thoroughly. Add boiling water and stir until well blended. Add cold water. Let stand until cool, then pour over first layer. Chill until firm.

Third Layer

- 1 (3 ounce) package strawberry gelatin
- 1 cup boiling water
- 1 (17 ounce) can apricots, drained and pureed

Dissolve gelatin in boiling water. Stir in apricot puree. Let stand until cool, then pour over second layer. Chill until firm.

Note: This is an attractive and delicious salad to serve during the holidays.

Yield: 12 to 15 servings

Frozen Cranberry Salad

- 1 (16 ounce) can whole cranberry sauce
- 1 (8 ounce) can crushed pineapple, drained
- 1 cup sour cream
- ¼ cup sifted powdered sugar
- Lettuce leaves

Combine cranberry sauce and pineapple. Blend sour cream and powdered sugar. Add to fruit. Spoon mixture into paper-lined muffin pans. Freeze until firm. To serve, remove paper liners and place on lettuce leaves.

Yield: 12 servings

Cranberry Holiday Salad

1 (12 ounce) package fresh cranberries
2 cups sugar
1½ cups halved red grapes
1½ cups chopped celery
1½ cups chopped pecans
1 cup whipping cream
½ cup sugar

Using food processor, chop cranberries. Mix sugar with cranberries and let stand for 2 hours. Drain cranberries. Add grapes, celery and pecans, tossing to mix. Whip cream with sugar. Fold sweetened cream into cranberry mixture. Spoon into serving bowl and chill until served.

Note: An attractive salad, this is a nice change from the traditional congealed cranberry salad.
Yield: 8 to 12 servings

Cranberry Fluff

2 cups fresh cranberries, ground
3 cups miniature marshmallows
¾ cup sugar
2 cups seedless grapes
½ cup chopped walnuts
¼ teaspoon salt
1 cup whipping cream, whipped
2 cups diced unpeeled apples
1 (20 ounce) can crushed pineapple
Lettuce leaves

Combine cranberries, marshmallows and sugar. Chill, covered, overnight. Add grapes, walnuts, salt, whipped cream, apples and pineapple, mixing thoroughly. Chill well. Serve on lettuce leaves.
Yield: 8 to 10 servings

Pineapple Delight

2 (15 ounce) cans pineapple chunks, drained
1 cup sugar
¼ cup plus 2 tablespoons all-purpose flour
1 cup (4 ounces) grated sharp or mild Cheddar cheese
18 to 20 round buttery crackers, crushed
¼ cup butter, melted

Combine pineapple, sugar, flour and cheese. Pour into buttered 1½-quart casserole. Sprinkle crackers on fruit mixture and drizzle butter on crackers. Bake at 350° for 20 to 30 minutes.
Yield: 4 to 6 servings

Frozen Fruit Salad

Salad

1 cup sour cream
2 tablespoons lemon juice
¾ cup sugar
1 teaspoon salt
1½ large bananas, sliced
40 white seedless grapes, halved
1 (8 ounce) can crushed pineapple
½ cup chopped pecans

Combine sour cream, lemon juice, sugar and salt. Fold bananas, grapes, pineapple and pecans into sour cream. Spread mixture in 12x8x2-inch freezer-safe dish or spoon into paper-lined muffin pans. Freeze until ready to serve. Cut into squares and serve with dressing.
Yield: 8 to 10 servings

Dressing

½ cup vinegar
½ cup vegetable oil
½ cup ketchup
½ cup sugar

Combine vinegar, oil, ketchup and sugar, blending thoroughly.
Yield: 1 ¾ cups

Broccoli Salad

Salad

10 slices bacon
2 bunches broccoli
½ medium-sized red onion, chopped
½ cup raisins

Cook bacon until crisp, drain well and crumble. Cut broccoli floweret portion into bite-sized pieces, reserving stems for another use. Combine bacon, broccoli, onion and raisins. Prepare dressing, add to vegetables and mix well. Flavor improves if prepared a day in advance and chilled until ready to serve.
Yield: 6 to 8 servings

Dressing

½ cup mayonnaise
2 tablespoons vinegar
1 tablespoon sugar

Combine mayonnaise, vinegar and sugar, blending well.
Yield: ⅔ cup

Fresh Broccoli Salad

1 bunch broccoli
½ cup chopped pimento-stuffed olives
1 small onion, chopped
4 hard-cooked eggs, chopped
⅔ cup mayonnaise
Lettuce leaves

Cut broccoli flowerets and about ½ of stems into bite-sized pieces. Combine broccoli, olives, onion and eggs. Fold mayonnaise into vegetables, mixing lightly but thoroughly. Serve on lettuce leaves.
Yield: 6 to 8 servings

Pam's Vegetable Salad

Salad

1 bunch broccoli, cut in bite-sized pieces
1 head cauliflower, cut in bite-sized pieces
1 red bell pepper, sliced
1 yellow squash, sliced

Prepare dressing. Combine broccoli, cauliflower, bell pepper and squash. Add chilled dressing and toss to coat thoroughly.
Yield: 8 servings

Dressing

1 large onion (Vidalia preferred), cut in chunks
1 teaspoon salt
½ teaspoon black pepper
1 teaspoon celery seed
⅓ cup sugar
½ cup olive oil
⅓ cup vinegar
1 tablespoon prepared mustard

Combine onion, salt, black pepper, celery seed, sugar, oil, vinegar and mustard in blender or food processor container. Blend thoroughly. Chill for at least 2 hours or overnight.
Yield: 1½ cups

Sunshine Carrot Salad

2 cups grated carrots
1 (11 ounce) can mandarin oranges, drained
1 cup pineapple chunks, drained
1 cup flaked coconut
½ cup raisins
1 cup sour cream
Lettuce leaves

Combine carrots, oranges, pineapple, coconut and raisins, mixing well. Chill for 2 to 3 hours. Stir in sour cream. Serve on lettuce leaves.
Yield: 6 to 8 servings

Carolina Salad

- ½ cup raisins
- Hot water
- Cold water
- 1 cup shredded cabbage
- 1 large red apple, diced
- 1 cup chopped celery
- ½ cup (2 ounces) shredded sharp Cheddar cheese
- ½ cup mayonnaise

Soak raisins in hot water for several minutes, rinse in cold water and drain well. Combine raisins, cabbage, apple, celery and cheese. Add mayonnaise, mixing lightly but thoroughly.

Note: For larger quantity, use more cabbage and raisins. Salad is very good with pork entree.
Yield: 4 servings

Oriental Cabbage Salad

Salad

- 2 (3 ounce) packages oriental flavor ramen noodle soup
- 1 pound cabbage, shredded
- 1 cup slivered almonds
- ½ cup sunflower seeds
- 2 bunches green onions, finely chopped

Reserving seasoning packets for dressing, break ramen noodles into small pieces. Combine noodles, cabbage, almonds, sunflower seeds and onion. Add dressing and toss to coat thoroughly. Chill for 1 to 2 hours before serving.
Yield: 8 servings

Dressing

- ¾ cup canola oil
- ½ cup red wine vinegar
- 3 tablespoons plus 2 teaspoons sugar
- Soup seasoning packets

Combine oil, vinegar, sugar and seasoning, mixing well.
Yield: 1¼ cups

To remove lime deposits from teakettles, fill with equal parts vinegar and water. Bring to a boil and allow to stand overnight.

Cole Slaw

Salad

3 pounds cabbage, chopped
2 medium-sized onions, chopped
1 medium-sized green bell pepper, chopped
2 cups sugar

Combine cabbage, onion, bell pepper and sugar. Prepare dressing. Pour over vegetables and mix thoroughly.
Yield: 10 to 12 servings

Dressing

1 cup vinegar
1 cup vegetable oil
2 tablespoons sugar
2 tablespoons salt
2 tablespoons celery seed

Combine vinegar, oil, sugar, salt and celery seed in saucepan. Bring to a boil. Remove from heat. Dressing can be stored in refrigerator indefinitely.
Yield: 2 cups

Mrs. Jackson's Potato Salad

Salad

8 or 9 medium potatoes
Water
2 stalks celery, chopped
1 carrot, grated
1 medium-sized onion, chopped
2 tablespoons pickled tomatoes
1 hard-cooked egg, chopped

Cook potatoes in "jackets" in water to cover. Drain, peel and dice while warm. Add celery, carrot, onion, tomatoes and egg. Fold dressing into warm potato mixture.
Yield: 10 servings

Dressing

1¼ cups mayonnaise
1 teaspoon sugar
1 teaspoon garlic salt
1 teaspoon Worcestershire sauce

Combine mayonnaise, sugar, garlic salt and Worcestershire sauce, blending until smooth.
Yield: 1 ⅓ cups

Potato Salad

Salad

7 medium potatoes
Water
3 hard-cooked eggs, chopped

Cook potatoes in "jackets" in water to cover. Drain, peel and dice. Chill for about 6 hours. Prepare dressing. Combine potatoes and eggs. Fold dressing into mixture. Chill until ready to serve.

Note: A very old recipe, it is worth the extra effort. It's especially good with ham entree.

Yield: 6 to 8 servings

Dressing

½ cup milk
⅓ cup sugar
¼ cup vinegar
1 egg
¼ cup butter
1 tablespoon cornstarch
¾ teaspoon salt
¾ teaspoon celery salt
¼ teaspoon dry mustard
¼ cup chopped onion
¼ cup mayonnaise

Combine milk, sugar, vinegar, egg, butter, cornstarch, salt, celery salt and dry mustard in saucepan. Cook over low heat, stirring frequently, until thickened. Remove from heat. Blend in onion and mayonnaise. Let stand until cool.

Yield: 1½ cups

Jane's Vegetable Potato Salad

8 to 10 red potatoes
1 cup broccoli flowerets
¾ cup thinly sliced carrots
½ cup LeSueur baby peas
Chopped tomatoes (optional)
Chopped onion (optional)
1 (8 ounce) bottle buttermilk creamy salad dressing
½ teaspoon black pepper

Cook potatoes in "jackets" in water to cover. Drain and slice. Potatoes should measure 6 cups. Add broccoli, carrots, peas, tomatoes and onion. Pour salad dressing over vegetables and add black pepper, tossing lightly to mix.

Yield: 10 to 12 servings

Antipasto Salad

- 3 cups caulifloweretes
- 1 cup thinly sliced carrots
- 1 cup chopped celery
- 1 medium-sized red bell pepper, chopped
- 1 medium-sized green bell pepper, chopped
- 1 cup sliced mushrooms
- 1 small onion, sliced
- ¾ cup tarragon or white wine vinegar
- ¼ cup water
- ¼ cup olive oil
- ¼ cup vegetable oil
- 1 tablespoon honey
- ½ teaspoon oregano
- ½ teaspoon basil
- Herb salt to taste
- Freshly ground black pepper to taste
- 1 (3 ounce) jar pimento-stuffed green olives, drained

In large saucepan, combine cauliflowerets, carrots, celery, bell pepper, mushrooms and onion. Add vinegar, water, olive oil, vegetable oil, honey, oregano, basil, herb salt and black pepper. Bring to a boil, reduce heat and simmer for 5 minutes. Pour into bowl and stir in olives. Chill, covered, overnight.
Yield: 8 servings

Healthy Garden Salad

- 1 small red bell pepper, chopped
- 1 small green bell pepper, chopped
- 1 small yellow bell pepper, chopped
- 1 small carrot, shaved or finely shredded
- 6 to 8 radishes, sliced
- 2 small yellow squash, sliced
- 2 stalks celery, finely chopped
- 1 small red onion, sliced
- Black pepper to taste
- Parsley flakes to taste
- 1 (8 ounce) bottle low-calorie Italian salad dressing
- Lettuce leaves
- Tomato wedges (optional)

Combine bell pepper, carrots, radishes, squash, celery, red onion, black pepper and parsley flakes. Add portion of dressing, mixing well. Chill until ready to serve. Add additional dressing and mix thoroughly. Serve on lettuce leaves and garnish with tomato.
Yield: 6 servings

Black Bean-Corn Salad

- 1 (16 ounce) can black beans, drained
- 1 (16 ounce) can Mexican corn, drained
- ¼ cup chopped celery
- Chopped parsley to taste
- Thinly sliced green onion (optional)
- Chopped mushrooms (optional)
- ¼ cup Italian salad dressing

Rinse beans and corn with cold water and drain. Add celery, parsley, onion and mushrooms. Stir in dressing, mixing well. Chill until ready to serve.

Note: This is a great salad for a summer picnic.
Yield: 4 servings

Black-Eyed Pea Salad

Salad

- 4 cups cooked black-eyed peas, drained, or 2 (16 ounce) cans, drained
- 2 cups cooked rotini pasta
- 1 medium-sized red bell pepper, chopped
- 1 medium-sized green bell pepper, chopped
- 1 medium-sized purple onion, chopped
- 1 (16 ounce) package sliced provolone cheese, cut in strips
- 1 (3 ounce) package sliced pepperoni, cut in strips
- 1 (2 ounce) jar pimento, drained and diced
- 1 (4½ ounce) jar sliced mushrooms, drained
- 2 tablespoons chopped parsley

Combine black-eyed peas, pasta, bell pepper, purple onion, provolone cheese, pepperoni, pimento, mushrooms and parsley. Prepare dressing. Add dressing to vegetables and mix thoroughly. Chill, covered, for at least 2 hours before serving.
Yield: 8 to 10 servings

Dressing

- 1 (0.7 ounce) package Italian salad dressing mix
- ½ cup vinegar
- ¼ cup vegetable oil
- ¼ cup sugar
- ¼ teaspoon black pepper

Combine dressing mix, vinegar, oil, sugar and black pepper in jar with tightly fitting lid. Shake until sugar is dissolved.
Yield: 1 cup

Mangum's Pottery Salad

Salad

1 (16 ounce) can crowder peas
1 (16 ounce) can black-eyed peas
1 (16 ounce) can black beans
1 (16 ounce) can shoe peg corn
1 (8 ounce) can water chestnuts, drained and chopped
1 (2 ounce) jar pimento, drained and chopped
½ cup chopped green bell pepper
½ cup chopped celery
½ cup chopped onion

Drain crowder peas, black-eyed peas, beans and corn in colander, rinse, drain again and transfer to large bowl. Add water chestnuts, pimento, bell pepper, celery and onion. Prepare dressing. Pour over vegetables and toss to coat thoroughly. Chill for at least 24 hours to blend flavors.
Yield: 12 servings

Dressing

¾ cup vinegar
¾ cup vegetable oil
½ cup sugar

Combine vinegar, oil and sugar, blending well.

Celia's Make-Ahead Salad

Dressing

1 (16 ounce) can LeSueur peas, drained
½ cup thinly sliced green onion
½ cup thinly sliced celery
1 (8 ounce) can sliced water chestnuts, drained
1½ cups ranch salad dressing
1 teaspoon sugar
1 teaspoon salt
⅛ teaspoon black pepper

Combine peas, green onion, celery and water chestnuts. Stir in salad dressing, sugar, salt and black pepper. Chill thoroughly.
Yield: 5 cups

Salad

1 head lettuce, shredded
1 cup cherry tomato halves
3 tablespoons bacon bits

Just before serving, place lettuce in individual serving bowls. Pour dressing over lettuce and garnish with tomato and bacon.
Yield: 6 servings

Scandinavian Salad

Salad

1 (16 ounce) can French-style green beans
1 (16 ounce) can small peas
1 (2 ounce) jar pimento, chopped
2 medium-sized onions, minced
2 cups finely chopped celery

Drain green beans, peas and pimento, reserving liquids. Combine beans, peas, pimento, onion and celery in heat-safe container. Prepare dressing. Pour hot liquid dressing over vegetables. Chill for 12 to 48 hours. Drain well before serving cold.
Yield: 8 servings

Dressing

1 cup vinegar
½ cup vegetable oil
1 tablespoon sugar
1 teaspoon salt
1 teaspoon celery seed
1 tablespoon mustard seed

Combine reserved vegetable liquid, vinegar, oil, sugar, salt, celery seed and mustard seed in saucepan. Bring to a boil. Pour over vegetable mixture.
Yield: 1½ cups

Chinese Vegetable Salad

Salad

- **1 (16 ounce) can fancy mixed Chinese vegetables, drained**
- **1 (16 ounce) can French-style green beans, drained**
- **1 (16 ounce) can English peas, drained**
- **1 (8 ounce) can water chestnuts, drained**
- **1 (8 ounce) can bamboo shoots, drained**
- **1 (4 ounce) can mushrooms, drained**
- **1½ cups diced celery**
- **1 medium-sized onion, chopped**

Combine Chinese vegetables, green beans, peas, water chestnuts, bamboo shoots, mushrooms, celery and onion. Prepare dressing. Pour over vegetables and chill overnight.
Yield: 12 to 16 servings

Dressing

- **¾ cup vinegar**
- **½ cup sugar**
- **1 teaspoon salt**
- **Black pepper to taste**

Combine vinegar, sugar, salt and black pepper, blending until sugar and salt is dissolved.
Yield: 1 cup

Georgia Lettuce Salad

- **1 head lettuce, torn in bite-sized pieces**
- **1 (16 ounce) can English peas, drained**
- **1 small green bell pepper, chopped**
- **1 stalk celery, chopped**
- **1 small red onion, thinly sliced**
- **Mayonnaise**
- **Grated Parmesan cheese**
- **Salad bits or crumbled bacon**

A day in advance of serving, place lettuce in serving bowl or dish. Combine peas, bell pepper, celery and onion. Spoon vegetables on lettuce. Spread mayonnaise over vegetables in smooth layer to seal salad. Sprinkle Parmesan cheese on mayonnaise and top with salad bits or bacon. Cover dish with plastic wrap. Chill for 24 hours.

Note: Because it is prepared in advance, this salad is very convenient for serving guests.
Yield: 6 to 8 servings

Marinated Vegetables

Salad

2 cups broccoli flowerets
2 cups thinly sliced carrots
1½ cups caulifloweret s
1½ cups thickly sliced fresh mushrooms
3 stalks celery, sliced diagonally
1 medium zucchini, sliced
½ medium cucumber, cut in half lengthwise and sliced
½ cup green bell pepper rings

Several hours or a day in advance, prepare dressing. Combine broccoli, carrots, cauliflower, mushrooms, celery, zucchini, cucumber and bell pepper. Pour dressing over vegetables and chill for at least 3 hours or overnight. For ease in handling, place vegetables in zip-closure plastic bags, add dressing and chill, turning bags often.
Yield: 10 servings

Dressing

½ cup sugar
½ cup vinegar
⅓ cup vegetable oil
1½ teaspoons salt
½ teaspoon mustard
½ teaspoon celery seed

Combine sugar, vinegar, oil, salt, mustard and celery seed in saucepan. Bring to a boil and stir to dissolve sugar. Let stand to cool slightly.
Yield: 1 cup

Easy Napa Valley Salad

4 cups lettuce, spinach or combination, torn in bite-sized pieces
2 hard-cooked eggs, chopped
1 cup (4 ounces) shredded sharp cheese
1 (16 ounce) can beets, drained and chilled
1000 Island salad dressing

Divide lettuce or spinach, eggs, cheese and beets equally among 4 individual salad plates. Drizzle dressing over salads.

Note: this recipe is served at a restaurant in Napa Valley, California.
Yield: 4 servings

No Egg Caesar Salad

Salad

1 large head Romaine lettuce
2 tablespoons grated Parmesan cheese
½ cup salad croutons

Trim core from lettuce, rinse in colander with cold running water, shake to remove excess moisture, wrap in paper towels and store in refrigerator; if more than 1 hour before serving, store in plastic bag. Prepare dressing. Just before serving, tear lettuce into bite-sized pieces. Pour dressing over lettuce, sprinkle with Parmesan cheese, toss quickly, sprinkle with croutons and serve immediately.
Yield: 4 to 6 servings

Dressing

½ cup low-fat Parmesan-Italian salad dressing
¾ teaspoon Mrs. Dash
¼ teaspoon dry mustard
1½ teaspoons Worcestershire sauce
¼ cup (1 ounce) crumbled blue cheese (optional)
2 tablespoons lemon juice

Combine salad dressing, Mrs. Dash, mustard, Worcestershire sauce, cheese and lemon juice. Chill until ready to use.
Yield: ¾ cup

Spinach Salad

Salad

½ pound bacon
2 bunches spinach, torn in bite-sized pieces
1 head iceberg lettuce, torn in bite-sized pieces
Blue cheese (optional)

Cook bacon until crisp, drain well and crumble. Combine spinach and lettuce. Prepare dressing. Pour over vegetables, add bacon and blue cheese and toss to mix thoroughly.
Yield: 6 to 8 servings

Dressing

¼ cup sugar
⅓ cup cider vinegar
1 cup vegetable oil
1 teaspoon salt
1 teaspoon dry mustard
1 tablespoon minced onion
1 tablespoon poppy seeds

Combine sugar, vinegar, oil, salt, mustard, onion and poppy seed in jar with tight-fitting lid. Shake well until sugar is dissolved.
Yield: 1½ cups

South Boston (Virginia) Salad

Salad

6 slices bacon
Slivered almonds
Butter
Sugar
6 to 8 cups mixed lettuce, torn in bite-sized pieces
1 (11 ounce) can mandarin oranges, drained
1 small red onion, sliced

Cook bacon until crisp, drain well and crumble. Toast almonds in butter and toss with sugar. Combine bacon, almonds, lettuce, oranges and onion. Prepare dressing. Pour over vegetables and toss to coat thoroughly. Store extra dressing in refrigerator.
Yield: 6 servings

Dressing

¼ cup sugar
¼ cup red wine vinegar
½ cup vegetable oil
1 tablespoon tarragon
3 drops hot pepper sauce
Salt and black pepper to taste

Combine sugar, vinegar, oil, tarragon, hot pepper sauce, salt and black pepper, blending until sugar is dissolved.
Yield: 1 cup

Green Salad Unique

Salad

1 pound assorted lettuce, torn in bite-sized pieces
1 pound spinach, torn in bite-sized pieces
2 large avocados, sliced
1 pint strawberries, cut in halves
1 cantaloupe, cut in balls
1 pint cherry tomatoes
2 cucumbers, sliced
1 (8 ounce) carton mushrooms, sliced

Combine lettuce, spinach, avocados, strawberries, cantaloupe, tomatoes, cucumbers and mushrooms. Prepare dressing. Pour over vegetables, tossing to coat thoroughly.
Yield: 6 to 8 servings

Poppy Seed Dressing

½ cup sugar
½ cup tarragon vinegar
1 cup vegetable oil
1 teaspoon grated onion
¾ teaspoon salt
1 tablespoon poppy seeds
1 teaspoon dry mustard

Combine sugar, vinegar, oil, onion, salt, poppy seed and mustard, blending well.
Yield: 2 cups

Blue Cheese Dressing

- 1 (2 ounce) package blue cheese
- 1 cup mayonnaise
- 2 tablespoons vinegar
- ¼ cup sour cream
- ⅛ teaspoon garlic powder

Combine blue cheese, mayonnaise, vinegar, sour cream and garlic powder in blender or food processor container. Blend thoroughly. Consistency will be thick.
Yield: 2 cups

Super Salad Seasoning Mix

- 2 cups grated Parmesan cheese
- ½ cup sesame seed
- 2 teaspoons salt
- ½ teaspoon freshly ground black pepper
- ½ teaspoon garlic salt
- 1 tablespoon minced onion flakes
- 1 tablespoon parsley flakes
- ½ teaspoon dill weed
- 2 tablespoons poppy seed
- 1 teaspoon monosodium glutamate (optional)
- 3 tablespoons celery seed
- 2 teaspoons paprika

Combine Parmesan cheese, sesame seed, salt, black pepper, garlic salt, onion, parsley, dill weed, poppy seed, monosodium glutamate, celery seed and paprika. Mix well. Store in cool, dry place for up to 4 months.

Note: Use as topping for tossed salads, baked potato, buttered bread and soups or as garnish for potato, macaroni or egg salads. For sour cream dip, combine 2 tablespoons mix and 1 cup sour cream.
Yield: 3 cups

A few peppercorns in pepper shaker will keep holes from clogging and give ground pepper a fresh taste.

Breads

Most Carolinians grew up with homemade biscuits at every meal and yeast rolls on Sunday. Southern women were known for their baking skills. Almost every one had a particular bread, cake or pie that they were associated with, and were expected to bring to each family gathering.

Many of us remember standing patiently while biscuits were being made and hoping that the biscuit maker would have some leftover dough. This leftover or scrap dough would be rolled out, cut into strips, buttered lightly, sprinkled with cinnamon and sugar, rolled up like a pinwheel and popped into the oven: Stickies! That is one name given to this serendipitous morsel.

We hope you will fill your home with the aroma of one of our delightful breads and create some "Stickies" of your own.

Breads

Different breads reflect variety in ingredients and the method of preparation, especially in terms of leavening agents. Classic bread preparation usually involves the use of yeast and the necessity of kneading in conjunction with timed periods between steps. Quick breads do not use yeast so they do not require kneading, thereby providing a shortcut alternative for cooks with less time. Sourdough bread appeals to persons who enjoy old-time baking procedures.

Flour

All-purpose Flour—A basic multi-purpose flour, all-purpose is usually a blend of hard and soft wheats with the bran and wheat germ removed.

Cake Flour—Made from soft wheat and whiter with a finer texture than all-purpose flour, cake flour is used in delicate cake recipes.

Combinations—Whole wheat or graham flour, rye and buckwheat flours, bran cornmeal and oatmeal can be used in combination with all-purpose flour for special bread recipes. Whole grain flours and meals are never sifted but stirred lightly to mix, then measured.

Self-rising Flour—As its name implies, this flour contains leavening and salt. It can not be used in yeast bread recipes and when used in quick bread recipes, the salt, baking soda and baking powder are omitted.

Whole Wheat Flour—This flour contains all the grain. The wheat germ is perishable so wheat flour should be used quickly or stored in the freezer.

Leavenings

Leavenings are ingredients that form gas bubbles—specifically carbon dioxide when combined with liquid and other ingredients. The gas, air or steam expands when dough is heated.

Baking Powder—All baking powders contain three basic ingredients: soda, some sort of acid and cornstarch or flour. Gas bubbles form when baking powder is combined with liquid and the batter is heated.

Baking Soda—Baking soda releases gas when combined with acidic ingredients such as buttermilk, sour milk, vinegar or lemon juice.

Yeast—A tiny plant organism, yeast produces carbon dioxide when combined with other ingredients. Temperature and moisture combine to promote is growth. Yeast comes in two varieties: active dry yeast and compressed cake yeast.

Bread Notes

Bread Crumbs—Save bread crusts and heels to toast, then process in a blender or food processor for dry bread crumbs. For fresh crumbs, process whole slices of fresh bread. Store crumbs in an airtight container or freezer to prevent drying.

Bread Cups—Using large round cookie cutter, cut rounds from bread slices. Press into muffin pans and bake at 375° until browned, watching closely to avoid overbrowning. Use small cutter and miniature muffin pans to make cups for appetizer servings.

Bread Fingers—Slice hot dog buns in halves crosswise, then in quarters lengthwise. Brush with butter and sprinkle with garlic and herbs. Broil or bake quickly in oven until lightly browned.

Croutons—Dice 2 cups stale bread, preferably sourdough or French. Toss with ¼ cup olive oil flavored with crushed garlic. Scatter cubes on baking sheet and bake at 350°, stirring once or twice, until browned. Drain on paper towels and store in airtight container until needed.

Garlic Bread—Blend ½ cup melted butter, ¼ teaspoon oregano, 1/4 teaspoon basil and 1 teaspoon garlic salt. Cut loaf of French bread in slices, brush cut surfaces with butter mixture and wrap in aluminum foil. Bake at 425° for 10 to 15 minutes.

Muffins

- Stir muffin batter just enough to moisten the dry ingredients. Batter will be lumpy.
- For lighter muffins, place greased muffin pan in preheated oven for a minute or two before pouring batter into cups.
- Remove muffins from pans while slightly warm to prevent sogginess.

Biscuits and Rolls

- Shape and freeze unbaked yeast rolls on a baking sheet. Package frozen dough in plastic bags and freeze. When ready to use, remove from freezer, let dough thaw and rise in a pan, then bake.
- Knead dough after mixing ingredients for baking powder biscuits to improve texture.

Pancakes and Waffles

- Never sift pancake, biscuit or cake mix.
- Pancakes and waffles brown more quickly if a pinch of sugar is added to the batter.
- Add partially frozen, rather than thawed, berries to pancake batter or bread mixture to prevent bleeding in cooking.
- For variety, add chopped pecans, crumbled bacon or grated cheese to a favorite waffle batter.

A new twist on Cinnamon Toast - Chocolate Toast. Mix 3 heaping teaspoons of sugar with ¼ teaspoon of cocoa and sprinkle it over buttered toast.

Dilly Bread

- 1 packet active dry yeast
- ¼ cup warm (105 to 115°) water
- 1 cup cream-style cottage cheese
- 1 tablespoon minced onion
- 2 tablespoons sugar
- 1 teaspoon salt
- 1 teaspoon baking soda
- 1 tablespoon melted butter
- 2 teaspoons dill seed
- 1 egg
- 2¼ to 2½ cups all-purpose flour
- Melted butter
- Salt

Dissolve yeast in warm water. Heat cottage cheese to lukewarm (105 to 115°). Combine yeast liquid, cottage cheese, onion, sugar, salt, baking soda, butter, dill seed and egg. Using electric mixer, beat at low speed until well blended. Add most of flour, ½ cup at a time, beating well after each addition; fold in final portion by hand to form soft dough. Place in well-greased bowl, cover and let rise in warm place for 50 to 60 minutes or until doubled in bulk. Punch dough down, shape to form loaf and place in well-greased 9x5x3-inch loaf pan. Cover and let rise until doubled in bulk, above rim of pan. Bake at 350° for 40 to 50 minutes. Brush hot loaf with melted butter and sprinkle with salt.
Yield: 1 loaf

Sally Lunn Bread

- ¼ cup water
- 1 cup milk
- ½ cup vegetable shortening
- 4 cups sifted all-purpose flour, divided
- ⅓ cup sugar
- 2 teaspoons salt
- 2 packets active dry yeast
- 3 eggs

Combine water, milk and shortening in saucepan. Heat until warm (120°); shortening does not need to be fully melted. Combine 1 ⅓ cups flour, sugar, salt and yeast in mixing bowl. Using electric mixer, blend warm liquid into dry ingredients and beat at medium speed for about 2 minutes. Gradually add ⅔ cup of the remaining flour and the eggs and beat at high speed for 2 minutes. Add the remaining flour and mix well. Cover and let rise in warm, draft-free place until doubled in bulk. Beat dough down. Place in greased 10-inch tube or fluted tube pan. Cover and let rise until doubled in bulk. Bake at 350° for 40 to 50 minutes. Use knife tip to separate loaf from pan edges, remove and place on wire rack to cool.
Yield: 1 loaf

Potato Sourdough Bread and Rolls

6 cups bread flour
⅓ cup sugar
1 packet active dry yeast
1 tablespoon salt
½ cup vegetable oil
1 cup Potato Sourdough Starter
1½ cups warm (120 to 130°) water
2 tablespoons melted butter

Combine flour, sugar, yeast and salt. Gradually add oil, potato sourdough starter and warm water, mixing to form dough. Place dough on floured surface and lightly knead 4 to 5 times. Place in well-greased bowl, turning to grease all surfaces. Cover and let rise in warm, draft-free place for 2 hours or until doubled in bulk. For bread, punch dough down, divide in 2 portions and shape each into a loaf. Place in 9x5x3-inch loaf pans. Brush tops with melted butter. Cover and let rise in warm, draft-free place for 1 hour or until doubled in bulk. Bake at 350° for 25 minutes or until loaves sound hollow when tapped. Remove from pans immediately and cool on wire racks. For rolls, punch dough down, divided in 2 portions and shape each into 12 balls. Place in greased 8-inch round baking pan. Brush tops with melted butter. Cover and let rise in warm, draft-free place, for 1 hour or until doubled in bulk. Bake at 350° for 15 minutes or until golden brown.
Yield: 2 loaves or 2 dozen rolls

Use a grater rather than a knife to scrape the bottom of burned biscuits.

Potato Sourdough Starter

- ¾ cup sugar
- 3 tablespoons instant potato flakes
- 1 packet active dry yeast
- 1 cup warm (120 to 130°) water
- Starter Food

Combine sugar, potato flakes and yeast. Stir in warm water. Cover with plastic wrap, then pierce wrap with sharp knife tip in 4 to 5 places. Store in refrigerator for 3 to 5 days. Before using, let stand at room temperature for 1 hour. Stir well. Remove 1 cup starter and use in a recipe or give to a friend. Prepare 1 recipe starter food. Stir in remaining starter and let stand, uncovered, for 8 to 12 hours. Cover with plastic wrap, then pierce wrap with sharp knife tip in 4 to 5 places. Store in refrigerator for 3 to 5 days. Repeat process 3 times. Use all or discard after 4 "feedings".
Yield: 3½ cups

Starter Food

- ¾ cup sugar
- 3 tablespoons instant potato flakes
- 1 cup warm (120 to 130°) water

Combine sugar, potato flakes and warm water.

Mammaw's Rolls

- 1 packet active dry yeast
- ¼ cup warm (105 to 115°) water
- 2 egg whites, lightly beaten
- ½ cup vegetable oil
- ½ cup sugar
- 1 teaspoon salt
- 1 cup lukewarm (100 to 110°) water
- 4 cups sifted all-purpose flour

Dissolve yeast in warm water. In order listed, combine egg whites, oil, sugar, yeast liquid, salt, lukewarm water and flour. Mix thoroughly to form dough. Cover and chill for at least 12 hours. Pinch or shape dough into rolls. Place in well-greased baking pan and let rise for 2 hours or until doubled in bulk. Bake at 375° for about 15 minutes or until crust is browned.
Yield: 3 to 4 dozen

Quick Herbed Rolls

- ½ cup butter
- 1½ teaspoons parsley flakes
- ½ teaspoon dill weed
- 1 tablespoon onion flakes
- 2 tablespoons grated Parmesan cheese
- 1 (10 ounce) can refrigerated buttermilk biscuits

Melt butter in 9x9x2-inch baking pan. Add parsley, dill, onion and cheese to butter, mixing evenly. Let stand for 15 to 20 minutes. Cut biscuits pieces in halves or quarters. Dredge each in herb butter mixture, coating on all surfaces. Place biscuit pieces in baking pan. Bake at 425° for 12 to 15 minutes. Serve hot.

Note: Do not use flaky-style biscuit dough. Rolls can be assembled, covered and stored in refrigerator for up to 3 hours before baking.
Yield: 10 servings

Cinnamon Meringue Coffee Cake

- 2 tablespoons sugar
- 1 packet active dry yeast
- ¼ cup warm (105 to 115°) milk
- 1 cup margarine, softened
- 3 egg yolks
- 2 cups all-purpose flour

Dissolve sugar and yeast in milk. Combine margarine, egg yolks and flour. Stir yeast liquid into dry ingredients and blend well. Chill, covered, overnight. Prepare meringue filling. Divide dough into 2 portions. On lightly-floured surface, roll each to 18x16-inch rectangle. Spread ½ of meringue on dough, sprinkle with 1 teaspoon cinnamon and ½ cup nuts. Roll up and place in greased 9-inch round baking pan in circle. Bake at 325° for 20 to 25 minutes. Let stand until cool. Drizzle with frosting.

Note: Circle can be decorated with red and green candied cherries to resemble Christmas wreath. Baked cakes can be frozen.
Yield: 16 servings

Meringue Filling

- 3 egg whites
- ¾ cup sugar
- 1 cup coarsely chopped nuts
- 2 teaspoons cinnamon

Beat egg whites until stiff but not dry. Add sugar and mix well.

Frosting

- 1 cup powdered sugar
- 1 tablespoon milk

Blend powdered sugar with milk until smooth.

Cream Cheese Braids

- **1 cup sour cream**
- **½ cup sugar**
- **1 teaspoon salt**
- **½ cup margarine, melted**
- **2 packets active dry yeast**
- **½ cup warm (105 to 115°) water**
- **2 eggs**
- **4 cups unsifted all-purpose flour**

Scald sour cream. Stir in sugar, salt and margarine. Let stand until lukewarm. Sprinkle yeast on warm water in large warm bowl and stir to blend. Add sour cream mixture, eggs and flour, mixing until well blended. Chill, tightly covered, overnight. Prepare filling. Divide dough into 4 portions. On lightly-floured surface, roll each to 12x8-inch rectangle. Spread ¼ of filling on each, leaving ½-inch margin along edges. Roll up, from long side, pressing ends together and folding under slightly. Place in baking pan or on baking sheet lined with aluminum foil and greased. Using scissors, cut roll about ¾ way through, alternating from side to side, to resemble braid. Let rise until doubled in bulk. Bake at 375° for 12 to 15 minutes or until lightly browned. Drizzle with glaze.
Yield: 16 servings

Filling

- **2 (8 ounce) packages cream cheese, softened**
- **1 egg, beaten**
- **¾ cup sugar**
- **⅛ teaspoon salt**
- **2 teaspoons vanilla**

Combine cream cheese, egg, sugar, salt and vanilla, beating by hand, electric mixer or blender until smooth.

Glaze

- **2 cups powdered sugar**
- **¼ cup milk**
- **2 teaspoons vanilla**

Combine powdered sugar, milk and vanilla, blending until smooth.

Muffins will slide right out of tin pans if the hot pan is placed on a wet towel first.

Refrigerator Rolls or Cinnamon Buns or Coffee Cake

- **1 cup vegetable shortening**
- **½ cup sugar**
- **1 cup boiling water**
- **2 packets active dry yeast**
- **1 cup warm (105 to 115°) water**
- **2 eggs, beaten**
- **6 cups all-purpose flour**
- **1 teaspoon baking powder**
- **1 teaspoon baking soda**
- **2 teaspoons salt**

Dissolve shortening and sugar in boiling water. Let stand until lukewarm. Dissolve yeast in warm water. Add to shortening mixture. Blend in eggs. Sift flour, baking powder, baking soda and salt together. Add dry ingredients to liquid and mix well. Chill, covered, for several hours or overnight. Pinch or shape dough into rolls. Place in well-greased baking pan and let rise for 2 to 3 hours or until doubled in bulk. Bake at 350° for about 15 minutes.
Yield: 5 to 6 dozen

Cinnamon Buns

- **Margarine, softened**
- **Brown sugar**
- **Cinnamon**
- **Raisins**

Prepare roll dough and chill as directed. Working with ½ of dough at a time, place on lightly-floured surface and roll to form rectangle. Spread with margarine and sprinkle with brown sugar, cinnamon and raisins. Roll up, cut into uniform slices and place in well-greased baking pan, flat side down. Let rise for 2 to 3 hours or until doubled in bulk. Bake at 350° for about 15 minutes. Spread frosting on hot rolls.
Yield: 3 to 4 dozen

Coffee Cake

- **1 (16 ounce) package brown sugar**
- **1 cup raisins**
- **½ cup margarine, softened**
- **1 cup chopped nuts**
- **½ cup candied cherries (optional)**
- **¼ cup plus 2 tablespoons flour**
- **⅓ to ¾ cups cinnamon**
- **Vegetable oil**
- **⅓ to ¾ cup margarine, melted**

Continued on next page

Refrigerator Rolls or Cinnamon Buns or Coffee Cake (continued)

Prepare roll dough and chill as directed. Divide dough into 6 portions. Place on lightly-floured surface and roll to ¼-inch thickness in rectangle shape. Combine brown sugar, raisins, softened margarine, nuts, cherries and flour. Divide into 6 portions. Spread each dough rectangle with 1 to 2 tablespoons cinnamon and 1 portion brown sugar mixture. Roll up and place on well-greased baking sheet to form ring, bringing ends together. Using scissors, cut roll at 1-inch intervals, almost through, and turn each to lie flat, overlapping slightly. Brush lightly with oil. Let rise until doubled in bulk. Bake at 350° for 15 to 20 minutes or until browned. Brush hot cake with 1 to 2 tablespoons melted margarine and spread with frosting.
Yield: 6 (6x8-inch) coffeecakes

Frosting

1 (16 ounce) package powdered sugar
Boiling water

Combine powdered sugar with small amount of boiling water to form paste. Spread on hot buns or coffee cake.

Monkey Bread

1 cup milk
1 cup butter or margarine, divided
¼ cup sugar
1 teaspoon salt
1 packet active dry yeast
3½ cups all-purpose flour

Combine milk, ½ cup butter, sugar and salt in saucepan. Heat until butter is melted, remove from heat and cool to 105 to 115°. Add yeast and stir until dissolved. Place flour in large mixing bowl, form well in center and pour liquid mixture into well. Stir until blended. Let rise, covered, for 1 hour and 20 minutes or until doubled in bulk. On lightly-floured surface, roll dough to ¼-inch thickness in rectangle shape. Cut into 3-inch squares. Melt remaining ½ cup butter and dip each square into butter. Layer squares in 10-inch tube or fluted tube pan. Let rise for 20 to 30 minutes or until doubled in bulk. Bake at 375° for 30 to 40 minutes.

Note: The recipe may appear complicated but after preparing once, is easy and quick.
Yield: 10 to 12 servings

Banana Sour Cream Coffee Cake

½ cup chopped pecans
1¼ cups sugar, divided
½ teaspoon cinnamon
½ cup vegetable shortening
2 eggs
1 cup mashed bananas
1 teaspoon vanilla
½ cup sour cream
2 cups all-purpose flour
1 teaspoon baking powder
1 teaspoon baking soda
¼ teaspoon salt

Combine pecans, ¼ cup sugar and cinnamon, mixing well. Cream shortening and remaining 1 cup sugar together until light and fluffy. Beat in eggs, bananas and vanilla. Stir in sour cream. Combine flour, baking powder, baking soda and salt. Add dry ingredients to creamed mixture and mix just until blended. Sprinkle ½ of pecan mixture in bottom of well-greased 10-inch fluted tube pan, spoon ½ of batter into pan and repeat layers. Bake at 350° for 40 to 45 minutes or until wooden pick inserted near center comes out clean. Cool cake in pan for 5 minutes, loosen from sides of pan if necessary and invert on serving plate. Serve warm or cold.
Yield: 12 to 16 servings

Blueberry Coffee Cake

½ cup butter or margarine, softened
1 cup plus 1 tablespoon sugar, divided
¼ teaspoon salt
1 teaspoon vanilla
2 eggs, separated
1½ cups plus 1 tablespoon all-purpose flour, divided
1 teaspoon baking powder
⅓ cup milk
1½ cups fresh blueberries

Cream butter or margarine with ¾ cup sugar and salt. Add vanilla and egg yolks and beat until creamy. Combine 1 ½ cups flour and baking powder. Alternately add dry ingredients and milk to creamed mixture, blending well. Beat egg whites until soft peaks form. Add remaining ¼ cup sugar, 1 tablespoon at a time, and beat until stiff. Sprinkle berries with remaining 1 tablespoon flour. Add to batter. Fold egg whites into batter. Spread batter in greased 8x8x2-inch baking pan. Sprinkle with remaining 1 tablespoon sugar. Bake at 350° for 50 minutes or until wooden pick inserted near center comes out clean.
Yield: 8 servings

Favorite Brunch Baked Blintz

- 1 cup sugar, divided
- 4 eggs, divided
- 1 cup all-purpose flour
- 1 tablespoon baking powder
- ¼ cup milk
- 1 teaspoon vanilla
- 1 cup butter or margarine, melted
- 1 (16 ounce) carton cottage cheese
- 2 (8 ounce) packages cream cheese, softened
- Juice of 1 lemon
- Sour cream
- Strawberries

Combine ½ cup sugar, 2 eggs, flour, baking powder, milk and vanilla, blending well. Add margarine. Pour ½ of batter into 13x9x2-inch baking dish. Combine cottage cheese, cream cheese, remaining 2 eggs, remaining ½ cup sugar and lemon juice, blending until smooth. Spoon cheese mixture evenly on batter. Pour remaining batter on cheese layer. Bake at 350° for 1 hour. Cut into squares. Serve with dollop of sour cream and strawberries.

Note: Blintz can be assembled in advance and frozen. Thaw overnight in refrigerator before baking. It can also be frozen after baking.

Yield: 12 servings

Cinnamon Flip

- 1 cup sugar
- 1 rounded tablespoon vegetable shortening
- 1 cup milk
- 1 egg
- 1½ cups all-purpose flour
- 2 teaspoons baking powder
- All-purpose flour
- Brown sugar
- Butter
- Cinnamon

Cream sugar and shortening together until smooth. Add milk, egg, flour and baking powder, blending well. Spread batter in greased 13x9x2-inch baking pan, smoothing surface. Sift small amount of flour lightly over surface, sprinkle generously with brown sugar, add dots of butter and sprinkle with cinnamon. Bake at 350° for 40 minutes. Serve hot or cold.

Yield: 12 to 16 servings

Cranberry Coffee Cake

½ cup butter, softened
1 cup sugar
2 eggs
2 cups all-purpose flour
1 teaspoon baking soda
½ teaspoon salt
1 cup sour cream
1 teaspoon vanilla
½ cup chopped walnuts
1 (8 ounce) can whole cranberry sauce

Cream butter and sugar together until smooth. Add eggs 1 at a time, beating well after each addition. Combine flour, baking soda and salt. Alternately add dry ingredients and sour cream to creamed mixture. Stir in vanilla and nuts. Spread ⅓ of batter in greased 9-inch tube pan, spoon ½ of cranberry sauce on batter, repeat layers and top with remaining batter. Bake at 350° for 55 minutes. Cool in pan for 5 minutes, then invert on wire rack to complete cooling. Prepare glaze and drizzle over cake.

Yield: 8 to 12 servings

Glaze

¾ cup powdered sugar
1 tablespoon milk
½ teaspoon almond extract

Blend powdered sugar, milk and almond extract until smooth.

Streusel Coffee Cake

½ cup butter, softened
1 cup sugar
2 eggs
2¾ cups all-purpose flour, divided
½ teaspoon baking powder
½ teaspoon baking soda
½ teaspoon salt
1 cup buttermilk
1 teaspoon vanilla
¼ cup butter, melted
1 cup firmly-packed brown sugar
1½ teaspoons cinnamon
1 cup chopped nuts

Cream softened butter, sugar and eggs until smooth. Combine 2½ cups flour, baking powder, baking soda and salt. Add dry ingredients, buttermilk and vanilla to creamed mixture. Pour ½ of batter into greased and floured 13x9x2-inch baking pan. Combine melted butter, brown sugar, remaining ¼ cup flour, cinnamon and chopped nuts, mixing to streusel consistency. Sprinkle on batter and top with remaining batter. Bake at 350° for 30 minutes.

Yield: 16 servings

Bridget Latimer's Strawberry Coffee Cake

- ½ cup margarine, softened
- 1 (8 ounce) package cream cheese, softened
- ¾ cup sugar
- 1 cup milk
- 2 eggs, beaten
- 1 teaspoon vanilla
- 2 cups all-purpose flour
- 1 teaspoon baking powder
- ½ teaspoon baking soda
- ¼ teaspoon salt
- 1 (18 ounce) jar strawberry preserves
- 1 tablespoon lemon juice
- ¼ cup firmly-packed brown sugar
- ½ cup chopped pecans

Cream margarine, cream cheese and sugar together until smooth. Blend in milk, eggs and vanilla. Sift flour, baking powder, baking soda and salt together. Add dry ingredients to creamed mixture, mixing well. Spread ½ of batter in lightly-greased 13x9x2-inch baking dish. Combine preserves and lemon juice. Drop teaspoonfuls of preserves on batter and lightly spread to cover batter; do not mix into batter. Spoon remaining batter over preserves layer. Sprinkle with brown sugar and pecans. Bake at 350° for 40 minutes.
Yield: 16 servings

Double Apricot Bread

- 1 (16 ounce) can apricot halves, drained
- 1¾ cups all-purpose flour
- ¾ cup whole wheat flour
- 1¼ cups sugar
- 3½ teaspoons baking powder
- 1 teaspoon salt
- ½ teaspoon pumpkin pie spice
- 2 eggs, beaten
- ½ cup milk
- 1 tablespoon vegetable oil
- 1 cup chopped dried apricots

Using blender or food processor, puree canned apricots and set aside. Combine flour, whole wheat flour, sugar, baking powder, salt and pumpkin pie spice in large mixing bowl. Combine eggs, apricot puree, milk and oil. Add liquid mixture to dry ingredients, stirring just until moistened. Stir in dried apricots. Pour batter into 2 greased 8x4x2½-inch or 7½x3½x2-inch loaf pans. bake at 350° for 45 to 50 minutes or until wooden pick inserted near center comes out clean. Cool in pan for 10 minutes, then remove to wire rack to complete cooling.
Yield: 2 loaves

Sweet Puffs

- 2 cups all-purpose flour
- 1 cup butter
- ½ cup sour cream
- 1 egg yolk
- Powdered sugar

Using food processor, position knife blade in bowl. Add flour and butter. Pulse 4 or 5 times until mixture resembles coarse meal. Add sour cream and egg yolk. Process until dough forms a ball and separates from sides of bowl. Divide pastry into 2 portions. Chill, covered, for 8 hours. Prepare filling and set aside. On lightly-floured surface, roll pastry to ¼-inch thickness in rectangle. Cut into 3-inch squares. Press each piece into 1 ¾-inch cup of muffin pan, corners extending above rim. Spoon 1 teaspoon filling into each shell. Fold and seal corners over filling. Chill for 30 minutes. Bake at 375° for 20 to 25 minutes. Remove from pan and cool on wire rack. Sprinkle with powdered sugar.
Yield: 3½ dozen

Filling

- 1 (8 ounce) package cream cheese, softened
- 1 egg
- ½ cup sugar
- 1 teaspoon vanilla
- 1 teaspoon grated lemon peel

Combine cream cheese, egg, sugar, vanilla and lemon peel. Using electric mixer, beat at medium speed until smooth and fluffy.
Yield: 1½ cups

Banana Nut Bread

- 1 cup sugar
- ½ cup vegetable oil
- 2 eggs, beaten
- 3 large bananas, mashed
- 2 cups all-purpose flour
- ½ teaspoon baking powder
- 1 teaspoon baking soda
- ½ teaspoon salt
- 3 tablespoons milk
- ¾ teaspoon vanilla
- ½ cup chopped pecans

Combine sugar and oil, beating until smooth. Blend in eggs and bananas. Sift flour, baking powder, baking soda and salt together. Alternately add dry ingredients and milk with vanilla to banana mixture, beating thoroughly. Stir in nuts. Pour batter into greased 9x5x3-inch loaf pan. Bake at 350° for 1 hour.

Note: For small loaves, bake in 4 greased 5½x3x2-inch loaf pans at 325° for 40 minutes.

Yield: 1 loaf

Banana Raisin Bread

- 3 cups all-purpose flour
- ¾ cup firmly-packed light brown sugar
- 1 tablespoon baking powder
- ¾ teaspoon baking soda
- ¾ teaspoon salt
- ½ cup low-fat corn oil margarine
- 1 ⅔ cups mashed bananas
- 1 cup dark seedless raisins
- 1 cup uncooked quick cooking oats
- ½ cup frozen egg substitute, thawed
- ½ cup applesauce
- 1 teaspoon vanilla

Combine flour, brown sugar, baking powder, baking soda and salt. Using pastry blender or 2 knives in scissor fashion, cut margarine into dry ingredients until consistency of coarse crumbs. Add bananas, raisins, oats, egg substitute, applesauce and vanilla, stirring just until moistened. Spread batter in greased 9x5x3-inch loaf pan. Bake at 350° for 1 ¼ hours or until wooden pick inserted near center comes out clean. Cool in pan for 10 minutes, then remove to wire rack to complete cooling. Serve warm or cold.

Note: To present over browning, loosely cover bread with aluminum foil tent for last 15 minutes of baking time.

Yield: 1 loaf

Strawberry Bread

- 3 cups all-purpose flour
- 2 cups sugar
- 1 teaspoon baking soda
- 1 teaspoon salt
- 1 teaspoon cinnamon
- 3 eggs
- 1 cup vegetable oil
- 1 teaspoon vanilla
- 2 (10 ounce) packages frozen strawberries, thawed and chopped
- 1 cup chopped pecans

Combine flour, sugar, baking soda, salt and cinnamon. Blend eggs, oil, vanilla and strawberries together. Add strawberry mixture to dry ingredients and mix well. Stir in pecans. Pour into 2 greased 9x5x3-inch loaf pans. Bake at 350° for 45 to 60 minutes. Cool in pans for 10 minutes, then remove to wire rack to complete cooling.

Yield: 2 loaves

Cranberry Orange Loaf

3 cups all-purpose flour
2 teaspoons baking powder
2 teaspoons baking soda
1 teaspoon salt
2 teaspoons cinnamon
1 cup sugar
¼ cup butter, melted
4 eggs
Grated peel of 2 oranges
1 cup fresh orange juice
2 cups fresh cranberries
1 cup chopped walnuts
1 cup golden raisins

Combine flour, baking powder, baking soda, salt and cinnamon. Using electric mixer, combine sugar, butter, eggs and orange peel, mixing well. Alternately add dry ingredients and orange juice to egg mixture, beating well after each addition. Stir in cranberries, walnuts and raisins. Spread batter in 2 buttered and floured 9x5x3-inch loaf pans. Bake at 350° for 1 ¼ hours or until wooden pick inserted near center comes out clean; do not overbake. Cool in pans for 10 minutes, then remove to wire rack to complete cooling.
Yield: 2 loaves

Lemon Bread

2¼ cups sugar, divided
¾ cup margarine, softened
3 eggs
2¼ cups sifted all-purpose flour
¼ teaspoon baking soda
¼ teaspoon salt
¾ cup buttermilk
Grated peel of 1 lemon
¾ cups chopped nuts
Juice of 2 lemons

Cream 1½ cups sugar and margarine together. Beat in eggs. Sift flour, baking soda and salt together. Alternately add dry ingredients and buttermilk to creamed mixture, beating well after each addition. Stir in lemon peel and nuts. Pour batter into greased and floured 9x5x3-inch loaf pan. bake at 325° for 1 hour and 20 minutes. While bread bakes, combine lemon juice and remaining ¾ cup sugar, allowing sugar to dissolve. Cool bread in pan for 15 minutes, then remove and place on wire rack over wax paper or plate. Using cake tester or skewer, pierce top of loaf. Spoon lemon glaze over loaf. Cool completely before slicing.
Yield: 1 loaf

Orange Nut Bread

3 cups all-purpose flour
¼ cup sugar
2 teaspoons baking powder
½ teaspoon salt
½ cup chopped walnuts
1 tablespoon grated orange peel
½ cup orange marmalade
1 egg, well beaten
1 cup milk

Sift flour, sugar, baking powder and salt together. Add walnuts, orange peel and marmalade to dry ingredients. Blend egg and milk. Stir into orange marmalade mixture. Spread batter in well-greased 9x5x3-inch loaf pan. Let stand 15 to 20 minutes. Bake at 350° for 1 hour. Cool in pans for 10 minutes, then remove to wire rack to complete cooling.
Yield: 1 loaf

Peach Bread

2 cups all-purpose flour
1½ cups sugar, divided
1 teaspoon baking soda
¼ teaspoon salt
1 teaspoon cinnamon
½ cup chopped nuts (optional)
3 cups crushed peeled peaches
⅓ cup vegetable oil
2 eggs, beaten
1 teaspoon vanilla

Combine flour, 1 ¼ cups sugar, baking soda, salt, cinnamon and nuts. Sprinkle remaining ¼ cup sugar on peaches. Mix peaches, oil, eggs and vanilla together. Combine dry ingredients and peach mixture, mixing until blended. Pour batter into 2 well-greased 9x5x3-inch loaf pans. Bake at 325° for 55 minutes. Cool in pans for 10 minutes, then remove to wire rack to complete cooling.
Yield: 2 loaves

Beer Bread

5 cups self-rising flour
¼ cup plus 1 tablespoon sugar
1½ cups sour cream
1 (12 ounce) can beer
Melted butter

Combine flour and sugar. Alternately add sour cream and beer. Spread batter in greased 9x9x2-inch baking dish. Bake at 350° for 1 hour, brush with butter and bake for additional 10 minutes.
Yield: 16 servings

Pumpkin Nut Bread

3½ cups all-purpose flour
½ teaspoon baking powder
2 teaspoons baking soda
1½ teaspoons salt
½ teaspoon cinnamon
¼ teaspoon ground cloves
2 ⅔ cups sugar
4 eggs
⅔ cup vegetable shortening
⅔ cups water
2 cups pumpkin
1 cup raisins
1 cup chopped pecans

Sift flour, baking powder, baking soda, salt, cinnamon and cloves together. Combine sugar and eggs, beating until light and fluffy. Blend in shortening. Add water and pumpkin, mixing well. Add dry ingredients, raisins and pecans to pumpkin mixture. Pour batter into 3 greased 9x5x3-inch loaf pans or 16-ounce coffee cans. Bake at 350° for 1 hour. Cool in pans, remove and slice.

Note: For smaller loaves, ideal for Christmas gifts, bake batter in 7 greased 5 ¾x3 ¼x2-inch loaf pans at 350° for about 50 minutes. Bread can be frozen.
Yield: 3 loaves

The Best Zucchini Bread

3 cups sifted flour, divided
1½ cups chopped nuts
1 cup golden raisins
2 teaspoons baking powder
½ teaspoon baking soda
2 teaspoons salt
2 teaspoons cinnamon
2 teaspoons nutmeg
3 eggs
2 cups sugar
1 cup vegetable oil, divided
2 cups shredded zucchini
1 teaspoon vanilla

Combine ¼ cup flour, nuts and raisins. Sift remaining 2 ¾ cups flour, baking powder, baking soda, salt, cinnamon and nutmeg together. Combine eggs and sugar, beating thoroughly. Divide dry ingredients into 4 portions. In order listed, add to egg mixture: 1 portion flour and ½ cup oil; 1 portion flour and zucchini; 1 portion flour , remaining ½ cup oil, vanilla, nuts and raisins; remaining 1 portion flour, beating well after each addition. Batter will be liquid. Pour into 2 greased 9x5x3-inch loaf pans. Bake at 325° for 1 hour. Cool in pans for 10 minutes, then remove to wire rack to complete cooling.

Note: For smaller loaves, bake in 2 greased 7x3½x2½-inch loaf pans and 2 greased 5½x3x2-inch loaf pans.
Yield: 2 loaves

Bran Banana Nut Muffins

- 1 cup boiling water
- 3 cups all bran cereal
- ½ cup vegetable oil
- ½ cup molasses
- 2 eggs or equivalent egg substitute
- 1 cup raisins
- 2 very ripe bananas, mashed
- 2 cups buttermilk
- 3 cups whole wheat flour
- ½ cup firmly-packed brown sugar
- 1 tablespoon baking soda
- 1 cup chopped walnuts

Pour boiling water over cereal and let stand until cool. Add oil, molasses, eggs, raisins, bananas and buttermilk to cereal. Combine flour, brown sugar and baking soda. Add to bran mixture. Stir in nuts. Let stand, covered with wax paper, for 1 hour. Spoon batter into lightly-greased muffin pans. Bake at 400° for 25 minutes.

Note: Baked muffins freeze well.

Yield: 2 dozen

Ginger Muffins

- 1½ cups all-purpose flour
- 2 teaspoons baking powder
- ¾ teaspoon salt
- ½ teaspoon ginger
- ½ teaspoon cinnamon
- ¼ cup vegetable shortening
- 1 egg, beaten
- ½ cup milk
- ½ cup molasses
- Sugar

Combine flour, baking powder, salt, ginger and cinnamon. Cut shortening into dry ingredients until consistency of fine crumbs. Combine egg, milk and molasses. Add to dry mixture, stirring just until moistened. Spoon batter into greased muffin pans, filling cups ⅔ full. Sprinkle with sugar. Bake at 400° for about 20 minutes.

Yield: 1 dozen

Jelly Cheese Drops

- 2 cups all-purpose flour
- 1 tablespoon baking powder
- ¾ teaspoon salt
- 3 tablespoons vegetable shortening
- 1 cup (4 ounces) grated mild Cheddar cheese
- 1 cup milk
- 2 tablespoons tart jelly or orange marmalade

Sift flour, baking powder and salt together. Add shortening, blending with fork. Stir in cheese. Add milk and mix to form soft dough. Spoon dough into lightly-greased muffin pans, filling cups ⅔ full and indenting centers. Spoon ½ teaspoon jelly or marmalade into center of each. Bake at 450° for 15 to 20 minutes.

Yield: 1 dozen

Morning Glory Muffins

2 cups all-purpose flour
1¼ cups sugar
2 teaspoons baking soda
½ teaspoon salt
2 teaspoons cinnamon
2 cups grated carrots
½ cup raisins
½ cup shredded coconut
½ cup chopped pecans
3 eggs
1 cup vegetable oil
1 apple, cored and shredded
2 teaspoons vanilla

Combine flour, sugar, baking soda, salt and cinnamon. Add carrots, raisins, coconut and pecans. Combine eggs, oil, apple and vanilla. Add egg liquid to dry ingredients, stirring just until moistened. Spoon batter into greased or paper-lined muffin pans. Bake at 350° for 15 to 20 minutes.
Yield: 1½ dozen

Orange Muffins

1½ cups all-purpose flour
1 cup whole wheat flour
1 ⅔ cups sugar
2 teaspoons baking powder
½ teaspoon salt
¾ cup butter, melted
3 eggs, beaten
⅔ cup orange juice
1 tablespoon orange marmalade
1 teaspoon vanilla
1 teaspoon orange extract
½ cup chopped walnuts or pecans

Combine flours, sugar, baking powder and salt. Add butter, eggs, orange juice, marmalade, vanilla, orange extract and nuts, stirring just until moistened. Spoon batter into greased muffin pans, filling cups ½ full. Bake at 350° for 15 minutes.

Note: Baked muffins freeze well.
Yield: 2 dozen

Toasted Onion Muffins

1¾ cups biscuit baking mix
2 tablespoons cornmeal
2 tablespoons toasted onion flakes
¼ teaspoon salt
¼ teaspoon fines herbes
1 egg
1 cup milk
2 tablespoons vegetable oil

Combine biscuit mix, cornmeal, onions, salt and fines herbes. Add egg, milk and oil, stirring just until moistened. Spoon batter into well-greased muffins pans. Bake at 400° for 25 minutes.
Yield: ⅔ dozen

Zeverly House Pumpkin Muffins

- 1⅔ cups all-purpose flour
- 1½ cups sugar
- ¼ teaspoon baking powder
- 1 teaspoon baking soda
- ¼ teaspoon salt
- ⅛ teaspoon ground cloves
- 1 teaspoon pumpkin pie spice
- ⅓ cup raisins
- ⅓ cup butter, melted
- ⅓ cup water
- 2 eggs
- 1 rounded cup mashed pumpkin

Combine flour, sugar, baking powder, baking soda, salt, cloves, pie spice and raisins. Blend butter, water, eggs and pumpkin. Add pumpkin mixture to dry ingredients, blending well. Spoon batter into greased miniature or regular muffin pans. Bake at 350° for 30 minutes for large pans or 20 minutes for miniature pans.

Yield: 1 dozen

Contributor: Salem Tavern Restaurant
Winston-Salem, North Carolina

Pumpkin Apple Streusel Muffins

- 2½ cups plus 2 tablespoons all-purpose flour, divided
- 2¼ cups sugar, divided
- 1 teaspoon baking soda
- ½ teaspoon salt
- 1½ teaspoons cinnamon, divided
- ½ teaspoon ginger
- ¼ teaspoon ground cloves
- 2 eggs, lightly beaten
- 1 cup pumpkin
- ½ cup vegetable oil
- 2 cups finely chopped peeled apples
- 1 tablespoon plus 1 teaspoon butter

Prepare streusel topping by combining 2 tablespoons flour, ¼ cup sugar and ½ teaspoons cinnamon. Cut butter into dry ingredients until consistency of crumbs and set aside. Combine remaining 2½ cups flour, 2 cups sugar, baking soda, salt, 1 teaspoon cinnamon, ginger and cloves. Blend eggs, pumpkin and oil. Add egg liquid to dry ingredients, stirring just until moistened. Stir in apples. Spoon batter into greased or paper-lined muffin cups, filling cups ¾ full. Sprinkle streusel crumbs on batter. Bake at 350° for 35 to 40 minutes.

Note: For 6 large muffins, use giant pans and increase baking time to 40 to 45 minutes; for 24 small muffins, bake in miniature muffin pans for 20 minutes.

Yield: 6 giant muffins or 2 dozen small

Raisin Bran Muffins

- 5 cups all-purpose flour
- 3 cups sugar
- 1 tablespoon plus 2 teaspoons baking soda
- 1 tablespoon salt
- 1 cup vegetable oil
- 4 eggs
- 4 cups buttermilk
- 1 (15 ounce) package raisin bran cereal

Combine flour, sugar, baking soda and salt. Blend in oil, eggs and buttermilk. Add cereal, mixing well. Store batter, covered, in refrigerator. To use, spoon batter into greased muffin cups, Bake at 400° for 20 minutes.

Note: Batter can be stored in refrigerator for several weeks.
Yield: 8 to 10 dozen small

Mini Corn Muffins with Honey Butter

- 1 egg
- ½ cup milk
- ½ cup butter or margarine, softened
- 1 (8 ounce) can cream style corn
- 1 cup all-purpose flour
- 1 cup yellow cornmeal
- 1 tablespoon sugar
- 1 tablespoon baking powder
- 1 teaspoon salt
- 2 or 3 dashes hot pepper sauce
- 3 tablespoons diced green chilies (optional)

Whisk egg, milk, butter and corn together. Add flour, cornmeal, sugar, baking powder, salt, hot pepper sauce and chilies, stirring just until moistened. Spoon batter into greased miniature muffin pans, filling cups ¾ full. Bake at 425° for 15 to 20 minutes or until tops are golden. Remove immediately from pans. Serve with honey butter.
Yield: 3 dozen

Honey Butter

- ½ cup unsalted butter, softened
- ¼ cup honey

Cream butter until light and smooth. Add honey and whip until fluffy. Store in refrigerator. Serve at room temperature.
Yield: ¾ cup

Super Easy Biscuits

2 cups self-rising flour
1 cup milk
2 rounded tablespoons mayonnaise

Combine flour, milk and mayonnaise, using fork to mix. Spoon dough into greased muffin pans. Bake at 450° for about 10 minutes.
Yield: 1 dozen

Kitty's Cheese Biscuits

2 cups self-rising flour
1 tablespoon sugar
½ teaspoon baking soda
⅓ cup shortening
1 cup (4 ounces) finely shredded Cheddar cheese
1 cup buttermilk

Combine flour, sugar and baking soda. Cut shortening into dry ingredients. Stir in cheese. Add buttermilk and mix lightly. On lightly-floured surface, roll dough to ½-inch thickness. Cut with biscuit cutter and place on baking sheet. Bake at 425° for 10 to 12 minutes.

For quick preparation, use food processor to cut in shortening and blend in cheese. Different cheeses and herbs can be used. Baked biscuits freeze well.
Yield: 1½ dozen

Country Baking Powder Biscuits

2 cups sifted all-purpose flour
1 teaspoon sugar
1 tablespoon plus 1 teaspoon baking powder
½ teaspoon salt
2 tablespoons vegetable shortening
⅔ cup milk
Melted butter

Sift flour, sugar, baking powder and salt together. Cut shortening into dry ingredients. Gradually add milk and mix to form soft dough, adding additional milk if necessary. On lightly-floured surface, knead dough slightly. Roll to ¾-inch thickness. Cut with biscuit cutter, brush with butter and place on baking sheet.. Bake at 450° for 15 minutes.
Yield: 2 dozen

Contributor: Dorothy Powers
Laura's Restaurant

Easy Biscuits

3½ cups self-rising flour
1 teaspoon sugar
1 teaspoon baking powder
6 tablespoons vegetable shortening
1½ cups buttermilk

Combine flour, sugar and baking powder. Cut shortening into dry ingredients. Add buttermilk and mix until dough forms ball. On lightly-floured surface, knead dough 5 to 7 times. Roll to ¾-inch thickness. Cut with biscuit cutter and place on baking sheet. Bake at 450° for 10 to 12 minutes.
Yield: 1½ to 2 dozen

Praline Biscuits

½ cup butter
½ cup firmly-packed brown sugar
36 pecan halves
Ground cinnamon
2 cups biscuit baking mix
⅓ cup applesauce
⅓ cup milk

Place 2 teaspoons butter, 2 teaspoons brown sugar and 3 pecan halves in each cup of 12-cup muffin pan. Sprinkle cinnamon in each cup. Heat in oven until butter and sugar are melted. Combine biscuit mix, applesauce and milk, mixing to form dough and beating 20 strokes. Spoon dough into prepared muffin pans. Bake at 450° for 10 minutes. Invert on serving plate.
Yield: 1 dozen

Cheese Bread

3 cups biscuit baking mix
2 tablespoons poppy seed
2 tablespoons onion flakes
2 cups (8 ounces) grated mild Cheddar cheese
2 eggs, beaten
½ cup vegetable shortening, melted
1 cup milk

Combine biscuit mix, poppy seed, onion and cheese. Stir in eggs, shortening and milk. Spread batter in greased 13x9x2-inch baking pan. Bake at 375° for about 25 minutes. Cut into squares.
Yield: 16 to 20 servings

Mississippi Corn Bread

1 cup self-rising cornmeal
1 teaspoon baking powder
½ teaspoon salt
1 cup sour cream
1 (8 ounce) can cream style corn
½ cup vegetable oil
2 eggs, beaten

Combine cornmeal, baking powder and salt. Add sour cream, corn, oil and eggs, blending thoroughly. Pour batter into lightly-greased 13x9x2-inch baking pan. Bake at 350° for 30 minutes.
Yield: 16 to 20 servings

Harry's Favorite Corn Bread

¼ cup vegetable oil
1 cup buttermilk
2 eggs, beaten
1 (8 ounce) can cream style corn
1½ cups self-rising cornmeal mix
1 (4 ounce) can jalapeno or green chilies, drained and chopped (optional)
2 cups (8 ounce) shredded sharp Cheddar cheese (optional)

Combine oil, buttermilk, eggs and corn. Stir in cornmeal mix, chilies and cheese. Pour batter into greased muffin pans or 10½-inch oven-proof black iron skillet. Bake at 425° for 25 minutes. If using cheese, let stand for about 10 minutes before cutting.
Yield: 1½ dozen

Old Fashioned Cornmeal Mush

1 cup cornmeal
½ teaspoon salt
1 cup cold water
2 cups boiling water
Milk to taste

Blend cornmeal and salt. Gradually add cold water, stirring to form smooth paste. Pour boiling water into top of double boiler. Stir cornmeal paste into hot water and cook for 3 to 4 hours. Serve with milk.

Note: Cold mush may be cut in ½-inch slices, fried until lightly browned and served with syrup for breakfast dish.
Yield: 4 to 6 servings

Guynn's Spoon Bread

½ cup grits
⅔ cup cornmeal
¼ cup butter
1 teaspoon salt
2 eggs
2 cups milk

Cook grits, according to package directions, for 10 minutes. Fold cornmeal into cooked grits. Stir in butter. Add salt. Let stand to cool. Blend eggs and milk into cornmeal mixture, mixing well. Pour batter into greased 1½-quart casserole. Bake at 350° for 45 minutes.
Yield: 6 servings

Spoon Bread

1 cup cornmeal
1 teaspoon baking powder
1 teaspoon salt
2 eggs, lightly beaten
2 cups milk
1 cup boiling water
1 tablespoon butter, melted
1 tablespoon vegetable shortening, melted

Combine cornmeal, baking powder and salt. Add eggs, milk and enough boiling water to form very thin batter. Stir in butter and shortening. Pour batter into well-greased 1½-quart casserole. Bake at 375° for 30 to 40 minutes. Delicious!
Yield: 6 servings

Dot's German Pancake

2 cups all-purpose flour
⅓ cup sugar
1 teaspoon salt
4 eggs, well beaten
2 cups milk
1 teaspoon vanilla
¼ cup powdered sugar
½ teaspoon lemon juice
½ to 1 cup fresh fruit
Syrup, heated (optional)
Butter

Combine flour, sugar and salt. Blend beaten eggs, milk and vanilla. Add dry ingredients and beat until smooth. Pour batter into well-buttered 12-inch ovenproof heavy skillet. Bake at 375° for 40 to 45 minutes. Sprinkle baked pancake with powdered sugar, lemon juice and fruit and drizzle with syrup.
Yield: 6 to 8 servings

Maryland Cream Waffles

2 cups all-purpose flour
2 teaspoons sugar
1 tablespoon plus 1 teaspoon baking powder
½ teaspoon salt
2 eggs, separated
1¾ cups milk
½ cup butter, melted

Sift flour, sugar, baking powder and salt together. Beat egg yolks, blend with milk and add to dry ingredients. Add butter and beat until smooth and creamy. Beat egg whites and fold into batter. Pour small portion of batter into hot waffle iron. Bake for 3 minutes or until steam disappears. Serve with butter and maple syrup.
Yield: 4 servings

Crêpes

1¼ cups all-purpose flour
Pinch of salt
3 eggs, beaten
1½ cups milk
2 tablespoons butter, melted

In blender container, combine flour, salt, eggs, milk and butter. Mix well. Let stand for 1 hour. Dip crepe pan into batter, lift, turn and place over burner. Cook until crepe no longer steams or bubbles.

Note: Crepes can be prepared in advance and frozen.
Yield: 4 servings

Killer Bread

1 loaf French bread
2 cups (8 ounces) shredded Monterey Jack cheese
1 cup regular or low-fat mayonnaise
1 teaspoon garlic powder
1 (4 ounce) can green chilies, drained and chopped (optional)
Grated Parmesan cheese

Split bread loaf in half lengthwise and place on baking sheet. Combine Monterey Jack cheese, mayonnaise, garlic powder and chilies. Spread on cut bread surfaces. Sprinkle generously with Parmesan cheese. Bake at 400° until hot, bubbly and golden brown. Cut into thick slices. Serve with roasted meats and poultry.
Yield: 16 servings

Windy's Popovers

½ cup all-purpose flour
1 teaspoon sugar
⅛ teaspoon salt
1½ teaspoons melted butter or vegetable oil
½ cup milk
1 egg

Combine flour, sugar, salt, oil, milk and egg in blender container. Blend thoroughly. Pour batter into well-greased muffin pans, filling cups about ½ full. Bake at 400° for 35 to 40 minutes or until browned and firm.
Yield: ½ dozen

Too ripe bananas:
• Make banana muffins or bread.
• Mash the bananas, stir in a little lemon juice and freeze until you're ready to do some baking.
• Make banana popsicles: mash bananas, pack into 3-ounce paper cups, stick a popsicle stick or spoon in center for handle and freeze.

Cheese, Eggs & Pasta

Some transformation comes over us. School starts several weeks before Labor Day, and through absolute willfulness, we determine that it is fall. Never mind that the temperatures hover in the high 80's or low 90's. We notice that the first leaf on a dogwood tree has turned red and we hurriedly make our plans for an October leaf viewing trip to Blowing Rock in the North Carolina mountains. Our Carolina Panthers NFL team begins its season in sweltering September heat. Charity Balls and fund raisers dot our calendars. Fall is the social season in the Carolinas. The ball gown and black tie attired couple on Friday night might be the same couple with orange stencilled paws on their cheeks on Saturday morning making their way with a heavy picnic basket to a Clemson, South Carolina football game. Somehow when we are dividing our time between our alma mater, our local high school, Charlotte's NBA team, the Hornets and the Carolina Panthers, we find the time to support the Symphony and Opera. The North Carolina Blumenthal Performing Arts Center, a magnificent performing arts center in Charlotte, is host to our Symphony and Opera and touring Broadway shows. Fall is family reunion time; for some groups it is the time to build a house for Habitat; it is church or Charity League Bazaar time. By nature one may be predisposed to a noble spirit; but most of us come from families where generosity and thoughtfulness were taught and encouraged behaviors. The tradition and example of a generous spirit persists and is one the Carolinas most appreciable resources.

Cheese

Preparing and Serving

Soft cheese should be served chilled. Hard and semi-firm cheese tastes best when served at room temperature.

- Remove hard or semi-firm cheese from refrigerator 30 minutes before serving. Warm in microwave at high (100%) setting for 15 seconds to speed process.
- Use microwave to soften spreads, such as pimento cheese or cream cheese, if they are too firm to spread easily or incorporate in a recipe.
- Four ounces hard cheese will produce 1 cup shredded cheese.
- Cheese grates more easily when chilled.
- When slicing hard or semi-firm cheese, warm knife under running water to make it slice more smoothly.

Storage

- Rewrap freshly cut cheese tightly to prevent drying.
- Store strong smelling cheese, such as Roquefort, in plastic container with tight-fitting lid in coldest part of refrigerator.
- Fresh, unripened cheese should be used as soon as possible after purchasing and should be carefully rewrapped.
- Natural and processed cheese will stay fresh for several months if unopened and wrapped tightly; it will last up to six weeks once opened.
- Hard and semi-hard cheese can be frozen for up to 2 months. Soft cheese is not recommended for freezing because the flavor and texture will be changed.
- If mold develops, simply cut off before using.

Cooking

Cheese is already cooked and needs just enough heat to melt or blend well.

- Low heat is preferred as high heat or overcooking may cause the cheese to toughen, form strips, separate the fat and lose flavor.

- When adding cheese to a sauce, grate or dice it so it will melt and blend quickly.
- Because it is too soft to grate, dice processed cheese before adding to a recipe.
- When topping a casserole with grated cheese, add during the last 5 minutes of baking time to prevent the cheese from becoming hard and brittle.
- When making an omelet, add grated cheese after the omelet is cooked, just before folding.

Eggs

Storage

- Refrigerated eggs separate more easily than those at room temperature.
- Egg whites will yield more volume if at room temperature before beaten.
- When using only the white, save the yolk by covering with cold water or oil and store in the refrigerator.
- To store egg whites, place in tightly sealed container and refrigerate. Egg whites can be kept for several weeks.
- To freeze egg whites, place 1 egg white in each section of an ice cube tray. Freeze, transfer to plastic bag and keep in freezer until ready to use.

Sizes

Jumbo: 30 ounces per dozen

Extra Large: 27 ounces per dozen

Large: 24 ounces per dozen

Medium: 21 ounces per dozen

Small: 18 ounces per dozen

Curdling

To prevent eggs from curdling when adding to custards and sauces, do not overcook or incorporate at too high heat. Use this technique, called tempering, when adding eggs to hot mixtures:

- Beat eggs slightly.
- Add about ¼ cup hot mixture to beaten egg, warming the egg gradually. This "tempers" the egg so it can be added to the remaining hot mixture.
- Gradually add egg mixture to hot mixture, stirring constantly and cooking until mixture is thickened, smooth and creamy.

Hard-Cooked Eggs

- Prick large end of fresh egg with pin before cooking. Peeling is easier and the egg is less likely to crack during cooking.
- Place up to 12 eggs in single layer in large saucepan. Cover the eggs with at least 1 inch cold water. Add 1 teaspoon salt or vinegar to prevent egg white from escaping a cracked shell.
- Quickly bring water to a boil. Remove from heat and set aside, covered. Let stand for 15 to 20 minutes.
- Drain hot water and immediately rinse with cold water for a few minutes to stop cooking process and prevent gray-green discoloration of yolk.
- Let stand in cold water for 20 minutes, then gently crack shells and peel.
- Hard-cooked eggs in shells can be stored in refrigerator for 2 to 3 days.
- When slicing hard-cooked eggs, wet the knife to prevent crumbling.

A really fresh egg will sink and a stale one will float.

Pasta

- Always add dry pasta to generous quantity of boiling water and cook at low-boil. Add small amount of vegetable oil to water to minimize boiling over or sticking to pan and to separate pasta as it cooks.
- Pasta is done when it is still firm or "al dente", Italian for "to the bite".
- When preparing pasta for a casserole, reduce the cooking time by ⅓. The cooking process will be completed during the baking of the casserole.
- If pasta is cooked for a casserole, rinsing is unnecessary. If for a cold salad, rinse in cold water, drain well and add salad dressing or marinade while pasta is warm, then chill.
- Generally, pasta forms can be interchanged measure for measure or by weight.
- Six or seven ounces or 2 cups macaroni yields 4 cups cooked pasta.
- Seven or eight ounces spaghetti yields 4 cups cooked or 4 to 6 servings.
- Eight ounces or 4 to 5 cups egg noodles yields 4 to 5 cups cooked or 4 to 6 servings.

Cleaning brass and copper: Prepare a mixture of equal parts of flour, white vinegar and salt or lemon juice. Make a paste and rub into container. Then rinse and dry.

Basic Omelet

3 eggs
2 tablespoons butter
Salt and black pepper to taste

Whisk eggs until well blended. Melt butter in omelet pan over medium heat. Pour eggs into pan and cook until edges begin to thicken. With fork, lift edges to allow uncooked egg to contact pan. Shake often to prevent sticking. When bottom surface is thickened but top is still moist, remove from heat. Let stand a few seconds, add filling and fold in half. Serve immediately.

Yield: 1 or 2 servings

Filling Combinations

Fried, drained and crumbled bulk pork sausage, lightly sautéed mushrooms and sour cream

Diced ham, chopped parsley and shredded American or Cheddar cheese

Cooked, crumbled bacon, minced onion and shredded Swiss cheese

Chopped avocado blended with mayonnaise and lemon juice, minced onion and alfalfa sprouts

Shredded Monterey Jack cheese, thinly sliced green onion, diced green chilies, diced tomato and sour cream

Chopped artichoke hearts and grated Parmesan cheese or Romano cheese

Sliced sautéed mushrooms and sour cream

Caviar and sour cream

Chutney and grated mozzarella cheese

Grated and drained zucchini, thinly sliced green onion, diced tomato, basil and shredded Swiss cheese

Asparagus Stuffed Eggs

8 hard-cooked eggs
3 to 4 tablespoons mayonnaise
3 teaspoons grated lemon peel
½ teaspoon salt
½ teaspoon curry powder
¼ teaspoon dry mustard
16 asparagus tips
Pimento strips

Cut eggs in halves lengthwise. Remove and mash yolks until smooth. Stir in mayonnaise, lemon peel, salt, curry powder and mustard, mixing until creamy and well blended. Check seasonings. Spoon or pipe mixture into egg whites. Top each with asparagus tip and pimento strip.

Yield: 1¼ dozen

Festive Eggs

8 hard-cooked eggs
2 tablespoons mustard
2 tablespoons horseradish
½ cup minced onion
½ cup chopped pimento-stuffed green olives with small amount of juice
½ to 1 cup mayonnaise
Cayenne pepper to taste
Parsley sprigs for garnish

Cut eggs in halves lengthwise. Remove and mash yolks until smooth. Stir in mustard, horseradish, onion, olives and mayonnaise, mixing thoroughly. Spoon mixture into egg whites. Sprinkle with cayenne pepper and place on serving plate garnished with parsley.
Yield: 16 egg boats

Eggs El Paso Casserole

3 (4 ounce) cans green chilies, drained and chopped
4 cups (16 ounces) grated Cheddar cheese
4 cups (16 ounces) grated Monterey Jack cheese
2 (10 ounce) cans tomatoes with chilies, drained
12 eggs, lightly beaten

In order listed, layer in 13x9x2-inch baking dish: 1½ cans green chilies, 2 cups Cheddar cheese, 2 cups Monterey Jack cheese and 1 can tomatoes; repeat layers. Pour eggs over top layer. Bake at 325° for 1¼ to 1½ hours. Let stand for 15 to 20 minutes before cutting into rectangles to serve.
Yield: 10 to 12 servings

Crustless Quiche

1 pound bulk pork sausage
½ cup sliced mushrooms
4 eggs, lightly beaten, or equivalent egg substitute
¼ cup sour cream
¾ cup milk
⅓ cup biscuit baking mix
1 cup (4 ounces) grated Cheddar cheese

Cook sausage, stirring to crumble, until lightly browned. Drain excess fat. Sprinkle sausage and mushrooms in 13x9x2-inch baking dish. Combine eggs, sour cream, milk and biscuit mix. Pour batter over sausage. Sprinkle with cheese. Bake at 325° for 45 minutes.

Note: For variation, use cooked chopped vegetables, diced ham or other cheeses.

Yield: 6 servings

Ham and Cheese Grits

1½ cups instant grits
6 cups boiling water
4 cups (16 ounces) grated or cubed sharp Cheddar cheese
¾ cup butter or margarine
1 teaspoon onion powder
1 teaspoon salt
1 cup diced ham (optional)
3 eggs, well beaten
Dash of hot pepper sauce
Paprika

Sprinkle grits into boiling water, reduce heat and cook for 3 to 5 minutes, stirring frequently. Add cheese, butter or margarine, onion powder, salt and ham, stirring until cheese is melted. Gently fold in eggs and season with hot pepper sauce. Pour grits mixture into greased 3-quart casserole. Sprinkle lightly with paprika. Bake at 350° for 1 hour.
Yield: 10 servings

Italian Casserole

1 (8 ounce) package shell pasta
1 pound ground beef
¼ cup butter (optional)
2 (3 ounce) packages cream cheese
1 cup cottage cheese
¼ cup sour cream
½ cup chopped green onion
1 tablespoon chopped green bell pepper
2 (8 ounce) cans tomato sauce

Assemble casserole a day in advance. Prepare pasta according to package directions. While pasta cooks, brown beef in butter, stirring to crumble. Drain excess fat. Add tomato sauce and simmer. Drain pasta. Combine cream cheese, cottage cheese, sour cream, green onion and bell pepper. In order listed, layer in buttered 2-quart casserole: ½ pasta, cheese mixture, ½ pasta and meat sauce. Chill overnight. Bake at 350° for 30 to 45 minutes.
Yield: 4 to 6 servings

For fluffier omelets, add a pinch of cornstarch before beating.

Pasta Spirals with Beef and Bacon

- 1 (8 ounce) package pasta spirals
- 1 pound ground beef
- ½ cup chopped onion
- 5 slices bacon
- 1 (4 ounce) can sliced mushrooms, drained
- 1 (16 ounce) can tomatoes, chopped
- ½ teaspoon oregano
- 1 cup (4 ounces) grated sharp Cheddar cheese
- Salt and black pepper to taste

Prepare pasta according to package directions and drain. While pasta cooks, brown beef and onion together. Separately brown bacon, drain and dice. Drain excess fat from beef, then add bacon, mushrooms, tomatoes and oregano, mixing well. Place ½ of pasta in well-greased 2-quart casserole, add ½ of meat mixture and sprinkle with ½ cheese; repeat layers. Season with salt and black pepper. Bake at 350° for 20 minutes.
Yield: 4 to 6 servings

Steak and Pasta Salad

- 1 (8 ounce) package rotini pasta
- ¾ pound flank steak
- 3 medium-ripe tomatoes, cut in large chunks
- 1 cup fresh or frozen corn, thawed
- ½ cup sliced red onion
- ¼ cup chopped parsley
- ½ cup prepared olive oil vinaigrette dressing

Prepare pasta according to package directions and drain. While pasta cooks, grill or broil steak for 5 minutes each side for medium rare doneness. Let stand for 5 minutes. Add tomatoes, corn, onion, parsley and dressing to pasta, mixing thoroughly. Thinly slice steak, across grain. Add strips to salad and toss to mix.
Yield: 4 servings

Adding a small amount of salt to water will make the water boil faster.

Spaghetti with Red Clam Sauce

12 little neck clams
2 cloves garlic, minced
¼ cup olive oil
1 (28 ounce) can tomatoes, strained
1 tablespoon chopped parsley
Salt and black pepper to taste
1 (16 ounce) package spaghetti

Scrub clams and rinse in cold running water to thoroughly remove sand. Insert thin knife edge between edges of shells and pry open. Remove clams, cut in small pieces and place in small bowl with clam liquid. Brown garlic in oil. Stir in clam liquid, tomatoes, parsley, salt and black pepper. Simmer for 40 minutes. While sauce cooks, prepare spaghetti according to package directions. Drain and keep warm. Add clams to tomato sauce, increase heat and cook for 2 minutes. Serve over spaghetti.
Yield: 4 to 6 servings

Spinach Lasagna

1 (10 ounce) package frozen chopped spinach, thawed and well drained
2 cups ricotta or small curd cottage cheese
3 cups (12 ounces) shredded mozzarella cheese, divided
1 egg, lightly beaten
1 teaspoon salt
⅛ teaspoon black pepper
1 teaspoon oregano
2 (15½ ounce) jars spaghetti sauce with mushrooms
1 (8 ounce) package lasagna noodles
1 cup water

Combine spinach, ricotta or cottage cheese, 1 cup mozzarella cheese, egg, salt, black pepper and oregano, mixing well. In order listed, layer in greased 13x9x2-inch baking dish: ½ cup spaghetti sauce, ⅓ uncooked noodles and ½ cheese mixture; repeat layers. Top with remaining noodles, spaghetti sauce and 2 cups mozzarella cheese. Pour water in sauce jars, shake to loosen remaining sauce and pour around edges of dish. Bake, tightly covered with aluminum foil, at 350° for 1¼ hours. Let stand 15 minutes before serving.
Yield: 8 servings

Lasagna

- 6 lasagna noodles
- 1 pound ground beef or turkey
- 3 (8 ounce) cans tomato sauce
- 1 (6 ounce) can tomato paste
- 1 teaspoon salt, divided
- 1 tablespoon dried oregano
- 2 teaspoons basil
- ¼ teaspoon garlic powder or 1 clove garlic, minced
- 2 cups ricotta or small curd cottage cheese
- 1 egg
- 1 tablespoon parsley flakes
- 1 (6 ounce) package sliced mozzarella or provolone cheese
- ¼ cup (1 ounce) grated Parmesan cheese

Prepare pasta according to package directions and drain. While pasta cooks, brown beef or turkey, stirring to crumble. Drain excess fat. Combine tomato sauce, tomato paste, ½ teaspoon salt, oregano, basil and garlic. Spread ½ cup sauce in 12x8x2-inch baking dish. Add remaining sauce to cooked meat. Combine ricotta or cottage cheese, egg, parsley and remaining ½ teaspoon salt. Layer 3 noodles on sauce in baking dish, add ½ cheese mixture, ½ mozzarella or provolone cheese and ½ meat sauce; repeat layers. Sprinkle with Parmesan cheese. Cover dish with wax paper. Microwave at high (100%) setting for 20 to 26 minutes, rotating dish a quarter turn every 8 minutes. Let stand for 10 minutes before cutting.

Note: If assembled in advance and stored in refrigerator, add 4 to 6 minutes to cooking time.

Yield: 8 to 12 servings

Chicken Spaghetti

Spaghetti

- **6 chicken breast halves, boned and skin removed**
- **½ cup sliced onion**
- **1 tablespoon margarine**
- **2 tablespoons olive oil, divided**
- **1 (8 ounce) package spaghetti**
- **2 teaspoons salt**
- **1 (3 4/5 ounce) can pitted ripe olives, drained and sliced**
- **1 (14½ ounce) can tomatoes, chopped**
- **2 teaspoons cornstarch**
- **1 tablespoon cold water**
- **¼ cup (1 ounce) grated Parmesan cheese**
- **1 tablespoon chopped parsley**

Prepare marinade. Cut chicken breasts in halves crosswise. Place in 13x9x2-inch baking dish with onion. Pour marinade over chicken. Chill for 2 hours or longer, occasionally spooning marinade over chicken. Drain well, reserving marinade. Brown chicken pieces in margarine with 1 tablespoon oil in skillet over medium-low heat. Add ¼ cup reserved marinade. Cook, covered, for 10 minutes or just until chicken is tender. Remove chicken from skillet and keep warm. Prepare spaghetti according to package directions, using 2 teaspoons salt in boiling water. While spaghetti cooks, add olives and remaining marinade to skillet liquid. Stir in tomatoes and bring to a boil. Blend cornstarch and cold water. Add to tomato mixture and cook for 1 to 2 minutes, stirring frequently. Add chicken and cook to thoroughly heat. Drain spaghetti and rinse with hot water. Add cheese, remaining 1 tablespoon oil and parsley to spaghetti. To serve, mound spaghetti on serving plate, arrange chicken around spaghetti and spoon sauce over both.
Yield: 6 servings

Marinade

- **⅔ cup white wine vinegar**
- **3 tablespoons olive oil**
- **1¾ teaspoons salt**
- **¼ teaspoon black pepper**
- **1¾ teaspoons minced garlic**
- **1 teaspoon Italian seasoning**
- **1 teaspoon paprika**
- **3 drops hot pepper sauce**

Combine vinegar, oil, salt, black pepper, garlic, Italian seasoning, paprika and hot pepper sauce in tightly-covered jar. Shake to blend.
Yield: 1 cup

Shrimp with Linguini

1 (2 ounce) jar minced garlic
⅓ (2½ ounce) jar Mrs. Dash
Pinch of cayenne pepper
½ to 1 cup butter
1 (2 ounce) jar or bag pine nuts
1 (8 ounce) box linguini
48 shrimp, cleaned and deveined
1 teaspoon cholula hot sauce or to taste

Combine garlic, seasoning, cayenne pepper and butter in saucepan. Simmer, stirring often, for 15 minutes; do not boil. Add pine nuts and simmer for 15 additional minutes or until nuts are softened. While sauce cooks, prepare linguini according to package directions; drain but do not rinse. Add shrimp to pine nut sauce and cook for about 5 minutes or until shrimp are done. Serve shrimp sauce over linguini.
Yield: 4 to 6 servings

Fettuccine with Pesto Sauce

1 (16 ounce) package fettuccine
3 tablespoons pine nuts or walnuts
2 cups fresh basil leaves
2 cloves garlic
¼ cup butter, melted
1 cup olive oil
¾ cup (3 ounces) grated Parmesan cheese
¼ cup (1 ounce) grated Romano cheese
½ teaspoon black pepper
Grated Romano cheese

Prepare fettuccine according to package directions and drain. While fettuccine is cooking, prepare sauce by combining pine nuts or walnuts, basil, garlic, butter, oil, Parmesan cheese, Romano cheese and black pepper in blender container. Blend at low speed, scraping sides of container with rubber spatula, until consistency of mayonnaise. Pour pesto sauce over hot pasta and top with additional Romano cheese.
Yield: 4 to 6 servings

Most sinks can be unclogged by pouring ½ cup baking soda followed by ½ cup vinegar down the drain. This is cheaper and safer than commercial cleaners.

Orange Shrimp with Linguini

- 1 (6 ounce) package linguini
- 1 medium-sized red bell pepper, cut in ¾-inch pieces
- 1 tablespoon vegetable oil
- ¾ pound shrimp, cleaned and deveined
- ½ teaspoon grated orange peel
- ⅔ cup orange juice
- 1 tablespoon cornstarch
- 1 teaspoon chicken bouillon granules
- ½ teaspoon sesame oil
- ⅛ teaspoon ground red pepper
- ¼ teaspoon salt
- 1 (6 ounce) frozen pea pods, thawed
- 2 oranges, peeled and sectioned

Prepare pasta according to package directions, drain and keep warm. Cook bell pepper in oil in large skillet for 1 to 2 minutes or until tender. Remove peppers and set aside. Cook shrimp in skillet for 2 to 4 minutes or until pink. Remove shrimp and drain. Combine orange peel, orange juice, cornstarch, bouillon, sesame oil, ground red pepper and salt. Add to skillet and cook, stirring often, until bubbly. Stir in shrimp and bell pepper, mixing to coat with sauce. Fold in pea pods and orange slices and heat thoroughly. Serve over pasta.

Yield: 4 servings

Ziti and Vodka

- ½ teaspoon hot pepper flakes
- ¼ cup vodka
- 2 tablespoons butter
- ¼ cup plus 1 tablespoon olive oil
- ¼ pound diced prosciutto
- 1 (28 ounce) can plum tomatoes, chopped
- ½ cup (2 ounces) grated Parmesan cheese
- 1 (16 ounce) package ziti

Soak red pepper flakes in vodka overnight. Melt butter in skillet and blend in oil. Sauté prosciutto lightly in butter oil. Add tomatoes and simmer for 10 minutes. Strain pepper flakes from vodka, add vodka to tomato sauce and simmer for 20 minutes. While sauce simmers, prepare ziti according to package directions and drain. Serve sauce over hot pasta.

Yield: 4 to 6 servings

Soups & Sandwiches

The bone chilling cold of a Carolina winter's day may be dismissed as not cold at all by our Northern or Mid-Western cousins; but the wet cold air we Carolinians feel during the two months of January and February can only be vanquished by walking into a kitchen filled with the aroma of our favorite soup or stew simmering on the stove. The soup may be a first course for the evening meal but more often than not, it is the main course, coupled with a salad and warm bread fresh from the oven. When the weather is dreadful outside, the coziest place to be is a kitchen warmed from an afternoon of cooking. Carolina cooks have long known that soup simmering and bread baking in the oven produce the smells that put the crankiest children and adults into a more pleasant mood. All is right, or can be, with the world!

Soups

Soups with varied ingredients, flavors and textures add interest to a meal..As a first course, soup should complement the entree. Light or bland soups should be served with highly seasoned entrees. Cream soups should not be served with other creamed dishes.

As a first course, allow 1 quart for 6 servings. When serving soup as a main course, allow 1 quart for 3 to 4 servings.

Warm bowls when serving hot soup. Chill bowls when serving cold soup.

Varieties

Bisque—Bisque is a thick rich soup consisting of pureed seafood (sometimes fowl or vegetables) and cream.

Chowders—Chowders consist of a thick fish, meat or vegetable base to which cream and other vegetables are added.

Clear Soup—Broth, bouillon or stock made from meat or vegetables are used for clear soup.

Cream Soup—Cream or milk and butter are added to a vegetable base to make cream soup. It can be thickened by the addition of barley, rice, oatmeal or eggs. Cream soups must not be boiled; heat only to boiling point or heat in top of double boiler.

Preparation

- To eliminate excess liquid from soup, place a large colander into the pot, pressing slightly into solid ingredients. Spoon or scoop away excess liquid that collects inside the colander.
- Spices that are removed at the end of the cooking process should be placed in a tea strainer and hooked to the side of the stock pot during cooking.
- To correct a salty soup, place raw peeled potato in soup, boil for a short time and remove potato before serving. Or allow salty soup to cool thoroughly, then add 1 teaspoon sugar and reheat.
- Remove grease from soup by placing a lettuce leaf in hot soup, then removing lettuce before serving. Or cool soup to room

temperature, chill and skim congealed fat from surface.

- To clarify stock, let stand until cool. For each 4 cups stock, allow 1 egg white and 1 crushed egg shell. Beat egg whites until soft peaks form. Stir egg whites and crushed egg shell into stock. Heat until foam forms. Remove from heat and allow to stand at room temperature for 1 hour. Strain through several layers of cheesecloth or fine strainer.
- Add leftover stuffing to soups to enhance flavor and to thicken.
- When using alcohol in soups, add 1 tablespoon for 1 cup soup just before serving; do not boil. Too much alcohol will make soup bitter.
- For extra flavor, add bouillon cubes or granules to canned or homemade soup.
- Cool soups uncovered.

Winter Blend Soup

1 cup dried small red beans
¼ cup dried white navy beans
¼ cup dried split peas
½ cup dried lentils
6 cups water
8 cups chicken broth
⅓ cup minced onion flakes
1 teaspoon black pepper
2 teaspoons dried basil
¼ teaspoon ground cumin
¼ teaspoon garlic powder
⅛ teaspoon ground ginger
1 bay leaf
⅓ cup regular rice
Sliced green onion tops for garnish (optional)

Wash and drain beans. Combine red beans, navy beans, peas and lentils with water in Dutch oven. Bring to a boil and cook for 5 minutes. Remove from heat, let stand for 30 minutes and drain. Combine beans, peas and lentils with broth, onion, black pepper, basil, cumin, garlic, ginger and bay leaf in Dutch oven. Bring to a boil, cover, reduce heat and simmer for 45 minutes. Add rice and simmer for additional 45 minutes. Check seasonings. Remove bay leaf. Garnish individual servings with green onion.
Yield: 8 to 10 cups

Avocado Soup

1 ripe avocado, peeled, pitted and mashed
3 cups chicken broth
Salt and black pepper to taste
Paprika to taste
1 cup half and half

Stir avocado into broth in large saucepan. Season with salt, black pepper and paprika. Bring to a boil. Add cream and heat thoroughly; do not boil.
Yield: 4 cups

Rita's Easy Soup

4 cups fresh chicken broth or equivalent canned broth
2 (28 ounce) cans tomatoes, chopped or mashed
5 medium potatoes, peeled and cubed
6 medium carrots, cut in chunks
Salt and black pepper to taste
1½ pounds ground beef
1 packet taco seasoning
2 (16 ounce) cans mixed vegetables

Combine broth, tomatoes, potatoes, carrots, salt and black pepper in stock pot. Bring to a boil, reduce heat to medium and cook for about 30 minutes or until vegetables are tender. While vegetables cook, brown ground beef, stirring to crumble. Drain excess fat. Add beef and taco seasoning to cooked vegetable mixture and simmer for 3 to 4 minutes. Add mixed vegetables and heat thoroughly.

Note: For variation, substitute ground chicken for beef, add rice or noodles or use chicken bouillon instead of taco seasoning.
Yield: 16 to 20 cups

Drop a lettuce leaf into a pot of homemade soup to absorb excess grease from the top.

Hamburger Soup

- **1 pound ground chuck**
- **5 cups water**
- **1 (14½ ounce) can tomatoes, chopped with juice**
- **1 cup chopped onion**
- **1 cup sliced carrots**
- **1 cup chopped celery**
- **⅓ cup pearl barley**
- **¼ cup ketchup**
- **1 tablespoon beef bouillon granules**
- **2 teaspoons seasoned salt**
- **Salt and black pepper to taste**
- **1 teaspoon dried basil**
- **1 bay leaf**

Brown ground beef, stirring to crumble, in Dutch oven. Drain excess fat. Add water, tomatoes with juice, onion, carrots, celery, barley, ketchup, bouillon, seasoned salt, salt, black pepper, basil and bay leaf. Bring to a boil, reduce heat and simmer, covered, for 1 hour or until vegetables are tender. Check seasoning and remove bay leaf.

Note: Soup freezes well.

Yield: 10 cups

Vegetable Beef Soup

- **1 pound ground round of beef or turkey breast**
- **1 medium-sized onion, chopped**
- **2 cups water**
- **2 (14½ ounce) cans stewed tomatoes**
- **2 or 3 medium potatoes, peeled and diced**
- **1 (16 ounce) package frozen mixed vegetables**
- **1 (8 ounce) package frozen corn**
- **1 (8 ounce) package frozen baby lima beans**
- **¾ to 1½ cups tomato juice (optional)**

Brown beef or turkey with onion, stirring to crumble. Drain excess fat. While meat cooks, pour water into stock pot and bring to a boil. Add tomatoes, potatoes, frozen mixed vegetables, corn and beans. Stir in meat and onion. Add tomato juice to desired consistency. Simmer for 1 to 2 hours.

Note: To cook beef or turkey using microwave, place in colander in 2-quart glass measuring cup. Crumble meat. Cook at high (100%) setting for 8 minutes, crumbling with fork every 2 minutes. Add onion for final 2 minutes. Fat collects in measuring cup. Soup can be frozen but do not add potatoes. Cook separately and add to thawed soup when reheating.

Yield: 12 to 15 cups

Broccoli Soup

- 1 large bunch broccoli
- 1 medium-sized onion, chopped
- 1 clove garlic, minced
- 3 tablespoons butter
- 1 large potato, peeled and diced
- 4 cups chicken broth
- 1 cup milk
- Salt and black pepper to taste

Trim flowerets from stalks. Steam flowerets until tender, drain and set aside. Scrape stalks and dice. Simmer chopped stalks, onion and garlic in butter in large saucepan, stirring frequently, for 10 to 15 minutes. Add potato and broth, bring to a boil and cook for 20 minutes or until vegetables are tender. Stir in milk, salt and black pepper. Remove from heat. Using blender, puree 1 cup vegetable mixture at a time. Return to saucepan, stir in flowerets and reheat.
Yield: 8 cups

Herbed Broccoli Soup

- 2 cups bite-sized pieces fresh broccoli or 1 (10 ounce) package frozen broccoli spears
- ½ cup water
- 1 medium-sized onion, chopped
- 2 stalks celery, diced
- ¼ cup butter
- ⅓ cup all-purpose flour
- 1 (14½ ounce) can chicken broth
- Salt and black pepper to taste
- Basil to taste
- Thyme to taste
- Marjoram to taste
- ⅓ cup half and half

Cook fresh or frozen broccoli in water until tender crisp. Drain, reserving liquid. Sauté onion and celery in butter. Stir in flour and cook, stirring constantly. Gradually add broth and cook, stirring frequently, until thickened. Season with salt, black pepper, basil, thyme and marjoram and simmer to blend flavors. Stir in broccoli, reserved broccoli liquid and half and half. Heat thoroughly; do not boil.
Yield: 7 to 8 cups

If stew or soup has too much garlic, place parsley flakes in a tea ball and set it in the stew or soup pot until it soaks up the excess garlic.

Beer and Cheese Soup

- 1 cup sliced leeks
- ½ cup finely chopped celery
- ¼ cup butter
- 2 tablespoons olive oil
- 4 medium-sized potatoes, peeled and finely diced
- 4 cups chicken broth.
- 2 (12 ounce) cans beer
- 4 cups (16 ounces) shredded Cheddar cheese
- 3 or 4 dashes hot pepper sauce
- Salt and black pepper to taste

Sauté leeks and celery in butter and oil until tender. Add potatoes and broth. Bring to a boil, reduce heat and simmer until potatoes are tender. Remove vegetables from broth. Using food processor or blender, puree vegetables and return to simmering broth. Stir in beer and bring to simmer. Gradually add cheese, stirring until melted. Season with hot pepper sauce, salt and black pepper. Simmer, stirring constantly, until soup is thickened; do not boil.
Yield: 12 to 14 cups

Avgholemono Soup—Greek Chicken Soup

Soup

- 1 (2½ to 3 pound) broiler-fryer
- 4 cups chicken broth or water
- 1 small onion
- 1 stalk celery
- Salt and black pepper to taste
- ¾ cup orzo noodles

Combine chicken, broth or water, onion, celery, salt and black pepper in stock pot. Bring to a boil, reduce heat and simmer for 1 hour or until chicken is tender. Remove chicken and let stand until cool. Discard bones and skin from chicken, chop meat and set aside. Strain and reserve broth. Prepare orzo according to package directions, cooking for about 20 minutes or until done. Rinse orzo and add to reserved broth. Prepare egg lemon sauce. Add to broth with chicken.
Yield: 8 to 10 cups

Egg Lemon Sauce

- 2 eggs, separated
- Juice of 3 lemons
- Broth

Beat egg whites until fluffy. Add yolks. Gradually add lemon juice and small amount of broth.

Cheesy Chicken Chowder

- **2 cups shredded carrots**
- **½ cup chopped onion**
- **½ cup butter**
- **½ cup all-purpose flour**
- **3 cups chicken broth**
- **4 cups milk**
- **2 cups diced cooked chicken**
- **1 cup fresh or frozen corn**
- **1 teaspoon Worcestershire sauce**
- **2 tablespoons white wine (optional)**
- **1 teaspoon salt**
- **½ teaspoon black pepper**
- **2 cups (8 ounces) shredded Cheddar cheese**

Sauté carrots and onion in butter until tender. Blend in flour. Add broth and milk. Cook, stirring frequently, until thickened and smooth; do not boil. Add chicken, corn, Worcestershire sauce, wine, salt and black pepper. Gradually add cheese and cook until cheese is melted.
Yield: 12 to 14 cups

Chicken Vegetable Soup

- **1 (2½ to 3 pound) broiler-fryer**
- **Water**
- **1 medium-sized onion, chopped**
- **½ cup chopped celery**
- **½ cup chopped carrots**
- **1 (16 ounce) package frozen mixed vegetables**
- **1 (10 ounce) package frozen okra**
- **1 (10 ounce) package frozen butter beans**
- **1 (10 ounce) package frozen corn**
- **2 (28 ounce) cans tomatoes, crushed**
- **2 chicken bouillon cubes**
- **Black pepper to taste**
- **Basil to taste**
- **Oregano to taste**
- **Nature's seasoning to taste**

Simmer chicken in water to cover in stock pot until tender and separating from bones. Drain chicken, reserving broth. Discard bones and skin from chicken, chop meat and set aside. Strain fat from broth. Cook onion, celery and carrots in broth. Stir in frozen vegetables, okra, butter beans and corn and cook until tender. Add tomatoes and chicken. Simmer until thoroughly heated. Add bouillon and season with black pepper, basil, oregano and nature's seasoning.

Note: Other frozen vegetables may be substituted.
Yield: 12 to 16 cups

Low Sodium Chunky Chicken Soup

- 1 pound chicken breast fillets
- 4 cups water, divided
- ¼ cup chopped green onion
- ½ cup chopped celery
- ½ cup diced carrots
- Celery leaves to taste
- 2 tablespoons chopped parsley
- Black pepper to taste
- ¼ teaspoon poultry seasoning
- ¼ teaspoon thyme
- 1 teaspoon chicken bouillon granules
- 1 cup egg noodles

Simmer chicken with 2 cups water in Dutch oven for 45 to 60 minutes. Remove chicken, cut in small chunks and return to broth. Stir in remaining 2 cups water, onion, celery, carrots, celery leaves, parsley, black pepper, poultry seasoning, thyme, bouillon and noodles. Cook for 45 minutes or until vegetables are tender.
Yield: 10 to 12 cups

Quick Brunswick Soup

- 1 (28 ounce) can Brunswick stew
- 1 (28 ounce) can tomatoes
- 1 (16 ounce) can lima beans, drained
- 1 (12 ounce) can shoe peg corn, drained
- 1 teaspoon brown sugar
- 1 tablespoon butter
- 2 (10 ounce) cans boned chicken
- Salt and black pepper to taste
- Hot pepper sauce to taste
- Worcestershire sauce to taste

Combine stew, tomatoes, lima beans, corn, brown sugar, butter and chicken in Dutch oven. Season with salt, black pepper, hot pepper sauce and Worcestershire sauce. Bring to a boil, reduce heat and simmer for 1 hour.
Yield: 12 to 14 cups

A teaspoon each of cider vinegar and sugar added to salty soup or vegetables will remedy the situation.

Brunswick Stew

1 (6 to 7 pound) hen or 2 (2½ to 3½ pound) broiler-fryers
Water
1 (16 ounce) package dried butter beans
3 pounds white potatoes, peeled and cut in chunks
3 (28 ounce) cans tomatoes
1 pound ground chuck
1½ pounds onions, sliced
Sugar to taste
Salt and black pepper to taste
1 (14 ounce) bottle ketchup
1 (10 ounce) bottle Worcestershire sauce
2 (16 ounce) cans small green butter beans or 2 (10 ounce) packages frozen butter beans
½ cup butter
2 (16 ounce) cans cream-style corn
1 packet instant potatoes (optional)

A day in advance, cook chicken in water to cover until tender. Strain broth and reserve. Discard bone and skin from chicken, dice and reserve. Prepare beans according to package directions. Store broth and chicken in refrigerator overnight. Cook potatoes and mash. Combine broth, cooked beans, tomatoes, uncooked beef, onion and mashed potatoes in large heavy pot. Cook for 1½ hours. Add sugar, salt, black pepper, ketchup, ½ bottle Worcestershire sauce, canned or frozen butter beans and butter. Cook over medium heat, stirring often, for 2 to 3 hours; mixture will thicken toward stew consistency. Add corn and chicken and continue stirring. If thin consistency, stir in instant potatoes. Add remaining Worcestershire sauce if desired.
Yield: 24 to 30 cups

Catsup will flow out of the bottle evenly if you will first insert a drinking straw, push it to the bottom of the bottle, and remove.

Virginia Brunswick Stew

- 1 (2½ to 3 pound) broiler-fryer
- Water
- 3 large potatoes, diced
- 1 pound stewing beef chunks
- 1 country ham bone
- 2 quarts water
- ½ cup sugar
- 1 bay leaf
- 1 teaspoon basil
- 1 tablespoon chopped parsley
- 2 medium-sized onions, sliced
- 2 cups chopped skinless tomatoes
- 1 cup chopped celery with tops
- 1 cup butter beans
- 2 cups fresh or frozen corn
- ½ cup butter
- 1 pod red pepper, crushed
- Salt to taste
- 1 teaspoon coarsely ground black pepper

Cook chicken in water to cover until tender. Discard bones and skin from chicken and cut into pieces. Cook potatoes in small amount of water until tender, drain and set aside. Combine chicken, beef, ham bone, water, sugar, bay leaf, basil and parsley in stock pot. Simmer until beef is tender and shreds easily. Add onion, tomatoes, celery and butter beans. Simmer until beans are tender, stirring frequently. Add corn and simmer for 10 minutes. Stir in butter, red pepper, salt and black pepper. Add potatoes and cook, stirring constantly, for about 20 minutes or until stew is thickened.

Yield: 24 to 30 cups

Spicy Chili Soup

- 1 (28 ounce) can whole tomatoes, cut up, with juice
- 1 (16 ounce) can red kidney beans, undrained
- 1 (7 ounce) can Mexican corn, undrained
- 2½ cups beef broth
- ⅔ cup salsa
- ½ cup water
- ½ teaspoon cumin
- ½ teaspoon chili powder

Combine tomatoes, beans, corn, broth, salsa, water, cumin and chili powder in Dutch oven. Bring to a boil, reduce heat and simmer, uncovered, for 45 to 60 minutes. Serve with cornbread.

Note: This fast and easy recipe came from Austin, Texas.

Yield: 10 cups

Clam Chowder

10 cups sifted all-purpose flour
4 cups vegetable oil
½ (16 ounce) package bacon
1½ tablespoons whole thyme
1½ tablespoons black pepper
15 potatoes, peeled and diced in¼-inch cubes
2 large onions, diced
3 (46 ounce) cans clam, chopped
2 (46 ounce) cans clam juice
6 quarts water
12 quarts hot water
1 pound clam base
2 quarts milk
2 quarts whipping cream

Prepare roux by mixing flour and vegetable oil. Spread in baking pan. Bake at 250° for 45 minutes, stirring after 20 to 25 minutes. Remove from oven. Cook bacon in stock pot until partially browned. Stir in thyme and black pepper. Cook for 30 seconds. Add potatoes and onions. Cook, stirring frequently, for 6 to 8 minutes. Add clams and juice, stirring well. Reduce heat to medium and cook until mixture reaches 165° on cooking thermometer. Add roux mixed with 6 quarts water and simmer for 30 minutes. In separate stock pot, combine 12 quarts hot water and clam base. When hot, thicken with roux and whip until smooth. Simmer over medium heat for 20 minutes. Stir in milk and cream. Let stand until cool and store in refrigerator. Reheat to serve.
Yield: 7 gallons

Contributor: Philip Rateliff, Chef
Sea Captain's House
Myrtle Beach, South Carolina

Easy Corn Chowder

1 medium to large onion, chopped
3 large potatoes, cut in cubes
Water
2 cups frozen corn
1 (16 ounce) can cream-style corn
1 (12 ounce) can evaporated milk
Salt and black pepper to taste

Cook onion and potatoes in water to cover until vegetables are almost tender. Stir in frozen corn and cook until tender. Drain liquid. Add cream style corn and milk to vegetables. Season with salt and black pepper. Heat thoroughly.
Yield: 7 to 8 cups

Nancy's Corn and Sausage Chowder

- **1 pound bulk pork sausage**
- **1 cup chopped onion**
- **1 (28 ounce) can tomatoes, mashed**
- **1 (16 ounce) can whole kernel corn, undrained**
- **1 (16 ounce) can cream-style corn**
- **3 medium potatoes, peeled and diced (optional)**
- **2 tablespoons dried basil leaves**
- **2 to 3 teaspoons sugar**
- **½ teaspoon black pepper**
- **1 (5 ounce) can evaporated milk**

Cook sausage, stirring to crumble, until browned. Drain excess fat. Combine sausage, onion, tomatoes, whole corn, cream-style corn, potatoes, basil, sugar and black pepper in stock pot. Simmer for 45 minutes or until potatoes are tender. Add milk and heat just to boiling.

Note: Chowder freezes well and recipe doubles easily.

Yield: 8 to 10 cups

Cheese, Crab and Broccoli Soup

- **1 cup grated carrots**
- **1 cup finely diced celery**
- **¾ cup minced onion**
- **1½ cups chicken broth**
- **1 bunch broccoli, diced**
- **3 cups milk**
- **1 cup margarine or butter**
- **1 cup all-purpose flour**
- **3 cups (12 ounces) shredded sharp Cheddar cheese**
- **1 teaspoon salt**
- **½ teaspoon black pepper**
- **3 tablespoons Worcestershire sauce**
- **¾ pound crab meat or imitation crab or combination**
- **Sherry**

Cook carrots, celery and onion in broth in stock pot until vegetables are tender. Steam broccoli until tender and add to other vegetables. Stir in milk and set aside. Melt margarine or butter. Add flour and cook, stirring constantly, until blended. Add to vegetables and cook until sauce is thickened and smooth. Add cheese, salt, black pepper and Worcestershire sauce, stirring until cheese is melted. Add crab meat and heat thoroughly. Add sherry to individual servings as desired.

Note: Additional milk can be added after the soup is cooked. Soup can be prepared a day in advance and reheated.

Yield: 15 to 16 cups

She Crab Soup

- 2 large onions, minced
- 1 cup clarified butter or margarine or vegetable oil
- 2 cups all-purpose flour
- 10 cups half and half
- 4 cups whipping cream
- 1½ teaspoons ground mace
- 1 cup sherry
- Salt and black pepper to taste
- 1 pound crab meat

Cook onions in butter in Dutch oven until transparent. Add flour, reduce heat and cook, stirring constantly, for 5 minutes. Add half and half and cream, stirring frequently. Add mace, sherry, salt, black pepper and crab meat. Simmer for at least 30 minutes, stirring frequently to prevent sticking.
Yield: 16 cups

Contributor: Philip Rateliff, Chef
Sea Captain's House
Myrtle Beach, South Carolina

Special Potato Soup

- 2 stalks celery, sliced
- 1 medium-sized onion, chopped
- 2 tablespoons butter or margarine, melted
- 6 medium potatoes, peeled and cubed
- 2 carrots, sliced
- 3 cups water
- 5 chicken bouillon cubes
- Dash of black pepper
- ¾ teaspoon seasoned salt
- ½ teaspoon crushed rosemary
- ½ teaspoon dried thyme
- 2 cups milk
- 1 cup (4 ounces) shredded longhorn Cheddar cheese

Sauté celery and onion in butter or margarine in Dutch oven until tender. Add potatoes, carrots, water, bouillon, black pepper, seasoned salt, rosemary and thyme. Simmer, covered, for about 20 minutes or until vegetables are tender. Remove from heat and mash vegetables, leaving part of potatoes in small chunks. Stir in milk and cheese. Cook, stirring constantly, until cheese is melted.

Note: Potato soup can be frozen.
Yield: 10 cups

Leek and Potato Soup

- 4 cups sliced leeks (green and white portions)
- 4 cups diced potatoes
- Water
- Salt to taste
- Low-fat milk

Combine leeks and potatoes in saucepan. Add water to cover and season with salt. Cook, partially covered, over medium heat for 20 to 30 minutes. Pour ½ of mixture in blender container, puree and return to saucepan. Add milk to consistency desired. Serve hot or cold.

Note: Soup is best if made a day prior to serving. Store in refrigerator overnight.

Yield: 6 to 8 cups

Cucumber Soup

- 2 large cucumbers, peeled
- 1 (10¾ ounce) can cream of chicken soup, undiluted
- 1 cup sour cream
- ¾ cup milk
- Salt to taste
- Celery salt to taste
- Red pepper to taste
- 10 drops lemon juice

Cut cucumbers in halves lengthwise, remove seeds and cut into chunks. Place in blender and add soup, sour cream, milk, salt, celery salt, red pepper and lemon juice. Blend briefly until smooth. Chill soup before serving.

Yield: 4 cups

Okra Soup

- 1 large beef bone
- 3 quarts water
- 2 medium-sized onions, chopped
- 3 pounds fresh okra, chopped
- 1 (4 ounce) piece breakfast bacon
- 8 large tomatoes, cut up, or 2 (40 ounce) cans tomatoes
- Salt and black pepper to taste
- 1 bay leaf

Simmer beef bone in water for 2 hours. Add onion, okra, bacon, tomatoes, salt, black pepper and bay leaf. Simmer for 2 hours, adding water if necessary to thin. Discard bay leaf. Serve with hot cooked rice and corn sticks or muffins.

Yield: 16 cups

Potato Chowder

- 5 cups hash brown potatoes
- 4 green onions with tops, sliced, or 2 small onions, sliced
- 4 cups water
- 4 slices bacon (optional)
- 1½ (8 ounce) packages cream cheese, softened
- 1 cup (4 ounces) freshly grated Parmesan cheese
- 2 cups milk

Combine potatoes, onion and water in large saucepan. Bring to a boil, reduce heat and simmer until potatoes are tender. If using bacon, cook until crisp, drain, crumble and set aside. Add cream cheese and Parmesan cheese to cooked potatoes, stirring until cream cheese is melted. Gradually add milk and heat thoroughly; do not boil. Serve with bacon bits.

Yield: 6 to cups

Mushroom Potato Chowder

- 1 stalk celery, chopped
- 1 (8 ounce) package mushrooms, sliced
- 1 small onion, chopped
- ½ small green bell pepper, chopped
- 2 tablespoons butter or margarine
- 2 cups red potatoes, peeled and diced
- 2 cups chicken broth
- ½ teaspoon dried thyme
- 2 cups milk, divided
- ½ teaspoon salt
- ½ teaspoon black pepper
- 3 tablespoons all-purpose flour

Cook celery, mushrooms, onion and bell pepper in butter or margarine until tender in a large Dutch oven, stirring frequently. Add potatoes, broth and thyme. Bring to a boil, reduce heat and simmer, uncovered, for 30 minutes or until potatoes are tender. Stir in 1½ cups milk, salt and black pepper. Combine remaining ½ cup milk with flour, blending until smooth. Add to chowder and simmer, uncovered and stirring frequently, until slightly thickened.

Note: This is a delicious hearty soup that has the taste and texture of a meat chowder without red meat.

Yield: 6 cups

Mediterranean Seafood Soup

- 1 (8 ounce) bottle clam juice
- 1 cup water
- 1 pound mussels, scrubbed and debearded
- 1 pound medium shrimp, shelled and deveined
- ½ pound scallops (cut if very large)
- 2 medium-sized onions, sliced
- ¼ cup olive oil
- 2 stalks celery, chopped
- 2 cloves garlic, minced
- 1 (28 ounce) can tomatoes, crushed
- 1½ cups dry white wine
- 1 tablespoon Worcestershire sauce
- 1 teaspoon sugar
- 1 teaspoon basil
- 1 teaspoon thyme
- Salt and freshly ground black pepper to taste
- ¼ pound squid, sliced

Combine clam juice and water in stock pot. Bring to a boil. Add mussels, bring to a boil, reduce heat and simmer for 3 to 5 minutes or until mussel shells open, shaking pot occasionally. Using slotted spoon, remove mussels and set aside. Strain cooking liquid through cheese cloth, add water to measure 3 cups and set aside. Cook onion in oil in stock pot until tender. Stir in celery and garlic and cook for 1 minute. Add reserved liquid, tomatoes, wine, Worcestershire sauce, sugar, basil, thyme, salt and black pepper. Bring to a boil, reduce heat and simmer for 15 minutes. Add shrimp, scallops and squid. Simmer for 3 to 5 minutes or just until seafood is cooked; do not overcook. Stir in mussels. Serve immediately.

Note: Soup can be prepared to point of adding seafood. Store in refrigerator or freezer. Complete cooking just before serving. Other seafood can be added or substituted. Serve with rice and a crusty French bread.

Yield: 10 to 12 cups

Squash Soup

- 1 pound squash, sliced
- 1 medium-sized onion, sliced
- 3 cups water
- 3 beef or chicken bouillon cubes
- 1 cup sour cream
- Black pepper to taste
- Dill weed to taste

Cook squash and onion in water with bouillon cubes until vegetables are tender. Let stand until cool. Pour into blender container, add sour cream and blend until smooth. Season with black pepper and dill weed. Serve hot or cold.

Yield: 7 to 8 cups

Seafood Chowder

- 1½ cups sliced carrots
- 1½ cups chopped celery
- 1 medium-sized onion, chopped
- 1 (32 ounce) package frozen hash brown potatoes
- 2 (14½ ounce) cans chicken broth
- Salt and black pepper to taste
- ¾ (16 ounce) carton Velveeta cheese, cubed
- ½ (8 ounce) carton hot pepper Velveeta cheese, cubed
- 2 cups milk
- 1 or 2 (6 ounce) cans crab meat
- 1 or 2 (4½ ounce) cans cocktail shrimp
- Dash of hot pepper sauce (optional)

Cook carrots, celery, onion and potatoes in broth until tender. Season with salt and black pepper. Add cheeses and stir until melted. Blend in milk. Add crab and shrimp. Season with hot sauce. Heat thoroughly but do not boil. Serve with fruit salad and rolls.
Yield: 12 to 14 cups

Bet's Gazpacho

- 3 cups tomato-based vegetable juice
- 1 cup no-fat beef broth
- 1 cup chopped seeded tomatoes
- ½ cup chopped seeded and peeled cucumber
- ¼ cup chopped green bell pepper
- 3 to 4 tablespoons chopped green onion
- 1 tablespoon fresh lemon or lime juice
- 1 tablespoon Worcestershire sauce
- 1 teaspoon hot pepper sauce or to taste
- Whole peeled garlic clove

Combine juice, broth, tomatoes, cucumber, bell pepper, green onion, lemon or lime juice, Worcestershire sauce and hot pepper sauce. Pierce garlic with toothpick and add to soup. Chill thoroughly or overnight. Remove garlic and serve very cold.
Yield: 6 cups

Fresh Tomato Soup

- 2 medium to large onions, diced
- 1 teaspoon dried thyme
- ¼ cup vegetable oil
- 2½ pounds ripe tomatoes, peeled and coarsely chopped
- ½ cup all-purpose flour
- ¼ cup sugar
- 3 cups chicken broth
- ½ cup tomato paste
- Salt and black pepper to taste
- ¼ cup dried basil or ½ cup chopped fresh basil
- Sour cream or yogurt (optional for garnish)

Sauté onion and thyme in oil in Dutch oven until transparent. Stir in tomatoes. Blend flour, sugar, broth and tomato paste. Add to vegetables and simmer, stirring occasionally, for 30 minutes. Using food processor, puree soup. Season with salt, black pepper and basil. Return to Dutch oven and heat thoroughly. Garnish individual servings with sour cream or yogurt.

Yield: 10 to 12 cups

Spicy Vegetable Soup

- 1½ pound meaty soup bone
- 6 cups water
- 2 teaspoon salt
- ½ to 1 teaspoon black pepper
- 2 small bay leaves
- 1 tablespoon garlic salt
- 1 teaspoon oregano
- 1 tablespoon parsley flakes
- 2 medium potatoes, peeled and cut in ½-inch cubes
- ¾ cup diced carrots
- ¾ cup frozen whole kernel corn or canned, undrained
- 1 (28 ounce) can tomatoes with juice, chopped
- ½ cup frozen English peas
- 2 medium-sized onions, quartered
- ½ to ¾ cup barley
- 1 packet dry onion soup

Combine bone, water, salt, black pepper, bay leaves, garlic salt, oregano and parsley flakes in Dutch oven. Bring to a boil, reduce heat and simmer for 30 minutes. Add potatoes, carrots, corn, tomatoes, peas, onion, barley and onion soup. Simmer for 1½ hours. Remove soup bone, trim meat and add to vegetables, discarding bone.

Yield: 12 cups

Italian Minestrone Soup

1 (16 ounce) package dried kidney beans
10 cups water
4 cups chicken broth
2 cups beef broth
2 cups tomato juice
1 ham hock (optional)
2 cups chopped onion
2 cloves garlic, minced
¼ cup olive oil
2 medium potatoes, peeled and cubed
4 medium carrots, thickly sliced
2 cups coarsely chopped cabbage (optional)
2 small zucchini, thickly sliced
2 small yellow squash, thickly sliced
1 (28 ounce) can whole tomatoes
¼ cup chopped fresh parsley
2 tablespoons sugar
1 teaspoon salt
½ teaspoon black or white pepper
1 tablespoon dried basil
2 tablespoons oregano
½ cup (2 ounces) grated Parmesan cheese (optional)

Soak beans in water overnight, drain and rinse or combine beans and water in stock pot, bring to a boil and cook for 2 minutes, remove from heat, cover, let stand for 1 hour, drain and rinse. Combine chicken broth, beef broth and tomato juice in stock pot. Add soaked beans and ham hock. Cook for 30 minutes. Sauté onion and garlic in oil until onions are softened. Add potatoes and carrots. Sauté for 3 to 5 minutes. Add sautéed vegetables to beans. Stir in cabbage, zucchini, squash and tomatoes. Simmer for 30 minutes. Add parsley, sugar, salt, black or white pepper, basil and oregano. Simmer for 20 to 30 minutes. Sprinkle individual servings with Parmesan cheese.

Note: Soup freezes well.
Yield: 18 to 20 cups

Add a cup of water to the bottom portion of the broiling pan before sliding into the oven to absorb smoke and grease.

Hot Asparagus Sandwiches

4 slices bread
4 slices American cheese
4 slices boiled ham
12 spears canned asparagus
1 egg white
½ cup mayonnaise

Place bread slices on baking sheet and lightly toast on one side under broiler. Turn toasted side down. Place slice of cheese, ham and 3 asparagus spears on untoasted side of each bread slice. Whip egg white until fluffy but not stiff. Stir mayonnaise into egg white and spoon mixture over asparagus. Place under broiler at a distance to allow thorough heating of sandwich while top browns slightly.
Yield: 4 servings

Hawaiian-Eye Sandwich

2 cups large curd creamed cottage cheese
1 tablespoon grated orange peel
½ cup coarsely chopped pineapple chunks
½ cup raisins (optional)
¼ cup chopped walnuts or pecans
6 club rolls
Small lettuce leaves
Shredded carrots (optional)

Combine cottage cheese, orange peel, pineapple, raisins, carrots and nuts, mixing well. Using sharp knife tip, cut slice from top of each roll and hollow out center, leaving walls about ½-inch thick. Arrange lettuce around edges, spoon ¼ cup filling into roll and garnish with carrots.

Note: Filling is also good on raisin bread.
Yield: 6 servings

Margo's Orange Sandwich Mix

1 (11 ounce) can mandarin oranges, drained
1 (8 ounce) package cream cheese, softened
½ cup chopped walnuts
¼ teaspoon cinnamon
20 slices bread

Cut orange slices into thirds. Combine oranges, cream cheese, walnuts and cinnamon, blending well. Spread filling on ½ of bread slices and top with remaining slices.
Yield: 10 sandwiches

Party Sandwiches

- 1 (8 ounce) package cream cheese softened
- 1 tablespoon ketchup
- ¾ cup chopped walnuts or pecans
- ¼ cup chopped green bell pepper
- ¼ cup chopped onion
- 3 tablespoons chopped pimento
- 3 hard-cooked eggs, finely chopped
- ¾ teaspoon salt
- Dash of black pepper
- 16 slices sandwich bread, lightly buttered

Combine cream cheese, ketchup, walnuts or pecans, bell pepper, onion, pimento, eggs, salt and black pepper, mixing well. Spread filling on ½ of bread slices and top with remaining slices. Trim crusts and cut each sandwich twice diagonally to form 4 triangles.
Yield: 2 ⅔ dozen

Shrimp Tea Sandwiches

- 1 (3 ounce) package cream cheese, softened
- 2 tablespoons mayonnaise
- 1 tablespoon ketchup
- 1 teaspoon prepared mustard
- Dash of garlic powder
- 1 cup chopped cooked shrimp
- ¼ cup finely chopped celery
- 1 teaspoon finely chopped green onion
- 10 slices sandwich bread
- Butter, softened

Combine cream cheese and mayonnaise. Blend in ketchup, mustard and garlic powder. Add shrimp, celery and green onion. Spread bread slices lightly with butter. Spread shrimp filling on ½ of bread slices and top with remaining slices. Trim crusts and cut each sandwich twice diagonally to form 4 triangles.
Yield: 1 ⅔ dozen

Oven Divan Sandwiches

6 slices bread, toasted
6 slices cheese
¾ pound sliced chicken
1 (10 ounce) package frozen broccoli spears, thawed and well drained
¾ cup mayonnaise
¼ cup (1 ounce) grated Parmesan cheese
1 teaspoon dry mustard
2 to 3 tablespoons milk
¼ cup chopped red onion

Place toast in 13x9x2-inch baking pan. Layer cheese, chicken and broccoli on toast. Combine mayonnaise, Parmesan cheese, mustard and milk, blending well. Spoon dressing on broccoli layer and sprinkle with onion. Bake, uncovered, at 400° for 15 to 20 minutes.
Yield: 6 servings

Chunky Pimento Cheese

1 (3 ounce) package cream cheese, softened
1 (4 ounce) jar pimento, diced and drained
1 cup mayonnaise
⅛ teaspoon black pepper
4 cups (16 ounces) finely shredded sharp Cheddar cheese

Combine cream cheese and pimento, mixing well. Add mayonnaise, black pepper and Cheddar cheese, stirring until well blended. Store, covered, in refrigerator.
Yield: 3½ cups

Broiled Crab Open-Faced Sandwiches

1 (6 ounce) can crab meat, drained and flaked
¼ cup mayonnaise or mayonnaise-type salad dressing
1 (3 ounce) package cream cheese, softened
1 egg yolk
1 teaspoon minced onion
¼ teaspoon prepared mustard
Dash of salt
3 English muffins, split and toasted
2 tablespoons butter, softened

Combine crab meat and mayonnaise and set aside. Combine cream cheese, egg yolk, onion, mustard and salt together, beating until smooth and creamy. Spread muffins halves with butter. Spoon crab mixture on muffin halves, top with cream cheese mixture and place on baking sheet. Broil 5 to 6 inches from heat source for 2 to 3 minutes or until bubbly and golden.
Yield: 3 servings

Tuna Melt

1 (3 ounce) can white water-pack tuna, drained
Chopped celery to taste
Chopped onion to taste
Chopped ripe olives to taste
Low-fat mayonnaise to taste
Salt and black pepper to taste
1 English muffin, split
1 slice Swiss cheese
Basil or dill weed to taste

Combine tuna, celery, onion, ripe olives, mayonnaise, salt and black pepper. Spread evenly on cut surfaces of muffin, top with cheese and place on baking sheet. Broil until cheese is melted. Sprinkle with basil or dill weed.

Note: Sandwich is wonderful for a Saturday lunch.
Yield: 1 serving

Tuna Salad Sandwich

- **1 (6 ounce) can white tuna, drained**
- **1 medium apple, diced**
- **½ cup diced celery**
- **2 hard-cooked eggs, chopped**
- **2 tablespoons chopped sweet pickle**
- **Dash of salt**
- **2 tablespoons sliced green olives**
- **½ cup chopped almonds**
- **2 tablespoons fresh lemon juice**
- **2 to 4 tablespoons mayonnaise**
- **6 to 8 slices bread**

Combine tuna, apple, celery, eggs, pickles, salt, olives and almonds. Mix lemon juice and mayonnaise, add to tuna mixture and blend well. Spread filling on ½ of bread slices and top with remaining slices.
Yield: 3 or 4 servings

Tuna Sandwich Toastoes

- **2 (6 ounce) cans white tuna, drained**
- **⅔ cup mayonnaise**
- **½ cup chopped ripe olives**
- **4 hard-cooked eggs, chopped**
- **24 slices bread**
- **2 (5 ounce) jars Old English cheese spread**
- **½ cup margarine**
- **2 eggs, beaten**

A day in advance of serving, combine tuna, mayonnaise, olives and eggs. Using tuna can for cutter, cut rounds from bread slices. Spread filling on bread rounds, stacking to use 3 in each sandwich. Place on baking sheet. Combine cheese spread, margarine and eggs in top of double boiler over hot water. Stir until cheese is melted. Frost sandwich stacks with cheese mixture. Chill overnight. Bake at 350°s for 10 minutes.
Yield: 8 servings

Turkey and Ham Deluscious

- 4 slices bacon
- 3 tablespoons butter
- 3 tablespoons all-purpose flour
- 1½ cups milk
- 1 teaspoon salt
- Dash of cayenne pepper
- 1 cup (4 ounces) grated sharp cheese
- 4 slices turkey
- 4 slices ham
- 8 slices tomato
- 2 English muffins, split and toasted

Broil or fry bacon, drain on paper towel and set aside. Melt butter in saucepan. Blend in flour. Gradually stir in milk, season with salt and cayenne pepper and cook until smooth and boiling. Reduce heat and add cheese. Assemble sandwiches by placing turkey, ham and tomato slices on muffins, topping with bacon and spooning cheese over bacon slices.

Note: This sandwich is a meal in itself.
Yield: 2 servings

Windy's Vegetable Sandwich

- 2 tablespoons lemon juice
- ¼ cup finely chopped green bell pepper
- ⅔ cup grated carrots
- ¼ cup finely chopped celery
- ¼ cup chopped cucumber
- ¼ cup minced onion
- 1 (8 ounce) package cream cheese, softened
- Mayonnaise
- Salt and black pepper to taste
- 40 slices bread

Pour lemon juice over bell pepper, carrots, celery, cucumber and onion. Let stand. Blend cream cheese with enough mayonnaise for spreading consistency. Drain vegetables and add to cream cheese mixture. Season with salt and black pepper. Spread filling on ½ of bread slices and top with remaining slices.
Yield: 20 sandwiches

Vegetables, Fruits, & Accompaniments

Verandas and porches were cool places to linger on sultry summer days. Walk around that Carolina home to the back porch and you would see a beehive of activity. The back porch was probably equipped with an assortment of straight ladder back chairs. Here was a convenient place to shell the peas and string and snap the beans. Wayward peas were tolerated more easily on the porch than in the kitchen. From this vantage point, playing children could be corralled into helping with the task at hand. A basket of sewing might be taken to the front porch but preparing vegetables was a back porch chore. A bushel of peas to be shelled seemed daunting until an aunt or cousin or neighbor dropped by to help. All hands were needed to prepare them quickly for canning. How rapidly that mountain of vegetables could be diminished with extra hands and lively conversation. And after the first frost had slowed the supply of fresh vegetables, how very sweet the reward.

Busy hands and lively conversation still exist and make the task less daunting as Charity League members gather in one another's air conditioned homes to craft articles for the fall Charity League Bazaar. Some members still contribute preserves, jams, jellies and pickles that they have made during the summer. Exquisite, hand sewn Christmas skirts and ornaments and fine needlework grace the booths. This huge event requires the year round effort of all its members.

Vegetable Cookery

Water Methods

There are several methods of cooking vegetables with water.

- Immerse green vegetables in a large pot of boiling water and cook uncovered. This French or Chip method preserves the color, flavor and texture of the vegetable.
- Cook vegetables, covered, in very small amount of water quickly. This preserves most of the nutrients of the vegetables.
- Parboiling is a process in which the vegetables are partially cooked in a small amount of water. The cooking is completed during a later step in preparation of a dish.
- Microwaving allows even cooking of vegetables in a very small amount of water and retention of color. Place fresh vegetables in shallow microwave-safe dish, add a few tablespoons of water and cover with plastic wrap, puncturing to vent steam. Cook until vegetables are tender.
- Steaming involves placing vegetables in pierced insert or basket, suspending over boiling water and cooking, covered, until tender.

Frying

There are two basic methods of frying: deep frying in a large amount of vegetable oil or frying in a very small amount of oil. When using either method, vegetables should be cut in small pieces to assure they will cook evenly.

- Consider heat tolerance and flavor when selecting an oil or fat in which to fry vegetables. Some varieties smoke at high temperatures and others give a distinct taste or flavor. Pure olive oil has the richest flavor but has low heat tolerance. Corn oil, soy bean oil, sunflower oil and peanut oil have high heat tolerance.
- Stir-frying, in which vegetables are cooked quickly in small amount of oil, can be done in a large heavy skillet as well as a wok.
- After frying, oil or fat can be strained and reused. Each time it is reused, the heat tolerance is lowered.

Stewing and Braising

Both methods involve cooking vegetables very slowly in a small amount of liquid to merge the flavors. Braising is the preparation of 1 vegetable in a small amount of liquid. Stewing is simmering or boiling slowly in very little liquid.

The liquid used in cooking vegetables by either method can affect the flavor and texture. When using wine or acidic liquids such as lemon juice, the vegetables remain soft and intact throughout the cooking process. Both methods rely on the use of delicate herbs and spices to enhance flavors.

Baking

Baking whole vegetables in their skins produces a mellow, yet concentrated flavor. The method is ideal for root vegetables such as potatoes, as well as winter squashes and eggplant. The vegetables have tough outer skins that protect the pulp of the vegetables from drying during cooking.

Besides baking vegetables whole, other baking methods provide a variety of texture and flavor. Filling or stuffing with a mixture of other vegetables uses the basic vegetable as a cooking container. Tomatoes, artichokes, bell peppers and onions are good with stuffing.

Gratin is a baking method that involves chopping the vegetables, then topping with crumbs or cheese to create a crisp browned top with delicately flavored vegetables beneath. Gratins can be cooked with cream to create a moist, rich flavor.

Puddings combine pureed vegetables with eggs, grated cheese and butter and are baked in a mold.

Soufflés use the same ingredients as vegetable puddings but add beaten egg whites to create the lightness of a soufflé.

Broiling

Broiling uses the intensive heat of the upper heating unit in an oven by cooking vegetables about 6 inches from the heat source. The method requires close attention as browning occurs very rapidly. Soft vegetables, such as summer squash, eggplant and tomatoes, should be lightly oiled to keep them moist. Preheat the broiler for 15 to 20 minutes to assure a hot, even temperature.

Grilling

Grilling outdoors over a charcoal fire is more difficult than other techniques because it is hard to control the heat of the coals. Vegetables can be cooked directly on the grill or sealed in aluminum foil and placed on the grill. They should be grilled 6 inches from the coals. Cooking times vary; test for tenderness by piercing with tines of a long-handled fork.

Asparagus-Pea Casserole

2 (14½ ounce) cans asparagus spears, drained
1 (20 ounce) can small party peas, drained
1 (4 ounce) package slivered almonds, blanched
2 (10¾ ounce) cans cream of mushroom soup, undiluted
3 cups (12 ounces) regular or low-fat grated Cheddar cheese

Arrange asparagus spears in 2-quart casserole. Pour peas over asparagus, sprinkle almonds on peas, spoon soup on almonds and sprinkle cheese on soup layer. Bake at 350° for about 45 minutes or until cheese is bubbly and casserole is beginning to brown around edges.

Note: Recipe can be halved.
Yield: 15 servings

Barbecued Baked Beans

½ cup dark molasses
2 tablespoons vinegar
2 tablespoons prepared mustard
4 (16 ounce) cans baked beans
1 medium-sized onion, sliced

Combine molasses, vinegar and mustard. Pour beans into 2½-quart casserole. Stir molasses mixture into beans. Arrange onion slices on beans. Bake at 350° for 30 minutes.

Note: Onion can be layered with beans.
Yield: 12 to 16 servings

Spicy Baked Beans

4 or 5 slices bacon
1 (28 ounce) can baked beans
2 (16 ounce) cans pork and beans
½ cup chopped celery with leaves
1 large onion, chopped
2 tablespoons molasses
¼ cup firmly-packed brown sugar
1½ teaspoons garlic salt
1 tablespoon Worcestershire sauce
½ teaspoon basil
¼ teaspoon oregano

Cook bacon until crisp, drain, crumble and set aside. Combine baked beans, pork and beans, celery and onion. Stir in molasses, brown sugar, garlic salt, Worcestershire sauce, basil and oregano, mixing well. Pour bean mixture into 3-quart casserole. Sprinkle bacon bits on beans. Bake at 350° for 50 minutes.
Yield: 16 servings

Bean Casserole

1 (10 ounce) package frozen lima beans
1 (16 ounce) can pork and beans, drained
1 (16 ounce) can red kidney beans, drained
1½ cups chopped green bell pepper
1½ cups chopped celery
1½ cups chopped onion
1½ cups firmly-packed brown sugar
1 cup ketchup
Salt to taste
½ teaspoon garlic salt
6 bacon slices

Prepare lima beans according to package directions and drain. Combine lima beans, pork and beans, kidney beans, bell pepper, celery and onion. Stir in brown sugar, ketchup, salt and garlic salt. Pour bean mixture into 13x9x2-inch baking dish. Arrange bacon slices on beans. Bake at 350° for 30 minutes or until bubbly.
Yield: 12 to 16 servings

Green Beans and Mushrooms

- 2 cloves garlic, minced
- ¼ pound small mushrooms, trimmed and sliced
- 1 tablespoon butter
- 1 medium-sized red onion, cut in thin strips
- 1 pound fresh green beans, trimmed
- Salt to taste and black pepper to taste
- 1 teaspoon dill weed
- 2 tablespoons toasted almonds or pine nuts

Sauté garlic and mushrooms in butter until tender. Add onion and set aside. Steam beans until tender-crisp and drain. Combine beans and mushroom mixture. Season with salt, black pepper and dill. Toss with almonds or pine nuts and serve warm.

Yield: 6 servings

All Puffed-Up Broccoli Casserole

- 2 (10 ounce) packages frozen chopped broccoli
- 3 eggs, separated
- 1 tablespoon all-purpose flour
- Pinch of nutmeg
- 1 tablespoon margarine, softened
- 1 cup fat-free mayonnaise
- ¼ cup plus 1 tablespoon (1 ounce) grated Parmesan cheese
- ¼ teaspoon salt
- ¼ teaspoon black pepper

Prepare broccoli according to package directions and drain well. Beat egg yolks thoroughly. Add flour, nutmeg and margarine, mixing lightly. Stir in mayonnaise, Parmesan cheese, salt and black pepper. Beat egg whites (at room temperature) until stiff but not dry. Gently fold whites into yolk mixture. Add broccoli. Pour into buttered 9x9x2-inch baking dish. Bake at 350° for 30 minutes.

Yield: 9 servings

Broccoli stems can be cooked in the same length of time as the flowers if you make 'x' incisions from top to bottom through stems.

Creamed Broccoli

2 (10 ounce) packages frozen chopped broccoli
1 (8 ounce) package herb seasoned stuffing mix
2 (10¾ ounce) cans cream of chicken soup, undiluted
6 tablespoons milk, divided

Prepare broccoli according to package directions and drain. While broccoli cooks, prepare stuffing mix according to package directions for dry crumbly method and set aside. Place cooked broccoli in 12x8x2-inch baking dish. Spoon soup over broccoli. Use 3 tablespoons milk to rinse soup from each can and pour over soup layer. Sprinkle stuffing evenly over soup. Bake at 350° for 45 minutes.
Yield: 6 to 8 servings

Broccoli Casserole

3 (10 ounce) packages frozen chopped broccoli
1 medium-sized onion, chopped
½ cup margarine
1 (6 ounce) roll garlic cheese food
1 (4 ounce) can mushrooms, drained and chopped
1 (10¾ ounce) can cream of mushroom soup, undiluted
1 (8 ounce) package herb seasoned stuffing mix or breadcrumbs

Prepare broccoli according to package directions and drain; do not overcook. Sauté onion in margarine in saucepan over low heat. Add garlic cheese and stir until melted. Add mushrooms and soup, blending well. Stir in broccoli. Spread broccoli mixture in 13x9x2-inch baking dish. Sprinkle stuffing mix over broccoli mixture. Bake, uncovered, at 350° for 20 minutes or until thoroughly heated.
Yield: 8 servings

Broccoli and Rice Casserole

2 (10 ounce) packages frozen chopped broccoli
2 cups cooked rice
1 (10¾ ounce) can cream of chicken soup, undiluted
1 (16 ounce) jar soft cheese spread
1 (8 ounce) can water chestnuts, drained and sliced

Prepare broccoli according to package directions and drain. Combine broccoli, rice, soup, cheese and water chestnuts, mixing well. Spread broccoli mixture in greased 2-quart casserole. Bake, covered, at 350° for 20 minutes, stir and bake for additional 25 minutes. Remove cover and broil for a few minutes to brown top.
Yield: 6 servings

Broccoli and Corn Casserole

1 (10 ounce) package frozen chopped broccoli, thawed
¾ cup dry breadcrumbs, divided
1 (20 ounce) can cream-style corn
1 egg, well beaten
1 tablespoon grated onion
1 tablespoon butter, melted
1 (3 ounce) can French fried onions
2 slices bacon, diced

Combine broccoli, ½ cup breadcrumbs, corn, egg, onion and butter. Spread broccoli mixture in greased 2-quart casserole. Sprinkle remaining ¼ cup breadcrumbs, French fried onions and bacon over broccoli mixture. Bake at 350° for 30 minutes.
Yield: 6 servings

Cabbage Casserole

1 small head cabbage, cut in bite-sized chunks
1 (10¾ ounce) can cream of celery soup, undiluted
1 cup milk
⅓ cup mayonnaise
¼ cup margarine
2 cups (8 ounces) grated sharp cheese
2 cups corn flakes

Steam cabbage for 5 minutes and drain. Combine soup, milk, mayonnaise, margarine and cheese in saucepan. Heat, stirring constantly, until smooth. Add cabbage to cheese sauce. Sprinkle ½ of corn flakes in 2-quart casserole, pour cabbage mixture over corn flakes and sprinkle with remaining corn flakes. Bake at 350° for 15 minutes.
Yield: 6 servings

Red Cabbage

- 1 head red cabbage, cored and quartered
- 2 unpeeled Granny Smith apples, cored and quartered
- 2 onions, quartered
- 4 whole cloves
- 2 tablespoons butter, melted
- ½ cup red wine vinegar
- 1 cup water
- 2 tablespoons sugar
- Salt to taste

Combine cabbage, apples, onions and cloves in Dutch oven. Add butter, vinegar, water, sugar and salt, mixing well. Simmer, stirring occasionally, for 3 to 4 hours. Drain liquid and serve vegetables hot.
Yield: 6 to 8 servings

Company Carrots

- 2 pounds carrots, peeled
- Water
- Salt and black pepper to taste
- ½ cup mayonnaise
- 1 tablespoon minced onion
- 1 tablespoon prepared horseradish
- ¼ cup fine breadcrumbs
- 2 tablespoons margarine, softened
- Paprika
- Chopped parsley

Cook carrots in salted water until tender. Drain, reserving ¼ cup cooking liquid. Cut carrots lengthwise and arrange in 12x8x2-inch baking dish. Combine reserved cooking liquid, mayonnaise, onion, horseradish, salt and black pepper. Pour sauce over carrots. Sprinkle breadcrumbs on carrots, dot with margarine and sprinkle with paprika and parsley. Bake, uncovered, at 350° for 20 minutes.

Note: Carrots can be prepared in advance and reheated.
Yield: 6 servings

Gingered Carrots

- 10 medium carrots, peeled and sliced
- ¼ cup butter
- ¼ cup honey
- 1 teaspoon salt
- ¼ teaspoon cinnamon
- ½ teaspoon ginger

Combine carrots, butter, honey, salt, cinnamon and ginger in saucepan. Cook, covered, over medium heat, stirring occasionally, for 20 to 30 minutes or until carrots are tender. Serve hot.
Yield: 8 servings

Honey-Mustard Carrots

- **1 pound carrots, peeled and sliced**
- **2 tablespoons low-fat margarine, melted**
- **1 tablespoon Dijon mustard**
- **1 tablespoon honey**
- **¼ teaspoon ginger**

Cook carrots in small amount of water until crisp tender. Drain and keep warm. Combine margarine, mustard, honey and ginger, mixing well. Pour sauce over carrots and toss gently to coat.

Note: A very colorful dish, the carrots can be prepared in advance and reheated by microwave.

Yield: 4 servings

Marinated Carrots

- **3 pounds carrots, peeled and thinly sliced**
- **1 medium-sized green bell pepper, diced**
- **3 medium-sized onions, sliced**
- **1 (10½ ounce) can tomato soup, undiluted**
- **¼ cup vegetable oil**
- **¼ cup vinegar**
- **¾ cup sugar**
- **1 teaspoon prepared mustard**
- **1 teaspoon Worcestershire sauce**

A day in advance of serving, cook carrots in small amount of water until tender. Drain well. Combine carrots, bell pepper and onion. In blender container, combine soup, oil, vinegar, sugar, mustard and Worcestershire sauce. Blend thoroughly. Pour marinade over vegetables. Chill overnight.

Yield: 10 to 12 servings

Estrid's Corn Soufflé

- **1 (16 ounce) can cream-style corn**
- **2 (10 ounce) cans Mexican whole corn, drained**
- **1 cup sour cream**
- **¼ cup plus 1 tablespoon butter, cut in bits**
- **1 (8½ ounce) package corn muffin mix**
- **1 cup (4 ounces) grated sharp Cheddar cheese**

Combine cream style corn, Mexican corn, sour cream, butter and muffin mix. Spread mixture in greased 1½-quart casserole. Sprinkle with cheese. Bake at 350° for 50 to 60 minutes.

Yield: 6 to 8 servings

Grilled Corn on the Cob

⅓ cup butter or margarine
2 tablespoons prepared mustard
2 tablespoons prepared horseradish (optional)
1 teaspoon Worcestershire sauce
¼ teaspoon lemon pepper
6 ears fresh corn on the cob

Melt butter in small saucepan over low heat. Stir in mustard, horseradish, Worcestershire sauce and lemon pepper, blending well. Place each ear corn on 12x9-inch rectangle heavy duty aluminum foil. Drizzle butter mixture over corn. Fold edges of foil to form pouch and seal securely, leaving room for steam expansion. Grill over medium-hot grills, turning occasionally, for about 15 minutes.
Yield: 6 servings

Corn Pudding

2 eggs, beaten
1 cup milk
1 (16 ounce) can whole or cream-style corn
2 tablespoons butter, melted
3 tablespoons sugar
¼ teaspoon salt
½ teaspoon vanilla
Dash of nutmeg (optional)

Combine eggs, milk, corn, butter, sugar, salt and vanilla in 1½-quart casserole. Bake at 350° for 50 minutes or until center is firm. Sprinkle with nutmeg.
Yield: 6 to 8 servings

Fresh Corn Pudding

3 eggs
3 cups corn, freshly cut from cobs
2 teaspoons minced onion
3 tablespoons all-purpose flour
1 teaspoon salt
Dash of cayenne pepper
¼ cup butter, melted and cooled
1½ cups half and half or milk
Boiling water

Using electric mixer, beat eggs until frothy. With wooden spoon, stir in corn and onion. Combine flour, salt and cayenne pepper. Gradually add to corn mixture, stirring constantly. Add butter and half and half, mixing well. Pour corn mixture into well-greased 1½-quart casserole. Place dish in roasting pan, place pan in oven preheated at 350° and add boiling water to ¼ depth of casserole sides. Bake pudding for 15 minutes, stir gently with fork to distribute corn evenly, and bake for additional 45 minutes or until golden brown and knife tip inserted near center comes out clean.
Yield: 6 servings

Excellent Eggplant Extraordinaire

4 cups cubed peeled eggplant, seeded
Boiling water
Salt
1 (10¾ ounce) can cream of celery soup, undiluted
⅔ cup milk
1 egg
⅓ cup chopped onion
1¼ cups herb seasoned stuffing mix, divided
1 cup (4 ounces) shredded Monterey Jack cheese
3 tablespoons butter, melted

Cook eggplant in boiling salted water for 6 minutes. Drain well. Blend soup and milk together. Add egg and mix well. Combine soup mixture, eggplant, onion and ¾ cup stuffing mix, tossing thoroughly. Spread eggplant mixture in greased 13x9x2-inch baking pan. Combine remaining ½ cup stuffing mix, cheese and butter. Sprinkle on eggplant mixture. Bake, uncovered, at 350° for 20 to 30 minutes or until hot and bubbly.
Yield: 6 servings

Sautéed Greens with Dijon Mustard and Sour Cream

1¼ pounds fresh collard, turnip, mustard or beet greens
Boiling water
Salt and freshly ground black pepper to taste
3 tablespoons butter, margarine or olive oil
1 medium-sized yellow onion, minced
¼ cup sour cream
1 tablespoon Dijon mustard
Pinch of cayenne pepper

Remove coarse stems from greens, wash leaves and dry thoroughly. Stack leaves and cut in slivers. Drop greens into boiling salted water and cook for just a few minutes or until tender. Drain well. Sauté onion in butter in large skillet, cooking just until softened. Add greens and toss to coat. Combine sour cream, mustard, black pepper and cayenne pepper, mixing well. Add to greens and cook for 3 to 5 minutes or until liquid has almost evaporated, stirring frequently. Serve warm.
Yield: 4 servings

Mushrooms Florentine

- 1 pound fresh mushrooms
- 2 (10 ounce) packages frozen chopped spinach
- ½ teaspoon salt
- ¼ cup chopped onion
- ¼ cup butter, melted
- 1 cup sour cream
- Fresh dill sprigs, chopped
- 1 cup (4 ounces) grated sharp Cheddar cheese, divided
- Garlic salt to taste

Slice stems from mushrooms. Sauté caps and stems in butter until browned, browning cap side of mushrooms first. Prepare spinach according to package directions and drain well. Combine spinach, salt, onion, melted butter, sour cream and dill. Lightly press spinach mixture to line a 10x6x2-inch baking dish. Sprinkle with ½ cup cheese, arrange mushrooms on cheese, season with garlic salt and sprinkle with remaining ½ cup cheese. Bake at 350° for 20 minutes or until cheese is melted and browned.

Note: Dish can be assembled in advance. Canned button mushrooms can be substituted for fresh mushrooms; drain well.

Yield: 6 to 8 servings

Vidalia Georgia Onion Casserole

- 1 cup cornbread or herb seasoned stuffing mix
- ½ cup butter or margarine, melted
- 2½ cups diced Vidalia onions
- 2 tablespoons vegetable oil
- 2 eggs, beaten
- ⅔ cup milk
- ¼ cup (1 ounce) grated sharp Cheddar cheese
- Salt and black pepper to taste
- Parsley flakes for garnish (optional)

Combine stuffing mix and butter. Press lightly in 8x8x2-inch baking dish. Sauté onions in oil until transparent. Spread onions over stuffing mix. Combine eggs, milk and cheese. Pour egg mixture evenly over onions. Season with salt, black pepper and parsley. Bake at 350° for 45 minutes.

Yield: 4 servings

Onion Casserole

4 large onions
1 (10¾ ounce) can cream of mushroom soup, undiluted
1 (4 ounce) package slivered almonds, toasted
¾ cup corn flake crumbs
¼ cup butter, melted

Slice 2 onions and arrange rings in greased 1½-quart casserole. Add ½ of soup and ½ of almonds. Repeat layers. Combine corn flake crumbs and butter. Sprinkle over almond layer. Bake, covered, at 375° for 45 minutes.
Yield: 4 to 6 servings

Onion Pie

4 slices bacon
5 or 6 medium-sized onions, thinly sliced
2 tablespoons all-purpose flour
¼ teaspoon salt
½ cup milk
2 eggs, beaten
1 unbaked 8 or 9-inch pastry shell

Cook bacon until crisp, drain on paper towel, crumble and set aside. Sauté onion in bacon drippings over medium heat until tender, separating into rings. Combine flour, salt, milk and eggs, beating until smooth. Sprinkle bacon bits in pastry shell, layer onion on bacon and pour egg mixture over onion. Bake at 375° for 30 minutes or until firm.
Yield: 6 to 8 servings

Barbecued Potatoes

4 pounds small new potatoes
Water
Salt to taste
⅓ cup olive oil
½ teaspoon freshly ground black pepper
2 teaspoons minced garlic

Cook potatoes in salted water for 10 to 12 minutes. Drain well. Toss potatoes with oil, black pepper and garlic. Thread potatoes on metal skewers. Grill or broil for 9 minutes, turning at 3-minute intervals and brushing with oil mixture, until browned.

Note: May be prepared and refrigerated up to 24 hours before grilling.
Yield: 8 to 10 servings

Blue Cheese and Bacon Potatoes

- 4 baking potatoes
- Vegetable shortening
- 4 slices bacon
- ½ cup sour cream
- ¼ cup (1 ounce) crumbled blue cheese
- ¼ cup milk
- ¼ cup butter, softened
- ½ teaspoon salt (optional)
- Black pepper to taste

Brush or rub potatoes with shortening. Bake at 400° for 1 hour or until potatoes are done. While potatoes bake, cook bacon until crisp, drain well, crumble and set aside. Cut lengthwise slice from top of each baked potato. Scoop out pulp, place in bowl and mash. Add sour cream, blue cheese, milk, butter, salt and black pepper. Using electric mixer, beat until fluffy. Lightly spoon mixture into potato shells and place on baking sheet. Bake for 15 minutes or until thoroughly heated. Sprinkle each potato with bacon bits.

Yield: 4 servings

Potato and Feta Cheese Soufflé

- 4 medium boiling potatoes
- Water
- Salt and freshly ground pepper to taste
- 4 eggs, separated
- ¾ cup half and half
- 1 small onion, minced
- 1 stalk celery, finely chopped
- 3 tablespoons butter
- 1 cup (4 ounces) finely crumbled feta cheese

Cook potatoes in salted water to cover for about 30 minutes or until tender. Drain and let stand until cool enough to handle. Peel, place in bowl and mash with fork. Add egg yolks and half and half. Using electric mixer, beat to smooth puree consistency. Sauté onion and celery in 3 tablespoons butter until tender. Add sautéed vegetables, cheese, salt and black pepper to potato mixture. Generously butter bottom and sides of 7x3-inch soufflé dish. Beat egg whites until stiff. Fold ⅓ of whites into potato mixture, then fold potato mixture into remaining whites. Spread potatoes in soufflé dish and place on baking sheet. Bake at 400° for 40 to 45 minutes or until puffed and golden brown.

Yield: 4 to 6 servings

Potatoes in Herb Flavored Salt

- 2 pounds potatoes, peeled and cubed
- ¼ cup plus 1 tablespoon olive oil
- ¼ cup plus 3 tablespoons butter
- 10 sage leaves, chopped
- Rosemary sprigs
- Salt and black pepper to taste
- 1 clove garlic

Brown potatoes in oil and butter in large oven-safe skillet until golden. Transfer to oven and bake at 450° for about 20 minutes. Combine sage, rosemary, salt and black pepper. Press garlic and add juice to herbs. Remove potatoes from oven and season immediately with herb mixture.

Yield: 4 or 5 servings

Potato-Spinach Casserole

- 6 to 8 large potatoes, peeled
- Water
- Salt and black pepper to taste
- 1 cup sour cream
- 1 medium-sized onion, chopped
- ¼ cup butter, softened
- 1 (10 ounce) package frozen chopped spinach, thawed and drained
- 1 cup (4 ounces) grated Cheddar cheese

Cook potatoes in salted water to cover until tender. Drain and mash. Combine potatoes, salt, black pepper, sour cream, onion, butter and spinach, mixing well. Spread mixture in greased 2-quart casserole. Bake, uncovered, at 400° for 20 minutes, sprinkle with cheese and bake for additional 5 minutes.

Yield: 8 servings

Mashed Potatoes

- 4 or 5 Idaho potatoes
- Water
- Salt and black pepper to taste
- ¼ cup butter
- 1 cup milk
- Dash of garlic salt

Cook potatoes in salted water to cover until tender. Drain, peel and mash. Combine butter and milk in saucepan. Heat until butter is melted. Add milk to potatoes and mix well. Season with salt, black pepper and garlic salt, whip and serve immediately.

Yield: 4 to 6 servings

Boursin Potato Gratin

- 2 cups whipping cream
- ⅔ cup fresh boursin cheese with black pepper or 1 (5 ounce) package boursin cheese with cracked black pepper
- 2 tablespoons minced shallots
- 1 clove garlic, minced
- 2½ pounds new red potatoes, cut in ¼-inch slices
- Salt and freshly ground black pepper to taste
- 2 tablespoons snipped chives
- 2 tablespoons chopped parsley

If using fresh boursin cheese, prepare as directed. Combine cream, boursin cheese, shallots and garlic in heavy saucepan. Heat over medium heat, stirring until cheese is melted. Arrange ½ of potato slices in well buttered 13x9x2-inch baking dish, slightly overlapping rows. Season generously with salt and black pepper, pour ½ of cheese sauce over potatoes and sprinkle with chives. Repeat all layers. Bake at 400° for about 1 hour or until potatoes are tender and golden brown. Sprinkle with parsley.

Yield: 8 to 10 servings

Boursin Cheese with Black Pepper

- 3 cloves garlic, minced
- ½ teaspoon salt
- 1 (8 ounce) package cream cheese
- ¼ cup butter
- 2 tablespoons finely chopped parsley
- 1 to 2 tablespoons coarsely ground black pepper

Mash garlic with salt to form paste and set aside. Combine garlic paste, cream cheese, butter, parsley and black pepper. Using electric mixer or food processor and blend until smooth. Store, covered, in refrigerator for up to 2 weeks. Serve at room temperature or place in oven-safe 2-cup bowl or ramekin and bake at 350° for about 10 minutes or until warm. Serve with crackers, croustades or as filling for appetizer puffs.

Yield: 1 ½ cups

Dutch Stewed Irish Potatoes

- 1 onion, sliced
- 1 tablespoon butter or vegetable shortening
- ½ teaspoon salt
- Dash of black pepper
- 1 teaspoon minced parsley
- 2 cups diced potatoes
- Boiling water
- 2 teaspoons all-purpose flour
- ¼ cup cold water

Sauté onion in butter or shortening for about 5 minutes. Add salt, black pepper, parsley and potatoes. Cover with boiling water and cook until potatoes are tender. Blend flour and cold water, add to potatoes and liquid and cook until slightly thickened.
Yield: 2 servings

Scalloped Potatoes

- 8 medium potatoes, peeled and sliced
- ¼ cup chopped green bell pepper
- ¼ cup minced onion
- 2 teaspoons salt
- ⅛ teaspoon black pepper
- 1 (10¾ ounce) can cream of mushroom soup, undiluted
- 1 cup milk

Using about ⅓ of ingredients at a time, layer potatoes, bell pepper and onion in greased 13x9x2-inch baking dish, seasoning each layer with salt and pepper. Blend soup and milk together and pour over vegetables. Bake, covered, at 350° for 1½ hours.
Yield: 8 servings

Cheese Scalloped Potatoes

- 3 tablespoons butter
- 3 tablespoons all-purpose flour
- 1½ cups milk
- 1 teaspoon salt
- Dash of cayenne pepper
- 1 cup (4 ounces) grated Cheddar cheese
- ¾ cup chopped green bell pepper
- ½ cup chopped pimento
- 4 cups thinly sliced potatoes

Melt butter in saucepan. Blend in flour, gradually add milk, season with salt and cayenne pepper and cook, stirring frequently, until smooth and bubbly. Reduce heat and stir in cheese. When cheese is melted, add bell pepper and pimento. Alternately layer potatoes and cheese sauce in greased 12x8x2-inch baking dish. Bake at 325° for 2 hours.
Yield: 6 servings

Party Potatoes

- 1 cup butter or margarine, melted, divided
- ¼ to ½ cup chopped onion
- 1 (10¾ ounce) can cream of chicken soup, undiluted
- 2 cups sour cream
- 2 cups (8 ounces) grated Cheddar cheese
- 1 tablespoon salt
- 1 teaspoon black pepper
- 1 (32 ounce) package frozen hash brown potatoes, slightly thawed
- 2 cups corn flakes, crushed

Combine ½ cup butter or margarine, onion, soup, sour cream, cheese, salt and black pepper. Place potatoes in greased 3-quart casserole. Pour soup mixture over potatoes. Mix corn flakes and remaining ½ cup butter. Sprinkle over potatoes. Bake at 350° for 1¼ hours.

Note: For smaller quantities, divide ingredients between 2 or more smaller casseroles. Potatoes can be frozen for up to 3 months.

Yield: 8 to 10 servings

Spinach Madelynn

- 2 (10 ounce) packages frozen chopped spinach
- ¼ cup butter
- 2 tablespoons all-purpose flour
- 2 tablespoons chopped onion
- ½ cup evaporated milk
- 1½ cups (6 ounces) diced Monterey Jack cheese with jalapeno peppers
- ⅛ teaspoon black pepper
- ½ teaspoon garlic salt
- ½ teaspoon celery salt
- 1 teaspoon Worcestershire sauce
- 1 (13¾ ounce) can artichoke hearts, drained and quartered
- ½ cup buttered breadcrumbs

A day in advance of serving, prepare spinach according to package directions. Strain well and reserve liquid. Melt butter in saucepan over low heat. Blend in flour and cook, stirring often, until smooth but not browned. Add onion and cook until softened. Gradually add ½ cup spinach liquid and milk, stirring constantly to prevent lumps, and cook until thickened and smooth. Season with black pepper, garlic salt, celery salt and Worcestershire sauce. Add cheese and stir until melted. Combine sauce and spinach. Scatter artichoke pieces in 8x8x2-inch baking dish. Pour spinach mixture over artichokes. Chill overnight. Before baking, sprinkle with breadcrumbs. Bake at 350° until hot and bubbly.

Yield: 6 to 8 servings

Spinach Ricotta Tart

- 1 unbaked deep dish 10-inch pastry shell
- 2 (10 ounce) packages frozen chopped spinach
- 1 small onion, minced
- 3 tablespoons butter
- ½ teaspoon salt
- Dash of black pepper
- ¼ teaspoon nutmeg
- 2 cups ricotta cheese
- 1 cup half and half
- ½ cup (2 ounces) freshly grated Parmesan cheese
- 3 eggs, lightly beaten
- Parsley sprigs for garnish
- Cherry tomatoes for garnish

Bake pastry shell at 400° until lightly browned. Cool on wire rack. Prepare spinach according to package directions. Drain well, pressing to remove all liquid. Sauté onion in butter until transparent. Add spinach, salt, black pepper and nutmeg. Combine ricotta cheese, half and half, Parmesan cheese and eggs, mixing thoroughly. Stir in spinach. Spread spinach mixture in pastry shell. Bake at 350° for 50 minutes or until firm and lightly browned. Garnish with parsley and cherry tomatoes.

Note: Extra spinach mixture can be used to stuff fresh mushrooms. Bake until mushrooms are tender and serve as appetizers.

Yield: 6 to 8 servings

Spinach Supreme

- 2 (10 ounce) packages frozen chopped spinach
- ½ cup margarine
- 1 (8 ounce) package cream cheese, softened
- 1 (8 ounce) can water chestnuts, drained and chopped
- 1 (13¾ ounce) can artichoke hearts, drained and chopped
- 1 cup breadcrumbs

Prepare spinach according to package directions, reducing cooking time to 5 minutes. Drain well. Combine margarine and cheese in saucepan. Cook over low heat until melted. Stir in spinach and water chestnuts. Spread artichokes in 2-quart casserole. Spoon spinach mixture over artichokes and sprinkle with breadcrumbs. Bake at 350° for 35 minutes.

Note: For a luncheon, serve this with fruit or asparagus salad and angel biscuits.

Yield: 4 to 6 servings

Stuffed Acorn Squash

- 2 medium acorn squash, split lengthwise and seeded
- Water
- 8 to 10 fresh mushrooms, sliced
- 1 tablespoon butter
- 3 or 4 green onions, sliced
- ¼ cup chopped pecans
- ¼ cup sour cream
- ¼ cup (1 ounce) grated sharp Cheddar cheese

Place squash, cut surfaces down, in shallow pan of water. Bake at 350° for 45 to 60 minutes or until tender. While squash bakes, sauté mushrooms in butter until tender. Remove from heat and add onion, pecans and sour cream, mixing well. Spoon mushroom mixture into cavities of cooked squash. Sprinkle with cheese. Place in baking pan. Bake for 10 minutes or until cheese is melted.

Yield: 4 servings

Squash Casserole

- 2 pounds yellow squash, diced
- 1 medium-sized onion, chopped
- 3 tablespoons vegetable oil
- 1 cup sour cream
- 1 (10¾ ounce) can cream of chicken soup, undiluted
- 1 large carrot, grated
- 1 medium-sized green bell pepper, chopped
- 1 cup (4 ounces) grated Cheddar cheese
- 1 (8 ounce) package herb seasoned stuffing mix
- ½ cup margarine

Sauté squash and onion in oil until tender. Drain excess oil. Add sour cream, soup, carrots, bell pepper and cheese. In separate pan, melt margarine, add stuffing and mix thoroughly. Add ½ of stuffing to vegetable mixture and spread in buttered 12x8x2-inch baking dish. Top with remaining stuffing.

This recipe came from Anderson's Restaurant.

Yield: 8 to 10 servings

Squash Casserole or Soufflé

- 6 medium-sized yellow squash, cut in chunks (2 pounds)
- Water
- 1 egg, beaten
- 1 medium-sized onion, minced
- 1 large clove garlic, minced
- ½ cup mayonnaise
- ½ cup sour cream
- ½ cup (2 ounces) freshly grated Parmesan cheese, divided
- ½ teaspoon salt
- Black pepper to taste

Combine squash with water to cover in saucepan, bring to a boil, reduce heat and simmer for about 20 minutes or until squash is tender. Drain in colander and mash well. Combine squash, egg, onion, garlic, mayonnaise, sour cream, ¼ cup plus 2 tablespoons cheese, salt and black pepper. Spread mixture in well-buttered 2-quart baking dish and sprinkle with remaining 2 tablespoons cheese. Bake at 350° for 35 minutes or until golden brown; do not overbake.
Yield: 4 servings

Summer Squash Creole

- 4 slices bacon, diced
- ½ cup chopped green onion
- 2 pounds summer squash, diagonally cut in ½-inch slices
- ¼ teaspoon salt
- Dash of black pepper
- 2 medium tomatoes, peeled and cubed

Sauté bacon until crisp, drain and set aside. In 1 tablespoon bacon drippings or 2 tablespoons butter, sauté green onion for about 3 minutes. Add squash, salt and black pepper, tossing lightly to mix. Cook, covered, over low heat for about 15 minutes or until squash is just tender. Add tomatoes and toss to combine. Cook, covered, for 1 minute. Pour into serving dish and sprinkle with bacon.

Note: Dish can be prepared early in day and stored in refrigerator. Remove from refrigerator 30 minutes before baking; bake at 350° for 15 minutes.
Yield: 6 servings

Stuffed Zucchini

4 medium zucchini, trimmed and cut in halves lengthwise
Boiling water
1 pound bulk pork sausage or 1 pound fresh mushrooms, sliced
1¾ cups minced onion
1 tablespoon minced garlic
½ teaspoon dried thyme
1 bay leaf
2 tablespoons olive oil
Salt and black pepper to taste
¼ cup chopped parsley
1 egg
1 cup fresh breadcrumbs
¼ cup plus 2 tablespoons (1½ ounces) finely grated Gruyere or other cheese

Scoop pulp from center of squash halves, reserving shells. Chop pulp (amount should be about ¾ cup) and set aside. Cook shells in boiling water for about 4 minutes and drain. If using sausage, brown slightly, stirring to crumble, and set aside. Sauté onion, garlic, thyme and bay leaf in oil. If using mushrooms, add to onion mixture and cook until softened. Add zucchini pulp, salt and black pepper. Cook for 4 minutes. Discard bay leaf. If using sausage, add to zucchini mixture. Stir in parsley, egg and breadcrumbs. Divide stuffing among shells, place in well-oiled 13x9x2-inch baking dish and sprinkle with cheese. Bake at 425° for 30 minutes.

Note: These take a bit of effort but make an impressive side dish or light summer meal.

Yield: 8 servings

A leftover baked potato can be rebaked if you dip it in water and bake in 350° oven for about 20 minutes.

Zucchini Squash Casserole

- 2 (8 ounce) packages refrigerated crescent roll dough
- ½ cup (2 ounces) grated Parmesan cheese, divided
- 1¼ pounds zucchini, cut in ¼-inch chunks
- 3 cups sliced fresh mushrooms
- 1 large onion, halved and sliced
- 2 cups sour cream
- ¼ cup all-purpose flour
- ¼ teaspoon salt
- ⅛ teaspoon black pepper
- 1 (6 ounce) jar marinated artichoke hearts, drained and chopped
- 1 cup (4 ounces) shredded Monterey Jack cheese

Unroll 1 package dough, place in bottom of lightly-greased 13x9x2-inch baking pan and arrange to form crust, pressing perforations and seams to seal. Sprinkle ¼ cup Parmesan cheese on dough. Bake at 350° for 10 to 15 minutes or until golden. Steam zucchini, mushrooms and onion for 8 to 10 minutes. Combine sour cream, flour, salt and black pepper. Add vegetables, artichoke hearts and cheese to sour cream mixture. Spread over partially baked crust. Top with remaining dough, separated into triangles, and sprinkle with remaining ¼ cup Parmesan cheese. Bake at 350° for 30 to 40 minutes.
Yield: 12 servings

Sweet Potatoes

- 5 to 7 pounds sweet potatoes
- Water
- 2 cups sugar
- ¾ cup water
- ½ cup butter

Cook potatoes in water to cover for 15 to 20 minutes or until tender. Drain and let stand until cool. Peel potatoes and cut in thick slices. Layer slices in 13x9x2-inch baking dish. Spoon sugar over potatoes and sprinkle water on sugar until evenly moistened. Dot with butter. Bake at 350° for 45 minutes, reduce heat to 250° and bake for 2 hours.

Note: A recipe from Alma Hipp of Hickory, N.C., it is the rave of that city.
Yield: 10 to 14 servings

Bourbon Sweet Potatoes

- 8 sweet potatoes or 1 (16 ounce) can sweet potatoes, drained
- Water
- Salt
- ¼ cup condensed milk
- 2 eggs
- 2 tablespoons bourbon
- ½ cup butter
- 1 cup firmly-packed light brown sugar
- 1 (12 ounce) can crushed pineapple, undrained
- 2 cups grapenuts cereal
- ¼ cup butter, melted
- ½ cup chopped pecans or almonds

If using fresh potatoes, cook in salted water until tender. Drain and peel. Combine cooked or canned potatoes, milk, eggs, bourbon, butter, brown sugar and pineapple, whipping until well mixed or use blender. Spread potato mixture in 2-quart casserole. Combine cereal, melted butter and pecans or almonds, mixing to form crumb topping. Sprinkle on potato mixture. Bake at 375° for 15 to 20 minutes.

Note: Dish can be assembled in advance and stored in refrigerator. Add crumb topping just before baking and extend baking time to about 30 minutes.

Yield: 10 servings

Virginia Asher's Sweet Potato Casserole

- 2½ to 3 pounds sweet potatoes
- Water
- 1⅓ cups milk
- 1¾ cups sugar
- 1 cup margarine, melted, divided
- ½ teaspoon nutmeg
- 1 teaspoon cinnamon
- 1 cup chopped pecans, divided
- ½ cup firmly-packed brown sugar
- 2 cups corn flakes, crushed

Cook potatoes in water to cover until tender. Drain, peel and mash potatoes. Add milk, sugar, ½ cup margarine, nutmeg, cinnamon and ½ cup pecans, mixing lightly. Spread mixture in greased 13x9x2-inch baking pan. Bake at 325° for 45 minutes. While potato mixture bakes, prepare topping by combining remaining ½ cup margarine, ½ cup pecans, brown sugar and corn flakes, tossing to mix. Sprinkle on baked potato mixture and bake for additional 15 minutes.

Yield: 12 to 15 servings

Sweet Potato Puffs

- 2 medium-large sweet potatoes
- Water
- 1 egg, lightly beaten
- 1 tablespoon butter
- 1 teaspoon lemon juice
- 1 tablespoon brown sugar
- 1 teaspoon salt
- Dash of black pepper
- 1 cup corn flakes, crushed
- 6 to 8 large marshmallows

Cook potatoes in water to cover until tender. Drain, peel and mash potatoes. Add egg, butter, lemon juice, brown sugar, salt and black pepper, mixing well. Using about ¼ cup potato mixture, shape into ball around 1 marshmallow. Roll each ball in corn flakes and place in buttered 8x8x2-inch baking dish. Bake at 350° for about 20 minutes.

Note: Puffs can be assembled and frozen. Thaw and bake as directed.

Yield: 6 to 8 puffs

Baked Tomatoes

- 2 large ripe tomatoes, cut in halves and stems removed
- Salt and black pepper to taste
- ¼ teaspoon basil
- ¼ teaspoon parsley
- ½ cup chopped pecans
- 1 cup coarsely crushed round buttery crackers
- ¼ cup butter or margarine

Place tomatoes in 1½-quart casserole. Season with salt, black pepper, basil and parsley. Combine pecans and cracker crumbs. Melt butter in small saucepan, add crumb mixture and brown slightly. Spoon crumb mixture on top of tomato halves. Bake at 350° for 20 minutes.

Yield: 4 servings

Refrigeration alters the taste of white and sweet potatoes. Temperatures below 50° cause starch changes, so store potatoes in cool dark place.

Fried Cornmeal-Coated Green Tomatoes

¾ cup yellow cornmeal
¼ cup all-purpose flour
1 teaspoon sugar
1 teaspoon salt
½ teaspoon black pepper
2 teaspoons paprika
1 egg
1 tablespoon milk or water
6 green (unripe) tomatoes, cut in ½-inch slices
3 to 4 tablespoons butter
3 to 4 tablespoons vegetable oil

Combine cornmeal, flour, sugar, salt, black pepper and paprika in shallow dish. Whisk egg and milk or water together. Dip tomato slices in egg liquid, let excess drain and dredge in cornmeal mixture. Melt 1 tablespoon butter and 1 tablespoon oil together in large heavy skillet over moderately high heat. Fry about ⅓ of coated tomato slices at a time, cooking for 3 to 4 minutes on each side or until golden brown, and remove to heated platter. Repeat twice to prepare all tomato slices. Serve as side dish with eggs or meat.
Yield: 6 to 8 servings

Tomato Pie

1 unbaked 9-inch pastry shell
5 firm tomatoes, sliced
Salt and black pepper to taste
½ teaspoon dried oregano
1 cup chopped green onions
2 cups (8 ounces) grated sharp New York State Cheddar cheese
1 cup mayonnaise
½ cup (2 ounces) freshly grated Parmesan cheese

Using fork tines, pierce bottom of pastry shell. Bake at 400° for 10 minutes and surface is dry. Reduce oven temperature to 325°. Place a double layer of tomato slices in partially-baked pastry shell. Sprinkle with salt, black pepper, ¼ teaspoon oregano and ½ cup green onions; repeat layers. Combine Cheddar cheese and mayonnaise. Spread over vegetable layers. Sprinkle with Parmesan cheese. Bake for 45 minutes.
Yield: 6 to 8 servings

Scalloped Tomatoes

- 1 (28 ounce) can tomatoes, crushed, undrained
- ½ cup butter or margarine
- ½ cup firmly-packed brown sugar
- 1 tablespoon cornstarch
- 2 cups white bread cubes

Reserving ¼ cup tomato juice, combine tomatoes, butter or margarine and brown sugar in saucepan. Bring to a boil. Dissolve cornstarch in reserved tomato juice and add to tomatoes. Cook until thickened. Place 1 cup bread cubes in greased 2-quart casserole, pour ½ of tomato mixture over bread cubes and repeat layers. Bake at 350° for 45 minutes to 1 hour or until thickened and firm.

Note: Men especially love this dish.
Yield: 8 servings

Vegetable Casserole Almondine

- 1 cup slivered almonds
- ¼ (16 ounce) package bacon, cut in 1-inch pieces
- 1 pound eggplant or summer squash, sliced
- 1 pound zucchini, sliced
- 1 large onion, cut in wedges
- 1 tablespoon all-purpose flour
- 1 pound tomatoes, peeled and diced
- 1 teaspoon minced garlic
- 1 teaspoon salt
- ½ teaspoon black pepper
- 1 teaspoon basil
- 1 (6 ounce) package sliced Swiss cheese

Sauté almonds and bacon together until bacon is crisp. Remove with slotted spoon and set aside. Combine eggplant or summer squash, zucchini and onions in skillet. Cook, covered, over low heat for 15 minutes. Blend in flour. Add tomatoes, garlic, salt, black pepper and basil. Layer vegetable mixture, almonds and bacon, and cheese in 2-quart casserole, ending with almonds and bacon. Bake, uncovered, at 400° for 15 minutes.

Note: Dish can be assembled in advance and stored in refrigerator. Bake at 400° for 30 minutes.
Yield: 6 to 8 servings

Vegetable Casserole

Vegetables

1 (10 ounce) package frozen small peas
1 (10 ounce) package frozen baby limas
1 (10 ounce) package frozen French style green beans
Salt and black pepper to taste
1 (4 ounce) package slivered almonds
Paprika (optional)

Prepare sauce a day in advance of serving casserole and store in refrigerator until about 2 hours before using. Combine and cook vegetables according to package directions until tender. Season with salt and black pepper. Drain. Add almonds, reserving a small amount for garnish, to vegetables and stir in sauce. Sprinkle with reserved almonds and paprika.
Yield: 12 servings

Sauce

3 tablespoons vegetable oil
1 cup mayonnaise
1 teaspoon spicy brown mustard
1 teaspoon Worcestershire sauce
1 medium-sized onion, chopped
2 hard-cooked eggs, chopped

Combine oil, mayonnaise, mustard, Worcestershire, onion and eggs in tightly-covered jar and shake to blend.
Yield: 2 cups

Garden Vegetable Casserole

2 small yellow squash, sliced
2 medium zucchini, sliced
1 tomato, sliced
1 small onion, sliced
2 tablespoons grated Parmesan cheese
½ teaspoon seasoned salt
½ teaspoon basil
½ teaspoon thyme

Combine squash, zucchini, tomato and onion slices in 2-quart casserole. Mix cheese, seasoned salt, basil and thyme together, add to vegetables and toss lightly to mix. Bake at 350° for 20 to 25 minutes or microwave, covered, at high setting (100%) for 8 to 10 minutes.
Yield: 4 servings

Christmas Vegetable Casserole

- 1 (12 ounce) can shoe peg corn, drained
- 1 (16 ounce) can French-style green beans, drained
- ½ cup chopped red bell pepper
- ½ cup chopped green bell pepper
- ½ cup chopped celery
- ½ cup chopped onion
- ½ cup sour cream
- 1 (10¾ ounce) can cream of mushroom soup, undiluted
- 1 (8 ounce) package Cheddar cheese crackers, crumbled
- ½ cup butter or margarine, melted
- 1 (2 ounce) package slivered almonds (optional)

Combine corn and beans in 2½-quart casserole. Add red and green bell pepper, celery, onion, sour cream and soup, mixing well. Combine ½ of crumbled crackers and melted butter or margarine. Stir into vegetables. Sprinkle remaining cracker crumbs on vegetables. Bake at 350° for 35 minutes.
Yield: 6 to 8 servings

Curried Rice Casserole

- 1 medium-sized onion, chopped
- 1½ cups uncooked regular rice
- ¼ cup margarine
- 1 (10¾ ounce) can beef consommé
- 1 (10¾ ounce) can onion soup, undiluted
- 1 teaspoon curry powder
- 1 (4 ounce) can sliced mushrooms, drained

Sauté onion and rice in margarine, stirring constantly, until golden brown. Add consommé, soup, curry powder and mushrooms. Pour mixture into greased 1½-quart casserole. Let stand at room temperature for several hours. Bake, covered, at 325° for about 1 hour.
Yield: 8 to 10 servings

Rice will be fluffier and whiter if you add one teaspoon of lemon juice to each quart of water. This will also keep the grains separate.

Green Rice

1 cup uncooked regular rice
3½ cups water, divided
1 teaspoon salt
1 (10 ounce) package frozen chopped broccoli
½ cup chopped onions
½ cup chopped celery
2 tablespoons margarine
1 (8 ounce) jar soft cheese spread
1 (10¾ ounce) can cream of celery soup, undiluted

Cook rice in 2½ cups water with salt until tender. Cook broccoli in remaining 1 cup water for 5 minutes; do not drain. Sauté onions and celery in margarine until softened. Combine cooked rice, broccoli, onions and celery, mixing well. Pour into 2-quart casserole. Bake at 325° for 45 minutes or until bubbly.
Yield: 6 to 8 servings

Karen's Mexican Rice

2½ cups cooked rice
1 (4 ounce) can chopped green chilies, drained
3 green onions, chopped
1 cup (4 ounces) grated Monterey Jack cheese
1 cup sour cream
Salt and black pepper to taste

Combine rice, chilies, green onion, cheese and sour cream. Season with salt and black pepper. Spread mixture in 6-cup ring mold prepared with vegetable cooking spray. Bake at 350° for 25 minutes.
Yield: 4 or 5 servings

Saffron Rice

¼ cup chopped onion
⅓ cup butter
5 cups water
1 cup rice
1 teaspoon salt
¼ teaspoon saffron

Sauté onion in butter until golden. Bring water to boil in saucepan. Stir in rice, salt and saffron and cook, uncovered, over medium heat, until water is nearly absorbed and rice is tender. Drain. Add rice to onion mixture in skillet and heat until very hot. Serve with beef curry.
Yield: 4 servings

Wild Rice

- 1 (8 ounce) package thin noodles
- ½ cup margarine
- 1 (10¾ ounce) can onion soup, undiluted
- 1 (10¾ ounce) can chicken broth
- 1 (10¾ ounce) can chicken and rice soup, undiluted
- 1 (8 ounce) can bamboo shoots, drained
- 1 (8 ounce) can water chestnuts, drained
- 1 cup uncooked regular rice
- 1 tablespoon soy sauce

Cook noodles in margarine until browned. Add onion soup, broth, chicken and rice soup, bamboo shoots, water chestnuts, rice and soy sauce, mixing well. Pour mixture into 13x9x2-inch baking dish. Bake, covered, at 350° for 45 minutes to 1 hour.
Yield: 10 to 12 servings

Nassau Grits

- 1 (16 ounce) package bacon, cut in 1-inch pieces
- 1 medium-sized green bell pepper, finely chopped
- 2 small onions, minced
- 4 cloves garlic, chopped
- 1 cup uncooked grits
- 2 (14½ ounce) can tomatoes, juice reserved
- ¼ cup fresh basil leaves, cut in julienne strips
- ½ teaspoon salt
- ½ teaspoon black pepper
- ½ teaspoon oregano
- ½ teaspoon dried thyme
- ½ teaspoon hot pepper sauce

Cook bacon in black cast-iron skillet over medium-high heat until crisp. Remove bacon, drain, cool, crumble and set aside. Sauté bell pepper and onion in bacon drippings until tender, remove with slotted spoon, drain on paper towel and set aside. Discard bacon drippings but do not wipe skillet dry. Sauté garlic in skillet for about 1 minute or just until soft; do not brown. Add bell pepper and onion to garlic. Stir in grits. Strain seeds from tomato liquid (about 1 cup) and add to grit mixture. Chop tomatoes, remove seeds and add tomatoes to grits mixture. Cook for 20 minutes or until grits are done. Stir in basil, salt, black pepper, oregano, thyme, bacon and hot pepper sauce. Simmer for 30 minutes. Serve with fish, pork, chicken or ham.

Note: Dish can be prepared in advance and reheated.
Yield: 8 to 10 servings

Scalloped Apples

- 7 Granny Smith apples, peeled and thinly sliced
- ¼ cup plus 2 tablespoons water
- 1 tablespoon lemon juice
- ½ cup all-purpose flour
- ½ cup sugar
- ¼ teaspoon salt
- ¼ cup margarine, softened
- 1½ cups (6 ounces) grated sharp Cheddar cheese

Toss apple slices, water and lemon juice together and set aside. Combine flour, sugar and salt. Cut margarine into dry ingredients until coarse consistency. Place apples in lightly-greased 13x9x2-inch baking dish and sprinkle with crumb mixture. Bake at 350° for 35 minutes. Sprinkle cheese on apples and bake for additional 5 minutes.
Yield: 8 to 10 servings

Apple Cheese Casserole

- ⅔ cup sugar
- ¼ cup butter, softened
- 1 cup (4 ounces) grated sharp Cheddar cheese
- ½ cup all-purpose flour
- 1 (16 ounce) can sliced unsweetened apples, drained

Cream sugar and butter together until smooth. Add cheese and flour, mixing well. Layer ½ of apples in greased 9x9x2-inch baking pan, add ⅓ of cheese mixture, repeat layers and top with remaining cheese mixture. Bake at 325° for 40 minutes.
Yield: 6 servings

To remove the burned flavor from rice, place a piece of fresh white bread, preferable the heel, on top of the rice and cover the pot. In minutes the bad taste should disappear.

Fruit in Wine Sauce

- **1 (16 ounce) can pears, drained and juice reserved**
- **1 (16 ounce) can pineapple chunks, drained and juice reserved**
- **1 (16 ounce) can sliced peaches, drained and juice reserved**
- **1 (16 ounce) can apricots, drained and juice reserved**
- **1 (14 ounce) jar apple rings, drained and juice reserved**
- **½ cup margarine or butter**
- **2 tablespoons all-purpose flour or cornstarch**
- **½ cup firmly-packed brown sugar**
- **1 cup sherry, white wine or reserved fruit juice**

A day in advance of serving, layer fruit in buttered 13x9x2-inch baking dish, placing apple rings on top. Combine margarine or butter, flour or cornstarch and brown sugar in saucepan. Cook until thickened. Stir in sherry, wine or reserved fruit juice. Bring to a boil, let stand until cool and pour over layered fruit. Chill, covered, overnight. Bake at 350° for 30 minutes or until bubbly.

Note: A festive, colorful dish, the fruit is especially good with ham or turkey during the holiday season or as a brunch dish.

Yield: 8 to 10 servings

Warm Praline Fruit Compote

- 1 (16 ounce) can sliced peaches, drained and juice reserved
- 1 (16 ounce) can sliced pears, drained and juice reserved
- 1 tablespoon cornstarch
- 1 (16 ounce) apricot halves, drained
- ⅓ cup coarsely chopped pecans, toasted
- ¼ cup golden raisins
- ¼ cup orange marmalade
- ¼ cup praline liqueur
- 3 tablespoons butter, softened

Combine peaches, pears, apricots, pecans and raisins in lightly-buttered 2-quart casserole. Blend cornstarch and ¾ cup reserved fruit juice, mixing well, and set aside. Combine marmalade and liqueur and pour over fruit. Pour cornstarch liquid over fruit and stir to blend. Cover and refrigerate. Let stand at room temperature for 30 minutes before baking as directed. Bake at 350° for 30 minutes or until thoroughly heated.

Note: Good with ham or turkey entree, also wonderful brunch dish.

Yield: 6 to 8 servings

Pickled Beets

- 6 cups cooked beets
- Water
- 6 to 12 hard-cooked eggs, peeled (optional)
- 1½ cups white vinegar
- 1½ cups sugar
- 1 stick cinnamon
- 20 whole cloves
- 5 allspice berries

Cook beets in water until tender. Drain, reserving 2 cups cooking liquid. Place beets and eggs in glass container. Combine reserved beet liquid, vinegar, sugar, cinnamon, cloves and allspice in saucepan. Heat until sugar is melted and seasonings blended. Pour over beets and eggs. Chill overnight. Eggs will acquire rubbery texture and can be stored in refrigerator for at least 1 week. Beets, if placed in separate glass container, can be stored longer in refrigerator.

Yield: 8 to 10 cups

Bread and Butter Pickles

- 4 quarts cucumbers (about 6 pounds), cut in ¼-inch slices
- 6 medium-sized onions, thinly sliced
- ⅓ cup salt
- 4½ cups sugar
- 1½ teaspoons turmeric
- 1½ teaspoons celery seed
- 2 tablespoons mustard seed
- 3 cups cider vinegar

In large container, alternately layer cucumber and onion slices, sprinkling each layer with salt. Cover top with crushed ice, mix ice with vegetables and let stand for 3 hours. Drain thoroughly. Combine sugar, turmeric, celery seed, mustard seed and vinegar in enamel pot. Bring to a boil. Add vegetables and bring to a boil. Pack vegetables in hot sterilized standard canning jars, fill with hot syrup to ¼-inch from top, seal and store in cool place.
Yield: 8 pints

Mary's Cucumbers

- 4 cucumbers, unpeeled and very thinly sliced
- 1 tablespoon salt
- Ice water
- 2 cups sugar
- 1 cup white vinegar
- 2 cups water

Cover cucumber slices with salted ice water. Let stand for 2 hours to crisp. Combine sugar, vinegar and water in saucepan. Bring to a boil, remove from heat and cool. Drain cucumbers, rinse lightly and drain. Pour cooled syrup over cucumbers and let stand 24 hours. Serve as salad or side dish.
Yield: 5 to 6 cups

Pickled Figs

- 3 quarts ripe figs
- 2 quarts boiling water
- 1 cup cold water
- 5 cups sugar
- 1 cup cider vinegar
- 1 tablespoon whole cloves
- 1 cinnamon stick

Place figs in large stock pot. Cover with boiling water and let stand for about 5 minutes. Combine cold water, sugar and vinegar in large stock pot. Enclose cloves and cinnamon in cheese cloth bag and add to sugar water. Bring to a boil. Drain figs, add to syrup and boil for 25 minutes. Place figs in hot sterilized standard canning jars, fill with hot syrup to ¼-inch from top, seal and store in cool place.
Yield: 4 to 6 pints

Crystal Pickles

- **2 cups pickling lime**
- **8 quarts water**
- **8 pounds pickling (Kirby) cucumbers, unpeeled, cut in ¼-inch slices**
- **9 cups sugar**
- **2 quarts white vinegar**
- **¼ cup salt**
- **3 tablespoons mixed pickling spices**

Mix lime with water in large enamel pan. Submerge cucumber slices in lime water. Let stand for 24 hours. Drain cucumbers in colander, then rinse several times in large pan or sink of water. Wash enamel pan thoroughly with soap, rinse and fill with cold water. Add cucumbers and let stand for 3 hours. Drain thoroughly. Combine sugar, vinegar and salt in large enamel pot. Enclose pickling spices loosely in cheesecloth bag and add to sugar liquid. Bring just to boiling, add well-drained cucumbers and remove from heat to cool. Let stand for 24 hours, stirring often. On the third day, reheat cucumbers with liquid, bring to a boil, reduce heat and simmer for 10 to 15 minutes or until cucumber is transparent. Place cucumber slices in hot sterilized standard canning jars, fill with boiling syrup to ⅛-inch from top, seal immediately and let cool undisturbed. Store in cool place and let mellow for several weeks before serving. Serve ice cold.

Yield: 9 or 10 pints

Pickled Okra

- **4 teaspoons dill seeds**
- **3 pounds small okra, thoroughly rinsed**
- **4 small hot red peppers**
- **4 small hot green peppers**
- **8 cloves garlic**
- **1 quart white vinegar**
- **1 cup water**
- **¼ cup plus 2 tablespoons salt**

Using four 1-pint sterilized standard canning jars, place ½ teaspoon dill seed in bottom of each. Pack okra in jars; do not bruise. Add ½ teaspoon dill seed, 1 red pepper, 1 green pepper and 2 garlic cloves to each jar. Combine vinegar, water and salt in large saucepan. Bring to a boil. Fill jars with hot liquid to ¼-inch from top, seal and store in cool place for at least 1 month before serving. Serve cold.

Yield: 4 pints

Peach Pickles

- 8 pounds small peaches, peeled
- 2 tablespoons whole cloves
- 4 (2 inch) cinnamon sticks
- 4 cups sugar
- 1 quart vinegar

Cut peaches nearly to pit, twice around and once near center; slits allow syrup to penetrate fruit. Enclose cloves and cinnamon sticks in cheesecloth and secure tightly. Combine sugar, vinegar and spice bag in stock pot and cook for 10 minutes. Add peaches and simmer until tender but not broken. Let stand for 12 hours. Remove spice bag. Drain syrup into saucepan, bring to a boil and cook until thickened. Pack peaches in hot sterilized standard canning jars, fill with hot syrup to ¼-inch from top, seal and process for 10 minutes at 180°.
Yield: 6 to 7 pints

Pickled Peaches

- 3 cups white vinegar
- 4 cups sugar
- 5 cinnamon sticks
- 4 quarts small firm peaches
- Boiling water
- Cloves

Combine vinegar, sugar and cinnamon sticks in large saucepan. Bring to a boil, reduce heat slightly and cook, stirring occasionally, for 20 minutes or until syrup is slightly thickened. While syrup cooks, dip peaches in boiling water and remove peel when withdrawing peaches from water. Stud each peach with 2 cloves. Add peaches, several at a time, to hot syrup. Increase heat slightly and cook for 5 to 10 minutes or until tender but not overcooked. Pack peaches in hot sterilized standard canning jars, fill with hot syrup to within ¼-inch of top, seal and store in cool place for at least 2 months before serving.
Yield: 5 pints

Squash Pickles

10 cups very thinly sliced small squash
6 or 7 medium-sized white onions, very thinly sliced
2 medium-sized green bell peppers, very thinly sliced
2 medium-sized red bell peppers, very thinly sliced
Water
⅓ cup salt
2 cups white vinegar
3 cups sugar
1 tablespoon mustard seed
1 tablespoon celery seed

Combine squash, onions, green and red bell peppers in stock pot. Cover with water mixed with salt. Let stand for 1½ hours. Drain well. Combine vinegar, sugar, mustard seed and celery seed in stock pot. Bring to a boil, add drained vegetables, bring to a boil and cook for 4 to 5 minutes. Pack vegetables and liquid in hot sterilized standard canning jars, seal and store in cool place.
Yield: 8 to 10 pints

Watermelon Rind Pickles

6 pounds watermelon rind
1 cup pickling lime
Water
1 tablespoon alum
½ pound ginger root
12 cups sugar
6 cups white vinegar
1 tablespoon whole allspice
1 tablespoon whole cloves
2 (3 inch) cinnamon sticks

Remove all dark green rind and pink flesh from watermelon rind and cut into 2-inch fingers. Place in large enamel or glass container. Dissolve lime in 4 quarts water, pour over melon, cover with plastic wrap and let stand overnight. Combine alum with 4 quarts cold water in large container. Transfer melon to alum liquid, soak for 5 minutes and drain. In large enamel pot, combine ginger root, 4 quarts water and melon. Bring to a boil, reduce heat and simmer for 30 minutes. Drain water and remove ginger root. Rinse melon under cold running water for 5 minutes or longer. Rinse pot. Combine sugar, vinegar, 3 cups water, allspice, cloves and cinnamon in pot. Bring to a boil, add melon, bring to a boil, reduce heat and simmer for 3 hours. Pack melon in hot sterilized standard canning jars, fill with hot syrup to ¼-inch of top, seal and store in cool place for at least 2 months before serving. Serve cold.
Yield: 7 pints

Icy Sweet Green Tomato Pickles

7 to 8 pounds green tomatoes, sliced
3 cups slack lime
8 quarts water
10 cups sugar
6 cups vinegar
1 teaspoon allspice
1 teaspoon cinnamon
1 teaspoon cloves
1 teaspoon ginger
1 teaspoon mace

Soak tomato slices in lime mixed with water overnight. Drain, rinse tomatoes in clear water, 4 hours, changing water every hour. Combine sugar, vinegar, allspice, cinnamon, cloves, ginger and mace to form syrup. Drain tomatoes, pour syrup over tomatoes and let stand overnight or at least several hours. Cook tomatoes in syrup for 1 hour. Pack tomatoes in hot sterilized standard canning jars, fill jars with hot syrup to ¼-inch of top, seal and store in cool place.

Note: Cucumbers can be preserved using this method.
Yield: 12 pints

Red Flowering Crab Jelly

Crab apples
Water
Sugar

Wash apples well, leaving peel and stems intact. Place in large pot, add water to cover and cook until peel begins to break. Turn heat off, cover and let stand for several hours or overnight. Strain juice through colander. Measure and bring to a boil. For 1 cup juice, add ¾ cup plus 2 tablespoons sugar. Cook for 30 to 45 minutes or until jelly consistency. Pour into jelly jars and seal with paraffin.

Cranberry Relish

1 orange
1 pound fresh cranberries
1 (15 ounce) package golden raisins
3 cups sugar
½ cup vinegar
½ teaspoon cinnamon
½ teaspoon ground cloves
½ teaspoon ginger

Remove seeds from unpeeled orange, place orange in blender and chop. Combine orange, cranberries, raisins, sugar, vinegar, cinnamon, cloves and ginger in saucepan. Simmer, covered, until cranberries pop. Chill before serving. Store in refrigerator.
Yield: 6 to 8 cups

Blueberry Preserves

6 cups blueberries, washed, drained and dried
White wine (optional)
3 tablespoons lemon juice
7 cups sugar
2 pouches fruit pectin

Crush berries in food processor. Measure, adding white wine if necessary to obtain 4½ cups. Add lemon juice to berries. Blend berry mixture with sugar in large saucepan. Bring to a full boil (too rapid to stir down) and cook for 1 minute. Remove from heat and immediately add pectin. Skim any foam from top. Pour into sterile jelly jars, seal and process in hot water bath for 5 minutes or seal with paraffin.
Yield: 7 to 8 cups

Pepper Jelly

½ cup chopped hot green pepper, seeded and stemmed
1½ cups chopped green bell pepper, seeded and stemmed
1½ cups cider vinegar, divided
6½ cups sugar
1 (6 ounce) container pectin
Red or green food coloring

Combine hot and bell peppers with ½ cup vinegar in blender container. Blend until liquefied. Pour pepper mixture into large pot. This mixture can boil over quickly, so make sure pot is large enough to handle expansion during cooking. Add sugar and remaining 1 cup vinegar. Bring to a rolling boil and cook for 1 to 6 minutes. Remove from heat and skim foam. Stir in pectin and food coloring. Pour into hot sterilized jelly jars, filling to ½-inch of top. Seal according to jar manufacturer's directions or with paraffin. Serve as appetizer with cream cheese and crackers.

Note: Wear gloves when removing stems and seeds from hot green peppers to avoid burning hands and eyes. For firm jelly, cook for 6 minutes.
Yield: 7 (½ pint) jars

Wine Jelly

2 packets unflavored gelatin
1 cup cold water
1½ cups boiling water
⅔ cup sugar
½ cup lemon juice
¼ teaspoon salt
½ to 1 cup sherry

Soften gelatin in cold water. Add boiling water, sugar, lemon juice, salt and sherry. Store in refrigerator until firm.
Yield: 3 cups

Cranberry Chutney

- 1 (12 ounce) package fresh cranberries
- 1½ cups sugar
- ¾ cup water
- ¾ cup orange juice
- ¾ cup raisins
- ¾ cup chopped English walnuts
- ¾ cup chopped celery
- 1 medium apple, chopped
- 1 tablespoon grated orange peel
- 1 teaspoon ground ginger

Combine cranberries, sugar and water in large saucepan. Bring to a boil, reduce heat and simmer for 15 minutes. Remove from heat. Stir in orange juice, raisins, walnuts, celery, apple, orange peel and ginger. Store, covered, in refrigerator. Serve with ham or poultry.
Yield: 8 cups

Sweet Pepper Relish

- 6 green bell peppers, chopped
- 6 red bell peppers, chopped
- 6 medium-sized onions, chopped
- Boiling water
- 1 cup vinegar
- 1 cup sugar
- 1½ tablespoons salt

Combine green and red bell peppers and onion in stock pot. Add boiling water to cover and let stand for 5 minutes. Drain. Stir in vinegar, sugar and salt. Bring to a boil and cook for 5 minutes. Pack vegetables in hot sterilized standard canning jars, fill with syrup to ¼-inch of top and seal.
Yield: 6 pints

Squash Relish

- 6 large yellow squash, cut in chunks
- 4 medium-sized onions
- 1 green bell pepper
- 1 red bell pepper
- ¼ cup salt
- Water
- 3 cups sugar
- 2 cups vinegar
- 2 teaspoons celery seed
- 2 teaspoons turmeric

Using food grinder with coarse blade or food processor, chop squash, onion, green and red bell pepper; do not overprocess. Place vegetables in large mixing bowl, add salt, cover with water and let stand for 1 hour. Rinse vegetables in colander under cold running water and drain well. Combine sugar, vinegar, celery seed and turmeric in large saucepan, bring to a boil and cook for 3 minutes. Stir in drained vegetables, bring to a boil, reduce heat and simmer for 3 to 5 minutes. Pour mixture in hot sterilized standard canning jars, filling to ¼-inch of top, seal and store in cool place.
Yield: 6 pints

Seafood

We Carolinians have a love affair with seafood. Though we may have grown up in the mountains, foothills or the Piedmont, we were taught how to gig for flounder, to shrimp and to crab during summer visits to the beach. We have favorite seafood restaurants from the Outer Banks of North Carolina to Savannah, Georgia. We often do not agree on who makes the best hush puppy, a small oblong fried cornmeal and flour bread. We just know that they must accompany a seafood dinner. Often restaurants will bring a steaming basket immediately to your table once you have ordered. Munching on hush puppies while you are impatiently waiting for your meal can make the wait more than bearable. More than one adult has consumed too many and completely ruined their appetite for their order of a large platter of shrimp or flounder and crab cakes. Yelping, sunkissed children are quietened just as easily as yelping dogs were once quietened around a Civil War campsite, when morsels of fried cornmeal were tossed at them with the command to "Hush puppies."

Seafood

Thanks to rapid transportation and improved preservation methods, a large variety of fish and shellfish are now available. A reliable fish market will receive daily deliveries and be willing to order any fish. It should prepare fish (cleaning and beheading) to the customer's specifications.

Fish Varieties

Fish can be classified as oily or lean, according to fat content.

Oily
Amberjack
Bonito Blue
Butterfish
Carp
Freshwater Catfish
Herring
King Mackerel
Lake Trout
Mullet (Red or Gray)
Rainbow Trout
Sablefish
Salmon
Sardines
Shad
Spanish Mackerel
Swordfish
Tuna
Whitefish

Lean
Black Seabass
Gill
Cod
Crappie
Croaker
Dolphin
Flounder
Grouper
Haddock
Halibut
Ocean Catfish
Ocean Perch
Pike
Pollack
Pompano
Red Snapper
Rock Fish
Scrod
Shark
Sheepshead
Sole
Speckled Sea Trout
Triggerfish
Turbot
Walleye
Whiting

Saltwater (Alternate names)
Bluefish (Tailor, Skipjack)
Butterfish (Harvest Fish)
Croaker (Hardhead, Tom Cod)
Black Drum (Oyster Cracker, Oyster and Sea Drum)
Red Drum (Channel Bass, Redfish and Sea Drum)
Grouper (Sea Bass)
Red Hake (Mud Hake)
White Hake (Common Hake)
King Mackerel (Cero, Kingfish)

Fresh fish does not smell "fishy". It should be firm, plump and elastic and should not leave an impression when pressed with fingertips. The eyes should be clear, not sunken or foggy.

Frozen fish may be a better choice because many fishermen have facilities to freeze fish immediately. Frozen fish should be stored quickly after purchase and not allowed to thawed. When thawed, it must be cooked on the same day. Thaw frozen seafood in the refrigerator.

Thawed or fresh fish and all seafood should not be kept more than 1 day in the refrigerator. Most of it is best when prepared as soon as possible after purchasing. Recipes containing seafood should be stored in the refrigerator and eaten within 3 days of preparation.

Shellfish

Shellfish includes clams, cockles, crabs, crayfish or crawfish, lobsters, mussels, octopus, oysters, scallops, shrimp, squid and whelks.

Clams—Clams can be purchased in the shell or shucked. Clam shells should be tightly closed; the shell will not close if the clam is dead. After cooking, discard any clams that have not opened. Allow 6 clams per serving.

Crab—Two types of crab are usually available: hard shell and soft shell. Most whole crabs on the market today are already cooked. The shells are usually tinged with red. When purchasing live crab, look for movement in legs and keep alive until ready to cook. After cooking, crabs should be red and have no unpleasant odor. Four pounds of crab in the shell yields about 1 pound crab meat. Whether fresh or thawed, crab should be used within a day after purchasing.

Lobster—Live lobster is available at many seafood markets. When purchasing live lobsters, look for leg movement. When picked up, the lobster tail should curve under the body. Lobster can be refrigerated briefly but should be cooked soon after buying. Many seafood markets will steam lobster while the customer waits. The shell should be bright red and there should be no unpleasant odor. One live 1¼-pound lobster yields ¼ to ½ pound of meat.

Oysters—When purchasing live oysters, shells should be tightly closed or spring closed when tapped. If shell doesn't close, oyster is dead and should be discarded. The shell opens when the oyster is cooked. Oysters can be kept alive for several days in refrigerator. When buying shucked (shelled) oysters, look for plump, cream colored ones. The liquor surrounding the oysters should be clear, not milky. Do not rinse the oysters as the liquor enhances the flavor. Oysters are graded by size with weight indicated on the package. Allow 6 to 12 oysters per person or about 4 ounces per person if served as an entree, less if an appetizer.

Scallops—Scallops are available fresh or frozen. The large common variety of sea scallop ranges in color from white to orange to pink. The small, delicately flavored bay scallops are creamy white, pink or light tan. They may be used interchangeably. Fresh scallops can be stored in the refrigerator for several days. If frozen, they should be thawed in the refrigerator. One pound scallops serves 3 to 4 persons.

Shrimp—Fresh shrimp are available raw or cooked (in the shell or peeled). Fresh shrimp should be firm and have no unpleasant odor. Frozen shrimp should be ivory colored. A white tinge indicates freezer burn. Store any shrimp, fresh, frozen or thawed, in the refrigerator and use within one day after purchase. Shrimp are sold by size, range from very small to jumbo and are graded on number per pound. Allow 10 small, 7 medium or 6 large shrimp per serving.

Shrimp per pound	Heads on count	Tails on count
Small	31 to 33	51 to 60
Medium	26 to 30	41 to 50
Large	19 to 21	31 to 35
Jumbo	13 to 15	21 to 25

Cooking Shellfish

Bring a stock pot of water to a boil. Add ½ cup vinegar (tarragon or wine) to the pot for each 6 crabs to eliminate odor and retard frothing. Use a boil seasoning for flavor. Plunge crab or shrimp into boiling water, return water to a boil and cook quickly just until done.

To eliminate the odor of boiling shrimp, add a few fresh celery leaves to the pot. Place shells, heads and tails in an airtight freezer bag and store in freezer until garbage collection day.

Basic Crab and Shrimp Boil

½ cup salt
3 tablespoons cayenne pepper
¼ cup celery salt
¼ cup dry mustard
¼ cup ground cloves
2 tablespoons mace
2 tablespoons ground ginger

Combine salt, cayenne pepper, celery salt, mustard, cloves, mace and ginger. Store in airtight container. Use ½ cup seasoning for each 6 to 8 crabs or 12 shrimp.

Beer Boil

2 quarts water
5 (12 ounce) cans beer
¼ cup plus 1 tablespoon salt
2 tablespoons black pepper
2 tablespoons dry mustard
2 tablespoons celery seed
2 cups tarragon vinegar
5 pounds unpeeled shrimp

Combine water, beer, salt, black pepper, mustard, celery seed and vinegar in stock pot. Bring to a boil. Add shrimp and cook for 8 to 10 minutes or just until shrimp turn pink. Drain shrimp. Leave in shells for 30 minutes before peeling.

Baked Fish

- 4 to 6 fish fillets
- 1 cup chopped onion
- 1 tablespoon chopped parsley or parsley flakes
- Salt and black pepper to taste
- 2 cups dry white wine
- 1 cup whipping cream
- 1 tablespoon lemon juice
- 2 egg yolks, beaten

Place fish in buttered baking dish. Sprinkle onion and parsley on fillets and season with salt and black pepper. Pour wine over fish. Bake at 350° until wine begins to boil, cover and bake for 15 minutes. Drain cooking liquid into saucepan. Blend in cream, lemon juice and egg yolks, stirring until thickened. Pour sauce over fish and serve.
Yield: 4 to 6 servings

Quick Mediterranean Fish

- 1 medium-sized onion, sliced
- 1 clove garlic, crushed
- 2 tablespoons olive oil
- 1 (14½ ounce) can Italian style stewed tomatoes
- 3 to 4 tablespoons medium-flavor green chili pepper salsa
- ¼ teaspoon cinnamon
- 1½ pounds halibut, red snapper, sea bass or cod
- 12 pimento-stuffed green olives, cut crosswise in halves

Combine onion, garlic and oil in microwave-safe 1½-quart casserole. Microwave, covered, at high (100%) setting for 3 minutes. Drain liquid. Add tomatoes, salsa and cinnamon to vegetables. Arrange fish and olives on tomato mixture. Microwave, covered, at high setting for 3 to 4 minutes or until fish flakes with fork tines.
Yield: 4 to 6 servings

Flounder Florentine

- 3 (12 ounce) packages frozen spinach soufflé, thawed
- 2½ pounds flounder fillets
- ½ cup mayonnaise
- ½ cup sour cream
- ¼ cup (1 ounce) grated Parmesan cheese

Spread soufflé in lightly-greased 13x9x2-inch baking dish. Arrange fish on spinach. Blend mayonnaise and sour cream together and spread on fish. Sprinkle with Parmesan cheese. Bake at 350° for 35 to 45 minutes.
Yield: 4 servings

Fish Fillets with Mushroom Stuffing

- 1 tablespoon butter
- 1 (4 ounce) can broiled mushrooms with liquid, chopped
- 1 teaspoon onion flakes
- ⅛ teaspoon marjoram
- 1½ cups soft white bread cubes
- Salt and black pepper to taste
- 4 flounder fillets (1½ pounds)
- 2 tablespoons butter, softened
- 1 teaspoon gravy flavoring
- ½ teaspoon salt
- 1 teaspoon lemon juice

Combine butter, mushrooms and liquid, onion and marjoram in small saucepan and bring to a boil. Pour hot mixture over bread cubes and mix lightly with fork until bread is slightly shredded. Season with salt and black pepper. Place 2 fillets in greased 8x8x2-inch baking dish. Spread stuffing evenly on fillets and top with remaining fillets. Blend softened butter, gravy flavoring, ½ teaspoon salt and lemon juice until smooth. Spread glaze on fillets. Bake at 375° for about 30 minutes or until fish flakes easily with fork tines. Cut stuffed fillets in halves before serving and serve immediately,

Yield: 4 servings

Sole with Lobster Sauce

- 12 sole fillets
- Salt and black pepper to taste
- 3 cups milk
- 2 tablespoons onion, minced
- ¼ cup plus 2 tablespoons butter
- 1½ teaspoons dry mustard
- 2 teaspoons salt
- ¼ cup plus 1 tablespoon all-purpose flour
- 1 tablespoon lemon juice
- 1½ tablespoons sherry
- 2 (6 ounce) packages frozen lobster, thawed

Season sole with salt and black pepper. Roll up each fillet and secure with wooden pick and place in large skillet. Add milk and cook, covered, over medium heat for 5 minutes. Using slotted spoon, remove fillets from milk and place in single layer in 13x9x2-inch baking dish. Pour milk into bowl and set aside. Using same skillet, sauté onion in butter until tender. Blend in mustard, 2 teaspoons salt and flour. Add reserved milk and cook until thickened. Stir in lemon juice, sherry and lobster. Pour sauce over fillets. Let stand until cool, cover with aluminum foil and store in freezer. Thaw in refrigerator for 3 to 4 hours. Bake at 350° for 30 to 40 minutes, then broil until lightly browned.

Yield: 12 servings

Tuna Cakes with Dill Tartar Sauce

¾ cup finely chopped celery
¾ cup minced white onion or green onion
2 tablespoons low-fat cream cheese, softened
2 teaspoons lemon juice
⅛ teaspoon white pepper
Dash of ground red pepper
⅓ cup fine dry bread crumbs
1 teaspoon dried dill weed
1 (9¼ ounce) can tuna
1 egg white

In large non-stick skillet prepared with vegetable cooking spray, sauté celery and onion over medium heat until tender. Remove vegetables and place in mixing bowl. Add cream cheese, lemon juice, white pepper and red pepper, mixing well. Stir in breadcrumbs, dill, tuna and egg white, blending thoroughly. Divide mixture into 8 portions and shape each into 2½-inch cake. In skillet prepared with cooking spray, cook over medium-high heat for 2 minutes on each side or until browned. Serve with dill sauce or prepared tartar sauce.

Note: Vegetables can be sautéed in small amount of olive oil.
Yield: 4 servings

Dill Tartar Sauce
2 tablespoons low-calorie mayonnaise
1 tablespoon plain fat-free yogurt
1 tablespoon minced onion
1 tablespoon finely chopped peeled cucumber
1 teaspoon dried dill weed
1 teaspoon lemon juice

Combine mayonnaise, yogurt, onion, cucumber, dill and lemon juice, blending well. Serve with tuna cakes.
Yield: ⅓ cup

Orange Sauce for Fish

½ teaspoon grated orange peel
Juice of 2 oranges
1 tablespoon butter
Dash of nutmeg
1 tablespoon minced fresh dill
4 fish fillets

Combine orange peel, juice, butter, nutmeg and dill in small saucepan. Cook over medium heat until simmering, stirring occasionally, for about 5 minutes. Bake, broil or poach fillets. Spoon sauce over cooked fillets.

Note: Sauce is suitable for any fillets but is especially good with salmon steaks.
Yield: 4 servings

Salmon-Noodle Casserole

- **1 (8 ounce) package egg noodles**
- **1 cup sour cream**
- **1 teaspoon ranch salad dressing mix**
- **1 (7½ ounce) can salmon, drained and flaked**
- **1 (4 ounce) can sliced mushrooms, drained**
- **3 tablespoons chopped green onion with tops**
- **¼ teaspoon dried dill weed, crushed**

Prepare noodles according to package directions and drain well. Combine sour cream, dressing mix, salmon, mushrooms, onion and dill. Add mixture to noodles. Spread in buttered 2-quart casserole. Bake at 325° for 10 to 12 minutes or microwave at medium-high (70%) setting for 5 minutes until hot and bubbly. Stir before serving.
Yield: 4 servings

Crabmeat Casserole

- **1 pound crabmeat**
- **4 hard-cooked eggs, chopped**
- **2 cups mayonnaise**
- **2 cups half and half**
- **2 cups herb seasoned stuffing mix, divided**
- **1 to 2 tablespoons minced onion**
- **Salt and black pepper to taste**
- **½ cup (2 ounces) grated sharp Cheddar cheese (optional)**
- **Grated Parmesan cheese (optional)**
- **3 tablespoons margarine, melted**

Combine crabmeat, eggs, mayonnaise, half and half, 1½ cups stuffing mix, onion, salt, black pepper and Cheddar cheese. Pour mixture into 1½-quart casserole. Combine remaining ½ cup stuffing mix, Parmesan cheese and margarine. Sprinkle over crab mixture. Bake at 350° for 45 to 60 minutes.

Note: Casserole is a great dish for a luncheon or brunch.
Yield: 8 servings

Seabrook Crab Supreme

- **8 slices bread, diced**
- **1 pound crabmeat, cleaned**
- **½ cup diced onion**
- **½ cup chopped green bell pepper**
- **1 cup chopped celery**
- **½ cup mayonnaise**
- **4 eggs, beaten**
- **3 cups milk**
- **1 (10¾ ounce) can cream of mushroom soup, undiluted**
- **Grated Cheddar cheese**
- **Paprika**

Place half of bread in 2-quart casserole. Combine crab, onion, bell pepper, celery and mayonnaise. Spread mixture on bread and top with remaining bread cubes. Combine eggs and milk. Pour over layered ingredients. Bake at 325° for 15 minutes, remove from oven. spoon soup on mixture, sprinkle with cheese and paprika, and bake for additional 1 hour.

Note: The recipe is from Laura Seabrook MacKay, who was from John's Island, South Carolina.

Yield: 4 servings

Crab in the Back

- **2 cups crabmeat**
- **¼ teaspoon nutmeg**
- **2 whole cloves**
- **¼ teaspoon mustard**
- **¼ teaspoon mace**
- **1 tablespoon butter, melted**
- **1 egg, separated**
- **½ cup cooking wine or sherry flavoring**
- **Salt and black pepper to taste**
- **Cracker crumbs**

Combine crabmeat, nutmeg, cloves, mustard and mace. Stir in butter and beaten egg yolk. Add wine or sherry flavoring and season with salt and black pepper. Beat egg white until stiff and fold into crab mixture. Spoon mixture into crab backs or into buttered 8x8x2-inch baking dish. Sprinkle with cracker crumbs. Bake at 350° for 30 minutes.

Note: The recipe was given by May Rose Laurens, a caterer in Charleston, South Carolina, to Alice Lucas for her recipe collection when she married Archibald Rutledge in 1936.

Yield: 4 servings

Diddy's Deviled Crab

- 1 pound crabmeat, cleaned
- 2 cups soft bread crumbs
- 3 stalks celery, finely chopped
- 1 medium-sized onion, minced
- 2 eggs, beaten
- 1 tablespoon lemon juice
- ½ cup Miracle Whip salad dressing
- 2 tablespoons prepared mustard
- Salt and black pepper to taste
- Dash of Worcestershire sauce
- Paprika (optional)

Combine crab, bread crumbs, celery, onion, eggs, lemon juice, salad dressing, mustard, salt, black pepper and Worcestershire sauce. If mixture is too dry, add small amount of milk. Spread mixture in 12x8x2-inch baking dish prepared with vegetable cooking spray. Sprinkle with paprika. Bake at 350° for 30 minutes.

Note: When crabbing at the beach, save the backs of crabs for stuffing. Wash thoroughly in soapy water. Let stand overnight in water to which baking soda has been added. Rinse shells well, spray with vegetable cooking spray and stuff with crab mixture. Stuffed shells can be frozen, thawed and baked. Large cockle shells can also be used.

Yield: 8 servings

Annette Widmer's Crab Cakes

- 1 pound crabmeat
- 2 slices bread, crusts trimmed
- 1 egg, beaten
- 2 tablespoons chopped onion
- 1 teaspoon dry mustard
- 2 tablespoons mayonnaise
- ½ teaspoon Worcestershire sauce
- 1 tablespoon horseradish
- 1 tablespoon parsley flakes
- Crushed corn flakes
- 3 tablespoons vegetable oil

Combine crabmeat, bread, egg, onion, mustard, mayonnaise, Worcestershire sauce, horseradish and parsley flakes, mixing well. Shape into cakes. Coat with crushed corn flakes, place on plate or baking sheet and chill for 1 hour. Fry in hot oil until golden brown on both sides.

Yield: 4 servings

New Orleans Style Crab Cakes

- 3 stalks celery, finely chopped
- 1 green bell pepper, finely chopped
- 1 red bell pepper, finely chopped
- 8 scallions or green onions, minced, divided
- 3 cups butter, divided
- ½ teaspoon salt
- 1 teaspoon dried thyme
- 1 teaspoon curry powder
- ½ teaspoon cayenne pepper
- ¼ cup white wine
- ¼ cup lemon juice
- ¼ cup chopped fresh chives
- ¼ cup chopped fresh parsley
- 2 pounds fresh backfin lump crabmeat
- 4 cups milk, warm
- 1¾ cups all-purpose flour, divided
- 4 cups fresh bread crumbs, divided
- ¾ cup (3 ounces) grated Parmesan cheese
- 4 eggs, lightly beaten
- Vegetable oil for frying

Sauté celery, green and red bell pepper and ½ of scallions or green onions in 1 cup butter in large saucepan until tender. Stir in salt, thyme, curry powder, cayenne pepper, white wine and lemon juice. Remove pan from heat and stir in chives, parsley and crabmeat. Pour into bowl and set aside. Prepare sauce by cooking remaining scallions or onions in 2 cups butter until tender. Stir in 1 cup flour and cook until thickened. Add milk and mix until smooth and thickened. Add cream sauce to crabmeat mixture, mixing well. Add 1 cup bread crumbs and cheese. Shape crab cakes to preferred shape and thickness. Freeze for 3 hours. Coat cakes in remaining ¾ cup flour, eggs and remaining 3 cups bread crumbs. Fry in hot oil until golden brown on both sides, place on baking sheet and bake at 350° for approximately 20 minutes or until done. Serve hot with tartar sauce and fresh lemon.

Yield: 8 to 10 servings

Contributor: Chef Stephen Daniello
Columbine Restaurant
Valle Crucis, North Carolina.

Crawfish Etouffee

- 1/4 cup butter
- 3 tablespoons all-purpose flour
- 1/2 cup chopped green onion
- 1 1/2 cups minced onion
- 1/2 cup chopped celery
- 2 cloves garlic, minced
- 1 teaspoon tomato paste
- 2 cups fish stock
- 1 cup tomatoes
- 2 cups crawfish meat
- 1/4 cup chopped fresh parsley
- 2 teaspoons salt
- 1/2 teaspoon black pepper
- 1/2 teaspoon cayenne pepper

Melt butter in large saucepan. Remove from heat, stir in flour and blend until smooth. Return to heat and cook, stirring constantly, until roux is dark brown. Stir in onions, celery and garlic. Cook for about 10 minutes. Blend tomato paste with fish stock and add mixture to roux. Stir in tomatoes, crawfish, parsley, salt, black pepper and cayenne pepper. Simmer, covered, for 20 minutes. Serve over rice.

Note: Shrimp can be substituted for crawfish.

Yield: 4 servings

Contributor: Hotel Charlotte
Charlotte, North Carolina

Quick Lobster Newberg

- 2 (10 3/4 ounce) cans cream of mushroom soup, undiluted
- 1/2 cup sherry
- 1 teaspoon paprika
- 2 (6 1/2 ounce) cans lobster chunks

Blend soup and sherry in top of double boiler, adding additional sherry if necessary for sauce consistency. Stir in paprika and place over hot water. Heat, stirring occasionally. Add lobster and heat thoroughly. Serve over rice, rusks, toast or in patty shells.

Note: Shrimp can be substituted for lobster.

Yield: 4 servings

Scalloped Oysters

- **1½ cups crushed saltine crackers**
- **1 pint oysters, shucked, undrained**
- **½ cup butter, melted**
- **¾ cup milk**
- **Salt and black pepper to taste**

Layer cracker crumbs and oysters in 3-quart casserole. Combine butter and milk. Pour over oysters and crackers. Season with salt and black pepper. Bake at 350° for 40 minutes. Serve immediately.

Note: This is a favorite side dish at Thanksgiving and Christmas.
Yield: 6 servings

Oysters à la Paulette

Oysters

- **¼ cup butter**
- **2 teaspoons Worcestershire sauce**
- **Salt and black pepper to taste**
- **1 pint oysters**
- **½ cup cream sauce (recipe follows)**
- **½ cup sherry**
- **½ teaspoon chopped fresh parsley**
- **Paprika to taste**
- **4 to 6 pastry shells**

Prepare sauce and set aside while preparing oysters. Melt butter in chafing dish or skillet. Add Worcestershire sauce, salt and black pepper. When hot, add oysters and cook until edges curl. Add ½ cup cream sauce, sherry and parsley. Stir in enough paprika for pink color. Serve in pastry shells.
Yield: 4 to 6 servings

Cream Sauce

- **2 tablespoons butter**
- **2 tablespoons all-purpose flour**
- **1½ cups half and half**
- **Salt and black pepper to taste**
- **1 (4 ounce) can sliced mushrooms, drained**
- **1 (8 ounce) can small English peas, drained**

Melt butter in top of double boiler. Blend in flour. Gradually add half and half. Season with salt and black pepper. Cook over hot water until smooth and thickened. Add mushrooms and peas and heat thoroughly.

Baked Scallops for Two

- ¾ pound scallops
- Salt and black pepper to taste
- 2 tablespoons sherry
- ½ cup margarine, melted
- 1 cup fresh bread crumbs

Cut scallops crosswise in halves and place in buttered 1½ quart casserole. Season with salt and black pepper. Pour sherry, then ¼ cup margarine over scallops. Cover with breadcrumbs and drizzle with remaining ¼ cup margarine. Bake at 375° for 15 minutes.

Note: Crabmeat or cooked lobster can be substituted for scallops.

Yield: 2 servings

Seafood Medley

- 2 tablespoons cornstarch
- 2 cups milk, divided
- 2 cups half and half
- 2 egg yolks, lightly beaten
- ½ cup butter or margarine
- 2 teaspoons salt
- 1 teaspoon black pepper
- Dash of red pepper
- Dash of onion salt
- 3 tablespoons white wine
- 1 pound crabmeat
- 1 pound shrimp, cooked and cleaned
- 2 cups diced cooked chicken
- ¾ pound bay scallops
- 1 (8 ounce) can mushrooms, undrained
- 1 (8 ounce) jar pimento, chopped
- 1 tablespoon chopped parsley
- 6 to 8 cups cooked rice or 10 to 12 puff pastry shells

Blend cornstarch with ½ cup milk, mixing until smooth. In top of double boiler, combine cornstarch, remaining 1½ cups milk, half and half, egg yolks, butter or margarine, salt, black pepper, red pepper and wine. Cook over hot water until thickened. Stir in crabmeat, shrimp, chicken, scallops, mushrooms, pimento and parsley. Cook just until scallops are done. Serve over rice or in puff pastry shells.

Yield: 10 to 12 servings

Thaw fish in milk. The milk draws out the frozen taste and provides a fresh caught flavor.

Baked Seafood Casserole

- 1 pound superior frozen crabmeat, thawed
- 1 pound frozen cooked shrimp, thawed under cold water
- 1 pound lobster meat (optional)
- ½ medium-sized green bell pepper, chopped
- 1 medium-sized onion, chopped
- 1 cup chopped celery
- 2 tablespoons butter
- ½ teaspoon salt
- Dash of black pepper
- 1 teaspoon Worcestershire sauce
- 1 cup mayonnaise
- 1 cup buttered breadcrumbs

Drain thawed seafood well. Sauté bell pepper, onion and celery in butter until translucent. Combine crabmeat, shrimp, lobster, vegetables, salt, black pepper, Worcestershire sauce and mayonnaise. Spread mixture in buttered 2-quart casserole and sprinkle with breadcrumbs. Bake at 350° for 30 minutes. Serve with rice.
Yield: 4 to 6 servings

Royal Seafood Casserole

- ⅔ cup regular rice, uncooked
- 1½ pounds fresh green shrimp
- 1 (10¾ ounce) can shrimp soup, undiluted
- ¼ cup mayonnaise
- ½ small onion, minced
- ¾ cup milk, divided
- Black pepper to taste
- 1 (6½ ounce) can crabmeat, drained and cleaned
- 1 (8 ounce) can sliced water chestnuts, drained
- ¾ cup diced celery
- Paprika for garnish
- Slivered almonds

Prepare rice according to package directions. While rice cooks, cook, clean and peel shrimp. Blend soup with mayonnaise until smooth. Add onion, ½ cup milk, black pepper, shrimp, crabmeat, water chestnuts, celery and cooked rice. Add remaining ¼ cup milk if necessary to form moist mixture. Spoon into 13x9x2-inch buttered casserole. Sprinkle with paprika and almonds. Bake at 350° for 30 minutes or until hot and bubbly.

Note: Baked casserole freezes well.
Yield: 6 to 8 servings

Shrimp Thermidor

- ¼ cup chopped onion
- 2 tablespoons butter
- 1 (10¾ ounce) can frozen potato soup, thawed
- ¾ cup half and half
- ½ cup (2 ounces) shredded sharp American cheese
- 2 teaspoons lemon juice
- 1½ cups cooked shrimp, split lengthwise
- 1 to 2 teaspoons sherry
- 4 to 6 pastry shells

Sauté onion in butter until softened. Add soup and half and half. Heat slowly. Bring just to a boil and add cheese, lemon juice and shrimp. Stir in sherry. Serve in pastry shells.
Yield: 4 to 6 servings

Adlai Stevenson's Artichoke and Shrimp Casserole

- 1 (13¾ ounce) can whole artichoke hearts, drained
- ¾ pound medium shrimp, cooked
- ¼ pound fresh or canned mushrooms, sliced
- 6½ tablespoons butter, divided
- 4½ tablespoons all-purpose flour
- 1½ cups half and half
- 1 tablespoon Worcestershire sauce
- Salt and black pepper to taste
- ¼ cup dry sherry
- ¼ cup (1 ounce) grated Parmesan cheese
- Paprika
- Chopped parsley for garnish

Arrange artichokes in buttered 12x8x2-inch baking dish. Spread shrimp over artichokes. Sauté mushrooms in 2 tablespoons butter for 6 minutes. Spoon over shrimp. Melt remaining butter, blend in flour, stir in cream and add Worcestershire sauce, salt, black pepper and sherry. Cook to form cream sauce. Pour over layered shrimp and vegetables. Sprinkle with cheese and paprika. Bake at 375° for 20 minutes. Garnish with parsley.
Yield: 6 servings

Shrimp Unadilla

- 3 tablespoons butter or margarine, softened
- 3 tablespoons all-purpose flour
- ¼ teaspoon salt
- ¼ teaspoon paprika
- 2 cups half and half
- 1 teaspoon Worcestershire sauce
- 1 teaspoon steak sauce
- 1 teaspoon sherry
- ¼ teaspoon curry powder
- 2 tablespoons butter or margarine, melted
- 1½ cups cornflakes
- 1 pound shrimp, shelled, deveined and cooked
- 3 cups cooked rice

Blend softened butter or margarine with flour to form paste. Add salt and paprika and blend in half and half. Cook over low heat until thickened. Add Worcestershire sauce, steak sauce, sherry and curry powder. Drizzle butter or margarine over cornflakes and mix thoroughly. In order listed, in 2-quart casserole, layer half each of cream sauce, shrimp and cornflakes; repeat layers. Bake at 325° for 20 minutes. Serve over hot rice.

Yield: 4 servings

Easy Shrimp Casserole

- 1 (7½ ounce) package wild and white rice mix
- 2 to 3 pounds shrimp, cooked and shelled
- 1 cup (4 ounces) shredded Cheddar cheese
- 1 (10¾ ounce) can cream of mushroom soup, undiluted
- 1 cup chopped onion
- 1 cup chopped green bell pepper
- 1 cup chopped celery
- ¼ cup plus 2 tablespoons butter
- Salt and black pepper to taste
- 4 lemons, thinly sliced
- Salt and black pepper to taste

Prepare rice according to package directions. Combine rice, shrimp, cheese and soup. Sauté onion, bell pepper and celery in butter until softened. Add vegetables to shrimp mixture and spread in 12x8x2-inch baking dish. Season with salt and black pepper. Arrange lemon slices on mixture to cover completely. Bake, covered with aluminum foil, at 375° for about 20 minutes. Let stand a few minutes before serving.

Note: Casserole and tomato aspic makes an excellent menu for bridge luncheons.

Yield: 6 to 8 servings

Shrimp with Pasta and Feta

- 1 teaspoon minced garlic
- 5 tablespoons olive oil, divided
- 2 cups chopped peeled and seeded tomato
- ½ cup dry white wine
- ½ cup minced fresh basil leaves
- 1 teaspoon crumbled oregano
- Salt and black pepper to taste
- 2 pounds uncooked shrimp, shelled and deveined
- ½ teaspoon red pepper flakes or to taste
- 1 (8 ounce) package Feta cheese, crumbled
- 1 (16 ounce) package rigatoni or other tube-shaped pasta
- 2 tablespoons unsalted butter

Sauté garlic in 2 tablespoons oil in heavy skillet for 30 seconds. Add tomato and cook, stirring constantly, for 1 minute. Add wine, basil, oregano, salt and black pepper. Simmer, stirring occasionally, for 10 minutes. In separate skillet over high heat, cook shrimp in remaining 3 tablespoons oil for 2 minutes, stirring frequently. Season with red pepper. Spoon shrimp mixture into 8x8x2-inch baking dish and sprinkle with cheese. Spoon sauce over shrimp. Bake at 400° for 12 minutes. While shrimp bakes, prepare pasta, drain and toss with butter. Serve shrimp sauce over pasta.
Yield: 6 to 8 servings

Shrimp and Chicken Casserole

- ¼ cup plus 2 tablespoons butter or margarine
- ¼ cup plus 2 tablespoons all-purpose flour
- 1 cup chicken broth
- 1 cup half and half
- 2 cups (8 ounces) grated sharp cheese
- ⅓ cup sherry
- 3 cups cubed cooked chicken breast
- 3 cups cooked shrimp
- Grated onion to taste

Combine butter and flour in 1-quart glass measure. Microwave at high (100%) setting for 1 minute, stir and cook for additional 1 minute. Gradually blend in broth and half and half. Microwave at high setting for 3½ to 4½ minutes, stirring at 1 minute intervals, until thick and bubbly. Add cheese and sherry, stirring to melt cheese. Add chicken, shrimp and onion to sauce. Pour into 2-quart casserole. Bake at 350° until bubbly. Serve over rice or pasta, in pastry shells or plain.
Yield: 6 servings

Chinese Fried Rice with Shrimp and Eggs

- 1 cup uncooked regular rice
- ¼ cup vegetable oil, divided
- 1 packet chicken noodle with white chicken soup mix
- 2½ cups boiling water
- 1½ pounds uncooked shrimp, shelled, deveined and chopped
- 2 eggs, lightly beaten
- Salt and black pepper to taste
- 3 tablespoons soy sauce
- 5 small green onions, sliced

Sauté rice in 2 tablespoons oil in large skillet until golden brown. Combine soup mix and boiling water. Stir in rice and simmer, covered, for 25 minutes or until liquid is absorbed. In separate skillet, sauté shrimp in remaining 2 tablespoons oil for 1 minute. Add eggs and cook, stirring constantly, for 1 to 2 minutes. Stir in salt, black pepper and soy sauce. Stir shrimp mixture into rice mixture, sprinkle with green onion and let stand, covered, for 3 minutes.

Yield: 4 servings

Hotel Charlotte's Shrimp Creole

- 1 cup chopped onion
- 1 cup chopped celery
- ½ cup chopped green bell pepper
- ¼ cup butter
- 3 cloves garlic, minced
- 2 tablespoons flour
- ¼ cup cold water
- 2½ cups diced tomatoes
- 3 tablespoons chopped fresh parsley
- 1 teaspoon salt
- ¼ cayenne pepper
- 3 bay leaves
- 3 cups water
- 3 pounds uncooked shrimp, shelled and deveined
- 3 to 4 cups hot cooked rice

Sauté onion, celery and bell pepper in butter for about 5 minutes or until softened. Add garlic and sauté for about 5 minutes. Remove skillet from heat. Blend flour with cold water and gradually add to sautéed vegetables. Add tomatoes, parsley, salt, cayenne pepper, bay leaves and 3 cups water. Simmer for 15 minutes. Stir in shrimp and simmer, covered, for 30 minutes. Remove bay leaves. Serve over rice.

Yield: 4 to 6 servings

Contributor: Hotel Charlotte
Charlotte, North Carolina

Shrimp Scampi

- 1 pound uncooked shrimp, shelled and deveined
- 1 medium-sized onion, chopped
- 4 to 6 cloves garlic, minced
- 2 tablespoons butter or margarine
- 1½ cups water
- 1 packet chicken gravy mix
- 1 red bell pepper, chopped
- 1 tablespoon lemon juice
- ½ teaspoon salt
- 1½ cups uncooked instant rice
- ¼ cup chopped fresh parsley

Sauté shrimp, onion and garlic in butter in large skillet until shrimp are pink. Blend water and gravy mix until smooth. Add gravy liquid, red pepper, lemon juice and salt to shrimp mixture. Bring to a boil. Stir in rice and parsley, remove from heat and let stand, covered, for 5 minutes. Fluff with fork.

Note: To prepare using microwave oven, combine onion, garlic and butter in 12x8x2-inch microwave-safe dish. Cook, covered, at high (100%) setting for 2 minutes. Blend water and gravy mix. Add shrimp, gravy liquid, red pepper, lemon juice, salt and rice to sautéed vegetables. Cook, covered, at high setting for 4 minutes, stir and cook for 3 to 4 additional minutes. Let stand for 5 minutes. Add parsley.

Yield: 4 servings

Italian Style Shrimp

- ½ cup chopped onion
- 2 tablespoons olive oil
- 1 (28 ounce) can Italian style plum tomatoes, drained and cut in chunks, or 2 (14½ ounce) cans Italian seasoned stewed tomatoes
- ⅓ cup dry white wine
- 2 teaspoons dried oregano
- 1 tablespoon cornstarch (optional)
- 1 pound uncooked shrimp, shelled and deveined
- 1 cup (4 ounces) crumbled mild feta cheese
- 2 tablespoons chopped fresh parsley
- 3 cups cooked rice

Sauté onion in oil in large skillet over medium-high heat until softened. Add tomatoes, wine and oregano. Reduce heat and simmer for 5 minutes or until thickened, adding cornstarch if necessary. Stir in shrimp and cook for about 3 minutes or until shrimp are pink. Add cheese and parsley and cook for 1 minute. Serve over rice.

Yield: 4 servings

Okra Shrimp Creole

- ¾ cup chopped green bell pepper
- 1 cup diced celery
- 1 large onion, chopped
- ½ cup margarine
- ½ teaspoon sugar
- 2 teaspoons salt or to taste
- ¼ teaspoon black pepper
- ¼ teaspoon hot pepper sauce
- 2 teaspoons Worcestershire sauce
- 2 tablespoons all-purpose flour
- 1 cup water
- 1 cup tomato sauce
- 1 (12 ounce) can vegetable cocktail juice
- 1 (16 ounce) okra and tomatoes
- 1 cup tomato puree
- 2 pounds uncooked shrimp, shelled and deveined
- ½ cup sliced water chestnuts
- 6 to 8 cups hot cooked rice
- Parsley for garnish

Sauté bell pepper, celery and onion in margarine until softened. Blend in sugar, salt, black pepper, hot pepper sauce, Worcestershire sauce and flour. Stir in water, tomato sauce, vegetable juice, okra and tomatoes and tomato puree. Simmer for 20 minutes. Add shrimp and water chestnuts. Simmer for 10 to 15 minutes. Serve over rice and garnish with parsley.

Yield: 8 to 10 servings

Poultry, Beef & Pork

On the banks of the Catawba River stood Laura's Rozzelle House, built in the late 1840's by Richard Rozzelle to raise his growing family of nine children. His daughter Laura inherited the home and land and began running it as an inn in the early 1900's. In 1941, Laura's Rozzelle House began a long career of serving old-fashioned, mouth-watering country meals, family-style. Many Carolinians from both sides of the Catawba River have devoured the fried chicken and dumplings, candied yams, fluffy biscuits and cobbler served there. Laura's burned to the ground in 1990, but we have her recipe for country ham and red eye gravy.

Our food choices are more sophisticated and lighter now. But if you're wondering what tempted our taste buds and brought us comfort, use Laura's recipes for Country Ham, Country Biscuits and Citron Custard. However, Mrs. Dorothy Powers tells us that out of all the times she visited and helped with the chores, she never knew any of the cooks to use a recipe! Thank you Dorothy for writing these down. When we pack our picnic baskets for tailgating at out alma maters, a few of us will still include country ham biscuits.

Poultry

As chicken and turkey have gained popularity as healthy sources of protein, a wide variety of cuts are available for convenience and preference. Allow ¾ to 1 pound person on a whole bird if purchased in raw weight; allow 4 to 6 ounces boneless chicken per serving.

- Thaw frozen poultry in the refrigerator, allowing plenty of time. Place bird in shallow pan to catch drippings and cover.
- Slightly freeze chicken to make removal of skin easier.
- Meat thermometers are handy but not completely reliable. Insert probe in large meaty muscle on inside of thigh and avoid touching the bone.
- For a golden glaze, brush bird with butter or special glaze during last 20 to 30 minutes of baking. Glazes can be made from juices, jams and sugar.

Meat

Meat must comply with specific government standards and pass inspection to be sold in the United States. For each variety, there are classifications and weight standards that determine the price. The meat is inspected and stamped at the wholesale level, before division into individual cuts for purchase at the meat counter.

Beef

Beef is the meat of mature cattle, specifically raised to be slaughtered. The classifications are prime, choice and good.

Prime—Prime is richly marbled with fat and is the most tender, flavorful and expensive of beef cuts.

Choice—Choice is the most available variety with less fat than prime but enough for a good flavor.

Good—Good is sold as economy or "lean" meat, has little fat marbling, is usually not as tender as other grades but is nutritionally as good.

Aged—Aged beef is stored and hung in meat locker for 2 to 6 weeks to allow natural process to tenderize. Because of shipping process, all beef is aged to some extent.

In addition to the various grades of beef, the cut of meat determines tenderness and dictates the cooking method. Less tender cuts require longer cooking at lower temperatures. Marinating helps tenderize tougher cuts. Tender cuts require only brief cooking to seal the natural juices and enhance the flavor.

Brisket—Brisket is cut from the breast and foreleg section and is tough, making it ideal for long, slow cooking to tenderize.

Chuck—Chuck is cut from shoulder and consists of neck, blade, arm and shoulder and is a tough cut.

Flank—Cut from the underside belly section, it is boneless but relatively tough and is used as flank steak or fajita meat.

Loin—Sirloin strips, filet mignon, tenderloin and tenderloin roast is cut from the mid-section, in front of the hips, and is the most tender portion.

Rib—Cut from the forequarter section, rib steaks, rib eyes and rib roasts comes from directly behind the shoulder and along the backbone.

Round—Round is cut from the rump and hind leg section, tends to be tougher and offers roasts and steaks.

Much of the tougher sections of beef are ground or chopped to make hamburger. Hamburger is lean or fat, based on the quantity of fat included in the grinding. Ground chuck contains the most fat and ground round has the least. Sirloin is sometimes ground for high quality hamburger.

All cuts can be prepared in many ways but the most popular method for steaks and hamburgers are quick cooking broiling and grilling. Broiling positions the meat in the oven directly under and 5 to 6 inches from the heat source. Grilling cooks the meat over a bed of coals or in cast iron griddle over a burner. Thickness of cut determines the cooking length to achieve rare, medium, medium or well-done.

Oven Broiling

Very Rare	3 minutes per side	Medium	6 minutes per side
Rare	4 minutes per side	Well-Done	7 minutes per side
Medium Rare	5 minutes per side		

Time is based on 3 to 4 inch distance from heat source and 1-inch thickness of meat. For each additional ½-inch thickness, double time per side.

Grilling

Very Rare	6 to 7 minutes per side
Rare	8 to 9 minutes per side
Medium Rare	10 to 12 minutes per side
Medium	14 to 16 minutes per side
Well-Done	18 to 20 minutes per side

Time is based on 4 to 5 inches above moderately hot coals and 2-inch thickness of meat. For each additional ½-inch thickness, add 3 to 5 minutes per side.

Roasting

Insert meat thermometer for brief period toward end of roasting process to check doneness.

Oven temperature is 325°.

Cut	Approximate Weight (pounds)	Meat Thermometer	Minutes Per Pound	Total Time (hours)
Rib Roast	4 to 6	104° (rare)	26 to 32	1¾ to 3¼
		170° (well)	40 to 42	2¾ to 4¼
	6 to 8	140° (rare)	23 to 25	2¼ to 3¾
		160° (medium)	27 to 30	2¾ to 4
		170° (well)	32 to 35	3¼ to 4¾
Rolled Rib Roast	5 to 7	140° (rare)	32	2¾ to 3¾
		160°(medium)	38	3 to 4½
		170° (well)	48	4 to 5½
Rib Eye Roast	4 to 6	140° (rare)	18 to 20	1¼ to 2
		160° (medium)	20 to 22	1¼ to 2¼
		170° (well)	22 to 24	1½ to 2¼
Rolled Rump Roast	4 to 6	150° to 170°	25 to 30	1¾ to 3
Sirloin Tip Roast	3½ to 4	150° to 170°	35 to 40	2 to 2¾
Tenderloin Roast*				
Whole	4 to 6	140° (rare)	45 to 60	3 to 6
Half	2 to 3	140° (rare)	45 to 60	1½ to 3

** Baked at 425°.*

Ham and Pork

Ham is available precooked or cured. Country cured ham must be soaked in cold water for 8 to 12 hours before roasting. These hams come with detailed instructions for preparation and cooking.

- Unwrap ham and remove any cording or cloth covering.
- Rinse under lukewarm water to remove any preservatives.
- Remove rind, if necessary. Trim layer of fat to ¼ to ½-inch thickness.
- Place on rack and cover with glaze of brown sugar, vinegar, honey or fruit preserves.
- Bake, using meat thermometer as most accurate guide to doneness.
- Roast ham or fresh pork at 325 to 350°.

Roasting Ham

Variety	Weight (pounds)	Meat Thermometer	Time (hours)
Uncooked	6 to 8	185°	3½
	8 to 10	185°	3½ to 4
	10 to 15	185°	4 to 5
Uncooked Picnic	4 to 6	170°	3 to 3½
	6 to 8	170°	3½ to 4½
Fully Cooked	6 to 8	150°	2½
	8 to 10	150°	2½ to 3
	10 to 15	150°	3 to 4
Picnic Fully Cooked	3 to 5	150°	1½ to 2½
	5 to 7	150°	2½ to 3
Boneless Rolls	8 to 10	150°	3 to 3½
	10 to 12	150°	3½ to 4
Canned	3 to 7	150°	2 to 2½

Roasting Pork

Variety	Weight (pounds)	Meat Thermometer	Time (hours)
Loin Center	3 to 5	170°	2½ to 3
Loin Half	5 to 7	170°	3½ to 4¼
Loin Blade	3 to 4	170°	2¼ to 2¾
Loin Center Rolled	3 to 4	170°	2½ to 3
Boston Shoulder	4 to 6	185°	3½ to 4½
Boston Shoulder Rolled	3 to 5	185°	3 to 3½
Leg (Fresh Ham)	10 to 14	185°	5½ to 6½
Leg Half (Fresh Ham)	5 to 7	170°	3½ to 4½

Chicken Barbecue

- 10 pounds chicken leg quarters
- Water
- 1 (32 ounce) bottle ketchup
- 4 cups cider vinegar
- 1½ cups firmly-packed brown sugar
- ¾ cup prepared mustard
- Texas Pete to taste
- ¼ cup plus 2 tablespoons liquid smoke
- 1 tablespoon black pepper

Simmer chicken in water to cover in stock pot for 2 hours. While chicken cooks, prepare barbecue sauce by combining ketchup, vinegar, brown sugar, mustard, Texas Pete, liquid smoke and black pepper in saucepan. Simmer for 45 minutes. Drain broth from chicken, reserving for soup. Remove chicken from bones and chop finely or tease by shredding with fork tines. Place in 13x9x2-inch baking pan. Add barbecue sauce to moisten well. Bake at 325° for 1 hour. Drain any broth. Serve on sandwich buns with additional sauce.

Note: Barbecued chicken tastes like pork.

Yield: 16 to 20 servings

Charlotte's Grilled Chicken with Barbecue Sauce

- ¼ cup vinegar
- ½ cup Worcestershire sauce
- 2 tablespoons prepared mustard
- ½ cup margarine
- ¼ cup sugar
- ½ teaspoon salt
- 1 (2½ to 3 pound) broiler-fryer, cut in pieces

Combine vinegar, Worcestershire sauce, mustard, margarine, sugar and salt in saucepan. Simmer for 20 minutes. Grill chicken, brushing barbecue sauce on pieces while cooking.

Yield: 4 to 6 servings

Cola Broiled Chicken

- 1 (2½ to 3 pound) broiler-fryer, cut in pieces, or 4 chicken breast halves
- 1 cup ketchup
- 1 (12 ounce) carbonated cola soft drink

Place chicken in skillet. Blend ketchup and cola, pour over chicken and simmer for 1 hour.

Yield: 4 servings

Arroz Con Pollo (Chicken with Rice)

- 1 (4 pound) broiler-fryer, cut in pieces
- 1¼ teaspoon salt, divided
- ½ teaspoon black pepper
- ⅛ teaspoon paprika
- ¼ cup olive oil
- 1 medium-sized onion, chopped
- 1 clove garlic, minced
- 2 cups water
- 3½ cups canned tomatoes
- 2 chicken bouillon cubes
- ¼ teaspoon powdered saffron
- 1 bay leaf
- ½ teaspoon oregano
- 2 cups uncooked regular rice
- 1 (8 to 10 ounce) package frozen peas or artichoke hearts, thawed
- 3 pimentos, chopped

Season chicken with 1 teaspoon salt, black pepper and paprika. Brown chicken in oil in skillet, turning to brown on all sides. Place pieces in 13x9x2-inch baking dish. Sauté onion and garlic in skillet until onion is tender. Add water and heat, scraping to loosen browned bits from skillet. Stir in tomatoes, bouillon, saffron, bay leaf and oregano. Bring to a boil and pour over chicken. Stir in rice. Bake, tightly covered, at 350° for 25 minutes. Remove bay leaf, fluff rice, stir in peas, place pimento on surface and bake, covered, for 10 additional minutes.
Yield: 6 to 8 servings

Garlic Chicken

- 3 pounds chicken thighs, legs or breast halves
- ¼ cup butter or margarine
- 2 tablespoons olive oil
- 2 teaspoons salt or less to taste
- Freshly ground black pepper to taste
- 1 or 2 cloves garlic, minced
- ¼ cup minced onion
- 2 tablespoons lemon juice
- ½ teaspoon marjoram
- ¼ cup white wine

Brown chicken on all sides in butter and oil in large skillet. Combine salt, black pepper, garlic, onion, lemon juice and marjoram. Pour over chicken. Simmer, covered, for 30 minutes or until tender. Remove chicken to warm platter. Add wine to pan drippings and heat thoroughly. Pour over chicken. Serve with white or brown rice.
Yield: 4 or 5 servings

Baked Chicken with 40 Cloves of Garlic

4 pounds chicken pieces, skin removed
Salt and black pepper to taste
1 tablespoon olive oil
40 large cloves garlic, unpeeled
1¾ cups dry white wine
¼ teaspoon thyme
¼ teaspoon rosemary
2 tablespoons cognac
Fresh chopped parsley to taste
12 (½-inch thick) slices coarse bread

Season chicken with salt and black pepper. Heat oil in large shallow flame-proof casserole over medium heat, add chicken, brown for 5 minutes, turn and brown other side for 5 minutes. (Slight scorching will not affect flavor of dish.) Remove chicken from casserole and set aside. Reserving 1 clove garlic, sauté remaining garlic in casserole, stirring frequently, for 3 to 5 minutes or until garlic begins to brown. Spread garlic in single layer, place chicken on garlic and add wine, thyme and rosemary. Bake, tightly covered, at 350° for 45 minutes, check for doneness and bake up to additional 15 minutes if necessary. Remove from oven. Heat cognac in small saucepan, ignite and pour over chicken, shaking casserole until flames die down. Check sauce, adjust seasonings and sprinkle with parsley. Toast bread slices at 350° for about 10 minutes or until lightly browned. Rub both sides of slices with cut side of reserved garlic. To serve, place two slices bread on individual plates, top with 1 or 2 pieces chicken, spoon sauce over chicken and add several cloves garlic, to be pressed onto bread slices.
Yield: 6 servings

To get the skin off garlic before chopping, pound each clove with the side of a heavy knife. The skin pops off.

To banish onion, garlic and bleach odors from hands, put all five fingers on the handle of a stainless-steel spoon and run cold water over fingers.

Chicken Potato Roast

1 (3 to 3½ pound) broiler-fryer
1 medium-sized onion
2 or 3 medium baking potatoes
¼ cup margarine, melted
¾ teaspoon salt
1 teaspoon dried thyme
2 teaspoons paprika

Fold wings of chicken across back, place onion in chicken body cavity and tie legs together. Place breast side up on rack in shallow roasting pan. Cut potatoes crosswise in ¼-inch slices about ¾ way through. Place on rack with chicken. Blend margarine, salt, thyme and paprika. Brush on all sides of chicken and potatoes. Bake at 375° for 1¼ hours, basting with seasoned margarine after 35 minutes; roast until juices run clear. Let chicken stand 10 minutes before carving.
Note: A good accompaniment is Waldorf salad. This has taken the place of fried chicken for us.
Yield: 2 or 3 servings

Italian Oven-Easy Chicken

¼ cup all-purpose flour
2 teaspoons salt
¼ teaspoon garlic salt
¼ teaspoon oregano
½ teaspoon paprika
1 (2½ to 3 pound) broiler-fryer, cut in pieces
½ pound bulk pork sausage, cut into small pieces
1½ cups cooked or canned tomatoes, divided

Combine flour, salt, garlic salt, oregano and paprika. Dredge chicken pieces in seasoned flour. Bake sausage in 13x9x2-inch baking pan at 400° for 5 minutes; do not drain liquid from pan. Stir in ½ cup tomatoes. Place chicken, skin side down, in single layer on sausage and tomato mixture. Bake at 400° for 30 minutes, turn chicken, add remaining 1 cup tomatoes and bake additional 30 minutes or until chicken is tender.
Yield: 3 or 4 servings

Chicken Waikiki Beach

8 pieces chicken
All-purpose flour
Salt and black pepper to taste
¼ cup vegetable oil, or more to fry chicken
1 (20 ounce) can pineapple chunks
Water
½ cup sugar
½ cup firmly-packed brown sugar
2 tablespoons cornstarch
¾ cup vinegar
2 tablespoons soy sauce
¼ teaspoon ginger
1 large green bell pepper, cut in strips

Dredge chicken with flour and season with salt and black pepper. Brown chicken pieces on all sides in oil. Place in shallow roasting pan. Drain pineapple syrup into 2-cup measure, reserving chunks. Add water to syrup to measure 1¼ cups liquid. Combine sugar, brown sugar, cornstarch, syrup liquid, vinegar, soy sauce and ginger in saucepan. Bring to a boil, stirring constantly, and cook for 2 minutes. Pour over chicken. Bake, uncovered, for 30 minutes, add pineapple chunks and bell pepper and bake for additional 30 minutes or until chicken is tender.
Yield: 4 servings

Chicken à la Maria

¾ cup Italian-seasoned fine dry breadcrumbs
¼ cup (1 ounce) grated Parmesan cheese
12 chicken breast halves, skin removed and boned
½ cup sliced green onion
2 tablespoons butter or margarine
2 tablespoons all-purpose flour
1 cup milk
1 (10 ounce) package frozen chopped spinach, thawed and well drained
1 (4 ounce) package sliced boiled ham, diced

Combine breadcrumbs and cheese. Lightly coat chicken pieces with crumb mixture and arrange in lightly greased 13x9x2-inch baking pan; reserve any excess crumbs. Cook onion in butter or margarine in saucepan until tender. Blend in flour, add milk and cook, stirring constantly, until thickened. Stir in spinach and ham. Spread spinach mixture on chicken and sprinkle with reserved crumbs. Bake, uncovered, at 350° for 40 to 45 minutes or until done.
Yield: 12 servings

Creamy Baked Chicken Breasts

- 8 chicken breast halves, skin removed and boned
- 8 slices Swiss cheese
- 1 (10¾ ounce) can cream of chicken soup, undiluted
- ¼ cup dry white wine
- 1 cup herb-seasoned stuffing mix, crushed
- ¼ cup butter or margarine, melted

Arrange chicken pieces in 13x9x2-inch baking dish. Place cheese on chicken. Blend soup and wine and spoon evenly over cheese layer. Sprinkle with stuffing mix and drizzle with butter or margarine. Bake at 350° for 45 to 55 minutes.
Yield: 8 servings

Catalina Chicken

- 1 (8 ounce) bottle Catalina salad dressing
- 1 (1 4⁄5 ounce) packet onion soup mix
- 1 (5 ounce) jar pineapple preserves
- 1 (5 ounce) jar apricot preserves
- 12 chicken breast halves, skin removed and boned

Combine salad dressing, soup mix, pineapple and apricot preserves. Arrange chicken in 14x10x2-inch baking dish. Pour salad dressing mixture over chicken. Bake, uncovered, at 300° for 1½ hours or until chicken is tender.
Yield: 12 servings

Herbed Chicken and Vegetables

- 4 chicken breast halves, skin removed and boned
- 4 medium-sized onions, quartered
- 2 or 3 medium-sized white potatoes, cut in chunks
- 2 carrots, sliced
- Salt and black pepper to taste
- 1 teaspoon dried thyme
- ½ teaspoon dried rosemary
- ½ cup chicken broth

Arrange chicken pieces in 2-quart casserole. Place onion, potatoes and carrots on chicken. Combine salt, black pepper, thyme and rosemary. Sprinkle seasonings on vegetables. Pour chicken broth over vegetables and chicken. Bake, tightly covered, at 375° for 1 hour.
Yield: 4 servings

Moo Goo Gai Pan

- 4 chicken breast halves, skin removed and boned
- ½ teaspoon salt
- ⅛ teaspoon black pepper
- 2 teaspoons cornstarch, divided
- 2 tablespoons vegetable oil
- 2 tablespoons thinly sliced green onion
- 1 (10 ounce) package frozen snow peas
- 1 (4 ounce) can sliced mushrooms
- 2 tablespoons sliced pimento
- 2 tablespoons minced preserved ginger (optional)
- ½ cup chicken broth
- 1 tablespoon water
- 4 to 5 cups cooked rice

Cut chicken into 1x1x¼-inch cubs. Sprinkle with salt, black pepper and 1 teaspoon cornstarch. Let stand for a few minutes. Stir-fry chicken, a small portion at a time, in oil just until done, remove from skillet and set aside. Stir-fry onion for 1 minute. Add snow peas, mushrooms, pimento and ginger, stirring rapidly, until peas are crisp tender. Add broth and bring to a boil. Blend remaining 1 teaspoon cornstarch and water until smooth. Stir quickly into liquid with vegetables and cook over medium heat until bubbly and clear. Add chicken and heat thoroughly. Serve over rice, adding soy sauce as desired.

Note: If precooked chicken is used, add with vegetables and heat until very hot.

Yield: 6 servings

Chicken Saltimbocca

- 6 chicken breast halves, skin removed and boned
- 6 thin slices boiled ham
- 3 slices mozzarella cheese, cut in halves
- ½ cup chopped tomatoes
- ½ teaspoon crushed sage
- ⅓ cup fine dry breadcrumbs
- 2 tablespoons grated Parmesan cheese
- 2 tablespoons minced parsley
- ¼ cup butter, melted

Enclose each chicken piece in plastic wrap and pound lightly to flatten to 5-inch square. Discard plastic. Place ham slice and ½ slice cheese on each chicken piece. Top with tomato and sage. Fold in side, roll up jelly roll style and secure with wooden pick. Combine breadcrumbs, cheese and parsley. Dip chicken rolls in butter, then in crumb mixture and place in shallow baking pan. Bake at 350° for 40 to 45 minutes.

Yield: 6 servings

Chicken Casserole Supreme

- **1 (4 ounce) package chipped beef**
- **6 chicken breast halves, skin removed and boned**
- **3 slices bacon, cut in halves**
- **Black pepper to taste**
- **1 (10¾ ounce) can cream of mushroom soup, undiluted**
- **1 cup sour cream**

Spread chipped beef in 13x9x2-inch baking dish. Wrap each chicken piece with ½ slice of bacon, place on chipped beef and season with black pepper. Blend soup with sour cream and pour over chicken. Bake, tightly covered with aluminum foil, at 275° for 3 hours.

Note: To include rice, pour ¼-inch uncooked rice in casserole, add chicken pieces, season with black pepper, add 1 cup water and top with soup mixture. Casserole can be baked, uncovered, at 350° for 1 hour, then covered and baked for an additional 30 minutes. Fat-free sour cream and low-calorie soup can be substituted to reduce fat content of recipe.

Yield: 6 servings

Chicken Stroganoff

- **2 tablespoons chopped onion**
- **3 teaspoons butter or margarine, divided**
- **1 pound chicken cutlets, cut in ½-inch strips**
- **3 cups (8 ounces) sliced fresh mushrooms**
- **¼ cup chicken broth**
- **¼ cup dry white wine**
- **¼ teaspoon salt**
- **¼ teaspoon black pepper**
- **¼ teaspoon dried thyme**
- **¼ cup sour cream**
- **3 to 4 cups cooked rice or noodles**

Sauté onion in 2 teaspoons butter or margarine in large skillet over medium-high heat for 2 minutes, stirring constantly. Add chicken and cook, stirring constantly, for 2 to 3 minutes or until browned. Remove chicken from skillet. Stir-fry mushrooms in remaining 1 teaspoon butter or margarine in skillet for 2 minutes. Add broth, wine, salt, black pepper and thyme. Reduce heat and simmer for 7 to 10 minutes or until mushrooms are tender and liquid is slightly evaporated. Add chicken to mushrooms, heat thoroughly and stir in sour cream. Serve over rice or noodles.

Yield: 4 servings

Chicken Surabaja

6 chicken breast halves, skin removed, boned and cut in 1-inch chunks
1 (3 ounce) can French fried onion rings (optional)

Prepare marinade. Place chicken in shallow baking dish and pour marinade over pieces. Chill for 1 hour. Thread chicken on 12 skewers. Grill for 12 to 15 minutes, turning frequently; if cooking indoors, broil 6 inches from heat for 6 minutes on each side. While chicken cooks, prepare sauce. Pour over cooked chicken and garnish with onion rings.
Yield: 4 servings

Marinade

¼ cup soy sauce
2 tablespoons lemon juice
1 clove garlic, minced
Dash of white pepper
¼ cup water

Combine soy sauce, lemon juice, garlic, white pepper and water.

Sauce

2 tablespoons butter or margarine
½ cup soy sauce
2 tablespoons lemon juice
½ teaspoon salt
Dash of cayenne pepper

Combine butter or margarine, soy sauce, lemon juice, salt and cayenne pepper in saucepan. Bring to a boil, reduce heat and simmer for 2 minutes.

Easy Chicken Casserole

4 chicken breast halves
Water
1 cup sour cream
1 (10¾ ounce) can cream of celery soup, undiluted
2 tubes Ritz crackers, crumbled
½ cup butter or margarine, melted

Place chicken in medium saucepan, add water to cover and simmer until tender. Reserve ½ cup broth, discard skin and bones and cube chicken. Combine sour cream, soup and reserved broth. Mix cracker crumbs and butter or margarine. Place chicken in 12x8x2-inch baking dish. Spoon soup mixture over chicken and top with buttered crumbs. Bake, uncovered, at 350° for 30 minutes.
Yield: 6 servings

Chicken Wellington

- 1 (6 ounce) package long grain rice
- 2 teaspoons grated orange peel
- 12 chicken breast halves, skin removed and boned
- Salt and black pepper to taste
- 2 egg whites
- 12 sheets phyllo pastry
- ¼ cup plus 2 tablespoons butter, melted
- 2 (10 ounce) jars currant jelly
- 1 tablespoon prepared mustard
- 3 tablespoons port wine
- ¼ cup lemon juice

Prepare rice according to package directions. Add orange peel and set aside to cool. Enclose each chicken piece in plastic wrap and pound lightly to flatten to 5-inch square. Season with salt and black pepper. Beat egg whites until soft peaks form and fold into rice. For each serving, spread about ¼ cup rice on chicken piece and roll up jelly roll style. Brush single sheet of phyllo pastry with butter, place rolled chicken on pastry, fold top over chicken, press lightly to seal, fold edges over chicken and roll up to form pocket shape. Brush with butter and place on baking sheet. Bake at 375° for 35 minutes, loosely covering with foil if pastry browns too quickly. While chicken bakes, prepare sauce by heating jelly in saucepan and gradually adding mustard, port wine and lemon juice. Heat until well blended and serve over chicken pastry.

Note: Chicken packets can be assembled and frozen. Thaw in refrigerator for 30 minutes, then bake at 375° for 40 to 45 minutes.

Yield: 12 servings

Perk up the flavor and texture of plain ordinary rice:

Parmesan Rice*: Stir 3 tablespoons of cut-up butter and ¼ cup of freshly grated Parmesan cheese into 3 cups hot cooked rice.*

Nutty Rice*: Sauté 2 tablespoons coarsely chopped walnuts, almonds or pecans in 1 tablespoon olive oil or butter. Sprinkle over hot cooked rice just before serving.*

Lemon Rice*: Stir 2 tablespoons fresh lemon juice, 1 tablespoon unsalted butter and ½ teaspoon grated lemon zest into 3 cups hot cooked rice before serving.*

Chicken Tetrazzini

2 or 3 chicken breast halves
Water
1 (8 ounce) package spaghetti
2 tablespoons chopped onion
¼ cup chopped green bell pepper
2 tablespoons margarine
¼ cup milk
1 (10¾ ounce) can cream of chicken soup, undiluted
1½ cups (6 ounces) grated sharp Cheddar cheese

Place chicken in saucepan, add water to cover and simmer until tender. Reserve broth, discard skin and bones and chop chicken; recipe requires 3 cups chicken. Prepare spaghetti according to package directions, using reserved broth. While spaghetti cooks, sauté onion and bell pepper in margarine. Blend milk and soup together. Drain spaghetti. Add chicken, vegetables and soup mixture. Spread in 3-quart casserole and sprinkle with cheese. Bake at 350° for 30 minutes or until thoroughly heated.
Yield: 4 servings

Chicken Pot Pie

1 (4 pound) chicken, cooked, skin removed, boned and chopped
Water
1 (10¾ ounce) can cream of chicken soup, undiluted
1 (10 ounce) package frozen green peas and carrots or 1 (16 ounce) can mixed vegetables, drained
1 cup self-rising flour
1 teaspoon salt or to taste
½ teaspoon black pepper
1 cup buttermilk
½ cup margarine, melted

Place chicken in saucepan, add water to cover and simmer until tender. Reserve broth, discard skin and bones and tear or chop chicken into bite-size pieces. Place chicken in 13x9x2-inch baking dish. Combine 2 cups reserved broth, soup and vegetables in saucepan and bring to a boil. Pour over chicken. Blend flour, salt, black pepper, buttermilk and margarine together until smooth. Spoon evenly over vegetable mixture. Bake at 425° for 30 minutes; crust will be browned.
Yield: 6 servings

Chicken and Wild Rice Casserole

3 to 4 pounds chicken pieces or breasts
2 to 3 cups water
1 cup sherry
1½ teaspoons salt
½ teaspoon curry powder (optional)
1 medium-sized onion, cut in chunks
½ cup diced celery
1 pound fresh mushrooms, washed, dried and chopped
¼ cup butter or margarine
2 (6 ounce) packages long grain and wild rice mix
1 cup sour cream
1 (10¾ ounce) can cream of mushroom soup, undiluted.

Place chicken in stock pot and add water, sherry, salt, curry powder, onion and celery. Bring to a boil, reduce heat and simmer, tightly covered, for 1 hour. Strain and reserve broth, discard skin and bones and cut chicken into bite-size pieces. Prepare rice mix according to package directions, using reserved broth as cooking liquid in amount directed. Sauté mushrooms in butter or margarine until browned. Combine chicken, rice and mushrooms. Blend sour cream and soup together. Add to chicken mixture and toss to mix. Spread mixture in 13x9x2-inch baking dish. Chill, covered, until ready to bake. Bake at 350° for 1 hour.

Note: Chilling overnight improves flavor of casserole. Casserole can also be assembled and frozen. Thaw before baking as directed.
Yield: 6 to 8 servings

Chicken and Rice

1¼ cups coarsely chopped green bell pepper
¾ cup thinly sliced onion
3 tablespoons olive oil
¼ cup cornstarch
2 cups chicken broth
3 tablespoons soy sauce
2 cups chopped cooked chicken
3 ripe tomatoes, cut in thin wedges
3 to 5 cups hot cooked rice

Sauté bell pepper and onion in oil in covered skillet over low heat until tender but not browned. Blend cornstarch and ½ cup chicken broth until smooth. Add remaining 1½ cups broth and soy sauce. Stir liquid and chicken into vegetables. Cook, stirring frequently, until sauce is clear and thickened. Add tomatoes and cook just until heated. Serve over rice.
Yield: 4 to 6 servings

Gourmet Chicken Pie

- 2 medium-sized onions, chopped
- ¼ cup butter or margarine
- 4 cups diced cooked chicken
- 6 large fresh mushrooms, sliced, or 1 (4 ounce) can sliced mushrooms, drained
- 2 cups diced potatoes or frozen hash brown potatoes
- 1 cup frozen English peas
- 3 large carrots, thinly sliced
- 2 stalks celery, chopped
- 2 cups chicken broth
- ⅔ cup white wine
- ½ teaspoon dried parsley or 1 teaspoon chopped parsley
- 1 teaspoon chopped fresh chives
- ½ teaspoon dry mustard
- ½ teaspoon garlic powder
- ½ teaspoon white pepper
- ½ teaspoon black pepper
- 2 tablespoons Worcestershire sauce
- 2 bay leaves
- 3 tablespoons cornstarch
- ¼ cup water
- 2 (10¾ ounce) cans cream of mushroom soup, undiluted
- 1 cup sour cream
- ¼ cup (1 ounce) grated Parmesan cheese
- ½ cup margarine, melted
- 1 cup buttermilk
- 1 cup self-rising flour

Sauté onion in butter or margarine in large skillet for 3 minutes. Add chicken and sauté for 5 minutes. Stir in mushrooms and sauté for 3 minutes. Combine potatoes, peas, carrots, celery, broth, wine, parsley, chives, mustard, garlic, white pepper, black pepper, Worcestershire sauce and bay leaves. Add to chicken and simmer, covered, for 15 minutes. Remove bay leaves. Blend cornstarch and water until smooth. Stir into chicken mixture and bring to a boil, stirring constantly. Remove from heat and add soup, sour cream and cheese. Spread mixture in greased 13x9x2-inch baking dish. Blend margarine and buttermilk. Using electric mixer, gradually blend in flour until smooth. Pour batter over chicken mixture. Bake at 400° for 30 to 45 minutes or until lightly browned.
Yield: 8 servings

For quick thickeners for gravies, add some instant potatoes to your gravy and it will thicken beautifully.

Chicken Salad Oriental

- 1 (8 ounce) package rotini pasta
- Boiling water
- 1½ cups chopped celery
- ½ cup chopped green onion
- ¼ cup margarine
- 1 (10¾ ounce) can cream of chicken soup, undiluted
- ½ cup mayonnaise
- 2 tablespoons soy sauce
- 2 cups cubed cooked chicken
- 1 (8 ounce) can water chestnuts, drained
- 1 cup chow mein noodles

Cook pasta in boiling water for 5 minutes and drain well. Sauté celery and green onion in margarine until tender. Combine pasta, vegetables, soup, mayonnaise, soy sauce, chicken and water chestnuts. Spread mixture in 3-quart casserole. Bake at 350° for 20 minutes, sprinkle with noodles and bake for additional 5 minutes.
Yield: 8 servings

Crescent Chicken Squares

- 1 (3 ounce) package cream cheese, softened
- ¼ cup plus 1 tablespoon margarine, melted and divided
- 2 cups cubed cooked chicken breasts
- ¼ teaspoon salt
- ⅛ teaspoon black pepper
- 2 tablespoons milk
- 1 tablespoon chopped onion
- 1 (8 ounce) can refrigerated crescent roll dough
- ¾ cup crushed seasoned croutons

Blend cream cheese and 3 tablespoons margarine until smooth. Add chicken, salt, black pepper, milk and onion. Separate roll dough into 4 rectangles and press perforations on each to seal. Place ½ cup chicken mixture in center of each rectangle, pull corners of dough to center and press to seal. Brush tops with remaining 2 tablespoons margarine, dip into crushed croutons and place on ungreased baking sheet. Bake at 350° for 20 to 25 minutes.
Yield: 4 servings

Add a teaspoon of peanut butter to cover up the burned flavor in gravy.

Chicken and Stuffing Scallop

Scallop

- **1 (8 ounce) package herb-seasoned stuffing mix**
- **4 cups cubed cooked chicken**
- **½ cup margarine**
- **½ cup all-purpose flour**
- **¼ teaspoon salt**
- **Dash of black pepper**
- **4 cups chicken broth**
- **6 eggs, lightly beaten**

Prepare stuffing according to package directions for dry stuffing. Spread stuffing in 13x9x2-inch baking dish. Spoon chicken evenly on stuffing. Melt margarine in large saucepan. Blend in flour, salt and black pepper. Add broth. Cook, stirring often, until thickened. Gradually add hot liquid to eggs, mixing until well blended. Pour over chicken. Bake at 350° for 40 to 45 minutes. While scallop bakes, prepare sauce. Let baked scallop stand for 5 minutes before cutting into squares and serving with hot sauce.
Yield: 12 servings

Pimento Mushroom Sauce

- **1 (10¾ ounce) can cream of mushroom soup**
- **¼ cup milk**
- **1 cup sour cream**
- **¼ cup chopped pimento**

Combine soup, milk, sour cream and pimento in saucepan. Cook, stirring frequently, until thoroughly heated.
Yield: 2½ cups

Mexican Chicken

- **1 (10¾ ounce) can cream of chicken soup, undiluted**
- **1 cup milk**
- **1 cup chopped onion**
- **1 (10 ounce) can tomatoes with chilies**
- **1 (4½ ounce) can chopped green chilies, drained**
- **1 (12 ounce) package Doritos, slightly crushed**
- **1 (2½ to 3 pound) broiler-fryer, cooked, boned and cut in chunks**
- **1 cup (4 ounces) grated Monterey Jack cheese**

Combine soup, milk, onion, tomatoes with chilies and green chilies. Spread chips in buttered 13x9x2-inch baking dish. Layer chicken and soup mixture on chips and top with cheese. Bake at 350° for 35 minutes.
Yield: 6 to 8 servings

Crunchy Chicken Casserole

- **3 cups chopped cooked chicken**
- **1 cup chopped celery**
- **2 tablespoons minced onion**
- **1 (8 ounce) can sliced water chestnuts, drained**
- **1 (4 ounce) can sliced mushrooms, drained**
- **1 (2¼ ounce) package slivered almonds**
- **1 cup mayonnaise**
- **1 (10¾ ounce) can cream of mushroom soup, undiluted**
- **2 tablespoons lemon juice**
- **1 tablespoon parsley flakes**
- **¼ teaspoon paprika**
- **½ cup (2 ounces) grated cheese**
- **1 (8 ounce) can refrigerated crescent roll dough**

Combine chicken, celery, onion, water chestnuts, mushrooms and almonds. Stir in mayonnaise, soup, lemon juice, parsley and paprika. Spread mixture in greased 3-quart casserole and sprinkle with cheese. Unroll dough and arrange on mixture. Bake at 375° for 20 to 30 minutes or until casserole is bubbly and dough is browned.
Yield: 8 servings

Chicken Tortilla Casserole

- **4 to 6 chicken breast halves, cooked, boned and chopped**
- **1 (10¾ ounce) can cream of chicken soup, undiluted**
- **1 (10¾ ounce) can cream of mushroom soup, undiluted**
- **1 (5 ounce) can evaporated milk**
- **2 (4½ ounce) cans chopped green chilies, drained**
- **1 small onion, chopped**
- **1 teaspoon salt**
- **10 to 12 corn tortillas**
- **2 cups (8 ounces) grated Monterey Jack cheese**

Combine chicken, chicken and mushroom soups, milk, green chilies, onion and salt. Cut tortillas into quarters. Layer ⅓ of tortilla pieces in 13x9x2-inch baking dish, add ½ of chicken mixture and repeat layers, ending with tortillas. Sprinkle with cheese. Bake at 350° for 30 to 40 minutes.

Note: Chicken can be cooked by stewing method or wrapped in aluminum foil and baked at 400° for 1 hour. For flavor change, substitute ½ teaspoon red chili pepper for 1 can green chilies and use sharp Cheddar cheese instead of Monterey Jack. Bake at 300° for 1 hour.
Yield: 4 to 6 servings

Poppy Seed Chicken

- 1 cup sour cream
- 2 tablespoons lemon juice
- 1 (10¾ ounce) can cream of chicken soup
- 5 chicken breast halves, cooked, skin removed, boned and cubed
- Poppy seed
- 1 tube Ritz crackers, crushed
- ½ cup butter, melted

Combine sour cream, lemon juice and soup. Fold in chicken, mixing carefully. Spread mixture in greased 13x9x2-inch baking pan. Sprinkle generously with poppy seed. Spread cracker crumbs evenly over mixture and drizzle with melted butter. Bake at 350° for 30 to 40 minutes.
Yield: 6 to 8 servings

Rock Cornish Game Hen

- 2 Cornish hens
- ¼ cup dry white wine or rose
- ¼ cup firmly-packed brown sugar
- ½ teaspoon salt
- 1 tablespoon vinegar
- 1 single-serving packet instant onion soup
- Dash of ground cloves

Wash and dry hens, cut in halves and place, cut side down, in baking dish lined with aluminum foil. Combine wine or rose, brown sugar, salt, vinegar, soup mix and cloves, mixing well. Drizzle 2 to 3 spoonfuls over hens. Bake at 350° for 1¼ hours, basting with remaining sauce at 20 minute intervals.
Yield: 4 servings

Frozen Turkey Breast

- 1 (6 to 7 pound) frozen turkey breast
- ½ teaspoon salt
- ½ teaspoon onion salt
- ½ teaspoon celery salt
- ½ teaspoon Accent or tenderizer
- 1 tablespoons sugar
- 2 tablespoons butter, melted

Wash and blot dry frozen turkey breast. Season with salt, onion salt, celery salt, Accent and sugar. Place turkey on heavy duty aluminum foil. Drizzle with butter. Overlapping foil 3 to 4 inches, wrap turkey and fold ends to enclose. Place in shallow baking pan. Bake at 450° for at least 3 hours for 6 pound turkey breast, open foil and bake for 20 to 30 minutes for browning; do not overbrown.
Yield: 8 to 10 servings

Crunchy Turkey Casserole

- 3 cups chopped cooked turkey
- 1 cup cooked rice
- 1 (8 ounce) can sliced water chestnuts, drained
- 1 cup chopped celery
- 2 tablespoons chopped onion
- ½ cup sliced almonds
- 1 (10¾ ounce) can cream of chicken soup
- ½ cup mayonnaise
- 1 cup corn flakes

Combine turkey, rice, water chestnuts, celery, onion, almonds, soup and mayonnaise, mixing thoroughly. Spread mixture in 2-quart casserole. Bake at 350° for 30 minutes, sprinkle corn flakes on top of mixture, and bake for additional 15 minutes.
Yield: 4 to 6 servings

Zesty Chicken Barbecue Sauce

- ½ cup chopped onion
- 1 clove garlic, crushed
- ¼ cup vegetable oil
- ½ cup water
- 1 cup ketchup
- ¼ cup firmly packed brown sugar
- 3 tablespoons Worcestershire sauce
- 2 teaspoons prepared mustard
- 1 lemon, thinly sliced
- 1 teaspoon salt
- ¼ teaspoon crushed dried thyme
- Dash of hot pepper sauce

Sauté onion and garlic in oil until tender. Stir in water, ketchup, brown sugar, Worcestershire sauce, mustard, lemon, salt, thyme and hot pepper sauce. Bring to a boil, reduce heat and simmer for 5 minutes. Use sauce to baste chicken during grilling.
Yield: 2½ cups

To remedy greasy gravy, add a small amount of baking soda.

Beef Tenderloin

- ¼ cup Worcestershire sauce
- Juice of 2 lemons
- 1 (7 to 8 pound) whole beef tenderloin, fat removed
- Ground celery seed
- Hickory smoke salt
- Seasoned salt
- Garlic powder
- Freshly ground black pepper
- Thyme
- Paprika

Combine Worcestershire sauce and lemon juice. Rub liquid into surface of tenderloin. Sprinkle tenderloin with celery seed, hickory smoke salt, seasoned salt, garlic powder, black pepper, thyme and paprika, rubbing each into surface. Chill for several hours or overnight. Preheat oven to 500°. Tuck thin tail of tenderloin under and secure with wooden pick. Place in shallow baking pan. Bake at 500° for 10 minutes, reduce heat to 350° and bake for about 25 additional minutes for rare roast. Use a meat thermometer for more precise roasting.
Yield: 8 dinner servings
12 to 16 cocktail buffet servings

Brandied Steak

- 1 pound (1-inch thickness) top round of beef
- Coarsely ground black pepper
- 1 tablespoon vegetable oil
- Salt
- 3 tablespoons brandy
- 3 tablespoons Worcestershire sauce
- 3 tablespoons margarine or butter

Using mallet, tenderize beef. Sprinkle with black pepper. Sear meat in oil in skillet at 350°, cooking 4 to 5 minutes on each side. Remove from skillet and sprinkle both sides with salt. Deglaze skillet with brandy. Bring to a boil and stir in Worcestershire sauce. Reduce heat and add butter or margarine. Slice beef in ½-inch strips and return to skillet. Heat until warm. Serve with toasted French bread and pour extra sauce into individual cups for dipping.
Yield: 2 servings

Slottsstek (Swedish Pot Roast)

- **4 pounds rump or round roast**
- **2 tablespoons butter**
- **2 tablespoons vegetable oil**
- **1 cup minced onion**
- **3 tablespoons all-purpose flour**
- **1 tablespoon dark corn syrup**
- **2 tablespoons white vinegar**
- **2 cups fresh or canned beef broth**
- **1 teaspoon peppercorns**
- **1 large bay leaf**
- **6 flat anchovy fillets, washed and dried**
- **Salt and black pepper to taste**
- **Red currant jelly**

Sear beef, turning to brown all sides, in butter and oil in oven-proof casserole or Dutch oven. Remove meat and set aside. Cook onions for 6 to 8 minutes or until medium brown. Remove casserole from heat and stir in flour, blending well. Add syrup, vinegar and broth. Crush peppercorns and secure in cheesecloth bag; add with bay leaf and anchovies to liquid mixture. Place meat in liquid, cover and bring to a boil. Transfer to oven and bake at 325 to 350° for 3 hours or until tender. Skim to remove excess fat and remove bay leaf. Serve with jelly.
Yield: 8 servings

Beef Milano

- **2 cloves garlic, minced**
- **2 tablespoons vegetable oil**
- **2½ pounds lean stewing beef, cut in 1½-inch cubes**
- **1 packet onion soup mix**
- **1 (6 ounce) can tomato paste**
- **1 tablespoon all-purpose flour**
- **1 teaspoon chili powder**
- **1 teaspoon oregano**
- **1 cup water**
- **2 (14½ ounce) cans tomatoes**
- **1 (16 ounce) package noodles**
- **Grated Parmesan cheese**

Sauté garlic in oil in Dutch oven or heavy skillet until golden. Add beef and brown well on all sides. Stir in soup mix, tomato paste, flour, chili powder, oregano, water and tomatoes. Bring to a boil, stirring frequently, then reduce heat and simmer for 2 to 2½ hours. Prepare noodles according to package directions. Serve beef with sauce over noodles and sprinkle with cheese.
Yield: 6 to 8 servings

Indonesian Beef Curry

- 2 pounds beef round steak, cut in 1-inch cubes
- ¼ cup plus 1 tablespoon vegetable oil, divided
- 1⅓ cups chopped onion
- 2 or 3 cloves garlic, mashed
- 1 teaspoon salt
- ¼ teaspoon black pepper
- ½ teaspoon monosodium glutamate
- 2 tablespoons curry powder
- 2 tablespoons beef bouillon granules
- 2 cups hot water
- 1 (8 ounce) can tomato sauce
- 1 tablespoon lemon juice
- Saffron rice (see index)

Sear beef in 3 tablespoons oil in large skillet, turning to brown on all sides. Remove and set aside. Add remaining 2 tablespoons oil to skillet. Sauté onion and garlic in oil until soft and lightly browned. Combine salt, black pepper, monosodium glutamate, curry powder and bouillon. Add to sautéed vegetables and cook, stirring constantly, for 2 to 3 minutes. Add water, tomato sauce and beef. Simmer, covered, for 1½ hours; remove cover and cook for additional 30 minutes or until meat is tender and sauce is thickened. Stir in lemon juice. Serve with saffron rice.
Yield: 4 servings

Barbecued Beef

- ⅓ cup Worcestershire sauce
- ⅓ cup soy sauce
- 3 tablespoons liquid smoke
- 4 to 6 pounds chuck, pot, blade or shoulder beef roast
- Coarsely ground black pepper
- 1 cup prepared barbecue sauce (optional)

Combine Worcestershire sauce, soy sauce and liquid smoke; do not use any salt. Place beef in heavy oven-proof pot with tightly-fitting lid. Pour sauce over beef and sprinkle with black pepper. Bake at 275° for at least 3 hours; longer baking time improves the flavor. One hour before serving, remove from oven, discard bone and fat, shred beef and add barbecue sauce; return to oven for 1 hour. Serve on warmed buns with cole slaw.
Yield: 12 to 16 servings

Smothered Beef and Rice

1½ pounds lean stewing beef, cut in bite-size cubes
1 (8 ounce) can tomato sauce
½ cup water
1 teaspoon sugar
1 teaspoon salt
⅛ teaspoon black pepper
½ teaspoon garlic powder
¼ teaspoon dry mustard
1 pound small onions
4 cups hot cooked rice

Sear beef large skillet sprayed with vegetable cooking spray, turning to brown on all sides. Reduce heat to low. Add tomato sauce, water, sugar, salt, black pepper, garlic powder and mustard to beef. Cook, covered, for 45 minutes. Add onions and cook, covered, for 50 minutes. Serve over rice.
Yield: 4 to 6 servings

Beef Tips with Rice

1 (10¾ ounce) can French onion soup, undiluted
1 (10¾ ounce) can brown gravy
1 pound lean stewing beef, cut in bite-size cubes
Salt and black pepper to taste
3 to 4 cups hot cooked rice or noodles

Blend soup and gravy in saucepan. Add beef and season with salt and black pepper. Simmer, covered, for 2 hours. Serve beef and sauce over rice or noodles.
Yield: 4 servings

Steak San Marco

1 to 2 pounds cubed chuck steak
½ packet onion soup mix
1 (14½ ounce) can tomatoes
2 tablespoons olive oil
1 tablespoon wine vinegar
1 (4 ounce) can sliced mushrooms
1 clove garlic, minced
Black pepper to taste
½ teaspoon oregano

Combine beef, soup mix, tomatoes, oil, vinegar, mushrooms, garlic, black pepper and oregano in 2-quart deep casserole. Bake at 325° for 1½ hours or until beef is tender.
Yield: 4 servings

Slow Cooker Barbecue

- 1½ pounds lean beef roast, fat trimmed
- 1½ pounds lean pork roast, fat trimmed
- 2 cups chopped onion
- 3 medium-sized green bell peppers, chopped
- 1 (8 ounce) can tomato sauce
- ¼ cup vinegar
- ½ cup firmly-packed light brown sugar
- 2 teaspoons salt
- 1 teaspoon dry mustard
- ¼ cup chili powder
- 2 teaspoons Worcestershire sauce

Combine beef, pork, onion, bell pepper, tomato sauce, vinegar, brown sugar, salt, dry mustard, chili powder and Worcestershire sauce in slow cooker. Cook at low setting for 12 to 14 hours. Stir with wire whisk to shred meat.

Yield: 6 to 8 servings

Chinese Pepper Steak

- 1 pound round steak
- ¼ cup vegetable oil
- 3 cloves garlic
- ½ cup coarsely chopped onion
- 2 cups green bell pepper, bite-sized pieces
- ¼ teaspoon ginger
- ½ teaspoon salt
- ¼ teaspoon black pepper
- 1 tablespoon cornstarch
- 1 cup beef bouillon
- 1 tablespoon soy sauce or to taste
- 3 to 4 cups hot cooked rice or chow mein noodles

Cut steak diagonally across grain with knife at slanted angle. Sauté garlic in oil in skillet over medium heat for 3 minutes. Remove garlic. Add beef to skillet, increase heat slightly and stir to brown evenly. Add onion, bell pepper and ginger. Cook, stirring constantly, for about 3 minutes. Blend salt, black pepper, cornstarch, bouillon and soy sauce. Stir into beef and vegetables. Bring to a boil and cook, stirring constantly, until thickened. Serve over rice or chow mein noodles.

Note: For Chinese mushroom steak, substitute 1 pound sliced mushrooms for bell pepper; for potato steak, substitute 2 cups diced cooked potatoes plus 1 cup coarsely chopped celery leaves for bell pepper, and for mixed vegetable steak, substitute 1 cup sliced mushrooms, 2 (8 ounce) cans bamboo shoots, 2 (8 ounce) cans sliced water chestnuts and ½ cup diagonally-sliced celery for bell pepper.

Yield: 4 servings

Chinese Beef

- 1 pound sirloin tip, cut in thin strips
- 4 teaspoons sugar
- 2 teaspoons cornstarch
- 4 teaspoons soy sauce
- 2 teaspoons burgundy
- ½ cup plus 2 tablespoons vegetable oil, divided
- 3 small green bell peppers, cut in bite-size pieces
- 2 stalks celery, chopped
- 1 medium-sized onion, thinly sliced
- 6 cups hot cooked rice

Combine sugar, cornstarch, soy sauce, wine and ½ cup oil. Pour over beef and marinate for at least 30 minutes. Drain marinade from beef. Cook beef in remaining 2 tablespoons oil in large skillet for 2 minutes. Remove beef. Add bell peppers, celery and onion to skillet and cook for about 5 minutes or until crisp tender. While vegetables cook, prepare sauce. Add beef and sauce to vegetables and cook for 1 minute. Serve over hot rice.

Yield: 6 servings

Sauce

- 1 teaspoon cornstarch
- 2 teaspoons sugar
- 1 tablespoon ketchup
- 1 teaspoon soy sauce
- ½ teaspoon Worcestershire sauce

Combine cornstarch and sugar. Blend in ketchup, soy sauce and Worcestershire sauce.

Easy All Day Stew

- 2 pounds lean stewing beef, cut in bite-sized cubes
- All-purpose flour
- Salt and black pepper to taste
- 2 tablespoons vegetable oil
- 2 (10¾ ounce) cans cream of mushroom soup, undiluted
- 1 packet onion soup mix
- 1 cup red wine
- 1 (4 ounce) can mushrooms or ¼ pound fresh mushrooms

Sprinkle beef with flour, salt and black pepper. Sear cubes in oil, turning to brown on all sides. Place beef, soup, soup mix, wine and mushrooms in slow cooker. Cook at low setting for 8 to 10 hours. Serve stew over rice or noodles.

Yield: 4 to 6 servings

Korean Flank Steak

- 3 tablespoons soy sauce
- 3 teaspoons vegetable oil
- ¼ cup minced green onion
- 1 teaspoon minced garlic
- 1 tablespoon minced ginger
- 1 tablespoon sugar
- 2 tablespoons sesame seeds
- 1 pound flank steak

Combine soy sauce, oil, onion, garlic, ginger, sugar and sesame seeds. Place beef in glass dish, add sauce, cover and marinate in refrigerator overnight. Grill beef to desired doneness and cut in very thin slices to serve.

Yield: 4 servings

Beef Broccoli Wellington

- 1 pound lean ground beef
- 1 cup (4 ounces) shredded mozzarella cheese
- ½ cup chopped onion
- ½ cup sour cream
- ¼ teaspoon salt
- ¼ teaspoon black pepper
- 1 (10 ounce) package frozen chopped broccoli, thawed and drained
- 2 (8 ounce) cans refrigerated crescent roll dough
- 1 egg, beaten
- Poppy seeds

Brown beef, stirring to crumble, in medium skillet. Drain excess fat. Add cheese, onion, sour cream, salt, black pepper and broccoli to beef. Simmer for 10 minutes and set aside. Separate each can of dough into 4 rectangles, pressing perforations to seal. Overlap long sides of 2 rectangles by ½ inch and press firmly to seal. Place on ungreased baking sheet and roll to form 13x7-inch rectangle. Spoon ½ of beef mixture in center of dough, bring long edges to center over filling, overlapping slightly and pinch edges and ends to seal. Repeat with remaining dough and beef mixture. Brush with egg and sprinkle with poppy seeds. Bake at 375° for 18 to 22 minutes or until pastry is deep golden brown.

Yield: 6 to 8 servings

San Antonio Fajitas

- ½ cup vegetable oil
- ½ cup water
- 3 tablespoons lemon juice
- 1 tablespoon wine vinegar
- 2 tablespoons minced onion
- ½ teaspoon garlic powder
- ½ teaspoon dried thyme
- ½ teaspoon chili powder
- 1 teaspoon dried oregano
- 2 pounds skirt steak
- 8 to 10 flour tortillas

Combine oil, water, lemon juice, vinegar, onion, garlic powder, thyme, chili powder and oregano. Place beef in glass dish, add sauce, cover and marinate in refrigerator for 6 to 8 hours, turning every couple hours. Grill beef over hot coals for about 10 minutes. Cut in very thin slices. Serve in flour tortillas with condiments (lettuce, tomatoes, sour cream and onions).
Yield: 4 to 5 servings

Steak Supreme

- 1 pound round steak, cut in ¼-inch strips
- 2 tablespoons vegetable oil
- 1 (4 ounce) can sliced mushrooms, undrained
- 1½ cups diagonally sliced celery (½-inch pieces)
- 1 cup sliced green bell pepper (½-inch pieces)
- 1 cup coarsely chopped onion
- 1 (10½ ounce) can French onion soup
- 2 tablespoons low-salt soy sauce
- ½ cup water
- 1 rounded tablespoon cornstarch
- 3 to 4 cups hot cooked rice

Sauté beef strips in oil, turning to brown on all sides. Add mushrooms, celery, bell pepper, onion, soup and soy sauce. Simmer, covered, for 20 minutes. Blend water and cornstarch until smooth. Add to beef mixture and cook until thickened. Serve over rice.
Yield: 4 servings

Always heat the frying pan before adding oil or butter. This will keep things from sticking to the pan.

Roma Meat Roll

- 1½ pounds lean ground beef
- 1 egg, lightly beaten
- ¾ cup cracker or breadcrumbs
- ½ cup minced onion
- 1 teaspoon salt
- ⅛ teaspoon black pepper
- ½ teaspoon oregano
- 2 (8 ounce) cans tomato sauce with cheese or regular tomato sauce plus¼ cup (1 ounce) grated Parmesan cheese, divided
- 2 cups (8 ounces) shredded mozzarella cheese

Combine beef, egg, cracker or breadcrumbs, onion, salt, black pepper and oregano with ⅓ cup tomato sauce, mixing well. On wax paper, shape beef mixture into 12x10-inch rectangle. Sprinkle mozzarella cheese on beef. Lifting long edge of wax paper to guide, roll beef mixture jelly roll style and press ends to seal in cheese. Place in 13x9x2-inch baking dish. Bake at 350° for 1 hour, drain excess fat, pour remaining tomato sauce over roll and bake for additional 15 minutes.
Yield: 4 to 6 servings

Hartzell's Meat Loaf

- 1 pound ground beef
- 1 pound ground turkey
- ¾ cup quick-cooking oats, uncooked
- 1 medium-sized onion, chopped
- 1 cup ketchup, divided
- ¼ cup skim milk
- 2 eggs, lightly beaten, or equivalent egg substitute
- 2 tablespoons prepared horseradish, divided
- 1 teaspoon salt
- ¼ teaspoon black pepper
- 3 tablespoons brown sugar
- 2 teaspoons prepared mustard

Combine beef, turkey, oats, onion, ½ cup ketchup, milk, eggs, 1 tablespoon horseradish, salt and black pepper. Shape into two 7½x4-inch loaves. Place on broiler pan prepared with vegetable spray. Bake at 350° for 40 minutes. Combine remaining ½ cup ketchup, 1 tablespoon horseradish, brown sugar and mustard, spread over loaves and bake for additional 5 minutes.

Note: Loaves, cooled and wrapped in heavy-duty aluminum foil, can be frozen. Thaw in refrigerator overnight and bake in foil at 350° for 45 minutes.
Yield: 8 servings

Jackie's Meat Loaf

- 1 pound lean ground beef
- 1 cup breadcrumbs
- ½ medium-sized onion, chopped
- 1 (8 ounce) can tomato sauce, divided
- 1 egg, beaten
- 1½ teaspoons salt
- ¼ teaspoon black pepper
- ¼ medium-sized green bell pepper, chopped
- 2 tablespoons prepared mustard
- 2 tablespoons brown sugar
- ½ cup water
- 2 tablespoons vinegar

Combine beef, breadcrumbs, onion, ½ can tomato sauce, egg, salt, black pepper and bell pepper. Shape mixture into loaf and place in shallow baking pan. Combine remaining ½ can tomato sauce, mustard, brown sugar, water and vinegar. Bake loaf at 350° for 1 hour, basting with sauce several times.

Yield: 4 to 6 servings

William's Meat Loaf

- 4 slices bread or toast, torn in pieces
- 1 cup warm milk
- 2 eggs, beaten
- ½ cup minced onion
- 1 teaspoon salt
- ¼ teaspoon black pepper
- 1 teaspoon garlic salt
- ¼ cup steak sauce
- 1 (4 ounce) can sliced mushrooms, drained
- ½ cup chopped celery
- ½ cup chopped celery leaves
- ½ pound ground pork
- 1 pound lean ground beef
- ½ pound ground veal
- 1 tablespoon vegetable oil
- 1 beef bouillon cube
- ½ cup hot water
- 1 (14½ ounce) can Italian style tomatoes, crushed
- 1 medium-sized green bell pepper, sliced in ½-inch strips

Soften bread or toast in milk. Combine bread with milk, eggs, onion, salt, black pepper, garlic salt, steak sauce, mushrooms, celery, celery leaves, pork, beef and veal, mixing well. Shape into loaf and place in greased 13x9x2-inch baking pan. Drizzle oil over loaf. Dissolve bouillon in hot water and pour into pan. Add crushed tomatoes with juice. Bake at 350° for 1¾ hours to 2 hours, basting with pan juices at 15 minutes intervals during final 30 minutes baking time. Arrange bell pepper strips on loaf.

Note: Chunks of potato and carrots can be added around loaf before baking for a one-dish meal. Recipe makes a moist, well-flavored meat loaf.

Yield: 8 servings

Stuffed Peppers

- 1 small onion, minced
- 2 tablespoons bacon fat or butter
- 1 pound lean ground beef
- 1¼ cups breadcrumbs
- 1 teaspoon sugar
- 1½ teaspoons salt
- Pinch of black pepper
- 1 (16 ounce) can tomato puree
- 1 tablespoon vinegar
- 4 large or 6 medium-sized green bell peppers
- Boiling water
- ½ cup water
- Ketchup or chili sauce to taste

Sauté onion in fat or butter in skillet until softened and yellow. Add beef and cook until lightly browned and moisture is evaporated. Combine beef mixture, breadcrumbs, sugar, salt, black pepper, puree and vinegar. Cut large bell peppers in halves lengthwise or cut slice from tops of smaller bell peppers. Remove seeds. Cover peppers with boiling water, let stand for 5 minutes and drain. Spoon beef mixture into peppers and place in shallow baking dish. Add ½ cup water to skillet, heat and pour over stuffed peppers. Bake, covered, at 350° for about 20 minutes; remove cover, increase heat, add small amount of ketchup or chili sauce to top of each pepper and bake for additional 20 minutes or until browned. If necessary, add small amount of water to dish during baking to prevent sticking.
Yield: 6 to 8 servings

Beef Casserole

- 1 pound lean ground beef
- 1 small onion, chopped
- 1 (14½ ounce) can tomatoes, sliced or cut up
- ½ teaspoon salt
- 1 (10¾ ounce) can cream of mushrooms soup, undiluted
- ½ cup chopped green bell pepper
- ½ (8 ounce) package egg noodles
- 1 cup (4 ounces) grated Cheddar cheese, divided

Brown beef with onions in large skillet, stirring to crumble. Drain excess fat. Add tomatoes, salt, soup and bell pepper to beef. Simmer beef mixture while preparing egg noodles according to package directions. Drain noodles and add with ½ cup cheese to beef mixture. Spread in 9x9x2-inch baking dish and sprinkle with remaining ½ cup cheese. Bake at 350° for 15 minutes.
Yield: 4 servings

Italian Delight

- 2 pounds ground round steak
- 1 medium-sized onion, chopped
- 1 medium-sized green bell pepper, chopped
- 1 (8 ounce) package egg noodles or vermicelli
- 1 (16 ounce) can whole kernel corn, drained
- 1 cup condensed tomato soup
- 1 (8 ounce) can tomato sauce
- 1¼ cups (5 ounces) grated mellow Cheddar cheese

Brown beef with onion and bell pepper, stirring to crumble beef, until beef is done. Drain excess fat. Prepare noodles according to package directions and drain. Combine beef mixture, noodles, corn, tomato soup, tomato sauce and cheese. Spread mixture in 2 to 3-quart casserole. Bake at 350° for 30 to 45 minutes.
Yield: 6 to 8 servings

Six Layer Casserole

- 2 cups sliced raw potatoes
- 2 cups chopped celery
- 1 pound lean ground beef
- 1 cup chopped onion
- 1 cup finely diced green bell pepper
- 2 cups cooked tomatoes
- ¾ cup tomato juice (optional)
- 2 teaspoons salt
- ¼ teaspoon black pepper
- Green bell pepper rings (optional)

Layer potatoes, celery, beef, onion, diced bell pepper and tomatoes in greased 2-quart casserole, seasoning each layer with salt and black pepper. Garnish with bell pepper rings. Bake, covered, at 350° for 2 hours.

Note: Casserole can be varied by substituting ground turkey for beef, 2 (14½ ounce) cans stewed tomatoes for tomatoes, 1 teaspoon celery salt for chopped celery or by omitting bell pepper. To reduce fat in casserole, crumble ground beef or turkey in microwave-safe colander over bowl. Microwave at high (100%) setting for 8 minutes, stirring and breaking up meat with fork at 2 minute intervals. Add onion after 6 minutes. Assemble casserole by layering potatoes, celery salt, beef-onion mixture, tomatoes and tomato juice in dish. Season with black pepper. Bake at 350° for 2 hours.
Yield: 6 servings

Spicy Beef-Mac Casserole

3 medium-sized onions, sliced
¼ cup vegetable oil
1 pound ground round steak
2 (14½ ounce) cans tomatoes
2 teaspoons salt
¼ teaspoon black pepper
¼ teaspoon garlic salt
1 teaspoon dried rosemary
1 teaspoon parsley flakes
½ teaspoon celery seed
1 teaspoon hot pepper sauce
2 teaspoons Worcestershire sauce
1 cup milk
1 (10¾ ounce) can cream of mushroom soup, undiluted
2 cups (8 ounces) grated Cheddar cheese
1 (16 ounce) package small shell macaroni
¼ cup cracker crumbs

Sauté onion in oil in large skillet until lightly browned. Add beef and cook until lightly browned, stirring to crumble. Drain excess fat. Add tomatoes, salt, black pepper, garlic salt, rosemary, parsley, celery seed, hot pepper sauce and Worcestershire sauce to beef. Bring to a boil, reduce heat and simmer. In saucepan, blend milk with soup. Add cheese and heat until melted. Prepare macaroni according to package directions and drain well. Combine beef mixture, cheese mixture and macaroni. Spread in two 2-quart casseroles. Sprinkle with crumbs. Bake at 350° for 35 to 40 minutes or until browned and bubbly.

Note: Casserole can be assembled and frozen. Thaw before baking.
Yield: 12 servings

Ground Steak Casserole

1 pound ground round steak
1 (10¾ ounce) can cream of mushroom soup, undiluted
Salt to taste
Seasoning to taste

Shape beef into 4 patties. Sear on both sides in small amount of fat in skillet. Place in 9x9x2-inch baking dish. Blend soup with salt and preferred seasonings. Spoon soup over beef patties. Bake, covered, at 350° for 30 minutes. Serve with rice or whipped potatoes.

Note: Casserole can be assembled early in day and baked just before serving.
Yield: 4 servings

Company Casserole

1 (8 ounce) package narrow egg noodles
1 (10 ounce) package frozen chopped spinach
1 pound lean ground beef
1 (6 ounce) can tomato paste
1 teaspoon Worcestershire sauce
Few drops of hot pepper sauce
Salt to taste
¼ teaspoon oregano
1 cup low-fat cottage cheese
½ (8 ounce) package low-fat cream cheese, softened
½ cup low-fat sour cream
1 medium-sized onion, chopped
½ cup butter, melted
½ cup (2 ounces) grated sharp Cheddar cheese

Prepare noodles according to package directions, drain, rinse with hot water and set aside. Prepare spinach according to package directions, drain and set aside. Brown beef in skillet, stirring to crumble. Drain excess fat. Add tomato paste, Worcestershire sauce, hot pepper sauce, salt and oregano to beef, mixing well. Combine cottage cheese, cream cheese, sour cream and onions. In order listed in greased 2-quart casserole, layer ½ of noodles, ¼ cup butter, cheese mixture, spinach, remaining noodles, remaining ¼ cup butter and beef mixture. Sprinkle Cheddar cheese on beef layer. Bake, covered, at 350° for 30 to 40 minutes or until bubbly; remove cover for final 5 minutes baking time to brown.

Note: Casserole can be frozen.
Yield: 5 or 6 servings

For extra juicy, extra nutritious hamburgers, add ¼ cup evaporated milk per pound of meat before shaping.

Lasagna—Microwave

- 6 lasagna noodles
- 1 pound ground beef or turkey
- ½ cup chopped onion
- 1 tablespoon vegetable oil
- 3 (8 ounce) cans tomato sauce
- 1 (6 ounce) can tomato paste
- 1 teaspoon salt, divided
- 1 tablespoon dried oregano
- 2 teaspoons basil
- ¼ teaspoon garlic powder or 1 clove garlic, minced
- 2 cups ricotta cheese or small curd cottage cheese
- 1 egg
- 1 tablespoon parsley flakes
- 1½ cups (6 ounces) grated mozzarella or provolone cheese
- ¼ cup (1 ounce) grated Parmesan cheese

Prepare noodles according to package directions, drain and set aside. While noodles cook, brown beef or turkey, stirring to crumble. Drain excess fat and set meat aside. Sauté onion in oil until tender. Combine onion, tomato sauce, tomato paste, ½ teaspoon salt, oregano, basil and garlic, mixing well. Spread ½ cup sauce in 12x8x2-inch baking dish. Combine beef mixture with remaining sauce. In separate bowl, mix ricotta or cottage cheese, egg, parsley and remaining ½ teaspoon salt. Layer 3 noodles, ½ of cheese mixture, ½ of mozzarella or provolone cheese and ½ of tomato sauce in dish; repeat layers and sprinkle top with Parmesan cheese. Microwave, covered with wax paper, at high (100%) setting for 20 to 26 minutes, rotating dish ¼ turn at 8 minute intervals. Let stand 10 minutes before cutting to serve.

Note: Casserole can be assembled in advance and refrigerated. Add 4 to 6 minutes to cooking time for chilled casserole.

Yield: 8 to 12 servings

Jackie's Special Lasagna

- 3 pounds lean ground beef
- 1 cup chopped onion
- 1½ cloves garlic, pressed
- 1 tablespoon parsley flakes
- 3 (28 ounce) cans tomatoes, crushed
- 2 (14½ ounce) cans whole tomatoes
- 2 (15 ounce) cans tomato sauce
- 1 (6 ounce) can tomato paste
- 1 (6 ounce) can water
- 1 tablespoon salt
- ½ teaspoon black pepper
- 1 tablespoon dried oregano
- 3 tablespoons sugar
- 1½ (16 ounce) packages lasagna noodles, uncooked
- 2 cups cottage cheese
- 4 cups (16 ounces) shredded mozzarella cheese
- ¾ cup (3 ounces) grated Parmesan cheese

Brown beef in Dutch oven, stirring to crumble. Add onion, garlic and parsley and sauté for 5 minutes. Drain excess fat. Add tomatoes, tomato sauce, tomato paste, water, salt, black pepper, oregano and sugar to beef mixture. Bring to a boil, reduce heat and simmer for 3 to 4 hours. Spread small amount of sauce in greased 15x11x2-inch baking pan and 13x9x2-inch baking pan. Using about ½ of ingredients, layer uncooked noodles, cottage cheese, mozzarella cheese, sauce and Parmesan cheese in each pan; repeat layers. Bake, covered, at 350° for 45 minutes. Let stand before cutting to serve.

Note: Casserole can be assembled and frozen. Thaw before baking.
Yield: 16 servings

Mary Mason's Hamburger Quiche

- ½ pound lean ground beef
- ½ cup mayonnaise
- ½ cup milk
- 2 eggs, lightly beaten
- 1 tablespoon cornstarch
- 1½ cups (6 ounces) grated sharp cheese
- ⅓ cup sliced green onion
- Salt and black pepper to taste
- 1 unbaked 9-inch pastry shell

Brown beef, stirring to crumble. Drain excess fat. Combine mayonnaise, milk, eggs and cornstarch, mixing until smooth. Add beef, cheese, onion, salt and black pepper. Pour mixture into pastry shell. Bake at 350° for 35 to 40 minutes or until golden brown; knife tip inserted in center of quiche should come out clean.
Yield: 6 servings

Five Spice Beef in Rice

- 1 pound lean ground chuck
- 2 tablespoons olive oil
- ¼ cup minced onion
- 1½ teaspoons salt
- Dash of black pepper
- 1 bay leaf
- ⅛ teaspoon garlic powder
- ⅛ teaspoon thyme
- ⅛ teaspoon oregano
- 1 (10¾ ounce) can cream of mushroom soup, undiluted
- 1 (14½ ounce) can tomatoes
- 1 cup instant rice
- Grated cheese
- Sliced olives (optional)

Brown beef in Dutch oven, stirring to crumble. Add onion and cook until tender. Drain excess fat. Add salt, black pepper, bay leaf, garlic powder, thyme, oregano, soup, tomatoes and rice to beef. Bring to a boil, reduce heat and simmer for 5 minutes, stirring occasionally. Remove bay leaf. Pour mixture into 1½-quart casserole. Sprinkle with cheese and olives. Bake at 350° for 25 minutes.
Yield: 4 servings

Hominy Pie

- 1½ pounds lean ground chuck
- 1 medium-sized onion, chopped
- 2½ tablespoons margarine
- 1 large green bell pepper, chopped
- 1 clove garlic, chopped
- 2 tablespoons all-purpose flour
- 1 (28 ounce) can tomatoes
- Salt and black pepper to taste
- 1 tablespoon chili powder
- Pinch of sugar
- 2 (16 ounce) cans hominy, drained
- 1 cup (4 ounces) grated medium sharp cheese

Brown beef and onion in margarine, stirring to crumble. Add bell pepper and garlic. Sprinkle flour over beef mixture. Stir in tomatoes, salt, black pepper, chili powder and sugar. Simmer, covered, to blend flavors, stirring often. Add hominy to sauce. Pour mixture into 2½-quart casserole and sprinkle with cheese. Bake at 350° for 50 minutes.

Note: A good main dish for a cold evening, serve with fruit salad and cornbread.
Yield: 6 servings

Hamburger Pie

Filling

- 1 pound lean ground beef
- 1 medium-sized onion, chopped
- 2 cups cooked tomatoes or 1 (14½ ounce) can tomatoes
- 1 (8 ounce) can tomato sauce
- 3 tablespoons grated Parmesan cheese
- 1 tablespoon sugar
- ½ teaspoon salt
- ⅛ teaspoon black pepper
- 1 teaspoon basil
- ½ teaspoon garlic salt
- ½ teaspoon oregano
- 6 slices Cheddar cheese

Brown meat and onion together in large skillet, stirring beef to crumble. Drain excess fat. Add tomatoes, tomato sauce, Parmesan cheese, sugar, salt, black pepper, basil, garlic salt and oregano. Simmer, covered, for 30 minutes. While beef mixture cooks, prepare pastry. Pour beef filling into pastry shell. Arrange Cheddar cheese on filling. Roll out remaining pastry, cut with 2-inch cutter and place pastry circles on cheese, overlapping slightly. Bake at 400° for 35 minutes or until browned.

Yield: 4 to 6 servings

Pastry

- 1½ cups all-purpose flour
- 1 teaspoon garlic salt
- 1 teaspoon oregano
- ¼ cup (1 ounce) grated Parmesan or Romano cheese
- ½ cup butter
- ¼ cup plus 1 tablespoon cold water

Combine flour, garlic salt, oregano and Parmesan or Romano cheese. Using pastry blender, cut in butter until consistency of fine crumbs. Add water and mix to form dough. Roll out ⅔ of dough to fit 9-inch pie plate. Place in pie plate, trimming edges.

Adam's Stew

- 1 cup chopped onion
- 1 cup chopped green bell pepper
- ¼ cup olive oil
- 2 pounds lean ground beef
- 1 (16 ounce) can red kidney beans, drained
- 1 (16 ounce) can whole kernel corn, drained
- 1 (28 ounce) can Italian style tomatoes
- 2 (8 ounce) cans tomato sauce
- 1 tablespoon steak sauce
- Salt and black pepper to taste
- Dried basil to taste
- Dried mustard to taste

Sauté onion and bell pepper in oil in skillet until onion is golden. Add beef and cook, stirring often, until browned. Drain excess fat. Stir in beans, corn, tomatoes, tomato sauce, steak sauce, salt, black pepper, basil and mustard, mixing well. Simmer, covered, for 15 to 20 minutes.

Note: A family favorite, serve with a green salad and garlic bread.
Yield: 8 to 10 servings

Texas Chili

- 2 pounds lean ground beef
- 3 large onions, chopped
- 3 (16 ounce) cans chili hot beans
- 1 (8 ounce) can tomato sauce
- 1 (6 ounce) can tomato paste
- 2 teaspoons salt
- ½ cup chili powder
- 2 tablespoons cumin
- 1 teaspoon garlic powder
- 1 teaspoon paprika
- 2 to 3 teaspoons hot pepper sauce
- 4 cups water

Brown beef in skillet, stirring to crumble. Drain excess fat and place beef in 5-quart Dutch oven. Sauté onion until tender. Add onion, beans, tomato sauce, tomato paste, salt, chili powder, cumin, garlic powder, paprika, hot pepper sauce and water to beef. Bring to a boil, reduce heat and simmer for 1 to 1½ hours.
Yield: 10 to 12 servings

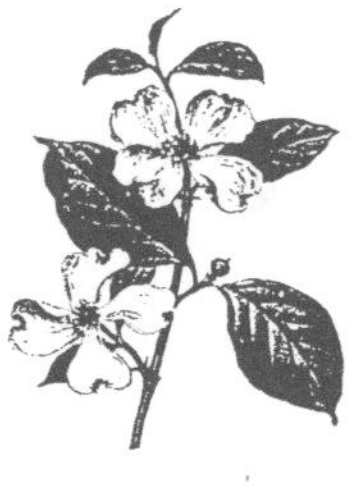

Three Bean Chili

- 1 pound lean ground beef
- 1 large onion, chopped
- 1 large green bell pepper, chopped
- 1 (14½ ounce) can diced tomatoes
- 1 (16 ounce) can black beans, undrained
- 1 (16 ounce) can pinto beans, undrained
- 1 (16 ounce) can kidney beans, undrained
- 1 teaspoon basil
- 1 teaspoon chili powder or to taste
- 1 teaspoon cumin
- 1 cup red wine or to taste

Sauté beef, onion and bell pepper together in Dutch oven until beef is browned. Drain excess fat. Combine beef mixture, tomatoes, black beans, pinto beans, kidney beans, basil, chili powder, cumin and wine. Simmer until thoroughly heated.

Yield: 6 to 8 servings

Barbecue Sauce

- 1 cup vegetable oil or butter, melted
- 1 cup chili sauce
- 1 cup tomato puree or tomato sauce
- ¼ cup vinegar
- 2 tablespoons lemon juice
- 2 tablespoons Worcestershire sauce
- ¼ cup firmly-packed brown sugar
- ¾ cup minced onion
- 1 teaspoon salt
- 1 teaspoon black pepper
- 1 teaspoon garlic powder
- 1 teaspoon horseradish
- ½ teaspoon dry or prepared mustard
- ⅛ teaspoon cayenne pepper (optional)

Combine oil or butter, chili sauce, tomato puree or sauce, vinegar, lemon juice and Worcestershire sauce in saucepan. Stir in brown sugar, onion, salt, black pepper, garlic powder, horseradish, mustard and cayenne pepper. Simmer for about 10 minutes. Store in refrigerator.

Note: Sauce is good with all meats, especially brisket, on the grill.

Yield: 4 cups

Dry Rub for Barbecue

Chicken

- **3 tablespoons salt**
- **1 tablespoon black pepper**
- **1 tablespoon paprika**
- **2 tablespoons garlic powder**
- **1 tablespoon dry mustard**
- **1 teaspoon crumbled bay leaf**

Ribs

- **3 tablespoons salt**
- **1 tablespoon black pepper**
- **1 tablespoon paprika**
- **1 tablespoon lemon powder**
- **¼ cup plus 2 tablespoons sugar**

Combine seasonings as listed. Rub mixture on all surfaces of meat before grilling.
Yield: ½ cup for chicken
¾ cup for ribs

Roast and Steak Marinade

- **1½ cups vegetable oil**
- **¾ cup soy sauce**
- **½ cup red wine vinegar**
- **⅓ cup lemon juice**
- **¼ cup Worcestershire sauce**
- **2 cloves garlic, minced**
- **1 tablespoon black pepper**
- **2 tablespoons dry mustard**
- **1½ teaspoons parsley flakes**

Combine oil, soy sauce, wine vinegar, lemon juice and Worcestershire sauce. Blend in garlic, black pepper, mustard and parsley. Marinate meat for 12 hours or overnight in refrigerator, turning at least once.
Yield: 3 ⅓ cups

Reuben Casserole

- **4 slices rye bread, cubed**
- **1 (16 ounce) package or can sauerkraut, drained**
- **1 (12 ounce) can corned beef, shredded**
- **1 cup sour cream**
- **¼ cup minced onion**
- **2 cups (8 ounces) shredded mozzarella cheese**
- **1 cup (4 ounces) shredded Swiss cheese**
- **¼ cup butter, melted**

Spread ½ of bread cubes in greased 2-quart casserole. In order listed, layer sauerkraut, corned beef, cream, onion, mozzarella cheese and Swiss cheese on bread cubes. Top with remaining bread cubes and drizzle with butter. Bake at 350° for 30 to 35 minutes.
Yield: 4 to 6 servings

Veal Parmesan

2 tablespoons butter
½ cup plus 2 tablespoons grated Parmesan cheese, divided
¼ cup all-purpose flour
¼ teaspoon salt
Dash of black pepper
4 veal cutlets
1 (5 ounce) can evaporated milk, divided
1 (8 ounce) can tomato sauce
1 tablespoon brown sugar

Melt butter in 12x8x2-inch baking pan. Combine 2 tablespoons Parmesan cheese, flour, salt and black pepper. Dip veal pieces in ⅓ cup evaporated milk and roll in seasoned flour. Place in baking pan. Bake, uncovered, at 350° for 30 minutes. Blend tomato sauce and brown sugar. Pour into pan around veal. Combine ⅓ cup evaporated milk and remaining ½ cup Parmesan cheese. Spoon mixture over veal. Bake for additional 20 to 25 minutes or until tender.
Yield: 4 servings

Veal Parmigiano

1 pound thinly sliced veal
Salt and black pepper to taste
1 egg, lightly beaten
¼ cup plus 1 tablespoon water
½ cup breadcrumbs
3 tablespoons vegetable shortening
1 (10½ ounce) can tomato soup, undiluted
¼ cup minced onion
1 small clove garlic, minced
Dash of thyme
4 slices mozzarella cheese
¼ cup (1 ounce) grated Parmesan cheese

Pound veal to flatten. Season with salt and black pepper. Beat egg and 1 tablespoon water together. Dip veal in egg mixture, then in breadcrumbs. Brown veal in shortening in skillet. Arrange pieces in 12x8x2-inch baking dish. Combine soup, remaining ¼ cup water, onion, garlic and thyme. Pour over veal. Arrange mozzarella cheese on veal and sprinkle with Parmesan cheese. Bake at 350° for 30 minutes.
Yield: 4 servings

Country Ham—Wood Stove Perfect

- Country ham
- 1 tablespoon sugar
- Water
- ½ cup coffee (optional)

Place country ham in cold heavy skillet. Cook over very low heat, browning on 1 side, then turning to brown on second side. Snip slits in fat but do not trim all of it from ham. To prepare brown gravy, remove ham from skillet. Heat sugar in skillet until browned. Add water and coffee, cooking until gravy consistency.

Contributor: Dorothy Powers
Laura's Restaurant

Ham and Artichoke Casserole

- ¼ cup butter or margarine
- ¼ cup all-purpose flour
- 2 cups milk, warmed
- Generous dash of seasoned salt
- Pinch of white pepper
- Generous dash of cayenne pepper
- ½ teaspoon nutmeg
- ⅔ cup (2½ ounces) shredded Swiss cheese
- ¼ cup dry sherry
- 2 (14 ounce) cans artichoke hearts, drained
- 12 thin slices boiled or baked ham
- ⅔ cup (2½ ounces) grated Parmesan cheese

Melt butter in saucepan over medium heat. Blend in flour until smooth. Remove from heat and gradually stir in milk until smooth. Cook, stirring constantly, until thickened. Add seasonings and Swiss cheese. Cook over low heat until cheese is melted. Remove from heat and stir in sherry. If artichoke hearts are large, cut in halves. Place 2 halves on ham slice, roll up and place in buttered 12x8x2-inch casserole. Pour sauce over rolls and sprinkle with Parmesan cheese. Bake at 350° for 30 minutes or until browned and bubbly.
Yield: 6 servings

Sweet and Pungent Pork

2 eggs, beaten
1 cup all-purpose flour
1 teaspoon salt
2 cups water, divided
1 1l2 pounds pork, cubed
Peanut oil
3 medium-sized green bell peppers, cut in strips
2 cups pineapple chunks, drained
¾ cup firmly-packed brown sugar
1 cup vinegar
3 tablespoons molasses
Freshly ground black pepper
3 medium tomatoes, peeled and quartered
½ cup chopped sweet pickle
1 tablespoon cornstarch

Combine eggs, flour, salt and ¼ cup water. Add pork and stir until coated. Fry pork in 2-inch depth of oil at 375° for 3 minutes or until golden brown. Drain well and keep warm. Combine bell peppers, pineapple, brown sugar, vinegar, molasses, black pepper and 1½ cups water. Bring to a boil, stirring constantly. Add tomatoes and simmer for 5 minutes. Stir in sweet pickles. Blend cornstarch with remaining ¼ cup water. Add to bell pepper mixture and cook until thickened, stirring constantly. Add pork and simmer for 15 minutes.

Note: Chicken can be substituted for pork.
Yield: 6 servings

Kitty's Barbecued Pork Tenderloin

½ cup soy sauce
2½ tablespoons sesame oil
2 teaspoons fresh lime juice
2 teaspoons rice wine vinegar
1½ tablespoons minced garlic
1½ teaspoons ground ginger
½ teaspoon sugar
1 (3 pound) pork tenderloin, fat trimmed

Combine soy sauce, oil, lime juice, vinegar, garlic, ginger and sugar. Place tenderloin in 13x9x2-inch baking dish. Pour marinade over tenderloin, turning several times to coat thoroughly. Cover with plastic wrap. Marinate in refrigerator for about 3 hours, turning at 1 hour intervals. Drain marinade from tenderloin. Grill, turning and basting often with marinade, over medium-hot coals for about 45 minutes to 1 hour or until meat thermometer reaches 150°. Let stand at least 10 minutes before cutting in thin diagonal slices, arrange on serving platter and drizzle with Kitty's Barbecue Sauce or serve sauce on side.

Note: Slow and medium-low are the secrets to cooking a whole pork loin on the grill. Turn and baste the meat often. Do not let burn.
Yield: 8 servings

Kitty's Barbecue Sauce

- 1 medium-sized onion, slivered
- 2 tablespoons vegetable oil
- 4 cloves garlic, cut in halves
- 1½ cups ketchup
- 1 cup fresh orange juice
- ¼ cup plus 2 tablespoons fresh lemon juice
- ¼ cup plus 2 tablespoons red wine vinegar
- ½ cup water
- ¼ cup honey
- 2 tablespoons all-natural liquid smoke
- 2 tablespoons dark molasses
- 1 tablespoon Worcestershire sauce
- ¼ cup firmly-packed dark brown sugar
- 3 tablespoons finely chopped crystallized ginger
- ¼ teaspoon hot pepper sauce or more to taste
- 2 tablespoons chili powder
- 1 tablespoon ground coriander
- 1 tablespoon dry mustard
- 1 teaspoon salt or more to taste

Sauté onion in oil in heavy saucepan over medium heat for 5 to 7 minutes or until golden, adding garlic during last minute of cooking time. Stir in ketchup, orange juice, lemon juice, vinegar, water, honey, liquid smoke, molasses, Worcestershire sauce, brown sugar, ginger, hot pepper sauce, chili powder, coriander, mustard and salt, mixing well. Bring to a boil, reduce heat and simmer, stirring often, for 45 minutes to 1 hour or until sauce is thickened and smooth. Using slotted spoon, remove onion and garlic and discard. Check seasonings and adjust as necessary. If sauce is too thick, add small amount of water. Cool to room temperature and store in refrigerator in covered container for up to 2 weeks.
Yield: 5 cups

Brown Rice and Pork Chop Casserole

- 1 cup uncooked brown or white rice
- 2 tablespoons butter or margarine
- 2 beef bouillon cubes
- 2 cups boiling water
- 4 pork tenderloin chops
- Salt and black pepper to taste

Brown rice in butter or margarine, stirring constantly. Add bouillon to boiling water and stir until dissolved. Pour over rice, then pour rice into 12x8x2-inch baking dish. Bake, tightly covered with aluminum foil, at 300° for 20 minutes. While rice is baking, season pork with salt and black pepper, then brown pork in skillet used for preparing rice. Place pork on partially baked rice, cover and bake for additional 20 minutes.
Yield: 4 servings

Desserts & Sweets

More than any other food, desserts seem to elicit memories. No matter what your age, if your favorite childhood dessert was banana pudding, grandmother, mother or great aunt still produces an elegant crystal bowl of humble banana pudding for you when you visit. There is so much love in the offering. It says, "I remember you when you were little and I love you now as I did then."

Carolina cooks are known for their banana puddings, rich pound cakes, fruit pies and cookies which are often heavy with pecans. Gone are the days when we stained our fingers shelling pecans; they are now beautifully packaged in the stores, already shelled. In days past we even had "pie safes" in the kitchen. The "pie safe" was not under lock and key but was a simply constructed cupboard with pierced tin doors into which were placed the freshly baked pies.

Though we now have enormous refrigerators for storage, we have so little time. So if it is not a tradition to always take Congo Bars on picnics or to travel to your son's college Parents' Weekend with his favorite Brown Sugar Pound Cake, perhaps it is time to choose to make one of our desserts. Take the time to start your own family tradition and make a warm food memory.

Cakes

Ingredients

The key to a good cake is in the batter. Allow butter, vegetable shortening, cream cheese and eggs to reach room temperature before using. Butter or shortening beaten with sugar should resemble whipped cream. Vanilla should be added to the creamed butter and sugar mixture as the butter will better absorb and distribute the flavor.

It is best to use cake flour for all cakes as it produces larger, more velvet-textured cakes with greater uniformity in texture. Combine dry ingredients in a bowl and whisk to mix thoroughly, instead of sifting. Coat raisins, dates and berries with a portion of the flour to prevent the fruit from settling to the bottom of the cake.

Pans

To make removal of the cake from the pan easier, grease or oil the bottom and sides and dust with flour. A large kitchen salt shaker is handy for that purpose. For chocolate cake, use cocoa rather than flour to dust the pan. Invert the pan over the sink and tap to dislodge loose flour. For even easier removal, grease bottom of pan, line with wax paper, grease the paper and then dust with flour. Cool cake in pan for 10 minutes, then invert and it will slip out easily.

If a recipe calls for:	You may use:
1 or 2 eggs with 1 to 2 cups flour	8x8x2-inch pan or two 8-inch round layer pans
2 eggs with 2½ cups flour	9x9x2-inch pan or 10x10x2-inch pan or two 9-inch round layer pans
4 eggs with 2 to 3 cups flour	13x9x2-inch pan or 12x10x2-inch pan or two 9-inch round layer pans or three 8-inch round layer pans
6 egg whites and 2½ cups flour	14x10x2-inch pan or three 9-inch round layer pans
8 or more egg whites with 2½ cups flour	14x10x2-inch pan

Pan Sizes

If a recipe calls for:	**Substitute:**
two 8-inch layers	2 thin 8x8x2-inch pans or 18 to 24 cupcakes
three 8-inch layers	two 9x9x2-inch pans
two 9-inch layers	two 8x8x2-inch pans, 3 thin 8-inch layers, 15x10x1-inch jelly roll pan or 30 cupcakes
8x8x2-inch pan	one 9-inch layer
two 8x8x2-inch pans	two 9-inch layers or 13x9x2-inch pan
9x9x2-inch pan	2 thin 8-inch layers
two 9x9x2-inch pans	three 8-inch layers
13x9x2-inch pan	two 9-inch layers or two 8x8x2-inch pans
12x8x2-inch layer	two 8-inch layers
9x5x3-inch loaf	9x9x2-inch pan or 24 to 30 cupcakes
8x4x3-inch loaf	8x8x2-inch pan
9x3½-inch tube	two 9-inch layers or 24 to 30 cupcakes
10x4-inch tube	two 9x5x3-inch loafs, 13x9x2-inch pan or 15x10x1-inch jelly roll pan

Frosting

When frosting a layer cake, place 2 pieces wax paper about 5 inches wide on plate, covering it. Place cake on paper and frost. When finished, slip wax paper from beneath cake, leaving plate clean.

To frost cupcakes quickly, dip top of each into soft frosting, twirl and turn right side up.

For party cupcake cones, fill flat-bottomed ice cream cones ½ full with cake batter. Place cones in muffin pans. Bake according to package directions. Cool before frosting and decorating.

Cookies

Preparation

Cookies are easy and fun to make and there are many favorite recipes. Keep these tips in mind to make preparation easier.

When making rich butter cookies, combine dry ingredients and creamed mixture thoroughly to avoid a crumbly dough. For recipes with chopped raisins and marshmallows, cut them with scissors instead of knife. Chill cookie dough for 10 minutes to reduce the amount of flour needed when rolling; excess flour makes cookies tough. Or use powdered sugar instead of flour on rolling surface; cookies will be sweeter. For thin rolled cookies, roll dough on greased and floured baking sheet, cut in shapes and remove excess dough between shapes.

Baking

Unrimmed baking sheets allow cookies to bake evenly and quickly. Shiny sheets in a size that clears the oven sides by at least 1 inch allows good heat circulation and even baking. Cool sheets before placing cookie dough on them. When using parchment paper, do not butter the pan or the paper. To remove cookies stuck to baking sheet, reheat quickly and cool for 1 minute, then remove with spatula.

Storage

Crisp cookies should be kept in airtight containers. If they become soft, place in 300° oven for 5 minutes to restore crispness. Keep soft cookies soft by placing a bread slice in the container.

Pies

Pastry

- Too much moisture in the dough will make the crust tough and cause the pie to steam rather than bake. Handle dough as little as possible after adding liquid.
- To avoid tough crusts, do not use all butter. To measure butter or shortening, fill a measuring cup with water less the amount desired, add butter or shortening and discard water.

- Combine ingredients for crust, then chill dough for 10 minutes. This reduces the amount of flour needed on the rolling surface.
- Use a pastry cloth and stockinet-covered rolling pin when rolling the pastry. It will be tender and flaky and less flour and strokes will be necessary.
- Pastry can be rolled between 2 sheets of wax paper. Peel off the top paper and invert circle of pastry into pie plate, removing the second paper. Make sure crust covers the surface smoothly, without air trapped beneath the surface. For a double crust pie, fold the top crust over the lower crust along the edges before crimping it to prevent juices from overflowing.
- To avoid a soggy bottom crust, brush surface with well beaten egg white before adding filling. Cool pie on wire rack after baking. When baking a pastry shell, place another pie pan on top of the pastry to prevent "bubbling" or prick pastry with fork tines to release heat. Avoid pouring filling into pastry shell until just before baking.
- Brush top pie crust with milk before baking to make it brown and glossy.
- Shiny metal pie pans do not bake bottom crusts as well as aluminum pans with a dull finish or an ovenproof pie plate. Place a sheet of aluminum foil directly under the pie pan to catch drippings from the pie.

Crumb Crusts

Crumbs	Sugar	Butter
Graham Crackers (18)	1½ cups	¼ cup
Vanilla Wafers (38)	1¼ cups	⅓ cup
Ginger Snaps (24)	1¼ cups	⅓ cup
Chocolate Wafers	1¼ cups	⅓ cup

Mix crumbs, sugar and butter well. Press mixture in 9-inch pie plate. Bake at 375° for about 10 minutes.

Never Fail Pie Shell

1 cup all-purpose flour
½ teaspoon salt
⅓ cup vegetable shortening
3 tablespoons cold water

Sift flour and salt together. Using pastry blender, cut shortening into dry ingredients until consistency of small peas. Sprinkle water over mixture and toss lightly with fork until mixture sticks together. Shape into a smooth ball, wrap in wax paper and chill. Lightly roll pastry into circle 1 inch larger than pie plate. Transfer to pie plate, pat to remove air, crimp edges and prick with fork tines. Bake at 450° for about 12 minutes. Cool before filling.
Yield: 1 (9-inch) pastry shell

Meringues

Meringue will not shrink if spread on the pie filling so that it touches the crust on all edges. Bake meringue in a moderate oven. Cool baked meringue slowly away from drafts; "tears" form if meringue is cooled too quickly.

Meringue

3 egg whites
¼ teaspoon cream of tartar
½ teaspoon baking powder (optional)
3 tablespoons sugar
½ teaspoon vanilla extract

Beat eggs with cream of tartar until foamy. Add ½ teaspoon baking powder if extra high meringue is desired. Gradually add sugar, beating until peaks are stiff and glossy. Spread meringue on pie, covering to seal all edges. Bake at 400° for 8 to 10 minutes or until lightly browned. Cool away from drafts.

Candy

Use a large pot when making candy. Butter the pot to a depth of 2 inches to prevent boiling over. Cover for the first 3 minutes of boiling to prevent formation of crystals. When making hard candies, remove pot from heat and allow to cool for 2 minutes before pouring. Avoid making candy in hot, humid weather. If candy becomes sugary, add a small amount of water and bring to a boil.

Sugar, Syrup and Candy Cooking Chart

Stage of Hardness	Temperature Range	Cold Water Test	Uses
Thread	223 to 234°	Forms a 2-inch soft ball	Cooked icings and syrups
Soft Ball	234 to 240°	Forms soft ball but doesn't hold shape	Fondant, fudge and penuche
Firm Ball	242 to 248°	Form firm ball that holds shapes unless pressed	Caramels
Hard Ball	250 to 268°	Forms a hard ball that holds shape yet is pliable	Divinity, popcorn balls, marshmallows, nougat and saltwater taffy
Soft Crack	270 to 290°	Separates into hard but not brittle threads	Butterscotch and taffies
Hard Crack	300 to 310°	Syrup separates into hard, brittle threads	Brittle glacé
Clear Liquid	320°	Thick clear liquid, sugar liquefies	Barley sugar
Caramel	338 to 350°	Thick brown liquid (do not drop into cold water)	Flavoring and color

All About Chocolate

Chocolate is derived from ground, roasted and shelled cocoa beans. It ranges from bitter to sweet in flavor.

Chocolate Morsels or Squares—A convenient form of chocolate, it must be melted to assure proper blending if used as a substitute for other forms of chocolate.

Cocoa—Commonly in powder form, cocoa is the solid substances remaining after cocoa butter has been removed from the chocolate.

Liquid Chocolate—Different from chocolate syrup, liquid chocolate can be substitutes in recipes calling for cocoa powder or unsweetened chocolate. It is usually packaged in 1 ounce packets, each equal to 1 square unsweetened or ¼ cup cocoa powder.

Storage

Store chocolate in a cool dry place (60 to 78° and about 50% humidity). Refrigeration makes it brittle and hard. If stored in refrigerator, allow chocolate to reach room temperature before using. Wrap airtight to avoid absorption of refrigerator odors and to prevent moisture from forming when it is removed from refrigerator.

Because of its high content of cocoa butter, chocolate may develop a gray film called "bloom" when stores at temperatures that fluctuate between hot and cold. It's caused by cocoa butter rising to the surface. Although unattractive, it does not affect the taste and melting will eliminate the film.

Melting Chocolate

When melting, chocolate may harden or tighten if the smallest amount of moisture is present in the melting container. Correct by adding 1 teaspoon vegetable shortening for each ounce of chocolate and blend well.

Microwave—Place 6-ounce package chocolate chips in 2-cup glass measure. Cook at high (100%) setting for 1 minute, stir with dry spoon and cook for 1 additional minute. Remove and stir until chocolate is smooth. For 12-ounce package, use a 4-cup measure and cook for 2 minutes, stir and cook for 1 minute. Melt 2 squares at a time, uncovered, at medium (50%) setting for 2½ minutes, stir and cook for ½ to 1½ minutes or until softened.

Oven—Place chocolate, in its own wrapper, on aluminum foil lined baking sheet and place in oven during preheating for recipe.

Top of Stove—Use a heavy saucepan over low heat if chocolate is combined with fat or liquid. When melting alone, avoid scorching by using a small bowl in hot water or by using a double boiler.

Apple Bavarian Torte

Pastry

½ cup butter, softened
⅓ cup sugar
½ teaspoon vanilla
1 cup all-purpose flour

Cream butter and sugar together until smooth. Stir in vanilla. Add flour and mix thoroughly. Spread in bottom and to 2-inch depth on sides of 9-inch greased spring form pan.

Filling

2 (8 ounce) package cream cheese, softened
½ cup sugar
2 eggs
1 tablespoon vanilla

Combine cream cheese and sugar, beating until smooth. Add eggs and vanilla, mixing well. Pour filling into prepared pastry. Prepare topping. Arrange apples in concentric circles on top of filling. Bake at 450° for 5 minutes, reduce oven temperature to 400° and bake for 25 minutes. Cool in pan before serving.

Note: Torte, with apples on top, is especially good for a brunch.
Yield: 8 servings

Topping

4 cups thinly sliced peeled golden Delicious apples
⅓ cup sugar
½ teaspoon cinnamon
½ cup chopped walnuts or pecans

Combine apples, sugar, cinnamon and nuts.

Angel Wings

1 9-inch angel food cake, torn in bite-size pieces
1 (3¾ ounce) package instant vanilla pudding mix
3¼ cups milk, divided
1 packet unflavored gelatin
2 cups whipping cream, divided

Place cake pices in 13x9x2-inch baking dish. Prepare pudding, using 3 cups milk instead of 2 cups. Dissolve gelatin in remaining ¼ cup milk. Whip 1 cup cream and fold into pudding. Pour mixture over cake pieces. Chill overnight. Whip remaining 1 cup cream and place dollop on individual servings of dessert.
Yield: 15 servings

Layered Banana-Pineapple Dessert

1½ cups graham cracker crumbs
¼ cup sugar
⅓ cup margarine
3 bananas, sliced
1 (8 ounce) package cream cheese, softened
3½ cups cold milk
2 (3¾ ounce) packages instant vanilla pudding mix
1 (20 ounce) can crushed pineapple, drained
1 (8 ounce) carton frozen whipped topping, thawed

Combine graham cracker crumbs, sugar and margarine. Press crumbs evenly in bottom of 13x9x2-inch baking dish. Arrange banana slices on crust. Whip cream cheese with wire whisk until smooth. Gradually add milk, beating until smooth. Blend in pudding mix. Pour mixture evenly over bananas. Spoon pineapple on pudding layer and spread whipped topping over pineapple. Chill until ready to serve.

Note: For low calorie version, use fat-free cream cheese, skim milk, sugar-free pudding mix and low-calories whipped topping. Sugar can be omitted from crust.

Yield: 12 to 16 servings

Coffee Charlotte

12 plain ladyfingers
2 tablespoons instant coffee granules
¼ teaspoon salt
⅔ cup sugar
2 packets unflavored gelatin
3 cups milk
¼ cup cognac
2 cups whipping cream, whipped
Grated semi-sweet chocolate

Prepare a day in advance of serving. Split ladyfingers in halves and line bottom and sides of 9 or 10-inch spring form pan with cut surfaces inward. Combine coffee, salt, sugar and gelatin in saucepan. Add milk and simmer until sugar and gelatin are dissolved. Remove from heat and stir in cognac. Chill until spoonful of filling mounds slightly. Fold whipped cream into filling and pour into prepared pan. Chill until firm. Remove sides of pan and garnish with chocolate.

Note: A beautiful and delicious dessert, this is especially good for a dinner party.

Yield: 10 servings

Chocolate Delight

Crust

¾ cup margarine, melted
1½ cups all-purpose flour
¾ cup chopped pecans

Combine margarine, flour and pecans, mixing well. Spread mixture in 13x9x2-inch baking pan, pressing to form crust. Bake at 375° for 15 minutes. Set aside to cool.

Filling

1 (8 ounce) package cream cheese, softened
1 cup powdered sugar
1 (12 ounce) carton frozen whipped topping, thawed, divided
1 (3¾ ounce) package instant vanilla pudding mix
1 (4½ ounce) package instant chocolate pudding mix
3 cups milk
Grated chocolate

Combine cream cheese, powered sugar and 1½ cups whipped topping, blending thoroughly. Spread filling over cooled crust. Chill. Combine vanilla pudding mix, chocolate pudding mix and milk. Spoon over cream cheese layer and top with remaining whipped topping. Garnish with chocolate.

Yield: 12 to 16 servings

Chocolate Fancy

1 (12 ounce) package semi-sweet chocolate chips
2 tablespoons water
3 eggs, separated
2 tablespoons sugar
1 cup whipping cream
1 teaspoon vanilla
1 small angel food cake, torn in bite-size pieces

Prepare in advance to permit chilling overnight. In top of double boiler over simmering water, melt chocolate with 2 tablespoons water. Add egg yolks and cook for 1 minute, stirring constantly. Remove from heat and set aside to cool. Beat egg whites with sugar. Whip cream. Add egg whites and vanilla to cream. Fold cooled chocolate liquid into whipped cream mixture. Add cake pieces, mix lightly and spread in 8x8x2-inch baking dish. Chill overnight.

Yield: 9 servings

Heavenly Strawberry Crunch

Crust

½ cup margarine
1 cup all-purpose flour
¼ cup firmly-packed brown sugar
½ cup chopped pecans

Melt margarine in 13x9x2-inch baking pan. Add flour, brown sugar and pecans, mixing well. Bake at 350° for 20 minutes, stirring often to prevent overbrowning. Set aside to cool.

Filling

2 egg whites
1 (10 ounce) package frozen strawberries, thawed
⅔ cup sugar
1 (16 ounce) carton frozen whipped topping, thawed

Beat egg whites until stiff peaks form. Add strawberries and sugar. Fold in whipping topping. Spread pecan mixture in 13x9x2-inch baking pan, reserving ½ cup. Spread strawberry mixture on crust and sprinkle with reserved pecan mixture. Chill at least 3 hours before serving.

Note: Dessert can be frozen. Remove from freezer 30 minutes before serving.

Yield: 16 servings

Ten Days Dessert

1 (16 ounce) can crushed pineapple, drained
1 (16 ounce) can sliced pineapple, drained and cut in chunks
1 (10 ounce) bottle maraschino cherries, drained
1 (16 ounce) can sliced peaches, drained and cut in chunks
Sugar
1 cup whiskey
Cake
Whipped cream

Prepare 10 days before serving. Measure pineapple, cherries and peaches and combine in large bowl. For each cup fruit, add 1 cup sugar to fruit. Pour whiskey over fruit. Store in refrigerator for 10 days. Serve on cake with whipped cream.

Yield: 8 to 10 servings

Raspberry Holiday Torte

- **1 cup butter, softened**
- **1½ cups sugar, divided**
- **5 eggs, separated**
- **2 tablespoons milk**
- **2 teaspoons vanilla, divided**
- **¾ teaspoon salt, divided**
- **½ teaspoon baking powder**
- **2 cups all-purpose flour, sifted**
- **1¼ cups raspberry preserves**
- **1⅓ cups flaked coconut**
- **2 cups sour cream**

Cream butter with ½ cup sugar until smooth. Blend in egg yolks, milk, 1 teaspoon vanilla, ½ teaspoon salt and baking powder, beating well. Add flour and mix well. Pour batter into three 9-inch round baking pans, bottoms greased only. Spoon ⅓ cup preserves on each layer, leaving 1-inch margin around edge. Beat egg whites with remaining ¼ teaspoon salt until soft mounds form. Gradually beat in remaining 1 cup sugar and beat until stiff peaks form. Fold in coconut and remaining 1 teaspoon vanilla. Spread mixture over preserves in each pan. Bake at 350° for 35 to 40 minutes or until light golden brown. Cool in pans for 15 minutes, remove and cool completely on wire racks. Spread sour cream on layers and stack, garnishing top with sour cream and remaining ¼ cup preserves. Chill for several hours or overnight before serving.

Yield: 10 to 12 servings

Old Fashioned Short Cake

- **2 cups self-rising flour**
- **½ cup sugar**
- **½ cup plus 2 tablespoons vegetable shortening**
- **1 egg**
- **Milk**
- **Strawberries**
- **Whipped cream**

Sift flour and sugar together. Cut shortening into dry ingredients. Add egg and mix well. Add just enough milk to form very stiff dough. Spread dough in 8x8x2-inch baking pan. Bake at 325° for 45 minutes. Cut hot cake in squares, split and butter. Serve with strawberries and whipped cream.

Yield: 9 servings

Helen's Strawberry Shortcake

- 1 unbaked 9-inch pastry shell
- 2 cups fresh strawberries, hulled and mashed
- Sugar to taste
- 2 tablespoons butter, melted
- 1 cup whipping cream, whipped

Bake pastry shell at 425° for 10 minutes. Cool, then break into 2-inch pieces. Combine strawberries and sugar. Chill until ready to serve. Place several pieces pastry on individual serving plate, add strawberries and repeat layers. Drizzle with butter and add dollop of whipped cream.
Yield: 2 servings

Cranberry and Apple Crunch

Topping

- ¾ cup uncooked regular oats
- ½ cup all-purpose flour
- ¼ cup firmly-packed brown sugar
- ¼ teaspoon cinnamon
- ½ cup butter, diced

Combine oats, flour, ¼ cup brown sugar and ¼ teaspoon cinnamon. Cut in ½ cup butter until well blended and crumb consistency. Set aside.

Filling

- 4 cups diced tart apples
- ¾ cup cranberries
- 2 tablespoons orange juice
- Pinch of salt
- ¾ cup firmly packed brown sugar
- ½ teaspoon cinnamon
- 2 tablespoons butter, melted
- Sweetened whipped cream (optional)

Combine apples, cranberries, orange juice, brown sugar, cinnamon and salt. Pour fruit mixture into buttered deep dish 9-inch pie plate or 8x8x2-inch baking pan. Sprinkle topping on fruit and drizzle with melted butter. Bake at 400° for 30 minutes, cover loosely with aluminum foil and bake for additional 30 minutes. Serve warm with whipped cream.
Yield: 8 servings

Peach Cobbler Supreme

- 8 cups peeled and sliced fresh peaches
- 2 cups sugar
- 2 to 4 tablespoons all-purpose flour
- ½ teaspoon nutmeg
- 1 teaspoon almond extract
- ⅓ cup butter, melted
- Pastry for double-crust 9-inch pie

Combine peaches, sugar, flour and nutmeg in saucepan. Let stand until syrup forms. Bring to a boil, reduce heat and simmer for 10 minutes or until peaches are tender. Remove from heat, add almond extract and melted butter, mixing well. Spoon ½ of peaches into lightly buttered 10x8x-2inch baking dish. On lightly-floured surface, roll ½ of pastry to 10x8x⅛-inch rectangle. Place on peaches. Bake at 475° for 12 minutes or until golden brown. Spoon remaining peaches on crust. Roll remaining pastry to ⅛-inch thickness, cut into ½-inch strips and arrange in lattice design on peaches. Bake for additional 10 to 15 minutes or until lightly browned.
Yield: 8 to 10 servings

Glazed Peaches

- 1 (29 ounce) can peach halves, drained and syrup reserved
- 2 teaspoons grated orange peel
- Juice of 1 orange
- 1 teaspoon grated lemon peel
- Juice of 1 lemon
- 1 (8 ounce) carton frozen whipped topping, thawed
- ½ teaspoon almond extract

Combine peach syrup, orange peel and juice and lemon peel and juice in heavy saucepan. Simmer, uncovered, until syrup volume is reduced by ½. Place peaches in syrup and simmer for about 15 minutes, constantly spooning syrup over peaches; avoid breaking peaches. Pour into bowl, let stand until cool and chill. Fold almond extract into whipped topping. Serve peaches with flavored topping.
Yield: 6 or 7 servings

Frosted Pumpkin Crisp

Cake

- **1 (16 ounce) can pumpkin**
- **1 (13 ounce) can evaporated milk**
- **3 eggs**
- **1 cup sugar**
- **½ teaspoon cinnamon**
- **Dash of ginger**
- **Dash of nutmeg**
- **Dash of ground cloves**
- **1 (18½ ounce) package yellow cake mix**
- **2 cups chopped pecans**
- **1 cup margarine, melted and cooled**

Combine pumpkin, milk, eggs, sugar, cinnamon, ginger and nutmeg, mixing well. Pour into 13x9x2-inch baking pan, prepared by greasing, lining with wax paper and greasing wax paper. Sprinkle cake mix evenly over pumpkin mixture. Spread pecans on cake mix. Drizzle margarine over pecans. Bake at 350° for 50 to 60 minutes. Invert pan on serving tray, remove wax paper and let stand until cool. Spread frosting on cooled cake and chill until served.

Note: Dessert can be served without frosting.

Yield: 12 to 16 servings

Frosting

- **1 (8 ounce) carton frozen whipped topping, thawed**
- **1 (8 ounce) package cream cheese, softened**
- **1½ cups powdered sugar**

Combine whipped topping and cream cheese, mixing thoroughly. Add powdered sugar and blend for spreading consistency.

Forgotten Dessert

- **6 eggs whites**
- **¼ teaspoon salt**
- **½ teaspoon cream of tartar**
- **1½ cups sugar**
- **1 teaspoon vanilla**
- **1 cup whipping cream, lightly sweetened and whipped, or frozen whipped topping, thawed**
- **Fresh or frozen fruit**

Preheat oven to 450°. Beat egg whites until foamy. Add salt and cream of tartar. Beat until stiff peaks form. Gradually add sugar, then vanilla, beating until stiff and glossy meringue forms. Spread meringue in buttered 13x9x2-inch baking dish. Place in oven, close door and turn oven off. Leave meringue in oven overnight; do not open door until morning. To serve, spread with whipped cream or topping and top with fruit.

Yield: 12 servings

Coffee Ice Cream Dessert

Crust

1 (8 or 9 ounce) package chocolate ice box cookies, crushed

⅔ cup margarine, melted

Combine cookie crumbs and margarine. Press mixture in bottom of 13x9x2-inch baking pan. Freeze.

Second Layer

½ gallon coffee ice cream, softened

Spread ice cream on frozen crust. Freeze.

Third Layer

5 (1 ounce) squares semi-sweet chocolate

2 tablespoons margarine

1 cup sugar

1 (12 ounce) can evaporated milk

Melt chocolate in saucepan over very low heat. Add margarine, sugar and milk. Bring to a boil and cook for about 3 minutes, stirring constantly. Cool completely. Pour sauce over ice cream layer. Freeze.

Note: Cookies are often placed with ice cream toppings, rather than in cookie section, at supermarket. Dessert is very rich so servings should be small.

Yield: 16 to 18 servings

Strawberry Ice Cream

1½ (3 ounce) packages strawberry gelatin

1¾ cups sugar

1 cup boiling water

3 (4 ounce) cans evaporated milk

1 (13 ounce) can sweetened condensed milk

4 cups strawberries, mashed

1 tablespoon vanilla

1 cup whole milk

Dissolve gelatin and sugar in boiling water. Let stand until cool. Combine gelatin liquid, evaporated milk, condensed milk, strawberries and vanilla in container of ice cream freezer. Add whole milk to reach fill line. Process according to freezer manufacturer's directions.

Yield: 1 gallon

Chocolate-Amaretto Raspberry Freeze

Crust

28 creme-filled chocolate sandwich cookies, crushed

¾ cup margarine, melted

Combine cookie crumbs and margarine. Spread in 13x9x2-inch baking pan prepared with vegetable cooking spray.

Second Layer

⅓ cup amaretto

½ gallon vanilla ice cream, softened

1 (16 ounce) jar raspberry preserves

Using electric mixer, blend amaretto into ice cream. Spread on cookie crust. Freeze. Spread preserves on frozen ice cream. Freeze.

Third Layer

1 cup sugar

1 teaspoon vanilla

4 (1 ounce) squares semi-sweet chocolate

¼ cup plus 2 tablespoons margarine

¼ cup amaretto

Combine sugar, vanilla, chocolate and margarine in heavy saucepan. Bring to a boil and cook, stirring constantly, for 1 minute. Remove from heat, blend in amaretto and chill. Spread cooled sauce on raspberry layer. Freeze.

Topping

1 cup pecans

Margarine

Salt

2 tablespoons amaretto

1 (8 ounce) carton frozen whipped topping, thawed

Lightly salt pecans and toast in margarine; do not overbrown. Chop pecans and add with amaretto to whipped topping. Spread topping on chocolate layer. Freeze. Let stand at room temperature for 10 minutes before serving.

Yield: 16 to 20 servings

Evelyn's Fruit Slush

1 cup sugar
2 cups boiling water
1 (12 ounce) frozen orange juice concentrate, thawed and undiluted
1 (10 ounce) jar maraschino cherries, halved or quartered
2 tablespoons concentrated lemon juice
3 ripe bananas, coarsely chopped
1 (16 ounce) can crushed pineapple

Dissolve sugar in boiling water. Add orange juice and cherries. Pour lemon juice over bananas and pineapple. Combine fruit mixture and cherry mixture. Chill overnight. Freeze for 3 to 4 hours. Let stand at room temperature for 30 minutes before serving. Stir or mash mixture until slushy. Serve in compotes or dessert dishes.

Note: Slush can be stored in freezer for 2 to 3 weeks.
Yield: 8 servings

Vanilla Wafer Banana Pudding

2 cups milk
2 eggs, separated
⅔ cup plus ¼ cup sugar, divided
⅛ teaspoon salt
2 tablespoons cornstarch
1½ teaspoons vanilla extract
48 vanilla wafers
4 or 5 ripe bananas

Pour milk in top of double boiler over boiling water and heat until scalded. Beat egg yolks. Add ⅔ cup sugar, salt and cornstarch to yolks. Blend about ½ cup scalded milk into egg mixture. Add egg mixture to remaining milk in double boiler and cook over boiling water for about 6 minutes or until smooth and thickened. Remove from heat and add vanilla. Alternately layer vanilla wafers and bananas in 9x9x2-inch baking dish or 1½-quart casserole. Pour hot custard over layers. Let stand until cool. Beat egg whites until stiff but not dry. Gradually add remaining ¼ cup sugar, beating until very stiff and glossy. Spread meringue over pudding. Bake at 425° for about 15 minutes; do not overbrown.
Yield: 6 to 9 servings

Blueberry Bread Pudding

4 cups milk
2 cups half and half
1¼ cups sugar
1 tablespoon vanilla extract
2 teaspoons grated lemon peel
¼ teaspoon cinnamon
6 eggs
1 (8 ounce) loaf Italian bread, cut in 1-inch chunks
1 cup fresh or frozen blueberries, thawed
Boiling water
Powdered sugar

Using wire whisk, combine milk, half and half, sugar, vanilla, lemon peel, cinnamon and eggs, mixing well. Add bread and toss gently to coat well. Let stand for 15 minutes, stirring occasionally. Spoon bread mixture into greased 13x9x2-inch baking dish. Spread blueberries on bread mixture. Place baking dish in large roasting pan, place on oven rack and add boiling water to roasting pan to ½ depth of baking dish. Bake at 350° for 1 hour or until knife tip inserted in center of pudding comes out clean. Carefully remove baking dish from pan and place on wire rack. Sprinkle with powdered sugar. Serve warm or chilled.
Yield: 16 servings

Lemon Sponge Custard

¾ cup sugar
1½ tablespoons butter, softened
2 teaspoons grated lemon peel
2 or 3 eggs, separated
3 tablespoons all-purpose flour
¼ cup lemon juice
1 cup milk

Cream sugar, butter and lemon peel together. Add egg yolks and beat thoroughly. Alternately add flour and lemon juice mixed with milk. Beat egg whites until stiff but not dry. Fold whites into yolk mixture. Spoon batter into buttered custard cups or 1-quart casserole. Place cups or casserole in pan filled with 1 inch hot water. Bake at 350° for 45 minutes for cups and about 1 hour for casserole or until custard is firm. Serve hot or cold.

Note: Custard magically separates while baking.
Yield: 4 to 6 servings

Cold Cherry Soup

2 cups water
3 cups sugar
1 stick cinnamon
4 cups pitted fresh sour cherries
1 tablespoon cornstarch
2 tablespoons cold water
¼ cup whipping cream, whipped
¾ cup dry red wine

Combine 2 cups water, sugar and cinnamon stick in saucepan. Bring to a boil. Add cherries, reduce heat and simmer for 40 minutes. Blend cornstarch with 2 tablespoons cold water until smooth. Stir into cherries, bring to a boil and cook for 2 minutes or until clear. Chill soup. Serve with dollop of cream and splash of wine.

Note: This is a very different but wonderful dessert.

Yield: 4 to 6 servings

Spanish Flan

4 eggs, well beaten
1 (13 ounce) sweetened condensed milk
1¾ cups homogenized milk
¼ cup sugar

Strain eggs into mixing bowl. Add condensed and homogenized milk, mixing thoroughly. Caramelize sugar by planing in saucepan over low heat and cooking, tilting pan, until sugar is dissolved and converts to syrup. Pour caramelized sugar into bottom of 1½-quart ring mold. Pour custard mixture over sugar. Place mold in shallow pan of water. Bake at 325° for 1 hour or until firm. Invert to unmold. Chill.

Yield: 8 servings

Rice Pudding

2 eggs, separated
½ cup sugar
½ teaspoon salt
2¼ cups milk
1 teaspoon vanilla
2 cups cooked rice
Raisins (optional)
Diced apple (optional)
Dash of nutmeg

Beat egg yolks. Add sugar, salt, milk, vanilla, rice, raisins and apple to yolks. Beat egg whites until stiff and fold into rice mixture. Spoon mixture into 8x8x2-inch baking dish. Sprinkle with nutmeg. Bake at 350° for 45 minutes.

Yield: 6 servings

Tiramisu

6 (8 ounce) packages cream cheese, softened
3 cups sugar
7 whole eggs
7 egg yolks
¾ cup rum
4 cups whipping cream, whipped
Lady fingers
Cold brewed espresso coffee
Semi-sweet cocoa

Combine cream cheese and sugar, beating until smooth. Add eggs and egg yolks, blending well. Add rum and fold in whipped cream. Dip lady fingers in coffee and arrange single layer in bottom of 12x12x2½-inch baking dish. Spread ½-inch layer of cream cheese mixture on ladyfingers. Repeat layers twice. Sprinkle top with cocoa.
Yield: 12 servings

Contributor: Chef Nick Fusco
Fusco's Restaurant
Beach Colony Resort
Myrtle Beach, South Carolina

Banana Pineapple Pie

Pastry
1½ cups graham cracker or vanilla wafer crumbs
3 tablespoons sugar
¼ cup plus 2 tablespoons margarine, melted

Combine crumbs, sugar and margarine, mixing well. Press crumb mixture into 9-inch pie plate. Bake at 375° for 8 minutes.

Filling
1 (8 ounce) can crushed pineapple, undrained
2 tablespoons flour
½ cup sugar
2 medium-sized bananas
½ cup chopped pecans
1 cup whipped cream, whipped, or frozen whipped topping, thawed

Combine pineapple, flour and sugar in saucepan. Heat over low heat until thickened. Let stand until cool. Slice bananas into pastry shell. Sprinkle nuts on bananas. Spoon pineapple mixture over nuts and bananas. Top with whipped cream.
Yield: 1 (9-inch) pie

Grated Apple Pie

2 cups peeled and grated apples
1 cup sugar
1 egg, beaten
¼ cup plus 2 tablespoons margarine, melted
1 tablespoon lemon juice
1 unbaked deep dish 10-inch pastry shell or 2 unbaked 8-inch pastry shells

Combine apples, sugar, egg, margarine and lemon juice. Spread apple mixture in pastry shell. Bake at 350° for 1 hour.

Note: For 3 small pies, double ingredients. Baked pie freezes well.
Yield: 1 deep dish pie

Easy Chocolate Cream Pie

2½ tablespoons unsweetened cocoa
2½ tablespoons cornstarch
1 cup sugar, divided
2 eggs, separated
¾ cup evaporated milk
¾ cup water
1 teaspoon vanilla
1 tablespoon butter
1 baked 8 or 9-inch pastry shell

Combine cocoa, cornstarch and ¾ cup sugar in top of double boiler. Lightly beat egg yolks. Add egg yolks, milk and water to dry ingredients and mix well. Cook over hot water over medium heat until thickened. Add vanilla and butter. Pour filling into pastry shell. Beat egg whites until stiff. Add remaining ¼ cup sugar and beat to form meringue. Spread over filling. Bake at 425° until lightly browned.
Yield: 1 (8 or 9-inch) pie

Chocolate Brownie Pie

1 cup sugar
½ cup all-purpose flour
⅓ cup unsweetened cocoa
¼ teaspoon salt
2 eggs
½ cup butter, melted
½ cup semi-sweet chocolate chips
½ cup chopped nuts
1 teaspoon vanilla
Powdered sugar (optional)

Combine sugar, flour, cocoa and salt. Add eggs and butter, mixing well. Stir in chocolate chips, nuts and vanilla. Pour batter into greased 8 or 9-inch pie plate. Bake at 325° for 25 to 30 minutes. Sprinkle with powdered sugar.
Yield: 1 (8 or 9-inch) pie

German Chocolate Pie

- 2 cups sugar
- 2 tablespoons all-purpose flour
- 2 tablespoons unsweetened cocoa
- 1 egg
- 1 tablespoon margarine, melted
- 1 (12 ounce) can evaporated milk
- 1 cup flaked coconut
- ¼ cup chopped pecans
- 2 unbaked 9-inch pastry shells

Combine sugar, flour and cocoa. Add egg and margarine, beating until smooth. Blend in milk, coconut and pecans. Pour filling into pastry shells. Bake at 350° for about 45 minutes.

Note: This recipe came from the old S&W Cafeteria of Charlotte.
Yield: 2 (9-inch pies)

Yummy Fudge Pie

- 2 (1 ounce) squares unsweetened chocolate
- ½ cup butter
- 2 eggs
- 1 cup sugar
- ¼ cup all-purpose flour
- 1 teaspoon vanilla extract
- ½ teaspoon almond extract
- 1 unbaked 9-inch pastry shell
- Whipped cream
- 6 to 8 maraschino cherries

Melt chocolate and butter together. Combine eggs, sugar, flour, vanilla and almond extract. Add to chocolate mixture. Pour into pastry shell. Bake at 350° for 30 minutes. Garnish individual servings with whipped cream and cherry.

Note: Pie can be chilled for 4 hours or more before serving. Absolutely sinful but so easy to make!
Yield: 1 (9-inch) pie

Put a layer of marshmallows in the bottom of a pumpkin pie, then add the filling. The marshmallows will come to the top and make a nice topping during baking.

Grandmother Hancock's Chocolate Chess Pie

- 1½ (1 ounce) squares unsweetened chocolate
- ½ cup butter
- 1 teaspoon vanilla extract
- ½ cup sugar
- 1 cup firmly-packed brown sugar
- 1 tablespoon all-purpose flour
- Pinch of salt
- 2 eggs
- ¼ cup milk
- 1 unbaked 9-inch pastry shell

Melt chocolate and butter in top of double boiler over hot water. Remove from heat and stir in vanilla. Combine sugar, brown sugar, flour and salt. Blend in eggs and milk. Add chocolate mixture to egg mixture, mixing well. Pour into pastry shell. Bake at 325° for 40 minutes.

Note: An old family recipe, the original calls for the milk to be measured as "3 eggshells full".

Yield: 1 (9-inch) pie

Sherry Cream Pie

- 6 egg yolks
- 1 cup sugar
- ½ teaspoon salt
- 1 packet unflavored gelatin
- ½ cup cold water
- 2 cups whipping cream, whipped
- ½ cup sherry
- 2 (9-inch) graham cracker crumb crusts
- ½ cup finely sliced almonds

Beat egg yolks until light. Blend in sugar and salt. Soften gelatin in cold water, pour into top of double boiler over boiling water and heat until dissolved. Add gelatin to egg mixture, stirring constantly. Fold whipped cream into egg mixture. Stir in sherry. Cool filling until it begins to thicken, then spread in crusts. Chill until firm. Sprinkle with almonds before serving.

Yield: 2 (9-inch) pies

Just Pie

- ½ cup butter or margarine, melted
- 1 cup sugar
- 2 eggs, beaten
- 1 teaspoon vanilla
- 1 teaspoon white vinegar
- ½ cup raisins
- ½ cup chopped nuts
- ½ cup flaked coconut
- 1 unbaked 9-inch pastry shell

Combine butter or margarine with sugar. Blend in eggs, vanilla and vinegar. Add raisins, nuts and coconut. Spread filling in pastry shell. Bake at 325° for 50 minutes.
Yield: 1 (9-inch) pie

Shoo Fly Pie

- ½ teaspoon baking soda
- ¼ teaspoon salt
- ¾ cup boiling water
- 1 cup dark corn syrup
- ½ cup firmly-packed light or dark brown sugar
- 1½ cups sifted all-purpose flour
- ¼ cup butter or margarine
- 1 unbaked 9-inch pastry shell

Stir baking soda and salt into boiling water. Add corn syrup, blend thoroughly and set aside. Combine brown sugar and flour. Cut butter or margarine into dry ingredients until crumb consistency. Pour ⅓ of syrup liquid into pastry shell, sprinkle ⅓ crumb mixture on liquid and repeat layers twice. Gently press top layer of crumbs to seal edges. Bake at 375° for 35 minutes. Serve warm or cold.

Note: This Pennsylvania Dutch pie is traditionally served as a breakfast pastry.
Yield: 1 (9-inch) pie

Southern Chess Pie

Pastry

- **1⅓ cups all-purpose flour**
- **1 teaspoon salt**
- **⅓ cup plus 2 tablespoons vegetable shortening**
- **¼ cup cold water**

Combine flour and salt. Cut shortening into dry ingredients until crumb consistency. Add cold water. Shape pastry into a ball. On lightly-floured surface, roll out to circle to fit 9-inch pie plate.

Filling

- **½ cup sugar**
- **1 cup firmly-packed brown sugar**
- **1 tablespoon all-purpose flour**
- **2 eggs**
- **2 tablespoons milk**
- **1 teaspoon vanilla extract**
- **½ cup butter, melted**
- **1 cup chopped pecans**
- **1 unbaked 9-inch pastry shell**

Combine sugar, brown sugar and flour. Using wire whisk, beat eggs, milk, vanilla and butter into dry ingredients. Fold pecans into mixture. Pour into pastry shell. Bake at 375° for 40 to 45 minutes.
Yield: 1 (9-inch) pie

S&W Chess Pie

- **1½ cups sugar**
- **3 tablespoons corn meal**
- **2 tablespoons all-purpose flour**
- **⅛ teaspoon salt**
- **¼ teaspoon nutmeg**
- **½ cup butter, softened**
- **6 egg yolks**
- **1 cup milk**
- **1 unbaked 9-inch pastry shell**

Combine sugar, corn meal, flour, salt and nutmeg. Add butter and beat until light. Blend in egg yolks. Add milk and mix well. Let mixture stand 30 minutes before pouring into pastry shell. Bake at 325° for about 40 minutes or until firm.

Note: This recipe came from the old S&W Cafeteria of Charlotte.
Yield: 1 (9-inch) pie

Coconut Custard Pie

½ cup butter or margarine, melted
2 cups sugar
Pinch of salt
5 eggs, beaten
¾ cup buttermilk
1 teaspoon vanilla extract
1¾ cups flaked coconut
2 unbaked 9-inch pastry shells

Pour butter or margarine over sugar and mix thoroughly. Blend in salt, eggs, buttermilk, vanilla and coconut, mixing well. Pour filling into pastry shells. Bake on low oven rack (about 4 inches above coils) at 350° for 40 to 45 minutes or until golden brown; filling puffs as it bakes, then settles as it cools.

Note: Baked pie can be frozen.
Yield: 2 (9-inch) pies

S&W Custard Pie

1¼ cups sugar
½ teaspoon salt
2 tablespoons butter, softened
4 eggs, beaten
2 cups milk
1 teaspoon vanilla extract
1 unbaked 10-inch pastry shell

Combine sugar and salt. Add butter and mix until smooth. Add eggs and mix well. Beat in milk and vanilla until smooth. Pour filling into pastry shell which has high fluted edges. Bake at 425° for 25 to 30 minutes; filling will be set around edges but soft in center. Cool completely before cutting.

Note: This recipe came from the old S&W Cafeteria of Charlotte.
Yield: 1 (10-inch) pie

For baking, it's best to use medium to large eggs. Extra large may cause cakes to fall when cooled.

Citron Custards

Pastry

3 cups all-purpose flour
¼ teaspoon salt
¾ cup vegetable shortening
½ cup or more ice water

Combine flour and salt. Using fork or pastry blender, cut shortening into dry ingredients. Add ice water and mix to form soft dough. Chill for several hours. Roll dough to 1/16-inch thickness. Cut with biscuit cutter large enough to fill cup of regular muffin pan. Fit pastry circles into muffin pans carefully. Recipe requires 32 muffin cups (three 12-cup pans). If using 1 or 2 pans, following instructions with filling for completing recipe.

Filling

½ cup butter, softened
1½ cups sugar
3 eggs at room temperature, separated
1 teaspoon vanilla

Cream butter with sugar until smooth. Add egg yolks, mixing just until blended. Reserve whites for topping. Stir in vanilla. Place 1 teaspoon filling in each pastry cup. Bake at 325° for about 15 minutes or until lightly browned. Cool in muffin pans. If reusing pans to complete recipe, gently remove baked custards from pans and place on baking sheet.

Meringue Icing

1½ cups sugar
⅓ cup light corn syrup
⅓ cup water
3 egg whites (reserved from filling recipe)
1 teaspoon vanilla

Combine sugar, syrup and water in saucepan. Cook for 5 to 10 minutes. Whip reserved egg whites until firm. Stream syrup into egg whites and blend carefully but thoroughly. Stir in vanilla. Spread 1 teaspoon meringue on each baked custard, sealing to edges. Bake at 200° for 1 hour, turn oven off and leave custards in oven overnight.

Yield: 32 servings

Contributor: Dorothy Powers
Laura's Restaurant

Daiquiri Pie

1 (3 4/5 ounce) package regular lemon pudding mix
1 (3 ounce) package lime gelatin
⅓ cup sugar
2½ cups water, divided
2 eggs, lightly beaten
⅓ cup light rum
1 (8 ounce) carton frozen whipped topping, thawed
1 (10-inch) graham cracker crust
Thin slices of lime

Combine pudding mix, gelatin and sugar in saucepan. Blend in ½ cup water and eggs. Add remaining 2 cups water. Bring to a boil, stirring constantly with wire whisk, over medium heat and cook until thickened. Remove from heat and stir in rum. Chill thoroughly. Fold in ½ of whipped topping. Spread filling in crust. Chill. Just before serving, spread remaining whipped topping on pie.

Note: Instead of chilling pie, pie can be frozen. Clean plastic cover that protects purchased crust, invert on filling and crimp edges to pie pan. Thaw before serving.
Yield: 1 (10-inch) pie

Lemon or Lime Pie

1 (6 ounce) can frozen lemonade or limeade concentrate, thawed
1 (13 ounce) can sweetened condensed milk
1 cup sour cream
1 (8 ounce) carton frozen whipped topping, thawed
Few drops yellow green food coloring
1 (10-inch) graham cracker crust

Combine lemonade or limeade concentrate, milk, sour cream, whipped topping and food coloring, mixing thoroughly. Spread filling in crust. Chill for at least 6 hours.
Yield: 1 (10-inch) pie

You'll get more juice from a lemon if you first warm it slightly in the oven.

Easy Peach Pie

Pastry

1¼ cups crushed graham crackers
2 tablespoons brown sugar
Dash of cinnamon
¼ cup plus 2 tablespoons butter, melted

Combine crumbs, brown sugar, cinnamon and butter, mixing thoroughly. Press crumb mixture into 10-inch pie plate. Bake at 350° for 8 minutes. You may use a bought crust; if so, follow directions on package.

Filling

2 cups sugar
½ cup cornstarch
2 cups cold water
2 tablespoons corn syrup
1 (3 ounce) package peach gelatin
2 cups peaches
1 (8 ounce) carton frozen whipped topping, thawed (optional)

Combine sugar and cornstarch in saucepan. Blend in cold water. Place over medium heat, add syrup and cook until slightly thickened. Blend in gelatin. Spread peaches in baked crust. Pour filling over peaches. Chill. Serve with whipped topping.
Yield: 1 (10-inch) pie

Peach Cream Pie

⅔ cup plus 3 tablespoons sugar, divided
¼ cup plus 1 tablespoon all-purpose flour
¼ teaspoon salt
3 eggs, separated
2 cups milk, scalded
1½ to 2½ cups sliced fresh peaches, sweetened
¼ teaspoon almond extract
3 dashes nutmeg
1 baked 9-inch pastry shell
½ teaspoon cream of tartar

Combine ⅔ cup sugar, flour and salt in top of double boiler. Beat egg yolks well. Add with scalded milk to dry ingredients and cook, stirring constantly, over hot water until thickened. Remove from heat and let stand until cool. Add peaches, almond extract and nutmeg, mixing lightly. Spread filling in pastry shell. Beat egg whites with cream of tartar. Gradually add sugar and beat until peaks form. Spread over pie filling, Bake at 400° until lightly browned. Cool before serving.
Yield: 1 (9-inch) pie

Pecan Pies

½ cup margarine, softened
1 cup sugar
4 eggs, beaten
1 cup dark corn syrup
1½ to 1¾ cups broken pecans
Dash of salt
1 teaspoon vanilla extract
2 unbaked 9-inch pastry shells

Cream margarine and sugar together until smooth. Add eggs, syrup, pecans, salt and vanilla. Spread filling in pastry shells. Bake at 425° for 10 minutes, reduce oven temperature to 350° and bake for 25 to 30 minutes.
Yield: 2 (9-inch) pies

Mama's Chocolate Pecan Pie

2 (1 ounce) squares unsweetened chocolate
3 tablespoons butter
1 cup light corn syrup
¾ cup sugar
½ teaspoon salt
3 eggs, lightly beaten
1 teaspoon vanilla extract
1 cup pecans
1 unbaked 9-inch deep dish pastry shell

Melt chocolate and butter together in top of double boiler or by microwave method. Combine syrup and sugar in saucepan. Simmer for 2 minutes. Add chocolate mixture and let stand until slightly cooled. Add salt and eggs, mixing thoroughly. Stir in vanilla and pecans. Spread filling in pastry shell. Bake at 375° for 35 to 40 minutes. This is a tried and true family favorite.
Yield: 1 (9-inch) deep dish pie

Easy Pie

1 (16 ounce) can crushed pineapple, drained
1 (14 ounce) can sweetened condensed milk
Juice of 2 lemons
1 (8 ounce) carton frozen whipped topping, thawed
2 (9-inch) graham cracker crusts

Combine pineapple, milk and lemon juice. Fold whipped topping into pineapple mixture. Spread filling in crusts. Chill for at least 30 minutes.
Yield: 2 (9-inch) pies

Special Derby Pie

- 1 cup sugar
- ½ cup all-purpose flour
- 2 eggs, beaten
- 1 teaspoon vanilla
- ½ cup butter, melted
- 1 cup chopped pecans
- ½ cup semi-sweet chocolate chips
- ½ cup butterscotch chips
- 1 unbaked 9 or 10-inch pastry shell
- 1 (8 ounce) carton frozen whipped topping, thawed
- 8 to 10 maraschino cherries

Combine sugar, flour, eggs and vanilla. Stir in butter, pecans, chocolate chips and butterscotch chips. Spread filling in pastry shell. Bake at 350° for 30 to 40 minutes. Garnish individual servings with whipping topping and cherry.

Note: For variation, roll pastry to 13x9x2-inch rectangle and press in bottom of baking pan. Double filling recipe and pour over pastry. Bake at 350° for 45 to 50 minutes. Cool and cut into squares.

Yield: 40 to 48 bars

Strawberry Pie

- 1 cup sugar
- ¼ cup strawberry gelatin
- 3 tablespoons cornstarch
- 1 cup boiling water
- 4 cups strawberries
- 1 baked 9-inch pastry shell

Combine sugar, gelatin and cornstarch in saucepan. Add boiling water and cook for 10 to 15 minutes or until thickened. Let stand until cool. Add strawberries to mixture and spread in pastry shell. Chill.

Yield: 1 (9-inch) pie

Penny's Dutch Baby

- ¼ cup margarine
- 3 eggs
- ¾ cup milk
- ¾ cup all-purpose flour
- Fresh fruit: strawberries, blueberries, kiwi, peaches, pineapple or combination
- Powdered sugar

Prepare 9-inch pie plate with vegetable cooking spray. Melt margarine in pie plate. Using electric mixer, beat eggs at high speed for 1 minute. Gradually add ¾ cup milk, then gradually add flour and mix for 30 seconds. Pour into prepared pie plate. Bake at 400° for 20 minutes. Arrange fresh fruit on crust and sprinkle with powdered sugar.

Yield: 4 servings

Apple Nut Cake

Cake

2 cups sugar
1½ cups vegetable oil
3 eggs
2 teaspoons vanilla extract
3 cups all-purpose flour
1 teaspoon baking soda
½ teaspoon salt
3 cups chopped apples
1 cup chopped nuts

Cream sugar and oil together until smooth. Blend in eggs and vanilla. Combine flour, baking soda and salt. Add dry ingredients to egg mixture, mixing to form stiff batter. Fold apples and nuts into batter. Spread evenly in 15x10x2-inch baking pan prepared with vegetable cooking spray. Bake at 350° for 45 to 55 minutes. Prepare frosting and spread on warm cake.
Yield: 20 to 24 servings

Frosting

½ cup butter
1 cup firmly-packed brown sugar
¼ cup milk

Melt butter in saucepan. Stir in brown sugar and milk. Bring to a boil and cook for 2 minutes.

Brown sugar won't harden if an apple slice is placed in the container.

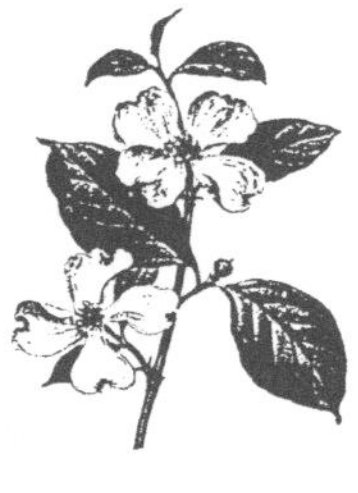

Apple Pecan Cake

Cake

3 eggs, beaten
2 cups sugar
½ cup vegetable oil
2 teaspoons vanilla
2 cups all-purpose flour
2 teaspoons baking soda
¼ teaspoon salt
2 teaspoons cinnamon
½ teaspoon nutmeg
4 cups diced unpeeled apples
1 cup chopped pecans

Beat eggs, sugar, oil and vanilla together until smooth. Combine flour, baking soda, salt, cinnamon and nutmeg. Blend dry ingredients into egg mixture. Fold apples and nuts into batter. Spread in greased and floured 13x9x2-inch baking pan. Bake at 325° for 1 hour or until cake tests done. Prepare frosting and spread on cooled cake.
Yield: 16 to 20 servings

Cream Cheese Frosting

2 (3 ounce) packages cream cheese, softened
1½ cups powdered sugar
½ teaspoon vanilla extract

Combine cream cheese, sugar and vanilla, whipping until smooth.

Banana Pan Cake

1 cup sugar
½ cup butter or margarine, softened
2 eggs or equivalent egg substitute
3 ripe bananas, mashed
1 cup all-purpose flour
1 teaspoon baking soda

Cream sugar and butter or margarine together until smooth. Blend in egg and bananas. Add flour and baking soda, mixing just until moistened; do not beat. Pour batter into 8x8x2-inch baking pan prepared with vegetable cooking spray. Bake at 375° for abut 25 minutes.
Yield: 9 servings

Apricot-Almond Upside Down Cake

- ¼ cup butter
- ¼ cup firmly-packed light brown sugar
- 1 (17 ounce) can apricot halves, drained and quartered
- ¼ cup slivered almonds
- ½ cup milk
- 1 cup sifted all-purpose flour
- 1 teaspoon baking powder
- ¼ teaspoon salt
- 3 eggs
- 1 cup sugar
- ¾ teaspoon almond extract
- Whipped cream (optional)

Melt butter in 9x9x2-inch baking pan over low heat. Remove from heat. Stir brown sugar into butter. Arrange fruit in pan in decorative pattern and sprinkle with slivered almonds. Scald milk and set aside. Sift flour, baking powder and salt together. Beat eggs for 3 minutes at high speed. Gradually add sugar and mix well. Blend in dry ingredients at low speed. Add warm milk and almond extract, beating until thoroughly mixed. Pour batter into prepared pan. Bake at 350° for 35 minutes. Using spatula or knife tip, separate cake from edges of pan, let stand for 5 minutes and invert on serving plate. Serve warm with whipped cream.
Yield: 9 servings

Date Nut Cake

- 1 cup sugar
- ½ cup vegetable oil
- 4 eggs
- 1 cup all-purpose flour
- 1 teaspoon salt
- 1 (16 ounce) package pitted dates, chopped
- 4 cups pecan halves

Combine sugar, oil and eggs, beating until smooth. Blend in flour and salt. Fold dates and nuts into batter. Pour batter into greased and floured 9x5x3-inch loaf pan or three 7x3½x2½-inch loaf pans. Starting in cold oven, bake at 300° for 2 hours for large loaf or 55 minutes for small loaves or until light golden brown; do not overbake. Immediately remove cake from pan and enclose in plastic wrap. Let stand until cool and wrap in aluminum foil.
Yield: 3 (1 pound) loaves or 1 (3 pound) loaf

Hospitality Fruit Cakes

1 cup sugar
1 cup butter, softened
5 eggs
¾ to 1 pound candied green and red cherries, chopped
¾ to 1 pound candied green and red pineapple, sliced and cubed
2 cups light raisins
4 cups chopped pecans
2 cups all-purpose flour, divided
1½ teaspoons baking powder
1 teaspoon salt
½ cup unsweetened pineapple juice
2 tablespoons vanilla extract
½ pound candied green and red cherries, cut in halves

Cream sugar and butter together until light and fluffy. Add eggs, 1 at a time, mixing well after each addition. Combine ¾ to 1 pound cherries, pineapple, raisins and nuts. Sprinkle with ½ cup flour, tossing to coat thoroughly. Sift remaining 1½ cups flour with baking powder and salt. Alternately add dry ingredients and pineapple juice to creamed mixture, beginning and ending with dry ingredients. Fold in fruit and vanilla, blending well. Spoon batter into greased and floured or paper-lined miniature muffin pans, filling cups about ⅔ full. Top each with cherry half, pressing slightly into batter. Bake at 300° for 20 to 30 minutes or until lightly browned. Place on wire rack to cool. Cakes can be stored in layers with wax paper separation in air-tight container.

Note: These do take time but are well worth the effort. I use 4 miniature pans in the oven at once, which helps time wise.

Yield: 12 to 13 dozen

VANILLA FLAVORING: To make your own vanilla flavoring, at a fraction of the cost of the supermarket brands, you simply need: A large bottle (1.75 liters) of inexpensive vodka and 2 whole vanilla beans. Place the whole vanilla beans in the bottle of vodka, close and store for six weeks. At this time you may discard the beans and use the flavoring as it is called for in your favorite recipes. To make great gifts, simply pour into small decorative bottles.

Fruitcake for People Who Don't Like Fruitcake

- 1½ pounds pecans
- ¾ pound candied pineapple, chopped
- ¾ pound whole candied cherries
- 1 (16 ounce) package light raisins
- 2¼ cups sugar
- 1 cup butter, softened
- 6 eggs
- 2 tablespoons brandy extract
- 4 cups sifted all-purpose flour
- 1 teaspoon salt
- 1½ teaspoons cinnamon
- 1 teaspoon nutmeg
- Honey or light corn syrup

Prepare cake about 3 weeks before serving. Combine pecans, pineapple and cherries, reserving portion to garnish top of cake. Cream sugar and butter together until smooth. Add eggs and brandy extract, beating well by hand or electric mixer. Sift flour, salt, cinnamon and nutmeg together. Add dry ingredients to egg mixture, mixing thoroughly. Using heavy spoon, add fruit mixture to batter. Spread batter in aluminum-foiled lined two 9x5x3-inch loaf pans, one 10-inch tube pan or four 16-ounce coffee cans, filling about ⅔ full. Bake at 275° for about 2 hours for loaf pans or cans or 3 hours for tube pan. About 30 minutes before end of baking time, brush top of cake with honey or syrup, decorate with reserved fruit, pressing to attach, and continue baking. Cool cake in pan, remove and peel away foil. Wrap in wine-dampened cloth. Store in airtight container in cool place for several weeks to allow flavors to blend and cake to mellow.

Note: Leaving pecans and cherries whole is a time-saver and contributes to the appearance and color of cake when sliced.

Yield: 20 to 30 servings

Tropical Cake

1 (22 ounce) can cherry pie filling
1 (8 ounce) can crushed pineapple, undrained
1 (3 ounce) can flaked coconut
½ cup chopped nuts
1 (18½ ounce) package white cake mix
½ cup butter, melted

Spread pie filling in bottom of greased 13x9x2-inch baking pan. Spoon pineapple, coconut and nuts evenly on filling, sprinkle with cake mix and drizzle with butter. Bake at 375° for 30 minutes.
Yield: 16 to 20 servings

Swedish Pineapple Cake

Cake
2 cups sugar
2 eggs
1 (20 ounce) can crushed pineapple in heavy syrup, undrained
2 teaspoons vanilla extract
2 cups all-purpose flour
2 teaspoons baking soda
1 cup nuts

Combine sugar, eggs, pineapple and vanilla, mixing thoroughly. Blend in flour and soda. Add nuts. Pour batter into 13x9x2-inch baking pan. Bake at 350° for 40 to 45 minutes. Prepare frosting and spread on cooled cake.
Yield: 16 to 20 servings

Cream de Arraba Frosting
½ cup butter or margarine, softened
1 (8 ounce) package cream cheese, softened
1½ cups powdered sugar
1½ teaspoons vanilla extract
½ cup nuts, raisins or coconut

Cream butter or margarine and cream cheese together until smooth. Gradually add sugar, mixing well. Stir in vanilla and nuts, raisins or coconut.

Pumpkin Cake

Cake

- **1 (18½ ounce) package yellow cake mix**
- **¾ cup sugar**
- **1 teaspoon cinnamon**
- **Dash of nutmeg**
- **4 eggs**
- **½ cup vegetable oil**
- **1 cup canned pumpkin**
- **¼ cup water**

Combine cake mix, sugar, cinnamon and nutmeg. Blend in eggs, oil, pumpkin and water. Using electric mixer, beat for 5 minutes. Pour batter into greased and floured 10-inch tube pan. Bake at 350° for 45 minutes. Cool in pan for 10 minutes, then remove to wire rack. Prepare frosting and spread on cooled cake.
Yield: 16 to 20 servings

Cream Cheese Frosting

- **½ cup margarine, softened**
- **1 (3 ounce) package cream cheese, softened**
- **1 (16 ounce) package powdered sugar**
- **½ teaspoon maple extract or 1 teaspoon vanilla extract**

Cream margarine and cream cheese together until smooth. Gradually blend in powdered sugar. Stir in maple extract or vanilla.

Pound Cake

- **1 cup butter (do not use margarine)**
- **½ cup vegetable shortening**
- **3 cups sugar**
- **6 large eggs or 7 medium eggs**
- **3¼ cups cake flour**
- **1 teaspoon baking powder**
- **½ teaspoon salt**
- **1 cup evaporated milk**
- **½ teaspoon vanilla extract**
- **½ teaspoon almond extract**

Cream butter and shortening together until smooth. Add sugar and beat until fluffy. Add eggs, 1 at a time, beating well after each addition. Combine flour, baking powder and salt. Alternately add dry ingredients and milk to egg mixture, Stir in vanilla and almond extract. Pour batter into greased and floured 10-inch tube pan. Bake at 300° for 2 hours. Cool in pan for 10 minutes, then remove to wire rack.
Yield: 16 to 20 servings

Simple Strawberry Cake

Cake

- **2 cups all-purpose flour**
- **½ teaspoon baking soda**
- **½ teaspoon salt**
- **3 eggs, beaten**
- **1 cup vegetable oil**
- **1 cup sugar**
- **1 (3 ounce) package strawberry gelatin**
- **1 cup buttermilk**
- **1 (10 ounce) package frozen strawberries, thawed**

Combine flour, baking soda and salt. Set aside. Combine eggs, oil, sugar, gelatin and buttermilk, mixing well. Blend in dry ingredients. Reserving ½ cup juice from strawberries, stir berries into batter. Pour batter into 2 greased and floured 8-inch round baking pans. Bake at 350° for 30 to 40 minutes. Prepare frosting and spread between layers and on top and sides of cooled cake.

Yield: 12 to 16 servings

Strawberry Frosting

- **¼ cup butter or margarine, softened**
- **1 (16 ounce) package powdered sugar**
- **⅓ to½ cup strawberry juice**

Combine butter or margarine with powdered sugar, beating until smooth. Add strawberry juice until spreading consistency, beating until creamy.

Brown Sugar Pound Cake

- **1 cup butter**
- **½ cup margarine or vegetable shortening**
- **1 (16 ounce) package light brown sugar**
- **1 cup sugar**
- **5 eggs**
- **3 cups all-purpose flour**
- **1 teaspoon baking powder**
- **½ teaspoon salt**
- **1 cup milk**
- **2 teaspoons vanilla extract**
- **1 cup finely chopped pecans**

Cream butter and margarine or shortening together until smooth. Gradually add brown sugar, beating well. Blend in sugar and beat until light and fluffy. Add eggs, 1 at a time, beating well after each addition. Sift flour, baking powder and salt together. Alternately add dry ingredients and milk to egg mixture, beginning and ending with dry ingredients. Add vanilla and pecans and beat for 2 minutes. Spread batter in greased and floured 10-inch tube or fluted pan. Bake at 325° for 1½ hours or until cake tests done.

Yield: 16 to 20 servings

Old Fashioned Pound Cake

2 cups sugar
2 cups butter, softened
10 eggs, separated
4¼ cups sifted cake flour
2 teaspoons vanilla, almond or lemon extract

Cream sugar and butter together until very light. Alternately add egg yolks and flour, beating thoroughly. Beat egg whites until stiff. Fold whites and extract into batter. Spread batter in 2 greased and floured 9x5x3-inch loaf pans or 10-inch tube pan. Bake at 325° for about 1¼ hours. Cool in pan for 10 minutes, then remove to wire rack.
Yield: 16 to 20 servings

No Crust Cheese Cake

Cake
3 (8 ounce) packages cream cheese, softened
5 eggs
1 cup sugar
¼ teaspoon salt
½ teaspoon almond extract

Using electric mixer, blend cream cheese with eggs, adding eggs 1 at a time. Blend in sugar, salt and almond extract. Spread batter in 9-inch spring form pan. Bake at 325° for 45 minutes, remove from oven, spread with topping, return to oven and bake for additional 10 minutes. Let stand until cool, then chill before serving.

Note: Cooled cake can be topped with pie filling or fresh fruit.
Yield: 12 to 16 servings

Topping
1½ cups sour cream
2 tablespoons sugar
½ teaspoon vanilla extract

Blend sour cream, sugar and vanilla together until smooth.

An ice cream scoop can be used to fill cupcake papers without spilling.

Grandmother's Applesauce Cupcakes

- **1 cup sugar**
- **½ cup vegetable shortening**
- **1 egg, well beaten**
- **1 (16 ounce) can applesauce**
- **2 cups all-purpose flour**
- **2 teaspoons baking powder**
- **1 teaspoon baking soda**
- **½ teaspoon salt**
- **1 teaspoon allspice**
- **½ teaspoon cinnamon**
- **½ teaspoon ground cloves**
- **½ teaspoon nutmeg**
- **1 cup raisins, soaked and drained**
- **1 cup chopped pecans**

Cream sugar and shortening together until light and fluffy. Beat in egg. Add applesauce and mix well. Combine flour, baking powder, baking soda, salt, allspice, cinnamon, cloves and nutmeg. Gradually add dry ingredients to creamed mixture. Stir in raisins and pecans. Spoon batter into paper-lined muffin pans. Bake at 350° for 20 to 25 minutes.

Note: Great for tailgate parties!

Yield: 1½ dozen

Orange Blossoms

Cake

- **2 cups sugar**
- **1 cup margarine, softened**
- **4 eggs**
- **4 cups sifted all-purpose flour**
- **2 teaspoons baking powder**
- **½ teaspoon salt**
- **1 cup milk**
- **1 teaspoon vanilla extract**

Cream sugar and margarine together until smooth. Add eggs, 1 at a time, beating well after each addition. Combine flour, baking powder and salt. Mix milk and vanilla together. Alternately add dry ingredients and milk liquid to egg mixture, mixing well. Pour batter into greased or paper-lined miniature muffin pans. Bake at 350° for 10 to 12 minutes. Prepare frosting. Dip tops of cakes into frosting and place on wax paper until frosting is firm.

Yield: 6 dozen

Icing

- **1½ (16 ounce) packages powdered sugar**
- **Grated peel of 1 orange**
- **Grated peel of 1 lemon**
- **Juice of 2 oranges**
- **Juice of 2 lemons**

Combine powdered sugar, orange and lemon peel and orange and lemon juice, blending well.

Caramel Frosting

- 2 (16 ounce) packages light brown sugar
- ¼ teaspoon salt
- ¾ cup plus 3 tablespoons evaporated milk
- 1 cup butter
- 2 teaspoons vanilla extract
- 1 teaspoon baking powder

Combine brown sugar, salt and milk in saucepan, mixing thoroughly. Add butter, bring to a boil and cook for 3 minutes. Remove from heat. Using electric mixer, blend in vanilla and baking powder. Beat until thickened to spreading consistency.

Note: Frosting is especially good on spice cake.
Yield: Covers 1 sheet or layer cake

Chocolate Frosting

- 1 (3 ounce) package cream cheese
- ½ cup butter
- 1½ (1 ounce) squares semi-sweet chocolate
- 1 (16 ounce) package powdered sugar, sifted twice
- 1 (12 ounce) can evaporated milk

Melt cream cheese, butter and chocolate together. Blend in powdered sugar. Add milk until spreading consistency.
Yield: Covers 1 sheet or layer cake

Best Fudge Frosting

- 2 cups sugar
- ½ cup unsweetened cocoa
- ½ cup butter
- ½ cup milk

Combine sugar, cocoa, butter and milk in saucepan. Bring to a boil and cook for 2 minutes. Remove from heat and beat with electric mixer until spreading consistency.
Yield: Covers 1 sheet or layer cake

Carrot Cookies

Cookies

- **¾ cup sugar**
- **¾ cup butter, softened**
- **1 egg**
- **2 cups all-purpose flour**
- **2 teaspoons baking powder**
- **Pinch of salt**
- **1 cup mashed cooked carrots**
- **1 teaspoon vanilla**

Cream sugar and butter together until smooth. Blend in egg. Combine flour, baking powder and salt. Add dry ingredients to creamed mixture. Stir in carrots and vanilla. Drop dough by teaspoonfuls on baking sheet. Bake at 350° for 15 minutes. Cool on wire rack. Prepare frosting and spread on cooled cookies.

Yield:

Orange Juice Frosting

- **1 (16 ounce) package powdered sugar**
- **¼ cup margarine, softened**
- **2 tablespoons orange juice**

Combine powdered sugar and margarine with enough orange juice for spreading consistency, beating until smooth.

Cherry Drop Cookies

- **1 (18½ ounce) package cherry cake mix**
- **½ cup vegetable oil**
- **2 tablespoons water**
- **2 eggs**
- **Few drops red food coloring (optional)**
- **1 cup chopped nuts**
- **Maraschino cherries, quartered**

Combine cake mix, oil, water, eggs and food coloring. Stir in nuts. Drop dough by teaspoonfuls on baking sheet. Bake at 350° for 10 to 12 minutes. Cool on baking sheets for about 12 minutes, then cool on wire rack.

Yield: 4 to 5 dozen

Easy Chocolate Chip Cookies

1 (18½ ounce) package white cake mix
1 egg
½ cup firmly-packed brown sugar
½ cup vegetable oil
½ cup water
2 (12 ounce) packages semi-sweet chocolate chips
1 (3½ ounce) can flaked coconut or 1 cup nuts (optional)

Using electric mixer, combine cake mix, egg, brown sugar, oil and water, mixing well. Stir in chocolate chips and coconut or nuts. Drop dough by teaspoonfuls on baking sheet. Bake at 350° for 10 minutes.
Yield: 4 dozen

$250 Cookie Recipe

2 cups sugar
2 cups firmly-packed brown sugar
2 cups butter
4 eggs
2 teaspoons vanilla
4 cups all-purpose flour
2 teaspoons baking powder
2 teaspoons baking soda
1 teaspoon salt
4 cups regular oats
2 (12 ounce) packages semi-sweeet chocolate chips
1 (8 ounce) Hershey bar, crumbled
3 cups chopped nuts

Cream sugar, brown sugar and butter together until smooth. Add eggs and vanilla, mixing well. Combine flour, baking powder, baking soda and salt. Place oats in blender or food processor container and process to fine consistency. Add dry ingredients and oats to creamed mixture. Stir in chocolate chips, candy and nuts. Shape and roll dough into 1-inch and place 2 inches apart on baking sheet. Bake at 375° for 6 minutes.

Note: Recipe can be halved for smaller quantity.
Yield: 9 to 10 dozen

A slice of soft bread placed in the package of hardened brown sugar will soften it again in a couple of hours.

Corn Flake Cookies

1 cup light corn syrup
1 cup sugar
1 (12 ounce) jar smooth or crunchy peanut butter
4½ cups corn flakes
1 (3½ ounce) can flaked coconut

Combine syrup and sugar in saucepan. Bring to a boil and cook, stirring until sugar is dissolved. Remove from heat, add peanut butter and stir until melted. Combine corn flakes and coconut in large bowl. Pour peanut butter mixture over cereal and mix thoroughly. Drop dough by teaspoonfuls on wax paper. Let stand until firm.
Yield: 3 to 4 dozen

Date Balls

1 cup margarine
2 cups firmly-packed brown sugar
1 (8 ounce) package chopped dates
1 (3½ ounce) can or 1 cup flaked coconut
2 cups chopped nuts
3 cups crispy rice cereal
Powdered sugar

Melt margarine in large saucepan. Add brown sugar, dates and coconut. Cook for 6 minutes. Remove from heat. Stir in nuts and cereal. Shape and roll mixture into 1-inch balls, then roll in powdered sugar. Store in air-tight container.
Yield: 8 to 9 dozen

Molasses Cookies

1 cup sugar
¾ cup margarine, softened
1 egg
¼ cup molasses
2 cups all-purpose flour
2 teaspoons baking soda
½ teaspoon salt
1 teaspoon cinnamon
¾ teaspoon cloves
1 teaspoon ginger

Combine sugar, margarine, egg and molasses, mixing until smooth. Combine flour, baking soda, salt, cinnamon, cloves and ginger. Add dry ingredients to molasses mixture, mixing well. Chill dough thoroughly. Shape and roll into 1-inch balls, roll in sugar and place on baking sheet. Bake at 350° for 10 to 15 minutes.
Yield: 7 dozen

Old Fashioned Molasses Cookies

¾ cup sugar
¾ cup vegetable shortening
¾ cup molasses
3¼ cups all-purpose flour
1½ teaspoons baking powder
¾ teaspoon baking soda
¾ teaspoon salt
2 teaspoons cinnamon
¼ teaspoon ground gloves
1 teaspoon ginger
½ teaspoon nutmeg

Combine sugar, shortening and molasses, mixing until smooth. Combine flour, baking powder, baking soda, salt, cinnamon, cloves, ginger and nutmeg. Add dry ingredients to molasses mixture, mixing well. Chill dough thoroughly. On lightly-floured surface, roll dough to ¼-inch thickness. Cut with cookie cutter and place shapes on baking sheet. Bake at 350° for about 8 minutes.
Yield: 3 to 4 dozen

French Lace Cookies

½ cup butter
1 cup sugar
1 egg
1 teaspoon vanilla
1 cup regular oats
3 tablespoons all-purpose flour
¼ teaspoon baking powder
½ teaspoon salt
¼ cup flaked coconut

Melt butter in saucepan and remove from heat. Stir in sugar, egg and vanilla, beating until smooth. Combine oats, flour, baking powder and salt. Add to egg mixture, mixing well. Stir in coconut. Drop dough by teaspoonfuls on aluminum-foil lined baking sheet. Bake at 350° for 10 to 12 minutes or until dark golden brown; cookies should be well browned but avoid burning. Cool on foil, then peel away from cookies.
Yield: 3 dozen

Oatmeal Cookies

1¼ cups sugar
½ cup vegetable shortening
½ cup molasses
2 eggs
1¾ cups all-purpose flour
1 teaspoon baking soda
1 teaspoon salt
1 teaspoon cinnamon
2 cups regular oats
1½ cups raisins

Combine sugar, shortening, molasses and eggs, beating until smooth. Sift flour, baking soda, salt and cinnamon together. Add dry ingredients to molasses mixture, mixing well. Stir in oats and raisins. Drop dough by teaspoonfuls on lightly-greased baking sheet. Bake at 375° for 8 to 10 minutes.
Yield: 6 dozen

Grammy Spicer's Oatmeal Refrigerator Cookies

- ½ cup sugar
- ½ cup firmly-packed brown sugar
- ½ cup vegetable shortening
- 1 egg
- ½ teaspoon vanilla
- 1 cup sifted all-purpose flour
- 1 teaspoon baking soda
- Pinch of salt
- 1 cup quick cooking oats
- ½ cup flaked coconut

Combine sugar, brown sugar, shortening, egg and vanilla, beating until smooth. Combine flour, baking soda and salt. Add dry ingredients, oats and coconut to egg mixture, mixing well. Divide dough in 3 or 4 portions and shape each into 1-inch diameter logs. Wrap in wax paper and chill or freeze. Cut logs in ¼-inch slices and place on greased baking sheet. Bake at 350° for 15 minutes. Store in tightly-covered container.

Yield: 4 dozen

Colossal Cookies

- 1½ cups sugar
- 1½ cups firmly-packed brown sugar
- ½ cup butter or margarine, softened
- 4 eggs
- 1 teaspoon vanilla
- 1 (18 ounce) jar or 2 cups crunchy peanut butter
- 6 cups quick cooking or regular oats
- 2½ teaspoons baking soda
- 1 (6 ounce) package semi-sweet chocolate chips

Cream sugar, brown sugar and butter or margarine together until smooth. Blend in eggs and vanilla. Add peanut butter and mix well. Stir in oats, baking soda and chocolate chips, mixing thoroughly. Drop dough by scant ¼-cup measure on ungreased baking sheet, spacing about 4 inches apart; flatten with fork tines to 2½ inches diameter. Bake at 350° for 10 to 12 minutes. Cool on baking sheet for 1 minute, then transfer to wire rack. Store in tightly covered container.

Note: To freeze dough, drop dough by scant ¼-cup measure on baking sheet but do not flatten. Freeze until firm, remove and place in plastic bags in freezer. Place frozen dough on ungreased baking sheet, let stand at room temperature for about 30 minutes, flatten with fork tines and bake as directed. For smaller cookies, drop by rounded tablespoonfuls on ungreased baking sheet and flatten with fork tines to 1¼-inch diameter. Bake at 375° for 8 to 10 minutes.

Yield: 9 dozen small
4½ dozen large

Peanut Butter Cookies

1 cup sugar
1 cup firmly-packed brown sugar
1 cup vegetable shortening
2 eggs
1 tablespoon vanilla
1 cup peanut butter
3 cups all-purpose flour
2 teaspoons baking soda
½ teaspoon salt

Cream sugar, brown sugar and shortening together until smooth. Blend in eggs and vanilla. Add peanut butter, mixing by hand. Combine flour, baking soda and salt. Work dry ingredients into dough, mixing well. Shape and roll into 1-inch balls, place on greased baking sheet and press with fork tines to flatten. Bake at 350° until golden brown.
Yield: 7 dozen

Scotch Shortbread

4½ cups all-purpose flour
⅓ cup rice flour
¾ cup sugar
1½ cups butter
Powdered sugar

Combine flour, rice flour and sugar. Add butter and knead until dough is firm paste consistency. Pat to ½-inch thickness in lightly-buttered 13x9x2-inch baking pan. Prick dough with fork tines in design. Bake at 275° for about 45 minutes; baked shortbread will be yellow, not brown. Sprinkle with powdered sugar. Store in covered container.
Yield: 2 dozen

Southern Teas

2 cups sugar
1 cup butter, softened
4 eggs
1 teaspoon vanilla
4 cups all-purpose flour
1 teaspoon baking soda
Sugar
Cinnamon (optional)

Cream sugar and butter together until smooth. Add eggs and vanilla, mixing thoroughly. Sift flour and baking soda together. Add dry ingredients to creamed mixture, blending to form soft dough. On lightly-floured surface, roll dough to ⅛-inch thickness. Cut with cookie cutter, place shapes on baking sheet and sprinkle with sugar and cinnamon. Bake at 375° for about 12 minutes.
Yield: 4 to 5 dozen

Butter Balls

- **½ cup powdered sugar**
- **1 cup butter, softened**
- **1 teaspoon vanilla**
- **2¼ cups all-purpose flour**
- **¼ teaspoon salt**
- **¾ cup chopped pecans**
- **Powdered sugar**

Cream sugar, butter and vanilla together until smooth. Sift flour and salt together. Add dry ingredients and pecans to creamed mixture. Chill thoroughly. Shape and roll dough into ¾-inch balls and place on ungreased baking sheet. Bake at 375° for 10 to 12 minutes. Roll warm balls in powdered sugar.
Yield: 7 dozen

Luscious Apricot Bars

- **⅔ cup dried apricots**
- **Water**
- **¼ cup sugar**
- **1⅓ cups all-purpose flour, divided**
- **½ cup margarine**
- **1 cup firmly-packed brown sugar**
- **2 eggs, beaten**
- **½ teaspoon baking powder**
- **½ teaspoon vanilla**
- **½ cup chopped nuts**
- **Powdered sugar**

Place apricots in small saucepan and add water to cover. Bring to a boil and cook for 10 minutes. Drain, let stand until cool, cut into small pieces and set aside. Combine sugar, 1 cup flour and margarine, mixing until crumbly. Press mixture into bottom of greased 9x9x2-inch baking pan. Bake at 350° for about 25 minutes or until lightly browned. Gradually add brown sugar to eggs, beating well. Combine remaining ⅓ cup flour and baking powder. Add to egg mixture, mixing thoroughly. Stir in vanilla, nuts and apricots. Spread mixture over baked crust. Bake at 350° for 30 minutes or until lightly browned. Cool slightly in pan, cut in bars and roll in powdered sugar.

Note: For a 13x9x2-inch baking pan, make 1½ recipes. These mail well.

Yield: 2 to 2½ dozen

Apricot Bars

1 cup sugar
¾ cup margarine, softened
2 cups all-purpose flour
1 cup grated or shredded coconut
¼ teaspoon salt
½ cup chopped pecans
1 egg
1 teaspoon vanilla
1 (12 ounce) jar apricot preserves

Blend sugar and margarine. Combine flour, coconut, salt and nuts. Add to sugar mixture. Set aside ⅓ of mixture. Mix egg and vanilla together. Add to remaining ⅔ of coconut mixture, stirring until crumbly. Press into well-greased 13x9x2-inch baking pan, pressing with spatula to cover bottom evenly. Spread preserves to within ¼-inch of edges. Sprinkle with reserved crumb mixture and press lightly with fork. Bake at 350° for 25 to 30 minutes. Cool before cutting into squares.
Yield: 3 dozen

Best Brownies

1 (15 ounce) package plain brownie mix
6 chocolate candy bars with almonds

Prepare brownie mix according to package directions. Spread ½ of batter in pan, arrange candy bars on batter and top with remaining batter. Bake according to package directions. Cool in pan, cut in squares and serve slightly warm; do not frost.

Note: If preferred, brownies batter can be prepared from a recipe instead of mix.
Yield: 24 squares

Blond Brownies

¼ cup butter or margarine
1 cup firmly-packed light brown sugar
1 egg
¾ cup sifted all-purpose flour
1 teaspoon baking powder
½ teaspoon salt
1 teaspoon vanilla
½ cup chopped nuts

Melt butter in saucepan and remove from heat. Stir in brown sugar and set aside to cool. Add egg and beat well. Sift flour, baking powder and salt together. Stir into brown sugar mixture. Add vanilla and nuts, mixing well. Spread batter in well-greased 8x8x2-inch baking pan. Bake at 350° for 30 to 35 minutes. Cut in diamonds or squares.
Yield: 1 ⅓ dozen

Caramel Fudge Brownies

- 1 (18½ ounce) package German chocolate cake mix
- ½ cup butter, melted
- ⅔ cup evaporated milk, divided
- 1 (12 ounce) package caramels
- 1 cup chopped pecans
- 1 (12 ounce) package semi-sweet chocolate chips

Combine cake mix, butter and ⅓ cup milk, mixing well. Spread ½ of batter in 13x9x2-inch baking dish. Bake at 350° for 6 minutes. In microwave-safe bowl, combine caramels and remaining ⅓ cup milk. Microwave at high (100%) setting, stirring several times, until caramels are melted and blended with milk. Stir in pecans and chocolate chips. Spread caramel mixture on partially baked crust. Top with remaining batter. Bake at 350° for 15 to 20 minutes.
Yield: 2 to 2½ dozen

Gold Rush Brownies

- 2 cups firmly-packed coarsely crushed graham cracker crumbs
- 1 (6 ounce) package semi-sweet chocolate chips
- ½ cup coarsely chopped pecans
- 1 (13 ounce) can sweetened condensed milk

Combine cracker crumbs, chocolate chips and pecans. Blend in milk. Pour batter into 8x8x2-inch baking pan prepared by greasing bottom, lining with wax paper and greasing wax paper. Bake at 350° for 30 to 35 minutes or until golden brown. Cool in pan for 10 minutes, remove, peel away wax paper and cut into squares or bars.
Yield: 1⅓ dozen

Toffee Bars

1 cup firmly-packed light brown sugar
1 cup butter
1 egg yolk
2 cups all-purpose flour
1 teaspoon vanilla
6 (1 ounce) squares milk chocolate
1 cup chopped pecans

Cream brown sugar and butter together until light and fluffy. Blend in egg yolk. Gradually add flour, mixing just until moistened. Add vanilla. Spread batter in lightly buttered 15x10x1-inch jelly roll pan. Bake at 350° for 20 to 25 minutes or until golden brown. Remove from oven, place chocolate on hot surface and spread smoothly. Sprinkle with nuts. Cut into squares while warm.
Yield: 3 dozen

Cinnamon Chocolate Bars

Bars

2 cups sugar
2 cups all-purpose flour
½ teaspoon salt
1 teaspoon cinnamon
½ cup margarine
½ cup vegetable oil
¼ cup unsweetened cocoa
1 cup water
½ cup buttermilk
1 teaspoon baking soda
2 eggs, beaten
1 teaspoon vanilla

Combine sugar, flour, salt and cinnamon in mixing bowl. Combine margarine, oil, cocoa and water in saucepan. Bring to a boil, pour over dry ingredients and mix until blended. Dissolve baking soda in buttermilk. Add buttermilk, eggs and vanilla to cocoa mixture. Spread batter in greased and floured 15x10x1-inch jelly roll pan. Bake at 350° for about 20 minutes. While cake bakes, prepare frosting. Pour frosting over hot cake. Cool before cutting into bars. Bars can be frozen.
Yield: 3 dozen

Frosting

½ cup margarine
¼ cup unsweetened cocoa
¼ cup plus 2 tablespoons milk
1 (16 ounce) package powdered sugar
1 teaspoon vanilla
1 cup chopped nuts

Melt margarine in saucepan. Add cocoa and milk. Bring to a boil. Remove from heat. Using electric mixer, beat in powdered sugar, vanilla and nuts.

Congo Bars

- 1 (16 ounce) package light brown sugar
- ½ cup plus 3 tablespoons margarine or butter
- 3 eggs
- 2¾ cups sifted self-rising flour
- 1 tablespoon vanilla
- ½ to 1 cup chopped pecans
- 1 (12 ounce) package semi-sweet chocolate chips

Cream brown sugar and butter or margarine together until smooth. Alternately add eggs and flour, beating well after each addition; batter will be thick. Stir in vanilla, pecans and chocolate chips. Spread batter in 13x9x2-inch baking pan, prepared by lining with wax paper and greasing wax paper. Bake at 325° for 40 to 45 minutes. Cool before cutting into squares.

Yield: 2 to 3 dozen

Coconut Goody Bars

- 1 (18½ ounce) package white or yellow cake mix
- ½ cup margarine, melted
- 1 egg
- ¾ cup chopped pecans
- 1 (8 ounce) package cream cheese, softened
- 1 (16 ounce) package powdered sugar
- 2 eggs
- 1 (3½ ounce) can flaked coconut

Combine cake mix, margarine and egg, mixing until crumbly. Press mixture in bottom of ungreased 13x9x2-inch baking pan. Sprinkle pecans on crumb layer and press down lightly. Combine cream cheese, powdered sugar and eggs, beating until smooth. Stir in coconut. Spread coconut mixture on crumb layer. Bake at 350° for 35 to 40 minutes. Cut into bars.

Yield: 2 to 3 dozen

Chinese Chews

- ¾ cup butter
- 2 cups firmly-packed brown sugar
- 2 eggs
- 1 teaspoon vanilla
- 1⅓ cups all-purpose flour
- 1½ teaspoons baking powder
- 1 cup chopped nuts

Melt butter in saucepan. Remove from heat and blend in brown sugar. Add eggs and vanilla, mixing well. Combine flour and baking powder. Add dry ingredients and nuts to brown sugar mixture, mixing thoroughly. Spread batter in 13x9x2-inch baking pan. Bake at 325° for 35 minutes. Cool for 1 hour in pan before cutting into squares.

Yield: 2 to 3 dozen

Orange Nut Bars

Bars

3 eggs
1 (6 ounce) can frozen orange juice concentrate, thawed and undiluted
1 cup sugar
2 cups graham cracker crumbs
1 teaspoon baking powder
¼ teaspoon salt
1 cup chopped nuts
1 (8 ounce) package chopped dates
1 teaspoon vanilla

Beat eggs until light and fluffy. Blend in orange juice concentrate. Add cracker crumbs, baking powder, salt, nuts, dates and vanilla to egg liquid, mixing well. Spread batter in greased and lightly floured 9x9x2-inch baking pan. Bake at 350° for 50 minutes. Cool in pan. Spread with frosting and cut into bars.
Yield: 2 to 2½ dozen

Orange Frosting

1½ cups powdered sugar
2½ tablespoons orange juice

Combine powdered sugar and orange juice, beating until smooth and spreading consistency.

Peanut Butter Incredibles

⅓ (16 ounce) package graham crackers, crushed
½ cup margarine, melted
1½ cups smooth or crunchy peanut butter
1 (16 ounce) package powdered sugar
1 (13 ounce) can sweetened condensed milk
2 (12 ounce) packages semi-sweet chocolate chips

Combine cracker crumbs, margarine, peanut butter, powdered sugar and milk. Spread dough in 15x10x1-inch jelly roll pan prepared with vegetable cooking spray. Melt chocolate chips and spread over peanut butter mixture. Cut into squares, then chill.

Note: Always cut before chilling to avoid crumbling chocolate. Bars can be frozen.

Yield: 3 dozen

Pineapple Cheesecake Bars

Crust

1 cup all-purpose flour
½ cup sugar
½ cup margarine, softened

Combine flour, sugar and margarine, mixing to crumb consistency. Press crumbs in bottom of ungreased 13x9x2-inch baking pan. Bake at 350° for 10 to 15 minutes or until lightly browned.

Filling

2 tablespoons sugar
1 (8 ounce) package cream cheese, softened
2 tablespoons milk
1 teaspoon vanilla
1 egg
1 (20 ounce) can crushed pineapple, drained
1 cup flaked coconut
1 tablespoon margarine, melted

Using electric mixer, beat sugar, cream cheese, milk, vanilla and egg at medium speed for 3 minutes or until smooth. Stir in pineapple. Pour over partially baked crust. Combine coconut and margarine. Sprinkle over filling. Bake at 350° for 15 to 20 minutes or until firm. Cool before cutting into bars. Store in refrigerator.
Yield: 3 dozen

Yummy Squares

1 (18½ ounce) package yellow cake mix
3 eggs, divided
½ cup margarine, melted
1 (8 ounce) package low-fat cream cheese, softened
1 (16 ounce) package powdered sugar

Combine cake mix, 1 egg and margarine. Spread mixture in bottom of 11x7x1½-inch baking dish. Beat 2 eggs. Add cream cheese and powdered sugar and mix until smooth. Spread filling on crumb layer. Bake at 325° for 50 minutes. Cool before cutting into squares.
Yield: 1¼ dozen

No Bake Candy Balls

1 cup peanut butter
1 cup powdered sugar
½ cup chopped nuts
2 tablespoons butter, softened
1 cup coconut

Combine peanut butter, powdered sugar, nuts and butter, mixing well. Shape and roll into 1-inch balls. Roll each ball in coconut. Chill.
Yield: 3 dozen

Pink Party Things

Bars

1 (16 ounce) package graham crackers
1 cup butter
1 egg
½ cup milk
1 cup sugar
1 cup chopped nuts
1 cup flaked coconut
1 cup graham cracker crumbs

Line bottom of 13x9x2-inch baking pan with graham crackers. Melt butter in heavy saucepan. Combine egg, milk and sugar together. Add to butter and bring to a boil. Remove from heat. Stir in nuts, coconut and cracker crumbs. Spread mixture evenly on cracker layer and top with layer of crackers. Prepare frosting and spread on cracker layer. Chill for at least 4 hours. Cut into bars.
Yield: 4 dozen

Frosting

½ cup plus 1 tablespoon butter, softened
3 cups sifted powdered sugar
1½ tablespoons milk
1½ teaspoons vanilla
Few drops red food coloring

Combine butter, powdered sugar, milk and vanilla, beating until smooth. Tint with food coloring.

Buckeyes

1 (12 ounce) jar creamy or crunchy peanut butter
1 cup butter, softened
1½ (16 ounce) packages powdered sugar, sifted
2 (12 ounce) packages semi-sweet chocolate chips
1 bar paraffin

Combine peanut butter and butter, mixing until smooth. Blend in powdered sugar. Shape and roll into small balls. Refrigerate. Melt chocolate and about ¼ of paraffin in top of double boiler. Using wooden pick, dip each candy ball into chocolate, place on wax paper and chill until firm.

Note: Dee Underwood, wife of WBTV's C.J. Underwood says this is absolutely one of his favorites.
Yield: 6 to 8 dozen

Butter Creams

- 1 (12 ounce) jar crunchy peanut butter
- ½ cup margarine, softened
- 1 teaspoon vanilla
- Pinch of salt
- 1 (16 ounce) package powdered sugar
- 1 (12 ounce) package butterscotch morsels
- ¼ block paraffin

Combine peanut butter, margarine, vanilla, salt and powdered sugar. Shape and roll into small balls. Melt butterscotch chips and paraffin together. Using wooden pick, dip each candy ball into candy coating and place on wax paper to cool.
Yield: 6 to 8 dozen

Chocolate Pecan Toffee

- 1 cup sugar
- ½ cup butter or margarine
- ½ teaspoon cream of tartar
- 1 cup pecan pieces
- 6 plain chocolate candy bars

Combine sugar, butter or margarine and cream of tartar in heavy medium-size saucepan. Cook, stirring constantly, until syrup reaches 300° on candy thermometer. Spread pecan pieces on baking sheet. Drizzle syrup on pecans, using back of spoon to spread and separate. Place candy bars on hot candy and spread evenly as it melts. Cool, then break into pieces.
Yield: 1½ pounds

Toffee Bar Candy

- 40 saltine crackers
- 1 cup butter
- 1 cup firmly-packed brown sugar
- 1 (12 ounce) package semi-sweet chocolate chips
- 2 cups chopped pecans

Prepare 13x9x2-inch baking pan by lining with aluminum foil and spraying with vegetable cooking spray. Place layer of saltines in bottom. Combine butter and brown sugar in saucepan. Bring to a boil and cook for 2 minutes. Pour hot mixture over crackers. Bake at 350° for 12 minutes. Remove from oven, let stand for 1 minute, sprinkle with chocolate chips and spread as chips melt. Sprinkle pecans over chocolate, pressing lightly. Chill for 2 to 3 hours. Break into pieces.
Yield: Approximately 1½ to 2 pounds

Martha's Chocolate Wonderfuls

1 (16 ounce) jar crunchy peanut butter
1 (16 ounce) package Ritz crackers
1 tablespoon vegetable oil or shortening
1 (16 ounce) package almond bark

Spread between ½ and 1 teaspoon peanut butter on each cracker. Place oil or shortening in heavy sauce pan. Add almond bark, melt over low heat and keep warm. Using fork and spoon, dip 1 cracker at a time, peanut butter side down, into almond bark, drain briefly and place on wax paper on baking sheet. Chill for about 15 minutes. Store in tightly-covered container or freeze.

Note: For variety, use 2 crackers with peanut butter to make "sandwich", dip in chocolate coating and top with pecan half. White or dark chocolate almond bark may be used.
Yield: 4½ dozen

English Toffee Butter Crunch

1 cup plus 2 tablespoons sugar
1 cup butter
1 (6 ounce) package semi-sweet chocolate chips

Prepare baking sheet by lining with aluminum foil and lightly buttering the foil. Combine sugar and butter in heavy iron skillet. Cook over medium heat, stirring constantly, until candy thermometer reaches 304° (hard crack stage); syrup will be deep amber. Immediately pour onto foil and spread thin. Melt chocolate in double boiler over simmering water and spread over cooled toffee. Break into pieces.
Yield: Approximately 1 pound

Condensed Milk

1 cup instant nonfat milk powder
⅔ cup sugar
⅓ cup boiling water
3 tablespoons butter or margarine, melted

Combine milk powder, sugar, boiling water and butter or margarine in blender container. Blend until smooth. Store in refrigerator.
Yield: Equal to 1 (13 ounce) can sweetened condensed milk

Peanut or Pecan Brittle

2 cups raw shelled peanuts or pecans
1½ cups sugar
½ cup light corn syrup
2 tablespoons water
1½ teaspoons baking soda

Prepare baking sheet by lining with aluminum foil and lightly buttering the foil. Preheat electric skillet to 350°. Place peanuts or pecan in skillet. Add sugar, syrup and water. Cook, stirring occasionally, for about 10 minutes or until syrup is golden. Stir in baking soda; mixture will foam and deepen in color. Quickly pour syrup onto baking sheet and spread thin. Cool until firm and no longer sticky. Break into bite-size pieces. Store in air-tight container.
Yield: Approximately 1 to 1½ pounds

Chocolate Fondue

1 (12 ounce) package semi-sweet chocolate chips
1 cup light corn syrup
2 teaspoons vanilla
Dash of salt
Strawberries, pineapple chunks or cake cubes

Combine chocolate chips, syrup, vanilla and salt in top of double boiler over simmering water. Stir until chocolate is melted and mixture is smooth. Transfer to chafing dish or fondue pot and keep warm. Dip strawberries, pineapple or cake in sauce.

Note: A great party recipe.
Yield: 2½ cups

Cherry Rum Sauce

½ cup sugar
1 tablespoon cornstarch
¼ teaspoon salt
1 (16 ounce) can water-packed red tart cherries
¼ teaspoon red food coloring
1 cup whipping cream, whipped
½ teaspoon rum extract

Combine sugar, cornstarch and salt in saucepan. Drain cherries, reserving juice. Add juice and food coloring to dry ingredients, mixing until smooth. Cook, stirring frequently, until thickened and clear. Stir in cherries and simmer for 5 minutes. Chill. Just before serving, fold whipped cream and rum extract into sauce. Serve on pudding, angel food cake or plain cake.
Yield: 6 to 8 servings

French Candy Loaf

First Layer

3 cups sugar
1 cup half and half
1 tablespoon butter
1 teaspoon vanilla
½ cup chopped blanched almonds

Combine sugar and half and half in saucepan. Bring to a boil and cook, stirring constantly, until stream of syrup forms small ball in cold water. Remove from heat to cool. Stir in butter. When lukewarm, add vanilla and beat until creamy. Stir in nuts. Pour into lightly greased 9x5x3-inch loaf pan. Set aside to harden while making the second layer.

Second Layer

3 cups firmly-packed light brown sugar
1 cup half and half
1 tablespoon butter
Pink food coloring
¼ teaspoon peppermint flavoring
½ cup chopped Brazil nuts

Combine brown sugar and half and half in saucepan. Bring to a boil and cook, stirring constantly, until stream of syrup forms small ball in cold water. Remove from heat to cool. Stir in butter. When lukewarm, add food coloring and peppermint flavoring and beat until creamy. Stir in nuts. Spread mixture over firm first layer in loaf pan. Let harden while making the third layer.

Third Layer

3 cups firmly-packed light brown sugar
2 (1 ounce) squares unsweetened chocolate
1 cup half and half
1 teaspoon vanilla
½ cup chopped pecans

Combine brown sugar, chocolate and half and half in saucepan. Bring to a boil and cook, stirring constantly, until stream of syrup forms small ball in cold water. Remove from heat to cool. Stir in vanilla and beat until creamy. Stir in pecans. Spread mixture over firm second layer in loaf pan. When third layer is firm, remove candy loaf from pan. Because of richness, slice thinly to serve.

Note: This recipe has been a family special treat at Christmas for generations.

Yield: 1 loaf

Helpful Hints

Measuring Ingredients

Individual cups are used to measure dry ingredients. Standard sets of cups come in 1 cup, ½ cup, ⅓ cup and ¼ cup sizes.

Clear cups, either plastic or glass, with a pouring spout are used to measure liquid ingredients. Standard liquid measures are 1 cup, 2 cup and 1 quart. Each indicates volume in cups and fluid ounces. Metric units may also be indicated.

Measuring spoons are used for small quantities of dry and liquid ingredients. Standard sets of spoons are 1 tablespoon, 1 teaspoon, ½ teaspoon and ¼ teaspoon.

Measuring Dry Ingredients

Regular measures: This method is used for foods such as all-purpose flour and granulated sugar. Scoop ingredient to overflow cup and level with a straight edge. When measuring flour, do not shake the cup to level the flour because it will pack.

Loosely packed measures: This method is used for cake flour and powdered sugar. Spoon ingredient into measuring cup and level with a straight edge. Cake flour and powdered sugar have a tendency to pack and should be sifted before measuring.

Firmly packed measures: This method is used for foods such as brown sugar, fats and shortening. Spoon ingredient into cup, firmly press to remove air pockets and level with a straight edge. For easier removal of fats and shortening, rinse cup with water before measuring.

For measuring spoons, pour or scoop ingredient into the spoon and level with a straight edge.

Measuring Liquid Ingredients

Place the measuring cup on a level surface. Pour ingredient into cup to desired level, checking the measurement at eye level and adjusting if necessary.

For measuring spoons, pour liquid into the spoon until brimful. When measuring sticky liquids, such as honey, molasses or syrup, rinse spoon with water or lightly grease.

Measurements and Equivalents

Measurement	Equivalent
pinch or dash	less than 1/8 teaspoon
60 drops	1 teaspoon
3 teaspoons	1 tablespoon
2 tablespoons	1 fluid ounce
1 jigger	1 1/2 fluid ounces
1/2 cup	8 tablespoons
1/2 cup	4 fluid ounces
5/8 cup	1/2 cup plus 2 tablespoons
5/8 cup	10 tablespoons
1/3 cup	5 tablespoons plus 1 teaspoon
2/3 cup	10 tablespoons plus 2 teaspoons
2/3 cup	5 1/3 fluid ounces
3/4 cup	12 tablespoons
3/4 cup	6 fluid ounces
7/8 cup	14 tablespoons
7/8 cup	3/4 cup plus 2 tablespoons
1 cup	16 tablespoons
1 cup	8 fluid ounces
1 cup	1/2 pint
1 1/4 cups	10 fluid ounces
1 1/3 cups	10 2/3 fluid ounces
1 1/2 cups	12 fluid ounces
1/3 quart	1 1/3 cups
3/8 quart	1 1/2 cups
1/2 quart	2 cups
5/8 quart	2 1/2 cups
3/4 quart	3 cups
7/8 quart	3 1/2 cups
1 quart	4 cups
1 quart	2 pints
1 quart	1/4 gallon
1 quart	32 fluid ounces
1 quart	.946 liters
1 2/3 cups	13 1/3 fluid ounces
1 3/4 cups	14 fluid ounces
2 cups	16 fluid ounces
2 cups	1 pint
2 1/2 cups	20 fluid ounces
3 cups	24 fluid ounces
3 cups	3/4 quart
3 1/2 cups	28 fluid ounces
3 1/2 cups	7/8 quart
4 cups	1 quart

Measurement	Equivalent
1/16 pint	2 tablespoons
1/8 pint	1/4 cup
1/4 pint	1/2 cup
1/3 pint	2/3 cup
3/8 pint	3/4 cup
1/2 pint	1 cup
2/3 pint	1 1/3 cup
5/8 pint	1 1/4 cups
3/4 pint	1 1/2 cup
7/8 pint	1 3/4 cups
1 pint	2 cups
1/16 quart	1/4 cup
1/8 quart	1/2 cup
1/4 quart	1 cup
1/4 gallon	1 quart
1/3 gallon	1 1/3 quarts
3/8 gallon	1 1/2 quarts
1/2 gallon	2 quarts
5/8 gallon	2 1/2 quarts
2/3 gallon	2 2/3 quarts
3/4 gallon	3 quarts
7/8 gallon	3 1/2 quarts
1 gallon	4 quarts
1 gallon	8 pints
1 gallon	16 cups
1 liter	1.06 quart
1 liter	4 cups plus 3 1/3 tablespoons
5 cups	40 fluid ounces
6 cups	1 1/2 quarts
6 cups	48 fluid ounces
10 cups	2 1/2 quarts
10 cups	80 fluid ounces
12 cups	3 quarts
12 cups	96 fluid ounces
3 quarts	12 cups
3 quarts	3/4 gallon
4 quarts	1 gallon
4 quarts	128 fluid ounces
1/16 gallon	1 cup
1/8 gallon	1/2 quart

Dry Weights

Measurement	Equivalent	Measurement	Equivalent
2 gallons	1 peck	1 bushel	32 quarts
8 quarts	1 peck	1 bushel	64 pints
1 peck	8 quarts	1 bushel	128 cups
1 peck	2 gallons	¼ pound	4 ounces
4 pecks	1 bushel	½ pound	8 ounces
1 bushel	4 pecks	1 pound	16 ounces
1 bushel	8 gallons	2.2 pounds	1 kilo

Grams: Ounce Equivalents

Grams	Ounce	Grams	Ounce
25	0.87	85	3.0
30	1.0	100	3.5
50	1.75	125	4.4
75	2.63	150	5.25
80	2.8		

Conversion Formulas

To convert	Multiply		Times		
ounces to grams	the ounces	x	28.35	=	grams
grams to ounces	the grams	x	0.035	=	ounces
liters to U.S. quarts	the liters	x	0.95	=	U.S. quarts
liters to British quarts	the liters	x	0.88	=	British quarts
U.S. quarts to liters	the quarts	x	1.057	=	liters
British quarts to liters	the quarts	x	1.14	=	liters
inches to centimeters	the inches	x	2.54	=	centimeters
centimeters to inches	the centimeters	x	0.39	=	inches

Ingredient Yields

apple	1 medium	1 cup chopped
	3 medium	3 cups sliced or 3½ cups pared
bacon	8 slices, fried	½ cup crumbled
bananas	2 small or 1 medium	1 cup sliced
beans: butter, green or wax	1 pound	3 cups of 1-inch pieces
bread: white	1½ pounds	19 slices
	1½ pounds	24 thin slices
	2 pounds	28 slices
	2 pounds	36 thin slices
whole-wheat	1 pound	16 slices
	2 pounds	28 thin slices
rye	1 pound	23 slices
butter	½ pound or 2 sticks	16 tablespoons

blue cheese	4 ounces	1 cup crumbled
carrots	2 medium	1 cup of ¼-inch slices
	1½ medium	1 cup shredded
cauliflower	1 pound	3 cups flowerets
celery	2 medium stalks	1 cup of ¼-inch slices
	1¾ stalks	1 cup thinly sliced
cheese	4 ounces	1 cup shredded
	1 pound	4 cups shredded
corn	2 medium ears	1 cup kernels
crab	1 pound in shell	¾ to 1 cup flaked
cream	1 cup	2 cups whipped
crumbs: bread	4 slices	1 cup fine
chocolate	19 cookies	1 cup crushed
graham cracker	16 squares	1¼ cups crushed
saltines	28 squares	1 cup fine
vanilla wafer	22 wafers	1 cup fine
eggs	1 medium	¼ cup or 2 fluid ounces
	2½ medium	⅔ cup
	39 medium	1 pound
egg whites	8 to 10	1 cup
egg yolks	16	1 cup
green bell pepper	1	1 cup chopped
lemon	1	3 tablespoons juice
lemon peel	1	1½ to 3 teaspoons grated
marshmallows	10 small	1 large
	11 large or 110 small	1 cup
mushrooms	8 ounces	3 cups of ¼-inch slices
olives	15 large	1 cup chopped
	36 small	1 cup chopped
onions: green	9	1 cup sliced
white	1 medium	1 cup chopped
orange	1	⅓ to ½ cup juice
orange peel	1	1 to 2 tablespoons grated
potatoes	1 medium	1 cup grated
raisins	15 ounces	2¾ cups
rice: brown	1 cup	4 cups cooked
parboiled	1 cup	3 to 4 cups cooked
instant	1 cup	2 cups cooked
regular	1 cup	3 cups cooked
wild	1 cup	3 to 4 cups cooked
shrimp	1½ pounds in shell	2 cups cooked
tomato	1 medium	1 cup chopped

Canned Foods

The manufacturer of canned foods is required to list all ingredients used in preparation of the contents. Nutritional information is also required.

Purchase cans that are in good condition; do not buy or use cans that are dented, rusted or bulging. Store canned goods at room temperature. The average shelf life of canned foods is one year.

Can Sizes

Size	Weight	Volume	Number of 4 oz. servings	Common Uses
6 ounces	6 ounces	¾ cup	6	frozen juice concentrates
8 ounces	8 ounces	1 cup	2	fruits, vegetables
No. 1	10½ to 12 ounces	1¼ cups	2 to 3	condensed soups
12 ounce	12 ounce	1½ cups	3 to 4	fish products
No. 300	14 to 16 ounces	1¾ cups	3 to 4	beans, spaghetti, fruits, cranberry sauce
No. 1½ or 303	15 to 17 ounces	2 cups	4	fruit cocktail
No. 1 tall	16 ounces	2 cups	4	vegetables
No. 2	20 ounces	2½ cups	4 to 5	fruits, juices, vegetables
No. 2½	28 ounces	3½ cups	7	fruits, tomatoes, pumpkin
No. 3	32 ounces	4 cups	8	fruits, vegetables
46 fluid ounces	46 ounces	5¾ cups	9 to 11	fruit and vegetable juices
No. 5	52 ounces	6½ cups	12 to 13	institutional size
No. 10	105 ounces	12 cups	25	institutional size

Ingredient Substitution

Chocolate

If a recipe calls for:	*Use:*
1 (1 ounce) square unsweetened chocolate	• 1 (1 ounce) envelope soft baking chocolate • ½ cup semi-sweet chocolate chips (reduce shortening by 1 tablespoon and sugar by ¼ cup) • 2 tablespoons cocoa plus ½ tablespoon butter
3 (3 ounce) squares semi-sweet baking chocolate	• ½ cup semi-sweet chocolate chips
¼ cup unsweetened cocoa	• 1 (1 ounce) envelope soft baking chocolate • ½ cup semi-sweet chocolate chips (reduce shortening by 1 tablespoon and sugar by ¼ cup)

Ingredient Substitution

Flour *If a recipe calls for:*	*Use:*
1 cup sifted cake flour	• 1 cup sifted all-purpose flour less 2 tablespoons
1 cup sifted self-rising flour	• 1 cup sifted all-purpose flour plus 1¼ teaspoons baking powder and less than ⅛ teaspoon salt (omit baking powder and salt in recipe)
1 cup all-purpose flour	• 1 cup plus 2 tablespoons cake flour • 1 cup graham flour • 1 cup rye flour • 1½ cups bran • 1½ cups bread crumbs • 1 cup rolled oats • ⅞ cup cornmeal
1 cup biscuit mix	• 1 cup flour plus 1½ teaspoons baking powder and 2 tablespoons shortening
Thickening Agents *If a recipe calls for:*	*Use:*
2 tablespoons flour	• 3½ eggs • 7 egg yolks • ¾ ounce bread crumbs • 1 tablespoon cornstarch
Leavening Agents *If a recipe calls for:*	*Use:*
1 teaspoon baking powder	• ¼ teaspoon baking soda plus ½ teaspoon cream of tartar • 2 egg whites • ¼ teaspoon baking soda plus ½ cup buttermilk or sour milk (reduce liquid in recipe by ½ cup)
1 packet active dry yeast	• 1 cake compressed yeast
1 cup whole milk	• ¼ cup dry whole milk plus 1 cup water • ¾ cup non-fat dry milk solids plus 1 cup water and 3 tablespoons butter • ½ cup evaporated milk plus ½ cup water • 1 cup buttermilk plus ½ teaspoon baking soda
1 cup light cream	• ⅞ cup milk plus 3 tablespoons butter
1 cup heavy cream	• ¾ cup milk plus ⅓ cup butter
1 cup sour milk or buttermilk	• 1 cup sweet milk plus 1 tablespoon lemon juice or vinegar (let stand for 5 minutes) • 1 cup sweet milk plus 1¾ teaspoon cream of tartar

Ingredient Substitution

1 cup heavy sour cream	• ⅓ cup butter and ⅔ cup sour milk recipe
1 cup thin sour cream	• 3 tablespoons butter and ¾ cup sour milk recipe

Butter

If a recipe calls for:	*Use:*
1 cup butter	• ¾ cup clarified bacon fat (increase recipe liquid by ¼ cup) • ⅔ cup clarified chicken fat (increase recipe liquid by ¼ cup) • ⅞ cup corn or nut oil plus pinch of salt • ⅞ cup lard or vegetable shortening plus ½ teaspoon salt • 1 cup margarine • 1¼ cups whipping cream • 2½ cups half and half

Seasoning and Spices

If a recipe calls for:	*Use:*
1 teaspoon dried herbs	1 tablespoon fresh herbs
1 teaspoon allspice	⅓ teaspoon each of cinnamon, cloves and nutmeg
1 teaspoon basil	1 teaspoon oregano
1 teaspoon caraway	1 teaspoon anise
1 teaspoon cayenne pepper	1 teaspoon chili powder
1 teaspoon chervil	1 teaspoon parsley or tarragon
1 teaspoon fennel	1 teaspoon anise or tarragon
⅛ teaspoon garlic powder	1 small clove garlic
1 tablespoon prepared mustard	1 teaspoon dry mustard
1 teaspoon nutmeg	1 teaspoon mace
1 tablespoon minced onion flakes	1 small fresh onion
1 tablespoon onion powder	1 medium-size fresh onion
1 teaspoon oregano	1 teaspoon marjoram
1 teaspoon sage	1 teaspoon thyme

Sugar and Sweeteners

If a recipe calls for:	*Use:*
1 cup sugar	• 1 cup molasses plus ½ teaspoon baking soda (reduce recipe liquid by ¼ cup) • ½ cup honey plus ½ teaspoon baking soda (reduce recipe liquid by ¼ cup) • 1 cup maple syrup plus ¼ cup corn syrup (reduce recipe liquid by ¼ cup) • 1 cup maple syrup plus ¼ teaspoon baking soda
1 cup brown sugar	• 1 cup white sugar plus ¼ cup molasses
1 cup corn syrup	• 1 cup sugar plus additional ¼ cup recipe liquid
1 cup honey	• 1¼ cups sugar plus additional ¼ cup recipe liquid • 1 cup molasses

Quantity Food Preparation

Servings for 50

Quantities are averages. Adjust each serving according to serving adults or children or both.

Food	Serving Unit	Quantity
Bread/Cereal		
biscuits	2 to 3	10½ to 11 dozen
bran cereal	½ cup	3 (16 ounce) packages
cinnamon rolls	1 (3 ounce) roll	4½ dozen
cornbread	2 (2x2-inch) pieces	4 (13x9x2-inch) pans
doughnuts	1 or 2	7 dozen
grits (cooked)	⅔ cup	3 pounds makes 2 gallons
hard rolls	1 (3 ounce) roll	4½ to 6½ dozen
10-inch layer cake	1 (2 inch) slice	3 (10 inch) cakes
muffins	1 or 2	6 dozen
noodles (cooked)	⅔ cup	4 pounds makes 2 gallons
saltines	2 crackers	1 pound
sandwich bread	2 slices	7 pounds
spaghetti (cooked)	⅔ cup	4 to 5 pounds makes 2 gallons
Dairy Products		
butter	1 to 2 pats	1 to 1½ pounds
eggs	1 or 2	4½ to 8½ dozen
cream for coffee	1 tablespoon	2 cups
milk	¾ cup	2½ gallons
Fruit Juices		
canned	½ cup	4 (46 ounce) cans
frozen	½ cup	4 (12 ounce) cans
Meats		
ground meat patties	3½ ounces	14 pounds
cold cuts	2 to 2½ ounces	6½ to 8½ pounds
hot dogs	2	10 to 12 pounds
fried chicken	¼ to½ chicken	13 to 25 fryers
Vegetables		
dried beans (cooked)		4 to 5 ounces 5 pounds
broccoli	3 ounces	12 to 16 pounds
carrots	3 ounces	12½ pounds
lettuce for salad	1½ to 2 ounces	8 to 10 heads
tomatoes to slice	3 ounces	10 to 12½ pounds
Miscellaneous		
olives	3 or 4	2 quarts (84 to 94 count)
3-inch pickles	½ to 1	1½ to 2 pounds
jam and jelly	2 tablespoons	3 pounds
syrup	¼ cup	3¼ quarts
sugar	1½ teaspoons	¾ pound

Volume Units

Food	Unit	Weight	No. Per Unit
apples, medium	box	48 pounds	88 to 138
	bushel	45 to 50 pounds	100
bananas, medium	box	40 pounds	120
cantaloupe	crate	70 pounds	23 to 45
corn, ears	sack	40 pounds	200
grapefruit	carton	36 pounds	18 to 48
lettuce	carton	40 to 50 pounds	24 to 30 heads
onions, medium	sack	50 pounds	250
oranges	carton	40 pounds	48 to 180
peaches	bushel	50 pounds	80 to 88
	lug	18 to 14 pounds	55 medium
pears	box	50 pounds	80 to 180
baking potatoes	carton	50 pounds	60 to 140
strawberries	flat	12 (1 pint) boxes	
	crate	16 (1 quart) or 32 (1 pint) boxes	

Oven Temperature Guide

Always PREHEAT oven before placing food in unless the recipe calls for a cold oven.

Term	Fahrenheit	Celsius
very slow	250 to 275°	121 to 135°
slow	275 to 325°	135 to 163°
moderate	325 to 375°	163 to 191°
hot	375 to 425°	191 to 219°
very hot	425 to 475°	219 to 246°
extremely hot	475 to 525°	246 to 274°

Oven temperatures may vary from the dial setting. Inexpensive oven thermometers, available at hardware stores, in cooking utensil departments or through catalogs, can be placed in oven to monitor the precise temperature. Make adjustments accordingly. When using glass ovenware, reduce oven temperature by 25°.

To Determine Oven Temperatures Without a Thermometer

Sprinkle a small amount of flour in a pan and place in a heated oven. A piece of white tissue may be used instead of flour.

250 to 325°	Flour or tissue turns delicate brown in five minutes.
325 to 400°	Flour or tissue turns golden brown in five minutes.
400 to 450°	Flour or tissue turns deep brown in five minutes.
450 to 500°	Flour or tissue turns dark brown in three minutes.

Conversion Formula

To convert centigrade to fahrenheit: multiply by 9, divide by 5 and add 32.
To convert fahrenheit to centigrade: subtract 32, multiple by 5 and divided by 9.

Temperatures and Baking Times

Product	Oven Temperature (Fahrenheit°)	Baking Time (Minutes)
breads		
biscuits	425 to 450	10 to 15
cornbread	400 to 425	30 to 40
cream puffs	375	60
muffins	400 to 425	20 to 25
popovers	375	60
quick loaf breads	350 to 375	60 to 75
yeast bread	400	30 to 40
yeast rolls (plain)	400 to 425	15 to 25
sweet	375	20 to 30
cakes		
cupcakes	350 to 375	15 to 25
layer	350	20 to 30
loaf	350	45 to 60
angel food or sponge	350 to 375	30 to 45
cookies		
drop	350 to 400	8 to 15
rolled	375	8 to 10
egg/meat/milk/cheese		
cheese soufflé (baked in pan of hot water)	350	30 to 60
custard (baked in pan of hot water)	350	30 to 60
macaroni and cheese	350	25 to 30
meat loaf	300	60 to 90
meat pie	400	25 to 30
rice pudding	300	120 to 180
scalloped potatoes	350	60
pies		
custard in unbaked shell	400 to 425	30 to 40
meringue or cooked filling in baked shell	350 to 425	12 to 15
pastry shell	450	10 to 12
uncooked filling in double-crust	400 to 425	45 to 55
cooked filling in double-crust	425 to 450	30 to 45

Food Storage

Dry Food Storage

Location is the most important consideration in shelf storage of dry foods. Generally, foods stored at room temperature and away from heat sources will keep well if resealed properly or placed in airtight storage containers or cannisters. Packaged foods stored close to the stove top and oven or dishwasher can have a shorter shelf life because of the heat distributed from the appliances.

Heat can destroy the essence of herbs and spices so they should be stored away from heat-generating appliances. They also have a relatively short shelf life so it is better to buy in small quantities or divide purchases with a friend. Note the purchase date on the container with a marker.

Food	Average Shelf Lfe	Storage Suggestions
baking powder and baking soda	18 months	date container
bouillon cubes or granules	1 year	away from moisture or heat
bread	5 to 7 days	reclose wrapped with twist tie, store in refrigerator during summer
cake mixes	1 year	away from moisture or heat
canned foods	1 year	date container
chili sauce	1 month	can be refrigerated
coffee (instant)	6 months	can be refrigerated or frozen
coffee (vacuum pack)	1 year	can be refrigerated or frozen
dry cereals	4 to 6 months	airtight container
crumbs	6 months	airtight container or freezer
flour	1 year	airtight container or freeze
gelatin	18 months	date container
herbs and spices	6 months	date container
honey	1 year	if honey crystallizes, heat jar in hot water or remove lid and microwave briefly
prepared horseradish	1 month	refrigerate
jams and jellies	1 year	can be refrigerated
ketchup	2 to 3 months	refrigerate
lard	8 months	can be refrigerated
mustard	2 to 3 months	refrigerate
noodles (egg)	6 months	away from moisture or heat
vegetable oil	3 months	can be refrigerated
pancake mix	6 months	airtight container
pasta	1 year	can be refrigerated

Dry Food Storage

Food	Average Shelf Lfe	Storage Suggestions
peanut butter (unopened)	6 to 12 months	refrigerate some varieties
rice	6 to 12 months	airtight container
sugar	4 to 24 months	airtight container
tea	6 months	airtight container

Moist Staple Storage

Refrigerator Storage

Food	Average Refrigerator Life (35 to 40°)	Storage Suggestions
butter	2 weeks	tightly covered
buttermilk	2 weeks	tightly reclosed
cheese		
cottage	3 to 5 days	tightly covered or wrapped
cream	2 weeks	tightly covered or wrapped
hard	2 months	tightly covered or wrapped
Parmesan	3 months	tightly covered or wrapped
sliced	2 weeks	tightly covered or wrapped
spreads	1 to 2 weeks	tightly covered or wrapped
cream	3 to 5 days	tightly reclosed
eggs	1 to 3 weeks	depends on freshness when purchased
half and half	1 to 2 weeks	tightly reclosed
mayonnaise	3 months	tightly reclosed
meats		
bacon	1 to 2 weeks	tightly wrapped
cold cuts	2 weeks	tightly wrapped
fresh	1 to 3 days	tightly wrapped
hot dogs	1 to 2 weeks	tightly wrapped
poultry	1 to 2 days	tightly wrapped
nuts	up to 3 months	airtight container
seafood	1 day	double wrap to contain odor

Freezer Storage

Foods should be wrapped in airtight moisture/vapor proof material or containers to prevent odors from penetrating the freezer and other foods. Mark dates on packages as a reminder to use them within the storage period. Defrost frozen foods in refrigerator. Do not refreeze after food has thawed. Partially thawed fruit can be refrozen if it shows no sign of spoilage or partially thawed vegetables can be refrozen if ice crystals are still visible. If unsure, use as soon as possible.

Food	Average Freezer Life (0° or lower)	Storage Suggestions
breads	2 to 3 months	moisture-proof wrapping
butter or margarine	4 to 6 months	unopened package
cakes		
baked, unfrosted	2 to 6 months	tightly wrapped
frosted	2 to 3 months	tightly wrapped
cheesecake	1 month	tightly wrapped
coffeecake	1 month	tightly wrapped
cheese	3 to 4 months	chopped or shredded
cookies	6 to 8 months	tightly wrapped
fruits	8 to 12 months	label and date container
ice cream	1 month	original container
juices	1 year	container
beef		
ground	2 to 3 months	heavy duty moisture/vapor proof wrapping
roasts, steaks	6 to 12 months	heavy duty moisture/vapor proof wrapping
stew	2 to 3 months	container
game	6 to 8 months	heavy duty moisture/vapor proof wrapping
hot dogs	2 months	original wrapping plus overwrap
pork		
bacon	1 month	heavy duty moisture/vapor proof wrapping
chops	3 to 4 months	heavy duty moisture/vapor proof wrapping
ham	2 months	heavy duty moisture/vapor proof wrapping
roast	4 to 6 months	heavy duty moisture/vapor proof wrapping
poultry		
cooked	3 to 4 months	heavy duty moisture/vapor proof wrapping
uncooked	4 to 9 months	heavy duty moisture/vapor proof wrapping
seafood		
fish	2 to 3 months	heavy duty moisture/vapor proof wrapping
lobsters, scallops or crab	1 to 2 months	heavy duty moisture/vapor proof wrapping
oysters (shucked)	1 month	heavy duty moisture/vapor proof wrapping
shellfish	3 to 4 months	heavy duty moisture/vapor proof wrapping
milk	3 to 4 months	original unopened carton
nuts (shelled)	6 to 12 months	tightly wrapped

Freezer Storage

Food	Average Freezer Life (0° or lower)	Storage Suggestions
pies, fruit	6 to 8 months	tightly wrapped
pizza	3 to 5 months	tightly wrapped
sandwiches	1 month	individually tightly wrapped and frozen
soups	8 to 12 months	airtight container

Foods Unsuitable for Freezing

bananas	cucumbers	pears	salad greens
cabbage	mayonnaise	processed meats	tomatoes
celery	onions	radishes	whites of hard-cooked eggs
cream cheese			

Freezing Fresh Vegetables

To freeze fresh vegetables, wash thoroughly and blanch. Unblanched vegetables should never be frozen.

Vegetable	Time in boiling water	Vegetable	Time in boiling water
asparagus	2 minutes	corn on cob	8 minutes
green beans	2 minutes	lima beans	2 minutes
broccoli	3 minutes	peas	1 minute
cauliflower	2 minutes	spinach	2 minutes

Plunge vegetables into boiling water, remove and immediately submerge in very cold water for 4 to 5 minutes to stop cooking action. Drain, place in containers, label and freeze.

Some vegetables, such as green bell peppers, chives and celery, can be chopped and frozen in 1 cup portions for convenient use in cooking.

Freezing Casseroles

If casserole is to be stored in freezer, undercook slightly. The casserole will complete cooking when reheated.

To avoid losing use of casserole dish to freezer storage, line dish with heavy duty aluminum foil, pour partially cooked casserole into foil-lined dish and cool. Freeze solid, remove from dish, wrap tightly with foil, label and date contents and return foil-wrapped casserole to freezer. When ready to use, remove foil and reheat in original dish.

Herbs and Spices

Herbs are the fragrant leaves of various annual or perennial plants that grow in temperate zones and do not have a woody stem. Spices are the aromatic seasonings derived from the bark, buds, fruit, roots, seeds or stems of various plants and trees. Herbs and spices can be categorized as follows:

True herbs: basil, bay leaves, chervil, chives, dill, marjoram, mint, oregano, parsley, rosemary, sage, saffron, savory, tarragon and thyme.

True spices: allspice, cayenne, cinnamon, cloves, ginger, mace, nutmeg, paprika, pepper, saffron and turmeric.

Spice blends: chili powder, curry powder, fine herbs, pickling spices, poultry and seafood seasonings, pumpkin and apple pie spices.

Aromatic seeds: anise, caraway, cardamom, celery, coriander, cumin, dill, fennel, mustard, poppy and sesame seeds. The seeds are not especially aromatic until cooked or crushed.

Other seasonings: dried celery flakes, garlic and onion in powdered or dehydrated forms.

Fresh Herbs

Recipes may call for a blend of herbs.

Sweet herbs: chives, mint, sage and thyme.

Pot herbs: beet tops, cabbage, dandelion greens and spinach.

Salad herbs: any herbs used to flavor salads.

Fines herbes: a blend of chervil, chives, parsley and tarragon, used in French cooking and often in egg and cheese dishes.

Herb bouquet or bouquet garni: blend of herbs wrapped in cheesecloth, secured at top and used, much like a tea bag in making tea, to season dishes such as soups, stews, sauces and vegetables during cooking.

> **Classic bouquet**: 2 sprigs parsley, ½ bay leaf, 1 sprig fresh thyme or ⅛ teaspoon dried thyme.
>
> **Bouquet for lamb**: celery, parsley and rosemary.
>
> **Bouquet for veal**: lemon peel, parsley and thyme.
>
> **Bouquet for beef**: basil, bay leaf, clove and parsley.

Cooking with Fresh Herbs

- Season lightly when using herbs as the aromatic oils are very strong and a tiny pinch can be very intense.
- Finely chop or mince herbs so the maximum flavor is released during blending, cooking or marinating process.
- Never blend strong herbs such as basil, rosemary or sage because the flavors compete and overwhelm, rather than enhance, the dish.
- With the following exceptions, add herbs for the final 15 minutes of cooking because longer cooking can cause bitterness to develop or the herbs may lose flavor completely.

  Bay leaves can be used throughout the cooking process. Remove before serving.

  Cold preparations such as salad dressings or marinades require more time for absorption of flavors (at least 15 minutes).

  Follow directions when recipe directs addition of herbs and spices early in process.

- Equivalents: 1 tablespoon minced fresh herbs equals ⅓ teaspoon ground or 1½ teaspoons crushed dried herbs.

Dried Herbs and Spices

- Dried herbs and spices have a shelf life of 4 to 6 months so purchase in small quantities or divide with a friend. Check once a month for freshness and discard if stale. Old herbs and spices can ruin a dish.
- Store in airtight containers away from light, heat and moisture. Light robs herbs and spices of color, heat affects their flavor and potency and moisture causes them to cake and harden.
- Use dried herbs and spices with caution. It's easy to add more but difficult to correct overseasoning.
- Avoid using too much of any herb or spice unless a recipe specifically calls for it, such as ginger in gingerbread wherein one spice dominates the flavor of the recipe. Herbs and spices are meant to enhance, not disguise, the flavor of the food.
- When doubling or tripling a recipe, do not double or triple the herbs and spices. When doubling, use 1½ times the amount of herbs or spices; when tripling, use twice the amount of herbs or spices.

Cooking with Dried Herbs and Spices

- Crush or crumble dried herbs or spices before adding to other ingredients. They'll release more flavor.
- When possible, use freshly ground spices instead of preground spices. Whole spices have a longer shelf life than the powdered and a more intense flavor when freshly ground.
- To reconstitute dried herbs, soak in any recipe liquid for 10 minutes to 1 hour. If recipe includes butter, simmer herbs in butter before adding.
- Add dried herbs and spices early in the cooking process of casseroles, soups and stews. In salad dressing recipes, add dried herbs and spices to the oil 15 to 30 minutes before serving.

Correcting Overseasoning

- Peel and quarter a potato, add to dish and simmer for 15 minutes. Remove and discard potato before serving.
- If seasoning is still intense, prepare a second recipe without seasoning and combine the two.
- If dish is too salty, add quartered raw potato and 1/4 teaspoon brown sugar, adding up to 2 teaspoons if necessary.
- If seasoning is too sweet, add ½ to 1 teaspoon lemon juice, cider or wine vinegar.

Herb and Spice Chart

Herb or Spice	Description	Uses and Tips
Allspice	flavor of clove, cinnamon and nutmeg	baked goods, pot roasts, pickles, soups, lamb, fruit pies, pumpkin pie
Anise	sweet, licorice-like greenish-brown seeds	baked goods, shellfish, poultry and veal, fruit and vegetable salads, cheese. Spanish, Italian and Mediterranean entrees
Basil	subtle, spicy distinctive flavor	Italian dishes, especially tomato dishes and sauces; salads, eggs, cheese, lamb, pork, veal and chicken
Bay leaf	aromatic laurel tree leaf, used whole	meat, fish, soups and pasta sauces (remove before serving)
Caraway seeds	dark brown seeds with warm, tangy taste	rye bread, sauerkraut, cheese, potato/cabbage dishes, beef and pork

Herb and Spice Chart

Herb or Spice	Description	Uses and Tips
Cardamom	blackish-brown seeds with green pods	baked goods, pastries, fruits, soups and curries, wine and hot coffee
Cayenne pepper	very hot ground red pepper (also called chilies)	Mexican and Italian dishes, seafood, eggs, chili, soups, pork ribs, sausages and chicken
Celery seeds	derived from special variety of celery	pickling, salads, cream cheese spreads, eggs and vegetables, stews and seafood
Chervil	lacy leaf fine herb	soups, salads, eggs and seafood
Chili powder	very hot blend of spices including cayenne pepper	Spanish and Mexican dishes, rice, beans, meat and chili
Chive	delicate onion flavor	salads, soups, sauces, eggs and fish
Cinnamon	spicy bark of tree, ground or sticks	baked goods, drinks, desserts, pickles, stewed fruits and syrups
Cloves	spicy, pungent dried flower buds	used whole to stud ham, onions and oranges or to flavor hot drinks; used like cinnamon when ground
Coriander	perfumed aromatic seed	curries, stews, pickling and baked goods
Curry powder	golden yellow spice blend	Indian and Middle Eastern dishes, eggs, chicken, lamb, fish and cheese
Cumin	seed with bitter and aromatic character	Mexican dishes and Indian chutneys
Dill	cucumber pickle flavor	poultry, seafood, eggs, salad dressing, pickles, soups and cheese
Fennel	licorice character and aroma	Italian and Swedish dishes, seafood, salads and eggs
Garlic	strong onion-like odor and taste; mild when unpeeled, stronger when minced, even stronger when crushed or mashed	Mediterranean, Italian and French dishes, meats, fish, poultry, salads, salad dressings, sauces, soups and breads
Ginger	root with sharp pungent| fragrance	Oriental dishes, baked goods, meats and preserves; crystal form for sweetness, ground for cooking and whole for texture

Herb and Spice Chart

Herb or Spice	Description	Uses and Tips
Marjoram	spicy but delicate member of mint family	eggs, fish, poultry, salads, sauces, soups, stews and vegetables, especially spinach
Mint	fresh cool taste with spearmint or peppermint character	drinks, desserts, jellies, sauces, salads, lamb, fruit and vegetables
Mustard	sharp and spicy	pickles, relishes, salad dressings, dips, meat glazes, chicken and fish
Nutmeg	mellow and spicy	bread, cakes, vegetables, eggs, sauces, soups and drinks
Oregano	aromatic	Greek and Italian dishes, especially pasta, sauces, salad dressings, eggs and cheese
Paprika	spicy red pepper with mild sweet peppery flavor	garnish, color and zesty taste for variety of foods, frequently used in Hungarian and Spanish dishes
Parsley	mildly bitter fine herb	meat, fish, poultry, soups, salads, stews and garnish
Pepper, black	zesty and pungent	often in combination with salt
Pepper, white	subtle but stronger than black pepper	when more subtle flavor is desired and when pepper should not show; use half as much when substituting for black pepper
Poppy seeds	tiny blueish-black seeds with grainy texture and nut flavor	bread, rolls, noodles, dips, dressings and some pork
Rosemary	aromatic taste	lamb, beef, chicken, Italian and French cuisine and eggs
Saffron	pleasantly bitter reddish-yellow spice, very expensive	seafood, rice, eggs and Spanish and French cuisine
Sage	spicy musty grayish-green leaf	pork, sausage, fish, game, veal, poultry, stuffings, soups and sauces
Savory	piquant dark green leaf in summer and winter varieties	poultry, eggs, salads and stuffings
Sesame seeds	nut flavor	bread, rolls, salads, soups and casseroles

Herb and Spice Chart

Herb or Spice	Description	Uses and Tips
Tarragon	slightly anise-like sweet green leaf	poultry, fish, salads, sauces, dressings, soups and marinade; use sparingly on meat to avoid sweetness
Thyme	pungent	stuffings, soups, seafood, meat, poultry, stews, clam chowder and salad dressings
Turmeric	rich, sweet and slightly spicy red-orange spice	curry blends and pickling; can be used for saffron for color but different flavor

Glossary

À la king—Method of preparing delicately flavored meat, fish or poultry, cut up or in chunks, in creamy seasoned sauce. Pimento and mushrooms frequently added.

À la mode—Ice cream served with pie or other dessert.

Al dente—Pasta cooked until tender but slightly firm.

Amandine—Made or served with almonds.

Antipasto—In Italian cooking, appetizer assortment of fish, vegetables and cold meat served as hors d'oeuvre, first course before pasta or main course.

Appetizer—Small serving of juice, fruit, seafood or other food served as first course of a meal or as party food.

Aspic—Flavored gel-like substances made from meat stock, vegetable stock or fruit juice to which gelatin has been added. Used to coat meat, poultry or fish to form a glaze or mold.

Aubergine—French word for eggplant.

Au gratin—Dish browned in oven or broiler, usually topped with cheese, bread crumbs or other crushed ingredients.

Au jus—French term applied to meat served with natural, unthickened pan juices developed during preparation.

Baba—Sweet yeast cake combined with raisins and dried fruit and soaked in brandy, kirsch or rum after baking.

Baguette—Long, narrow loaf of bread with crispy crust and chewy texture.

Bake—To cook, covered or uncovered, in an oven by dry heat.

Ball—To cut into balls.

Barbecue—To roast or broil on a rack or revolving spit over hot coals or in the oven and basting with sauce.

Bard—To wrap lean meat with bacon, suet or fatback to prevent drying during cooking.

Baste—To brush or spoon melted fat, meat drippings, sauces or other liquids over food as it cooks to keep surface moist and flavorful.

Batter—Uncooked mixture, usually consisting of eggs, flour, leavening and liquid, that is pouring consistency.

Beat—To stir or mix rapidly with a spoon, whisk or beater, using a circular or loop motion.

Bechamel—Basic white sauce of flour and butter to which milk and seasoning have been added.

Beignet—French term for fritter.

Bind—To thicken or smooth consistency of a liquid, usually using egg yolks, flour, potatoes or rice.

Bisque—Thick creamy soup, usually made from fish or vegetable purees.

Blanch—To immerse food briefly in boiling water, then in cold water, to set color and flavor, to loosen skin for partial pre-cooking or for preparing foods for canning, freezing or drying.

Blend—To mix two or more ingredients until thoroughly combined in flavor and color and smooth in texture.

Blintz—Thin pancake rolled or folded around a cheese or fruit filling, then fried or baked.

Boil—To cook in a boiling liquid or to heat liquid until bubbles rise continually to break at surface (212° for water at sea level).

Bombay Duck—Dried fish used to season curries.

Bone—To remove bones from fish, meat and poultry.

Bouillon—A clear stock or broth made by straining liquid in which vegetables, meat or fish has been cooked.

Bouquet garni—Small bundle of herbs, usually bay leaf, parsley and thyme, wrapped in cheesecloth bag or tied together, used for flavoring soups and stews.

Braise—To brown meat or vegetables in a small quantity of hot fat with small amount of liquid.

Bread—To coat food with dry bread or cracker crumbs before cooking.

Brine—Strong salt solution used for pickling or preserving food.

Brochette—Skewer for broiling small pieces of meat or vegetables or food cooked on a skewer.

Broil—To cook by direct heat under flame, red hot heating unit or over an open fire or grill.

Broth—Liquid in which fish, meat, poultry or vegetables have been cooked.

Brown—To cook at high heat in hot fat on top of stove or in oven or broiler, giving food an appealing color and sealing in meat juices.

Bruise—To pound or crush into fragments.

Brûlée—French word for burned, used in cooking to describe foods glazed with caramelized sugar.

Brunoise—French term to describe method of dicing or shredding vegetables used in flavoring soups and sauces.

Brush on—To apply a liquid to the surface of food with a small brush.

Butterfly—To split food down center, without cutting all the way through, so the two halves can be opened flat like butterfly wings.

Canapé—Thin piece of bread, toast or cracker topped with spread or tidbit.

Caramelize—To melt sugar or food containing a high percentage of sugar over low heat, without scorching or burning, until brown color and characteristic flavor develops.

Caviar—Salted roe of sturgeon or other large fish, usually served as an appetizer.

Chapon—Chunk or slice of French bread rubbed with garlic and seasoned with oil and vinegar, tossed with salad greens to give subtle garlic flavor and discarded before serving.

Chiffonade—Soup garnish consisting of vegetables cut in fine strips, such as mixture of sorrel and lettuce cooked in butter.

Chill—To cool but not freeze, in a refrigerator, on ice or in ice water.

Chinois—Fine-meshed conical strainer. Also small Chinese oranges preserved in brandy or crystallized.

Chop—To cut food into small pieces with knife or other sharp tool.

Chutney—Pungent sauce or relish containing fruits, spices and herbs.

Clarify—To clear a liquid, such as consommé, by adding slightly beaten egg white and egg shells, then straining.

Clove—One small section of a segmented bulb, such as garlic.

Coat—To cover the surface of food with either a liquid or dry substance.

Coat a spoon—Stage reached when a mixture forms a thin, even film on back of metal spoon.

Coddle—Slowly cook food in a liquid just below boiling point.

Combine—To mix together two or more ingredients until blended.

Compote—Fresh or dried fruits cooked and served in a sweetened, flavored syrup, usually a dessert, or a serving bowl on stem, footed base.

Condiment—Seasoning added to food to enhance flavor, often referring to a sauce, spice or relish eaten with food.

Consommé—Clear strong soup made by boiling meat and bones for a long time.

Cool—To remove from heat and allow to stand until heat is reduced.

Core—To remove the inedible center portion of a fruit or vegetable.

Correct seasoning—To taste food at various stages of cooking process and to add more seasoning if necessary.

Coq au vin—Chicken in red wine sauce with onions, mushrooms and bacon.

Coquille—Shell or small dish made in shape of a shell, used for baking and serving various fish or meat dishes prepared with sauce.

Court-bouillon—Well-seasoned broth flavored with vegetables, fish and meat, used for poaching and as a sauce.

Cream—To beat butter or other fat with sugar or other ingredients until soft, smooth and fluffy.

Crème fraîche—Thickened cream made from whipping cream and buttermilk and used as topping for fresh fruits and pastries.

Creole—Dish made with tomatoes and peppers, usually served over rice.

Crèpes—Thin, light delicate pancakes of egg and flour batter.

Crimp—To seal edges of pie or pastry by pinching to form a decorative edge.

Crisp—To make leafy vegetables, such as lettuce, firm by rinsing in water and chilling or dry foods, such as bread or crackers, by heating.

Croissant—Flaky crescent-shaped roll.

Croquette—Thick creamy mixture containing meat, vegetables and/or rice that is shaped, coated with eggs and crumbs, then fried.

Croûte—French term for crust or pastry, en croute means wrapped in or topped with a crust.

Croutons—Toasted or fried pieces of bread, used to garnish or in mixed green salads.

Crumb—To break into small pieces.

Crush—To pulverize by rolling with rolling pin or by mashing until dry food is consistency of coarse powder or to mash fruits, particularly berries, until they lose shape.

Cube—To cut into small squares, generally ½ to ¼ inch.

Cure—To preserve meat, fish or cheese by salting, aging or smoking.

Custard—Mixture of beaten eggs and milk, variously sweetened, flavored and cooked either over hot water or baked in oven.

Cut in—Method of mixing solid fat into dry ingredients, using two forks or pastry blender, until particles are desired consistency.

Dash—Less than ⅛ teaspoon.

Deep fry—To cook food immersed in deep hot fat at about 360°.

Deglaze—To loosen pan drippings and browned bits from bottom of pan by adding stock wine or other liquid and heating gently.

Degrease—To remove fat from surface of a liquid.

Demi-glace—Rich brown sauce or gravy made by boiling meat stock to reduce liquid and usually flavored with Madeira or sherry.

Devein—To remove the black vein along the back of a shrimp.

Devil—To mix with hot or spicy seasonings, usually mustard and cayenne.

Dice—To cut into very small pieces of uniform size and shape.

Dilute—To add liquid to another liquid or semi-solid in order to thin or weaken it.

Demitasse—Very small cup or a cup of very strong black coffee.

Disjoint—To cut or break fowl or meat into smaller pieces at bone joints.

Dissolve—To disperse a dry substance in a liquid to form a solution or to heat a solid until it melts.

Dot—To place small pieces of butter or other substances on surface of food.

Dough—Thick pliable mixture of flour and other ingredients, with or without a leavening agent, which is baked as bread, pastry, etc.

Dragées (nonpareilles)—Miniature candies to decorate cookies, cakes and candies.

Drain—To remove liquid, usually by allowing food to stand in colander until liquid has dropped off or by pouring off liquid.

Draw—To remove the internal organs of poultry, game or fish.

Dredge—To coat food with a dry mixture such as flour, bread crumbs or cracker crumbs.

Drippings—The juices and melted fat of meat that emerge during cooking.

Drizzle—To pour liquid over surface of food in a fine stream.

Dust—To sprinkle surface of food lightly with dry substance such as flour, crumbs or sugar.

Duxelles—Thick pastelike mixture of minced sautéed mushrooms, sometimes seasoned with shallots, salt and pepper, and that is mixed into sauces and other recipes.

Egg and crumb—To dip food into a lightly beaten egg and dredge with crumbs, preventing food from absorbing fat from frying.

En papillote—To cook and serve in a wrapping of foil or oiled paper, typically a fish preparation method.

Enrich—To add cream, eggs or butter to food.

Entrée—Main course of a meal.

Escalope—Thin slice of meat or fish that has been slightly flattened and fried.

Essence, extract—Concentrated flavoring.

Filet, fillet—Boneless strip of lean meat, fish or poultry.

Fines herbes—Mixture of minced herbs: parsley, chives, tarragon and chervil.

Flake—To break into small pieces with a fork.

Flambé (blaze)—To ignite a food flavored with brandy or liqueur.

Flan—Open tart filled with fruit, cream, stuffing or some other filling.

Flavor—To enhance the taste of food by adding aromatics, condiments and spices.

Flour—Finely ground meal of grain or to coat evenly with thin layer of flour.

Fold—To add ingredients of a delicate mixture to a thicker heavier mixture, using a gentle over-and-over motion.

Force meat—Paste-like mixture of finely ground meat, poultry or fish.

Fricassée—To cook pieces of meat or chicken by braising in fat and then in seasoned liquid until tender.

Fritter—Meat, vegetable or fruit dipped in batter and fried in deep fat.

Frizzle—To fry thinly sliced meat until crisp and curly.

Frost—To spread with frosting or coat with sugar.

Fry—To cook in hot fat.

Fumet—Very strong stock used as a base for sauces

Ganache—Extremely rich butter cream, usually chocolate or mocha, used for filling pastries or tarts.

Garnish—To decorate food by adding small pieces of colorful foods such as pimentos, mushrooms, olives and lemons before serving.

Gazpacho—Cold soup made of raw chopped vegetables, usually including tomatoes.

Gel—To form a jelly-like substance with gelatin.

Giblets—Edible heart, liver, gizzard and neck of a fowl.

Glacé—French word for sweet frozen liquid, usually ice cream.

Glace—French word for food coated with thin sweetened syrup and cooked at high heat until syrup forms hard coating that cracks.

Glace de viande—Concentrated brown meat glaze derived by boiling meat stock down until dark and thick. Used to add flavor and color to sauces and gravies.

Glaze—Mixture applied to food which hardens, adds flavor and gives glossy appearance.

Grate—To cut food into small particles by rubbing them on sharp teeth of grating tool.

Gratin—Thin crust that forms on surface of certain dishes when browned under broiler or grill.

Grease—To rub fat on surface of food or utensils.

Grill—To cook on gridiron over embers or to put under hot broiler.

Grind—To cut food into small pieces or reduce to powder.

Hollandaise—Delicate sauce of egg yolks, butter and lemon juice.

Hors d'oeuvres—Small amounts of food served before a meal or as a first course.

Ice—Frozen liquid dessert or to spread with icing.

Icing—Sweetened thick coating for cakes, cupcakes and cookies.

Infuse—To steep herbs or other flavoring in boiling liquid until liquid absorbs the flavor.

Jelly-roll style—To roll a flat piece of cake, meat or fish around a filling.

Julienne—To cut fruits, vegetables and meats into match-like strips.

Knead—To work dough with heel of hand, pressing, folding and turning until it is smooth and satiny.

Lard—To insert strips or pieces of fat into uncooked lean meat to keep moist and succulent throughout cooking. Can be placed on top of uncooked lean meat for same purpose.

Leaven—To lighten the consistency and increase the volume of breads, cakes and cookies, with agents such as baking soda, yeast or baking powder that react with heat and elements in the dough.

Legumes—Vegetables such as peas and beans which bear fruit or seeds in a pod.

Lyonnaise—A dish, usually potatoes, cooked with onions.

Macedoine—Mixture of fruits or vegetables, served hot or cold.

Macerate—To soften by steeping in liquid, often with heat, or to soak fruits in alcoholic liquors.

Madrilene—Clear soup flavored with tomato juice and generally served chilled.

Marinate—To allow food to stand in a liquid, prior to cooking, to enhance its flavor and make it more tender.

Marrow—Soft fatty substance that fills cavities of bones.

Marzipan—Confection made from ground almonds, egg whites and sugar. Frequently colored, flavored and molded into shapes and decorated.

Mash—To soften and reduce to pulp, usually with a potato masher, back of a spoon or by forcing food through a ricer or press.

Mask—To cover food completely with sauce or aspic before serving.

Medallion—Small, circular portions of meat.

Melt—To change fat and solid dissolvable foods into liquid by heating.

Meringue—Snowy white combination of beaten egg whites and sugar, used as topping on desserts and baked until browned or formed and baked in small cakes.

Mince—To chop or cut in very small pieces.

Minestrone—Thick vegetable soup.

Mirepoix—Mixture of finely diced carrots, onions, celery and sometimes meat, cooked slowly in butter and used as flavoring for sauces, stuffings, stews and other dishes.

Mix—To combine two or more ingredients until evenly distributed.

Mocha—Combination of chocolate and coffee flavors.

Mold—To chill, cook or freeze in a container so that food takes on shape of the container.

Mortar and pestle—Mortar is bowl-shaped container of stone metal or wood and pestle is heavy blunt instrument used to pound or grind mixtures against the sides of mortar.

Mousse—Delicate mixture containing whipped cream or beaten egg whites.

Mull—To heat beverages such as fruit juice, wine or ale and sweetened with sugar and flavored with spices.

Nap—To cover food with sauce.

Nesselrode—Iced sweet mixture, usually fruits and nuts, used as a sauce or in puddings, pies, ice cream and other desserts.

Offal—Various parts of the meat carcass or innards.

Paella—Spanish dish of rice, chicken, seafood, vegetables and often sausage, flavored with saffron and other seasonings.

Pan-broil—To cook, uncovered, on a hot surface with fat removed as it accumulates.

Pan fry—To cook, uncovered, in a small amount of hot fat. Similar to sauté.

Parboil—To boil in a liquid until partially cooked.

Pare—To remove outer covering and steam of a fruit or vegetable with knife or other sharp tool.

Partially set—To chill gelatin until consistency of egg white.

Pasta—Dough of either flour and water or flour and egg, produced in variety of forms such as macaroni, spaghetti, noodles, etc.

Paste—Smooth blend of dry ingredients and liquid, used as a thickener for sauces and gravies, or any food pounded to a paste.

Pâté—Rich, well-seasoned blend of ground meat, poultry or fish, sometimes baked in a crust.

Pâte à choux—Pastry of water, butter, flour and eggs, used for making puffs for desserts and hors d'oeuvres.

Pâté en croute—Pâté baked in a pastry crust.

Pectin—Mucilaginous substance occurring naturally in certain fruits, used as a jelling agent when boiled with sugar.

Peel—To strip off the outer covering.

Petits four—Small fancy cakes and biscuits iced and often decorated with frosting flowers.

Pickle—To preserve a food in a flavored solution such as brine or vinegar.

Pinch—Amount of salt, sugar, herb, spice, etc. that can be grasped between the thumb and forefinger, generally less than 1⁄8 teaspoon.

Pit—To remove seeds or stones from fruit or vegetables.

Poach—To cook food submerged in a hot simmering liquid, being careful to retain shape of food.

Polenta—Thick cornmeal mush often served with sauce, gravy or stew or cooked firm and sliced or cooked just to consistency of mashed potatoes.

Pots de crème—Delicate chilled dessert puddings, often chocolate, served in individual cups.

Pound—To flatten with a mallet.

Praline—Mixture of caramelized sugar and nuts that is allowed to harden.

Precook—To cook food partially or completely before final cooking and reheating.

Preheat—To heat oven or broiler to desired temperature before adding food.

Preserves—Thickened mixture of fruit and sugar in which fruit retains its original shape.

Press—Culinary utensil for extracting, by pressure, the juice from a food.

Purée—Paste or thick liquid obtained by mashing or sieving certain food.

Quiche—Savory custard poured in pastry shell and baked until puffy and browned.

Ragoût—Thick highly-seasoned stew of meat, fowl or fish.

Ramekin—Small individual baking dish, commonly made of earthenware.

Ratatouille—Stew of eggplant, green bell pepper, tomatoes and squash, seasoned with garlic.

Reduce—To lessen volume of a liquid by evaporation, generally through heat, to produce concentrated and intense flavor.

Refresh—To plunge hot food into ice water, quickly stopping the cooking process and setting the color and flavor of food.

Render—To slowly heat pieces of lard or other animal fat to obtain liquid fat, producing an almost pure fat which is smooth and creamy and is excellent for baking.

Ribbon—Mixture of well beaten sugar and egg yolks which forms ribbon-like folds when dropped from raised beater or spoon.

Rice—To force food through utensil called a ricer.

Rind—Outer skin of fruit and vegetable.

Rissole—Seasoned meat, fish or vegetable mixture enclosed in pastry, often in shape of a turnover, and generally fried in deep fat.

Roast—To cook, uncovered, in oven by dry heat.

Roe—Fish eggs.

Roulade—Thin slice of meat rolled up, with or without stuffing and cooked in a seasoned liquid or sautéed.

Roux—Mixture of flour and fat, usually browned and used as thickening agent in many sauces.

Salt—To add salt to food or to rub with salt.

Sauerbraten—Pot roast of beef marinated in spiced vinegar mixture, then braised.

Sauté—To brown or cook food in a small amount of fat, turning frequently.

Scald—To heat a liquid to just below the boiling point; small bubbles form at edge of pan.

Scallop—To bake food, usually cut in pieces, covered with a liquid or sauce and topped with crumbs.

Score—To cut ridges or slits part way through the surface of food, usually in a diamond pattern, serving as decoration or permitting seasons to permeate the food.

Sear—To brown surface of food quickly, using intense heat.

Season—To add salt, pepper, herbs, spices and other ingredients to increase the flavor of the food.

Seed—To remove seeds.

Semolina—Coarse granules of cereal from which various pastas, puddings and soups are made.

Separate—To divide egg yolks from egg whites.

Set, set up—Condition in which liquids coagulate by heat or cold and retain their shape.

Shirr—To cook whole eggs in ramekins with cream, occasionally topping with bread crumbs.

Shred—To form small thin strips by rubbing food on a grater.

Shuck—To remove outer covering of food, such as shell of clams, oysters or scallops or husk of corn.

Sieve—To strain liquid through a sieve.

Sift—To pass sugar or other dry ingredients through a fine sieve.

Simmer—To cook a liquid over very low heat (180°).

Singe—To burn away small feathers of poultry or winged game by passing plucked bird through a flame.

Skewer—Thin wooden or metal rod on which various foods can be threaded before grilling or frying.

Skim—To remove, with a spoon or skimmer, a substance which rises to surface of a liquid.

Sliver—To cut into long thin pieces.

Snip—To cut into very small pieces with scissors.

Soft peaks—To beat egg whites or whipping cream until peaks, with tips that curl over, form when beaters are lifted.

Soufflé—Puffy egg dish with flavored sauce or base into which stiffly beaten egg whites are folded.

Spit—Utensil on which meat is threaded and then roasted or grilled by direct heat.

Steam—To cook, covered, by means of vapor from boiling liquid rising through the food.

Steep—To place a substance in a liquid just below the boiling point for a period of time to extract flavor, color and other qualities.

Stiff peaks—To beat egg whites or whipping cream until peaks, with tips that stand straight, form when beaters are lifted; peaks should be moist and glossy.

Stir—To mix with a circular motion until ingredients are blended or reach uniform consistency.

Stir fry—Oriental method of quickly stirring foods as they fry.

Stock—Liquid in which meat, poultry, fish, bones, vegetable and seasoning have been cooked and for use as base of soups, sauces, stews and gravies.

Strain—To pass through a sieve to separate liquids from solids.

Stroganoff—Meat sliced thin and cooked with a sauce of broth, sour cream, seasonings and mushrooms.

Stud—To insert whole cloves, pieces of garlic or other seasoning into food.

Sukiyaki—Japanese dish made with thinly sliced beef and usually containing soy sauce, bean curds and greens.

Sweetbread—The thymus gland of an animal, such as a calf or lamb.

Tart—A small individual pie filled with fruit, jam, custard or other filling.

Terrine—Earthernware dish in which minced or ground meat, game or fish are cooked or reference to pâté baked in such a dish.

Thicken—To make a liquid mixture more dens by adding an agent such as flour, cornstarch, egg yolks, rice or potatoes.

Timbale—Custard-like mixture of finely chopped meats, fish or vegetables with eggs, milk and seasonings, usually baked in ramekins and served unmolded.

Toasting—Application of direct heat until surface of food is browned.

Toss—To lightly mix ingredients.

Tripe—Stomach tissue of ruminants used as foodstuff.

Truss—To secure poultry or other food with binding or skewers to hold shape during cooking.

Tryout—See render.

Unmold—To remove from mold.

Velouté—Basic white sauce, made from chicken or veal, used as a base for other sauces.

Vinaigrette—Sauce made with vinegar to which other seasonings and herbs are added.

Welsh rarebit—Melted cheese, usually mixed with milk, ale or beer, and served over toast or crackers.

Whip—To beat rapidly until stiff or to increase volume by the incorporation of air.

Wiener schnitzel—Cutlet of veal, coated with egg and bread crumbs and cooked in fat.

Zest—The colored part of citrus rind used for flavoring or the oil pressed from the rind.

Ideas for Entertaining

Serving Methods

Continental

Continental or formal service involves waiters serving guests from platters. The guest of honor or the female guest to the right of the host is served first, followed by all other female guests and the hostess. Then the male guests to the right of the hostess and all other gentlemen with the host last. The order of service is repeated for each course. Dinner guests are served from the left and plates are removed from the right. Beverages are served from the right.

Family Style

In family style service, dinner plates are stacked in front of the host. All serving dishes are placed at the end of the table and the host places serving portion of each dish on each plate and passes it to guests.

Country Style

All place settings are set and serving dishes are placed on the table. Each guest serves himself and passes the dish to the right.

Blue Plate

Portions are placed on individual dinner plates in the kitchen and brought to the table before guests are seated.

Formal Placesetting

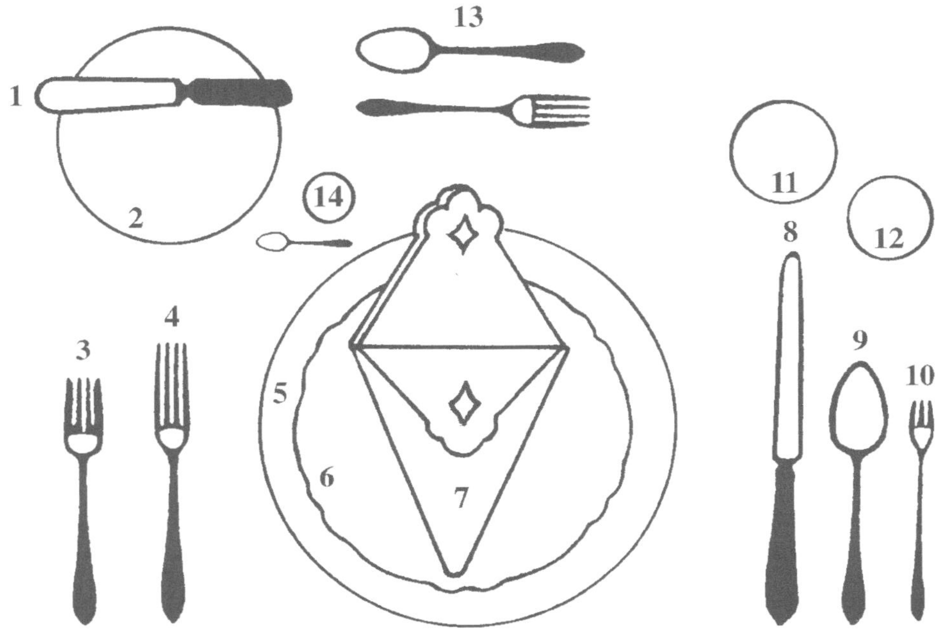

1. Butter knife
2. Bread plate
3. Salad fork
4. Dinner fork
5. Dinner plate
6. Salad plate or service plate
7. Napkin
8. Dinner knife
9. Dinner spoon
10. Cocktail fork or fish fork
11. Water glass
12. Wine glass
13. Dessert spoon and fork
14. Salt cellar and spoon

Buffet

Serving buffet style is versatile because it enables a hostess to serve a small dinner or large crowd with limited help. A hostess may ask a few friends to assist or may engage professional kitchen help.

Planning requires a step by step, mental dress rehearsal. Beverages, menu, traffic, serving, seating, clearing and cleaning should be carefully considered.

The number of guests is the first consideration. Decide whether guests will be seated at a table, eat from lap trays or stand while eating. Foods that require a knife should be served only at a seated buffet or if trays are provided. If a large number of people are being served, then all items on the menu must be served on one plate, with the exception of dessert.

Common sense and serving convenience should dictate menu selections. To avoid a messy plate, avoid foods that run or melt. Portions should be in individual servings when possible and served with all garnishes on them.

A buffet table requires that guests serve themselves in a logical sequence. Each dish should have a serving utensil next to it and portions should be pre-cut for individual servings.

Traffic is another key consideration. Determine space limitations and compensate for them, moving furniture to prevent congestion if necessary. Serve beverages in an area separate from the food. The arrangement should encourage guests to pick up their beverage after they have served themselves from the buffet table.

Several serving and clearing stations are more convenient for large buffets if space permits. If the weather is agreeable, move outdoors but do not rely on it. Be sure to have an alternate rain plan or date for outdoor occasions.

To simplify the clearing of dishes at a non-seated buffet, clearly designate a trolley or tray so guests can easily return their plates and the plates can be cleared from sight.

Central Buffet

The buffet is served from the dining table. Location of entry and exit determine where the beginning of the buffet should be placed. The sequence should allow each guest to pick up a dinner plate, proceed to self-serve the entree and then accompaniments such as vegetables and salads, to season foods with salt and pepper, pick up bread and finally add flatware and napkins. Dessert and coffee may be served from the table or placed in another room for convenience, allowing the buffet table to be cleared while dessert is served separately. Always remember to leave enough space beside the serving dishes for guests to set their plates while serving themselves.

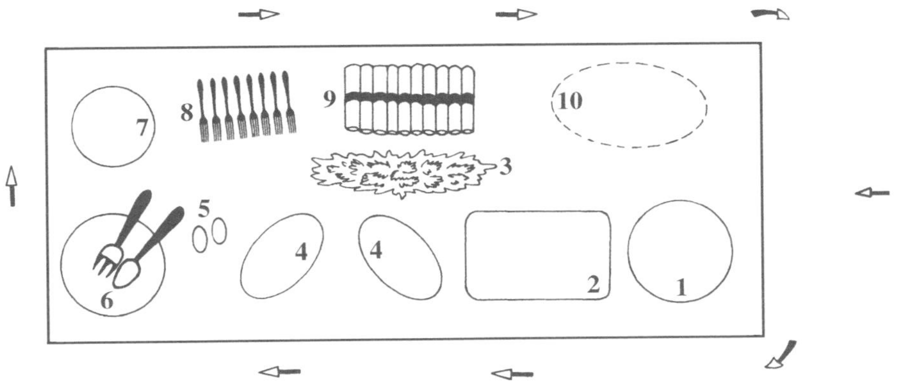

1. Dinner plates
2. Entree
3. Centerpiece
4. Vegetables
5. Salt and pepper
6. Salad and dressings
7. Bread
8. Flatware
9. Napkins
10. Dessert

Circular Buffet

A buffet on a round table works well for small groups. The tableware and food should be arranged in the same sequence as for the central buffet.

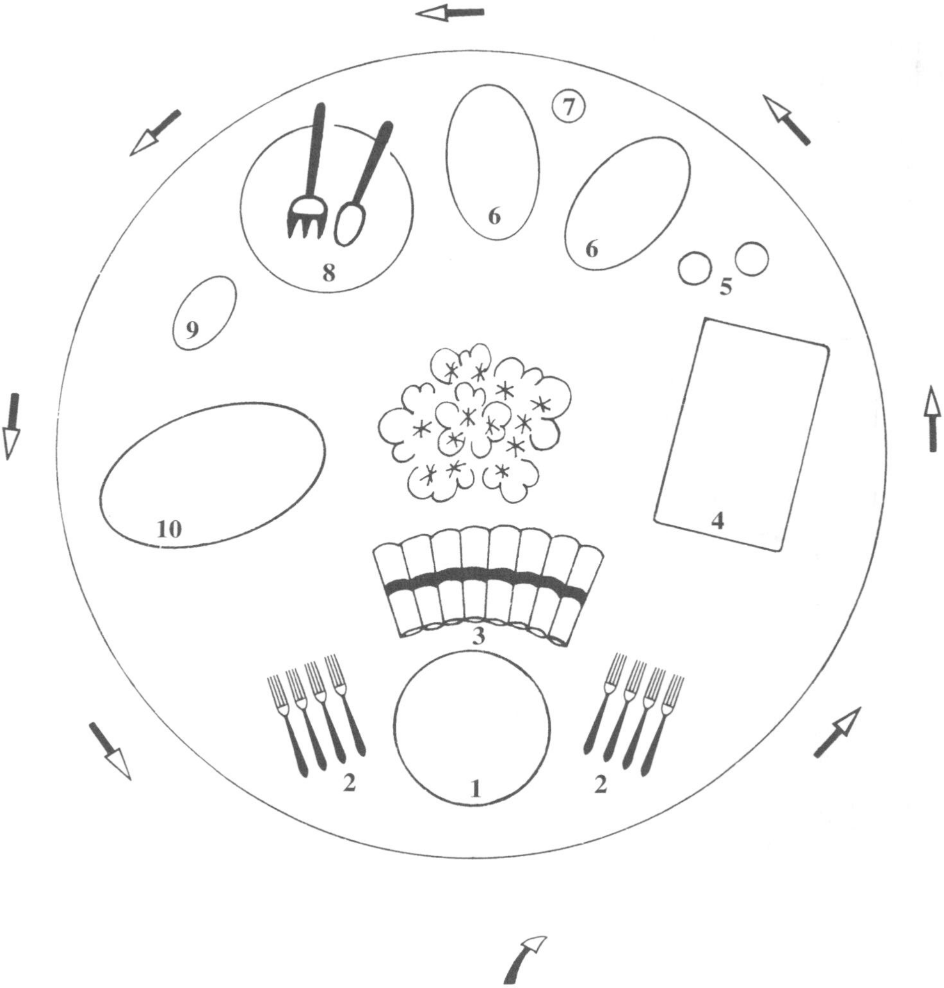

1. Dinner plates
2. Flatware
3. Napkins
4. Entree
5. Salt and Pepper
6. Vegetables
7. Accompaniments
8. Salad
9. Dressings
10. Bread

Napkin Folds

Folded napkins add a fanciful, festive touch to any dining table or occasion. Following are five distinctive folds, from simple to elaborate. A few days before the party, experiment with the napkins, select a fold suitable to the dinner and table decor, and fold the napkins, storing them on the table covered with tissue or plastic.

If serving buffet style with napkins on the serving table, consider the amount of space available. Experiment with different size napkins to see which folds work best with different size linens. Regardless of the size, the napkin should be square (a formal size is 22x22 inches). Folded napkins may be placed to the left, right, center, above or on the plate as well as in a glass.

Classic Fold

1. Open napkin and lay it flat.

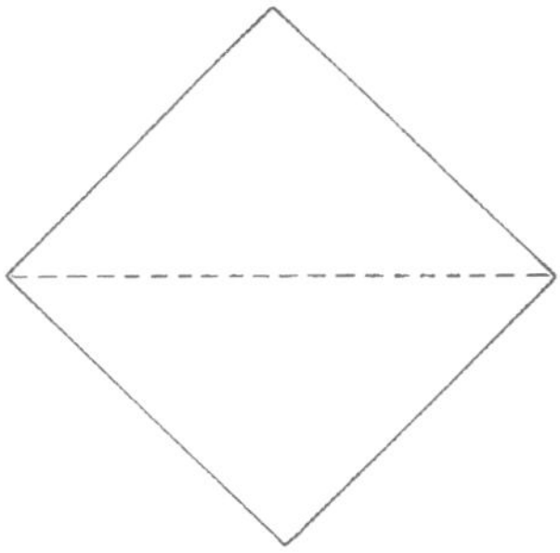

2. Fold into large triangle with point at the bottom.

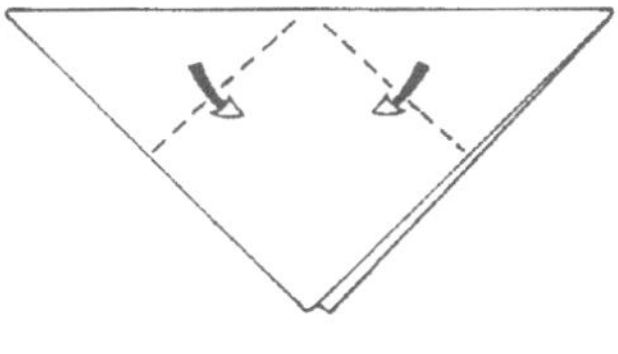

3. Fold left and right points to center point.

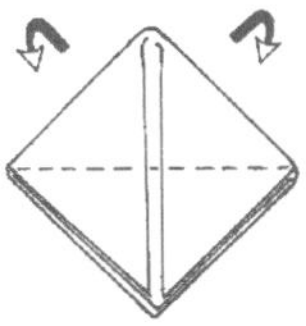

4. Turn napkin face side down and fold in half to form a small triangle.

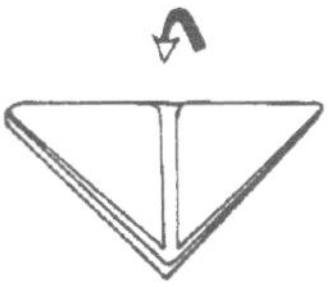

5. Fold triangle in half again to form smaller triangle. Stand on plate with decorative edge facing guest.

Flat Pocket or Lace Napkin Fold

1. Open napkin and lay it flat.

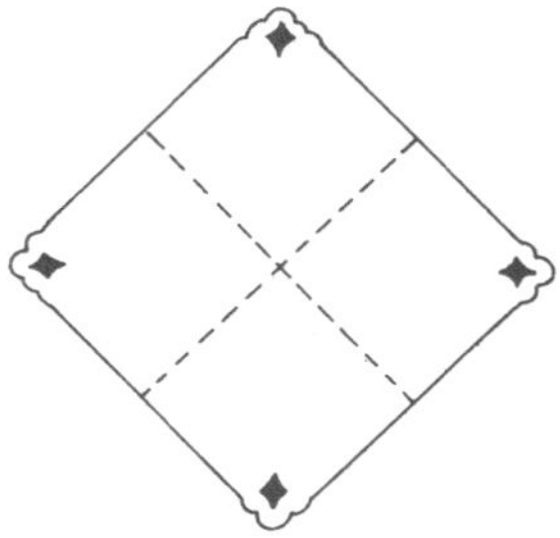

2. Fold in half and then fold again to form a square, with lace corners at the bottom.

3. Fold top point down.

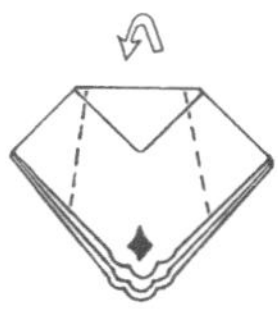

4. Fold left and right sides to overlap, tapering top edge. Then turn napkin over, placing lace points at the top.

5. Fold down a corner.

6. Leave as is or tuck flatware, flowers, favors, name tags, etc. in pockets.

Bishop's Hat or Fleur de Lis

1. Open napkin and lay it flat.

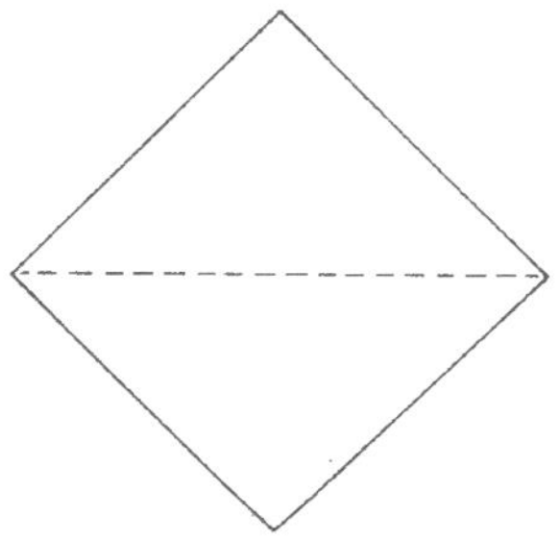

2. Fold open napkin into triangle, center point down.

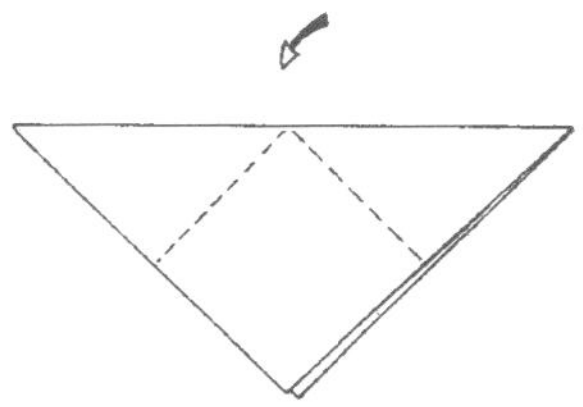

3. Fold left and right points to center point to create a diamond.

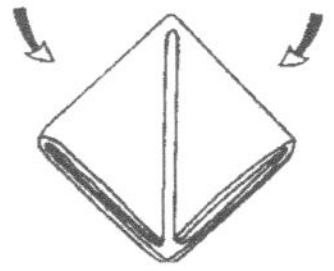

4. Fold top point down to within one inch of bottom point.

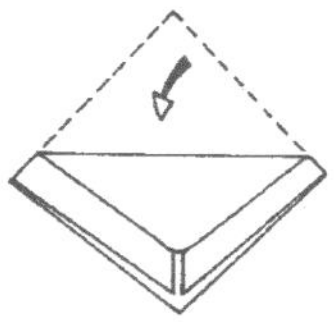

5. Fold same point up to edge. Fold left and right points under and overlap, tucking one inside the other.

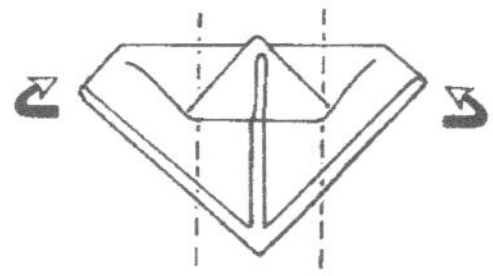

6. Stand upright, leave as is or turn down points to form a fleur de lis.

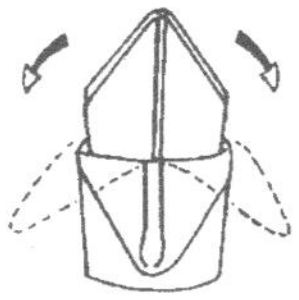

Standing Fan

1. Open napkin and lay it flat.

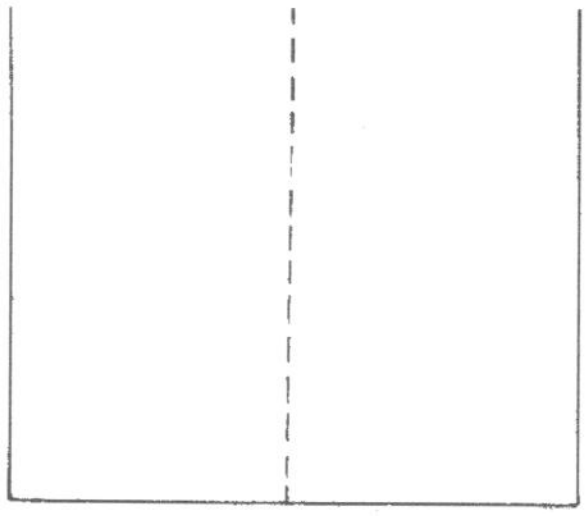

2. Fold napkin in half vertically with the fold side on the right.

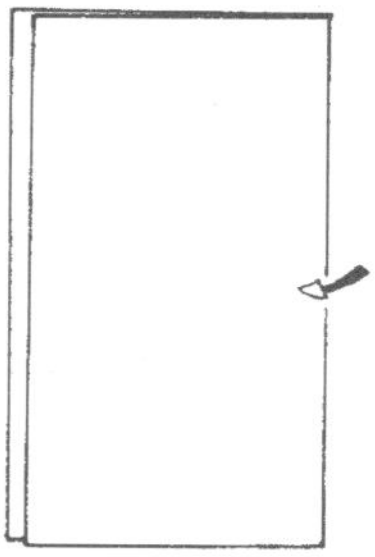

3. Beginning at the bottom, fold accordion style 2⁄3 way up.

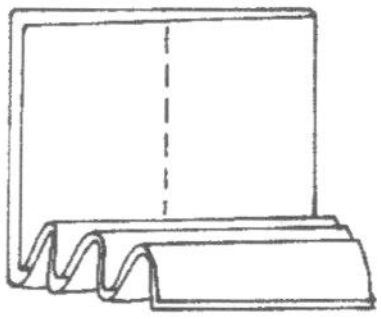

4. Fold in half with pleats on outside.

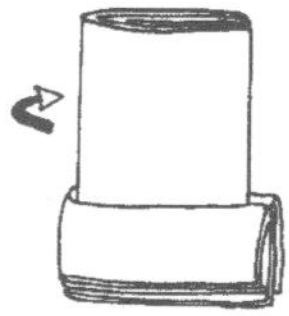

5. Fold upper right corners into triangle, overlapping side fold by one inch. Tuck overlap under to create base.

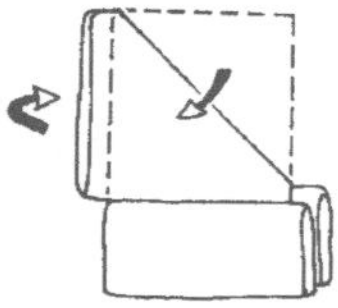

6. Stand upright and release pleats to form fan.

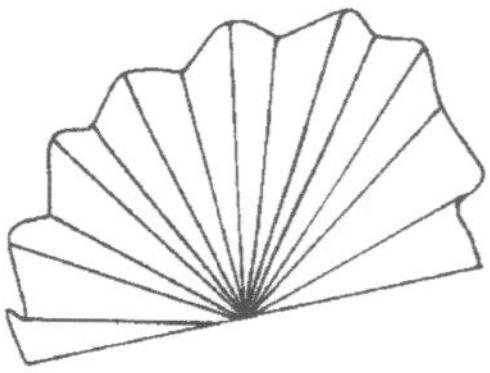

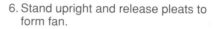

Fan in a Goblet

1. Open napkin and lay it flat.

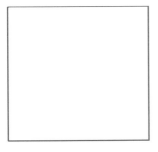

2. Fold entire napkin accordion style in one inch folds.

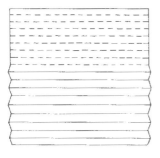

3. Find midpoint of napkin.

4. Fold in half at midpoint.

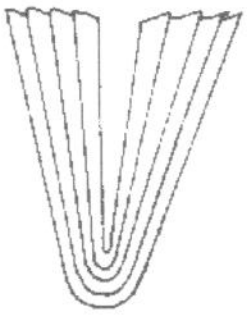

5. Hold folds at the desired depth and place in napkin ring or glass.

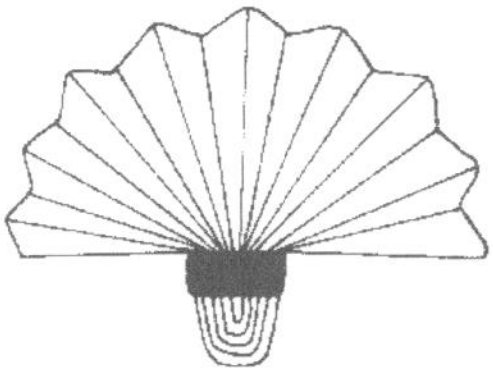

Individual Contributors

Bonnie Adams
Gretchen Allen
Mrs. Charles I. Allen
Elizabeth and Hunt Allen
Althea Barton
Carolyn M. Bass
Betty Beck
Mrs. L.A. Bell
Frances Black
Betty Boyd
Betty Brown
Jackie Brown
Agnes Browning
Kitty Bryson
Beverly Burgess
Helen Burkhardt
Jo Ann Clark
Fay Coker
Mrs. H.D. Cole
Eugenia Crotts
Judy Crowther
Saundra Culp
Margo Cummings
Miss Sarah Daniel
Mary H. Deyton
Jean Doerr
Linda Dowd
Charlotte B. Dunn
Lynda Eddy
Dorris J. Edmond
M.E. Edwards
Maryanne Evans
Guynn Francis
Kathryn Gray
Elizabeth Gribble
Priscilla "Prissie" Griffin
Julie Reed Hartzell
Mrs. Thomas Hatfield
Pearl Hearn
Sarah Hennessee
Anne Hipp
Ann Holman
Helen Horner
Sarah Hovis
Barbara Huckabee
Blanche Hunt
Diddy Irwin
Mrs. Maude Boren Jones
Jean Keitt
Jean Kirkpatrick
Barbara Stockton Knowles
Cynthia Kratt
Mrs. Bruce O. Leister
Caroline Lentz
Windy Leonard
Jerrie Lisk
Kat Lloyd
Edie Low
Mary Lumpkin
Beth Mangum
Bet Mangum
Mrs. George C. Marshall
WillieBell Martin
Jerry McAlister
Ethel McCraw
Nan McGlohon
Gloria McRorie
Polly Mickle
Betty Miller
Hazel Miller
Mary Lynn Morrill
Joan Moss
Nan Myers
Mary Nalley
Lucy Nance
Betty Nichols
Sharon Nivens
Susan Norris
Mrs. J.H. Northey
William Painter
Louise Painter
Tressa L. Pearson
Frances C. Pitts
Jackie Plott
Doris Pope
Ann Preston
Frances Puckett
Grace Reed
Jeannette Renfrow
Jeanne Reynolds
Connie Dorn Rist
Mrs. H.H. Robbins
Nancy L. Robinson
Gloria L. Roddey
Marie Rowe
Joyce Ruark
Pat Rush
Mrs. John Ryan
Mrs. E.W. Sachsenmaier
Evelyn Sanzenbacher
Doug Schnorr
Josephine "Jo" Schofield
Jacky Skipper
Ann Smith
Harry Smith
Ovid Smith
Mary Jo Spaugh
Merrily Spaugh
Barbara Spicer
Esther B. Stanfield
Faye Starnes
Mrs. W.T. St.Clair
Betty Stewart
Sherrill Suiter
Mrs. J.R. Surtman
Bess Terrell
Phyllis Thompson
Judy Thrash
Sandra "Chi Chi" Tourtellot
Dee Underwood
Helen Vales
Becky Vandergriff
Maxine Vandiver
Gloria Vaughan
Martha Villas
Eleanor S. Virkler
Mrs. A.A. Walker
Patricia Walker
Velma Wall
Nancy Wampler
Bonita "Bonnie" Ward
Sue Washam
Ida Weathers
Elizabeth "Liz" West
Ann Westlake
Jan Whittington
Toby Wilbur
Ann Wilson
Roberta Wiltbank
Carolyn Wolfe
Jean L. Wood
Mrs. J.W. Wood
Dorothy Wooten
Evelyn Yarbrough

Index

A

B

S

T

CAROLINA *Sunshine,* THEN & NOW
Charity League of Charlotte
P. O. Box 12495
Charlotte, North Carolina 28220

Please send me information on ordering additional copies of
CAROLINA *Sunshine,* THEN & NOW

Name ____

Address ____

City ______________________ State ________ Zip ______

Phone (   ) ___________________________________

CAROLINA *Sunshine,* THEN & NOW
Charity League of Charlotte
P. O. Box 12495
Charlotte, North Carolina 28220

Please send me information on ordering additional copies of
CAROLINA *Sunshine,* THEN & NOW

Name ____

Address ____

City ______________________ State ________ Zip ______

Phone (   ) ___________________________________

CAROLINA *Sunshine,* THEN & NOW
Charity League of Charlotte
P. O. Box 12495
Charlotte, North Carolina 28220

Please send me information on ordering additional copies of
CAROLINA *Sunshine,* THEN & NOW

Name ____

Address ____

City ______________________ State ________ Zip ______

Phone (   ) ___________________________________